The Tactical Guide for Building a PMO

By William D Dow, PMP

ISBN 978-0-9858695-0-2

Printed in the United States of America

Dedication

When I thought about dedicating this book, I wanted to focus on my family, both immediate and extended. You know who you are, so I will not go into a long list of names, but you all have to know how important you are to me. Everyone talks about the importance of family and I am no different, so this book is dedicated to my family, and I thank you all.

About the Author

William (Bill) Dow, PMP, is a published author and a certified Project Management Professional (PMP)® with more than 23 years of experience in information technology, specializing in software development and project management. Bill has a passion for project management, project management organizations (PMOs), and software development methodologies. Bill has a strong, successful background in project management specifically in understanding and developing project management methodologies. Bill started his career in the late 1980s as a Computer Programmer Analyst, he has also worked as a consultant all across North America, and has led large PMOs at AT&T Wireless/Cingular and at Microsoft Corporation.

Bill has taught project management and IT courses at both US and Canadian colleges. His favorite class centers on his first book, "Project Management Communications Bible."

To My Wife & Family

I want to thank my wife, Kath, and son, Bill, for their support while I wrote this second book. As you can imagine, book writing is a huge undertaking and requires support from them both. I hope they are both proud of me as much as I am proud of them.

I also want to thank my mother and my brothers and sister. Each of you are very important to me, great support mechanisms and I love you all.

Credits

Book Front, Back and Side Cover(s) Design—Elysia Chu

Book Foreword—Mark Perry Price

Book Editor—Sarah Rogers

PMO Leadership, Mentor, Friend—Al Callan, PMP

Portfolio Management Thought Leadership—Yorai Linenberg

Program Management & Thought Leadership—Mark Bestauros

Project Management Thought Leadership & Concepts—Jerry Baker, PMP

PMO Change Agents -Diana Lilla, M.A., PMP

PMO History, Mentor, Friend - Bruce Taylor

Table of Contents

Foreword

Starting in the early 1980s as a sales and marketing professional, I learned much about PMOs and how PMOs of all shapes and sizes can be of tremendous benefit to an organization. From my experience being in PMOs, managing a few PMOs and having PMOs report up to me or serve me along with other constituents, I have seen firsthand how PMOs can play a key role in meeting an unmet business need, fulfilling a mandate, achieving a set of defined objectives, and delighting stakeholders as measured by a very real and quantifiable business value.

Imagine my surprise when in the late 1990s, after two decades of very successful PMO-related experiences, all on the goal-oriented and objective rich line-of-business side, I entered the formal project management and PMO community. What I soon discovered within this formal project management community, adorned by its industry associations, standards and certifications, was far more than disappointing; it was nothing short of shocking and, I might add, disturbing.

In short, I found a myopic and self-serving project management community with a view of what a PMO should be that was characterized by cookie-cutter PMO models; simplistic and theoretical resources, procedures, and infrastructure strategies; misguided advice for selling the PMO and obtaining executive buy-in; exploitative promotion of knowledge-based certifications; and a view of a PMO that was more aligned to "the profession" and establishing a Center of Excellence of some kind that reflected that profession. Rather, a PMO should be characterized as a properly cast organization within a business, founded with a leadership team-determined mandate, supported further by a leadership team vision, mission, goals and measurable objectives for the PMO, their PMO.

Harsh words. But, as someone who over the last decade has worked with hundreds of PMOs in over forty-five countries, across six continents, I stand behind these words resolutely. And, I might add, various industry studies and research indicate that 25% of PMOs fail within year one, 50% of PMOs fail within year two, and 75% of PMOs fail within year three, which only confirms that within the formal project management community there is a significant problem with its view of what a PMO is.

The remediation of the industry's incorrect view of the PMO, and poor PMO track record, is not to throw out all that has been advanced within the formal project management community. As the saying goes, "With all of this *expletive-deletive*, there's gotta be a pony in here somewhere." Many people advocate that a PMO balance needs to be struck between "the means to the end" and "the end to be achieved." Or, put another way, until an organization casts the purpose of its PMO in terms of what business problem the PMO is solving and how the PMO will be held to account, there can be no sensible discussion about such things as PMO models; resources, procedures, and infrastructure strategies; how to sell the PMO; and on and on.

Perhaps there is no stronger advocate of this premise than Mark Langley, the CEO of the Project Management Institute®, who advised attendees of the Gartner PPM & IT

Governance Summit that if we continue to speak of project management in terms of such things as scope, time, and cost, then project management will fail us all. Langley went on to suggest that we need to speak of project management in terms of a new and more contemporary project management triangle, one that has at its three points: (1) technical project management per our standards and bodies of knowledge, (2) business acumen, and (3) leadership. And for this, there is no certification.

What Mark Langley and other project management and PMO experts know all too well, including the author of the book that you hold in your hand, is that when PMOs are driven by the needs of the business, they succeed; and when PMOs are driven by other motivations and biases, they are short-lived. Building an organizational entity of any kind within a company or enterprise is no small feat. The more collaborative and cross-silo'd that an organization needs to be, the more complex the endeavor will become, and arguably there is no more collaborative and cross silo'd of an organization than that of a PMO.

In response to this challenge, Bill Dow, in this book, provides a masterful guide for how to build a PMO: a tactical guide that is tempered with over two decades of his PMO and project management-related experience. Use this book to start a new PMO, refresh an existing PMO, or advance multiple PMOs of different types and sizes throughout the enterprise, but most importantly, use this book to address and solve business problems for which a PMO of some kind and project management techniques of some kind can be a viable, if not best, option. Kudos to Bill Dow for what will no doubt be a lasting PMO reference.

Mark Price Perry

How the Book Is Structured

Building a Project Management Organization (PMO) is a very difficult task for anyone—regardless of whether you have had many years of experience in the world of project management, this is not something that you can just wake up one morning and start doing. This book is actually catered to not just PMO Managers but many different roles in the world of project management and I would be willing to bet that you fit into one of the following roles as well:

- PMO Manager
- Portfolio Manager
- Program Manager
- Project Manager
- Project Coordinator
- Project Report Analyst

Did I guess right? Well, if you are in any one of those roles and you want to learn your role better, this book is for you. If you are curious about PMOs, this book is for you. If you are new to the project management industry, this book is for you. The subject is how to **build and implement PMOs**, but the book actually delves into so many more areas—while we go deep into the building of PMOs—that the book is not just for PMO Managers. The interesting note is that the book is definitely intended for PMO Managers, but it would be crazy to think that they are the only ones who would get value from it.

However, understand from the start, this book is tactical, so tactical, that it goes into a lot of detail. The book is set up for PMO Managers who are willing to get their hands dirty and get work done. If you are looking for a strategic book, put this book down right now, there are no concepts, no theories, and no high-level strategies. This book is purely tactical and for someone who needs to get started today and who is willing to do the work. There are many good, high–level books on the market. There are amazing presentations and lots of information that you can find on the Internet if you are looking to justify or strategize a PMO. However, if you need a book to help you get started tactically, this is your book. If you are looking for a step-by-step guide for building a PMO, this is your book. Is that what you are looking for?

The following are some helpful and friendly tips on how to use this book:

- Complete the templates in each chapter. In some of the chapters, you will find templates that are specifically provided as job aids to incrementally help you through the PMO creation process. Use the templates, do not ignore them.
- Document every PMO build decision right after you finish reading a chapter. It is a best practice to read the chapter, and then immediately document your decisions in the template at the end of the chapter. Then, when you get back to work, you can review your decisions and act upon them. But, if you do not document your decisions right away, you could easily forget what you decided.

- Look at the Chapter Review Questions & Answers: and make sure you can answer each question. They are there for you to review and do a self-check to ensure you understand the content. See if you can answer them immediately. If you cannot, go back and re-read that chapter. Being readily able to recall this information and knowledge will help you when you are at work and in the process of building or implementing your PMO.
- Do not assume you have to build and implement everything listed in the book. This is not possible. Your company will not accept that much process generally, so implement your PMO using the Crawl, Walk, Run theory.
- Do not assume that you are going to do just one role. The PMO Manager can be a Portfolio Manager, a Program Manager and Project Manager all at once. Read the book with an open mind and some flexibility of the various roles you can play as PMO Manager. The best PMO Managers are the ones who are the most flexible.

Part One: Project Management Office Fundamentals

The first part of this book is dedicated to providing PMO Managers the history and insight to the structure of PMOs. From PMO-type discussions, to providing the history of PMOs, to obtaining executive support—all of these areas set the foundation of the book and your new PMO. The goal of this brief part in the book is to provide some key information to the PMO Manager and to ensure everyone reading this book understands the basic fundamentals of building a PMO.

Part Two: Building a Project Management Office

The second part of this book focuses on teaching the core components of building or enhancing a PMO. Whether you are building a new PMO, or enhancing an existing PMO, this section covers both. This section of the book provides PMO Managers, who have never built a PMO, the details and specifics around building a PMO. This section also covers other scenarios, such as supporting existing PMOs where PMO Managers who are in the position to enhance their existing processes and techniques but don't know how. It is important to remember that building a new PMO, or enhancing an existing PMO, is essentially the same thing in this book. If you are leading an existing PMO, and you do not have something we covered in this book, then develop it. If you are leading a brand new PMO, and we cover something that will work for your new PMO, then develop it.

You will not find a large number of typical PMO templates in this book and that was done so for a very specific reason. The reason is that there are hundreds of templates on the web, and filling this book with templates that are already all over the web did not make sense. If your company has a specific template that they need you to use, it will be available and you won't have an issue finding it. What templates you do find in the book are specific to creating a PMO and all neatly explained as you discover them in each chapter.

As PMO Manager, you determine the right templates for your organization, and as you approach a particular subject area, such as risk management or change management, first look internally at what your company is currently using to see if that matches what you expect. If you see that the templates your Program/Project Managers are currently using require some tweaking or enhancing, look outside of your company—on the Internet, to a mentor, to another PMO Manager or a peer...etc.—and determine how you can enhance those templates.

In this part of the book, there are two key components to watch closely. These components are the **PMO Build Schedule**, which consists of sample rows from an actual Microsoft® Project.mpp file. These rows will show you the main components of that portion of the PMO that you are reviewing. For example, if you are reading the "PMO Training" chapter, you will see a PMO Build Schedule that highlights PMO training components. The second component is a section in chapters 4 through 12 called **PMO Build Decisions.** These are direct decisions that you, as PMO Manager, must make when implementing your PMO. For example, in Chapter 6, "PMO Staffing Models," one of the PMO Build Decisions for you to make is to name the staff you need for your PMO. When seeing these questions, spend the time and document your decisions, because as we get to the implementation phase of the PMO, you will need to call on your decisions to actually create your PMO. Sound fun? Well, it is. And, the book provides a very structured and organized approach to building your PMO. It is easy and a great way to create or enhance a PMO.

The following **Table 1.1 PMO Build Decision Chart** is a simple and easy-to-use chart to complete while you progress through the PMO-build chapters of the book and eventually use in the PMO Implementation chapter. Keeping this table current with your documented PMO decisions will be extremely helpful when entering the implementation phase of the PMO.

Table 1.1 PMO Build Decision Chart

PMO Build Chapters That Contain Build Decisions	PMO Build Decisions Questions #	Decisions Made
For example: Chapter 4	1, 5	My PMO Mission Statement is "To drive excellence in the management and delivery of projects" (5) My PMO will focus on Program & Project Management only and not include Portfolio Management
4		
5		
6		
7		
8		
9		
10		
11		
12		

Finally, in Part Two you will find that there are two different sections at the beginning and end of the chapter. At the beginning there is a section called **Questions you should be able to answer after reading this chapter** and at the end of the chapter you will find the answers in a section called **Chapter Review Answers:**. Take the time and go over these questions and answers in each chapter, as it is another fun way to help you learn the information.

Part Three: Implementing a Project Management Office

The third and final section of the book takes the concepts that are covered and explained in Part Two, and walks you through the implementation of your own PMO. However, Part Three does not generically say, "Implement everything we covered in Part Two," that's not how it works. But what Part Three does do is say, "Remember all the decisions you made in Part Two where you answered and documented those important **PMO build decisions in table 1.1**? Well, pull out those answers now because we are going to need them as we implement your PMO." This section should be straightforward, and you will find it very easy to go through the implementation process using the decisions you made earlier in the book in the design and build phases.

The Tactical Guide for Building a PMO

Finally, at the end of each of the chapters in Part Three, you will find the same section found in Part Two **Questions that you should be able to answers after reading this chapter** and the **Chapter Review Answers: at the end of the chapter.** Same scenario as with Part Two, spend the time and go over the questions at the beginning of the chapters and the answers at the end of each chapter. By going over these questions it will help you remember the information you have read and will help you learn and understand the information covered. Have fun with the questions as well; they are just there as reminders and as a recap to the chapter.

Tips & Best Practices and Bill's Thoughts

Throughout the book you are going to find two different types of learning aids that will help you through the PMO build process.

Tips & Best Practices—There are actually a large number of **Tips & Best Practices** scattered throughout this book. Each of these nuggets of information will help you through the PMO build process. Take the time and read these as they are short, but very valuable, and will help you be successful.

Bill's Thoughts:—You will also find **Bill's Thoughts** sections throughout the book that give you first-hand experience and personal accounts of what the author went through building a running his PMOs. This is just to set context and provide a little more background to the specific area being covered in that particular section.

These two learning aids will provide very valuable information as you go through the PMO building and implementing journey.

That's all there is to it, three parts to the book, each building on the other and each taking you through the journey of building and implementing a PMO.

Let's get started.

Chapter 1

PMO Introduction Now

Questions you should be able to answer after reading this chapter:

1. In the section, "The Top 5 Reasons Why PMOs Fail," what are two reasons that are most important to the *success* of a PMO?

2. In the "PMO Failure: Some Observations," survey what is the failure point called out for the executives around project management?

3. Typically, how long does a PMO Manager have to make an impression about a PMO's value?

4. Do PMO Managers need to be flexible in the roles they play?

5. Typically, how long do PMOs run before something negative occurs and they shut down or something major occurs and there is a change in direction?

The company has chosen you as the new PMO Manager. You are excited and ready to go, but have no idea how to start. Your intentions are good, you have been a Project Manager for years and have worked in many PMOs before, but this is the first time you are going to be running one yourself.

Frankly, you are a little scared and have no idea what to do. You are not the first person to have had this challenge and you will not be the last, but what is important is how you approach it. Luckily, you are reading the right book and I am going to help you tackle this massive challenge ahead of you. Relax, because this very difficult task can actually be very simple if you approach it in a very organized and structured way. You are a Project Manager, right? Well tackle building and implementing a PMO as if you would tackle a project. Fall back to the PMI's nine knowledge areas and consider each one's applicability when building your new PMO. Doing this will give you the confidence and wherewithal to at least give you some go-forward steps in this new adventure.

There are a number of books on the market that are written by some great project management thought leaders that I strongly encourage you to check out. For example, Mark Price Perry's book, *Business Driven PMO Setup: Practical Insights, Techniques and Case Examples for Ensuring Success* is an excellent PMO book that provides some great thoughts and strategies around some key areas for setting up and establishing PMOs from a very strategic level. It is highly recommend for anyone starting out and needing the initial strategic view of PMOs to read this book. Another recommended book, and a great resource, *The Strategic Project Office, Second Edition,* by Ken Crawford, is another excellent strategic book about building PMOs that provides some of the high-level ideas and concepts that PMO Managers run into when thinking about starting PMOs at their companies. One of the differences you will find in this book compared to the aforementioned books is that it comes from a different angle. This book is tactical and leaves the strategic side of building PMOs to the other two books, and other books like them. This book gives you step-by-step instructions for building a PMO. This book is so tactical that you will see snippets of a PMO project schedule throughout the book. As you progress through the book, you will continue to see snippets of different parts of that project schedule. Come visit the book's website **http://www.pmotacticalguide.com/** for more information about this PMO Build Schedule.

I recently attended a conference and spent a lot of time with many PMO Managers who were all looking for a tactical book about how to set up and manage PMOs, and they too had found that there was no single book that would give them that tactical information. Some of the PMO Managers I spoke to know Portfolio Management some know Project Management but are not as familiar with Program Management. Some know Program Management, but do not know Portfolio Management. It was all over the place, and it was very common for most people to be missing knowledge on one area or another; very few attendees seemed to know all of the areas in much depth. It is almost impossible for anyone to know everything across something as broad as Portfolio, Program, and Project Management.

Remember, as you are building your PMO that you are not alone and you do not have to figure this all out for yourself. The information in this book will get you through most scenarios at most companies, but if it doesn't, you can contact me, or you can contact the many experts in the industry who are running large-scale PMOs and are available to help and support you. Online project management sites, such as LinkedIn or Gantthead.com have lots of white papers and information that you can find to help you solve business problems. Take advantage of these resources; do not be afraid to ask questions. Remember that PMOs, in the big scheme of things, are still new in the project management industry, so there are many people like you who are learning and growing in this area and doing the best job they can. It is when industry leaders share their materials and lessons learned that allows everyone to be successful. Before we get started building your PMO, good luck, it is going to be a long journey but one that you will find valuable, frustrating, rewarding, and frankly, one of the best jobs in the world. You are going to do just fine and I am here the whole way.

Wait, before we go too far into creating or enhancing your PMO, let's look at some of the surveys and some of the industry discussions around successful PMOs and PMO failures. By heading into this new adventure with some knowledge and background, I hope you will avoid some mistakes that others made when they were in your same position.

Author, Elyse Nielsen, wrote the following article that does an excellent job explaining the top five reasons why PMOs fail. Have a look at this article.

The Top 5 Reasons Why PMOs Fail

1. **A lack of executive support**—There are many reasons for the lack of executive support and it arrives in many manners. There may be the public chiding, the noticeable loss of the inner circle. Discussions may occur around, no more changes at this time; the organization cannot make the leap. (Even though the only change was a project dashboard.) Another tactic is the inability to comprehend key concepts even after multiple explanations - like the PM lifecycle, perhaps you have heard the quote in a buy and implement shop. "We plan as we go implement". Another classic tendency is to cut funding support, new positions are denied or existing positions are reduced. Those experiencing it know it as a lack of executive support, and this one is always a nail in the coffin.

2. **They become policeman and auditors**—One purpose of a PMO is to bring value to the project managers, so auditing and policing for a bit is okay as long as it is used in an educational and mentoring manner. It helps drive the change to change resistant organizations. However, if the PMO has been doing it for a bit and is now viewed in the same light as the IRS, it was time to change out of this tactic a long time ago.

3. **They overburden the staff with process and documentation**—People drive project success. Processes and Technology should augment effectiveness not become obstacles. Additionally Process and Technology should help in the organization as communication and alignment improvement. Risk Management is a great process for identifying possible obstacles and gotcha's for the project. However if they aren't communicated to those accountable and empowered for managing the risk, the process is just more documentation on the already overburdened PM.

4. **No demand management or resource management**—This is basic management for it, and also recommended for the PMO. If you can't quantify demand, and priorities change all day long it will be impossible to project accomplished. Also if there are no resource for the projects, human heroics only

goes so far, and the projects will not be accomplished. The PMO can help assist developing a process for time tracking while remaining cognizant of the fact that in IT we hire for smarts, not for punching the clock at 7:30 am and at 4:00 pm. Also the demand for resources should not only include the IT staff, include your sponsors time as well.

5. **Benefits capture is not done**—This one is how you continue to facilitate and drive value. Yes it is a bit of marketing, but worth the time spent. The PMO should help to capture and quantify the business value of the completed projects. If you do not capture the benefits, it is more than likely they will not be captured. This cycles on down to individuals asking what is the value in the PMO overhead? Being proactive mitigates this argument altogether.

Printed with permission of Elyse Nielsen website:
http://www.anticlue.net/archives/000979.htm

Let us look at each of the reasons PMOs fail and discuss in detail why they are valid and relevant. Most PMO Managers experience these items, first-hand, so read these points carefully so that you understand and can avoid the pitfalls whenever possible.

1. **A lack of executive support**—This is a key point and I believe this is a top reason for PMO failures. I have had tremendous success when management supports PMOs and I have seen great failures when there is little–to-no support. I have dedicated an upcoming chapter in this book about this very subject.

2. **They become policeman and auditors**—This is another valid reason for PMO failures as well. However, I believe there is a need for balance around policing and auditing Project Managers and how they manage their projects and leaving them alone to run their projects their way. I believe you need a balance of monitoring the process and giving them leeway. PMOs with no policing in place are going to struggle, while PMOs with too much policing will fail.

3. **They overburden the staff with process and documentation**—Another point of failure, for sure, but we need to balance that failure with some rigor and processes for the Project Managers. PMOs that lack process, or have limited process, fail as well because there must be some consistency and rigor in how Project Managers manage their efforts. However, adding too much rigor or too many processes restricts Project Managers from completing their projects as they won't be able to manage their projects because they're so tied down with overhead or administrate work.

4. **No demand management or resource management**—This tends to be a failure for PMO Managers who do not have many years of experience and tend to get lost in driving the day to day of managing a PMO but not focus on their resources. PMO Managers often get so caught up in driving the PMO, or get so lost in the PMO's projects, that they let resource management occur on its own.

Unfortunately, resource management is a full-time concern for PMO Managers, and they need to have this as a top priority in running their PMOs.

5.   **Benefits capture is not done**—This is another very valid PMO failure point and something that supports the lack of executive sponsorship. When executives do not understand the value or the benefits that a PMO brings to an organization, the PMO can be one of the first things shut down or decentralized.

I hope the previous article got you thinking about some of the pitfalls and trouble areas you can run into when building your own PMOs. The article documents only five of the many different reasons why PMOs fail. I encourage PMO Managers to continue to search the Internet for various challenges that other PMO Managers and executives have experienced running a PMO.

The following article I really like as well because the observations parallel my own experience and what you might experience when building a PMO.

PMO Failure: Some Observations

By
David Tennant, PE, PMP

Having worked the last ten years assisting clients with setting up and running project management offices (PMOs), I've seen the value of a finely tuned PMO, but have also recognized areas of vulnerability. Recent articles have been promoting PMOs to solve many project and organizational problems.

In recent months, I have become aware of several key firms dismantling their Project Offices for a variety of reasons: the PMO could not demonstrate value, the cost was too great, projects were still not meeting target parameters, etc. Why did these PMOs fail? What were some of the root causes? I would like to offer the following observations for what I feel are key reasons of PMO failure:

1. **The PMO is looked upon as a temporary fixture**—to be closed down after a key project is completed. Consequently, there is very little, or zero, money targeted for methodology development, training, and process improvement. A successful PMO is not a short-term solution. In this case, the proper solution may have been a "special project" status or the use of a recovery team.
2. **Many upper level executives fail to understand what project management is all about and how it can help them**. And, based on what they have heard and read, they see the PMO as a fix to an immediate problem. The reality is that a PMO will take time to implement and effect change. Therefore, the PMO must be viewed as a commitment by management to incrementally improve their business processes over time. The PMO should have an impact company-wide across all projects.
3. **Project methodologies are too academic**. That is, they are loaded with great theories, lots of tools and templates, and volumes of information- but are out of touch with the way the organization needs to function. I have seen some organizations develop methodologies with close to 400 pages of instructions. Yet, because of the volume, combined with poor rollout, no one will use it. Having too much information is just as bad as not having enough. And, having the right information is what allows one to make good decisions. Without an effective PM process used by all, repeatable success is unlikely.
4. **The organization has a history of little accountability, lack of discipline on the part of PMs, and few requirements in the selection of project managers**. The organization's view of project management must change with the implementation of a PMO. If project managers in the new organization do not have authority (and responsibility) combined with a strong sense of purpose, then the same results will be achieved: failed projects. And, it is important that the organization think about the required skills necessary for each project manager. Having just the technical knowledge is not enough.

5. **Some PMOs in IT organizations were created as an outgrowth of the Y2K efforts in those firms.** Essentially, companies formed "crisis project teams" to get the code fixed. It was like sending the Marines in to take the beach at all costs. Costs and resources were not considerations as the systems had to be revised and tested by key dates-so the projects were schedule driven.

Now, fast forward to post-Y2K: the war is over, there are a lot of Marines left standing around, so now let's put them to work forming a PMO. The people used to working under crises conditions are now supposed to become methodology developers bringing structure and order to projects-quite the opposite of their recent experience. Consequently, the structure necessary to run a PMO in "peacetime" should have been developed by a different set of folks.

6. **Finally, a truly missed opportunity occurs in transforming an organization's culture when the PMO is not used as a change agent**. When new perspectives, approaches, and processes need to be implemented, the PMO is the perfect vehicle for organizational change.

However, implementing a PMO requires careful planning and consideration. In other words, a PMO should be planned just like a project: determine objectives, identify stakeholders, develop a WBS/Schedule/Budget, determine risks, identify roles and responsibilities, and..... well, you get the idea.

After all, if the PMO can't be well planned, you're already off to a bad start.

Printed with permission and can be found at this website:
http://www.threebridgesconsulting.com/article1.htm

Think long and hard about some of these points, most notably points 1-3. Both articles you just read are very valuable to review from time to time to keep in perspective the different challenges and problems PMO Managers face when building PMOs. It is really amazing how common these problems are from company to company and industry to industry. As PMO Manager, be prepared to face some of these same issues in your company. Knowledge is half the battle and having the knowledge to understand what can happen helps you be prepared in case it does happen.

As PMO Managers start building their brand new PMO, or in some cases are hired to fix and enhance an existing PMO, they start with not a care in the world. They have the needed executive support (temporarily) and the authority to do whatever they want to get the PMO started. Life is good and everything is clicking into place. Almost every PMO starts the same way. This typically lasts for about a year, but when projects go bad, or executives loose interest, or leave altogether, then the PMO is dismantled and PMO Managers move to different organizations. It happens that fast. The funny thing is that the discipline of project management is not lost, but what is lost is the rigor and structure that was initially so important to management. What management tends to focus on are quick results, and if the PMO does not deliver those results fast enough, the problems fall to the PMO and the one leading the PMO, you the PMO Manager.

PMO Managers and executives have to be aware of that PMOs are not all about getting quick results generally, and when starting to build a PMO if that is the main focus of the PMO Manager (you) and your management team, that is definitely something that can quickly sink a new PMO. As PMO Manager, you have to both market and bring value realization to your PMO as quickly as possible and work with your management team that PMOs are not all about quick results. I think it is important at least for the first year or so of your job, you need to continually market the value of the PMO. It is also important to market the results in the organization now that the PMO structure and process is in place. If done correctly, your PMO will dramatically improve your Program/Project execution success. Therefore, you should market and report that success.

You can see from the two articles above that your window to make an impression is short, and therefore you must regard marketing and selling your PMO as part of your full-time job. You have to balance this, though, with making sure your Program Managers and Project Managers are delivering their project results on time, on budget and with business value. When the programs and projects in your PMO do succeed, or if you as the PMO Manager and had to step in and help keep a program or project from going off track, ensure you market those successes as well.

The second point in PMO Failure: Some Observations article around executive support is also very relevant and important for you to realize. In Chapter 3, we dedicate some time on executive support and its importance to the success of a PMO. With limited or no executive support, you will struggle tremendously in running your PMO. If you talk to other PMO Managers, read PMO failure surveys, repeatedly the executive support reason continually comes up as one of the main factors for the success of any PMO. The fact that there are no quick fixes for PMOs is very true and is something that executives look for when approving PMO creation. Realistically, it is possible to quickly fix some component of project management, such as common status reports, lessons learned, and budget tracking, but it is simply not possible in other areas, including methodologies, leadership qualities, trust, and respect of a single Project Manager. These items take time to be successful.

The third point of the article PMO Failures: Some Observations it shows a very common problem that PMO Managers often face in their jobs. There is nothing worse than being too academic when building your PMO. Academics were the foundation of how PMOs originally started back in the 1960s, but it is important that PMO Managers turn academia into tactical practice as quickly as possible. A big, bloated PMO that is all "theory and best practices" is doomed to failure. PMO Managers cannot stand behind processes and best practices, but instead need to make the PMO work for the Program Managers and Project Managers who need to be supported as they execute their projects. A successful PMO is one that Program Managers and Project Managers can turn to for support and guidance, as well as process and procedures. An unsuccessful

PMO will enforce best practices and processes and expect both the Program Managers and Project Managers to blindly adopt them, no questions asked. PMO Managers must balance the academic side with the tactical side in the creation and implementation of their PMOs if they want to be successful. So, take real caution and look for a balance when you are building your PMO.

One of the common characteristics of a PMO Manager that is important to mention before you get too far into this role is that you are going to have to play many different roles. You can be both PMO Manager and Portfolio Manager. You can be both PMO Manager and Program Manager, or in some cases you can be called in to be a temporary Project Manager. You have to be prepared to play multiple roles while continually being the PMO Manager for the organization. This is such an important point because many executives or management types do not fully understand the PMO organizational structure, so when there are problems in the execution of a program or project, they will turn to you for support. Make sure to check your attitude at the door and be prepared to help with anything in your PMO. That is one of the important ways that you will show value to your management, and more importantly, to your employees. When they can turn to you for support and they know you are there for them anytime, it is going to go a very long way in how successful you are going to be as a people manager first, and then as a PMO Manager.

Bill's Thoughts:

I have managed two very large PMOs at two large corporations, here in the US, and I have been successful with both. To a degree, I have had success and I have had some failures, but the PMOs were not failures and that's important to note. The PMOs as a whole were successful. Not many people can say that truthfully. Each PMO ran 3–4 years which by PMO standards is a lifetime, and when each were closed down or dismantled for different reasons, it was based on executive support or organizational changes. Not one PMO was shut down because management did not perceive it was not valuable or that that it caused overhead or that it did not add value.

Summary

There are a number of PMO surveys on the Internet, and in every case they point to common reasons and areas that need considering when building a PMO: executive support, PMO process and policing, audits, and more. Surveys are generally the same, but written based on the experience or background of the person writing the survey, most likely an experienced PMO Manager. However, you will need to understand as you build your PMO that these surveys are something to consider and use as guiding principles in your journey, but not they don't represent everything. But as noted, there are common themes from company to company, so expect to run into some of them. These surveys are good because they give you the information so you do not run into the same traps. You should be constantly evaluating your PMO against the areas in the surveys to ensure ongoing success.

Chapter Review Answers:

1. It varies, but successful PMOs typically have executive support and do not overburden staff with too much process and documentation.

2. The failure point called out for executives is that they fail to understand what project management is all about and how it can help them.

3. There is a very brief window to make an impression, so PMO Managers must market the PMO and show value sooner rather than later.

4. Yes, PMO Managers need to be flexible because they play a variety of roles.

5. PMOs can thrive up to three–four years before there's a significant disruption in the PMO.

Chapter 2

History of PMOs

Questions you should be able to answer after reading this chapter:

1. Is everything we do considered a project?

2. What was the estimate time it took to build the Passage Tomb at Newgrange?

3. What was the first major building every constructed and to use Project Management practices?

4. What is the importance of the Gantt chart from a PMO Manager's perspective?

5. Why do we have PMOs?

One area that PMO Managers might not think about during their daily activities is the history of project management and the development of PMOs. What happened in the past is in the past and does not really matter, right? Well, that is just not the case. The accomplishments of the early pioneers of the project management industry helped put you in the position you are in today. As PMO Manager, you should know how the profession of project management began and how there was eventually the need for PMOs. This will provide a good foundation for you and give you some information and knowledge that you might not otherwise have had. It will also help you appreciate the challenges that others went through to move the industry forward.

As you can imagine, from the time man went on his first hunt for food, there was the need for project management. The hunt (the project) had a beginning, and hunger was the initiating process. Deciding which tools to use and how to prepare, organize, and execute the hunt was the planning process. Next, the hunting party used the plan to implement the hunt, which was the execution process. During the hunt, the hunting party was continuously monitoring and controlling the hunt. Any change, even the slightest change, was monitored, analyzed, and controlled. Then, there was the kill, cleaning, and eating of the animal. Finally, the closing of the project was performed by cleaning up and putting the hunting weapons away until the next hunt (the next project). Granted, this prehistoric example illustrates an unsophisticated project, but even unsophisticated projects go through the same project life cycle processes: initiating, planning, executing, monitoring/controlling, and closing out.

Project management has existed in some form for thousands of years, actually tens of thousands of years. Anything that requires an approach where humans organize, plan, and achieve specific goals can be roughly defined as a project.

Let us spend some time now and look at the history of PMOs and the history of project management.

Where We Came From

When we are looking at the history of project management, one of the first places to look is at the ancient projects. Let us look at them now.

Ancient Projects

When traveling the world and visiting ancient structures, such as the Egyptian pyramids, the Roman Coliseum, or the Great Wall of China, many people wonder how they were constructed. How could they build such magnificent and complex structures without the modern project management tools we have today? It is almost inconceivable, but they did it. How were these structures initially conceived? The initiation and planning process was set into motion. How were they constructed? They were built by using execution, monitoring and controlling processes, and when they finished, the close-out process.

Bill's Thoughts:

It is amazing to think that project management was applicable that many years ago. There clearly would have been a leader (PMO Manager) or someone in charge of an effort that size. PMOs, as we know them today, would not have been relevant at this time in history, but there had to have been a leader and that leader would have had to have some close people (leadership team) to coordinate everything they were building. Thing about a structure such as Newgrange, that certainly did not get built in a random way.

It is estimated that the construction of the Passage Tomb at Newgrange would have taken more than 20 years with resources of at least 300 men. Somehow, they used project management processes to construct this incredible structure. The real question here is how they constructed a stadium-like building with a corbelled roof that has not leaked for over 5,000 years. Today we can't even construct stadiums that last 30 or 40 years, sometime even less.

Going down the project management historic time path there were many large and complicated projects accomplished during this time. The next major project to be initiated, planned, and completed were the Egyptian pyramids.

Then Stonehenge was constructed in England about 50 years later, followed by the mega project that can be seen from space, the Great Wall of China. This project started 2,000 years after the pyramids.

During the Greek and Roman eras, the rate of development in architecture, engineering, and construction continued due to improved tools and materials, such as brick laying mortar and iron products. Project management was also due to more organized project workforce by trades. The Greeks with their amazing accuracy of measurement and applying the principals of simple quality management was demonstrated in the pantheon and again in the Parthenon. Due to the expanding Roman Empire, the Romans were superior organizers. This skill was mainly derived from the military, and then applied to their massive expansion of building projects, such as the construction of cities and towns that required roads, aqueducts, sewers, and a variety of buildings. Also, this was the time that the Roman Coliseum was constructed with its hundreds of different skills needing to be organized for that project.

Modern History

There has been such amazing progress in the history of project management that it is worth noting how we got here. **Figure 2.1 History of Project Management** represents a high-level timeline of the 20th century project management progress. As you can see, there has been major advancement in the profession of project management that includes the creation of PMOs.

Figure 2.1 History of Project Management

History of Project Management – How did we get here?

- 1910's Henry Gantt created the Gantt Chart
- 1960's PERT and CPM developed, PMI created
- 1970's MBO Manage by Objective
- 1980's Quality TQM Japanese cars & electronics
- 1990's Project Management – Microsoft ® Project introduced
- 2000's Project Management Organizations (PMO) created

The Gantt chart was developed in the 20th century, a time when the industry saw very few project management tools. During this time, there was no standard methodology or approach to managing a project. Henry Gantt changed that with his creation of the simplest, most important project management tool used today: **the Gantt chart**. The Gantt chart, also known as a bar chart, provides a graphic representation of a schedule for planning and controlling work, and recording the progress towards stages of a project. Gantt charts were employed on major infrastructure projects, including the Hoover Dam and the interstate highway system, and continue to be an important tool in project management. Since the advent of the computer, every automated scheduling system's main feature is the Gantt chart. As PMO Manager, the Gantt chart is going to be a tool you use daily across your programs and projects to understand how they are tracking and to see the progress of the efforts within your PMO. Especially, if you are using a Project Server environment, where all PMO programs and projects are loaded into project server and as PMO Manager you use the consolidated Gantt chart to see exactly how the efforts are progressing. This Gantt chart is a must have tool. You should be very thankful for this tool and for the work Henry Gantt did by creating and introducing this tool to the world 100 years ago. Imagine how different the industry would be without it.

Also in the 20th century, we saw the introduction of PERT analysis, the formation of PMI, MBO, TQM, and the creation of automated scheduling tools. When scheduling tools were placed in the hands of project managers, the industry shot forward and major advancements were made. This was the time when PMOs became viable, and PMO Managers (or leaders such as yourself) became staples in the industry. So, the role of PMO Manager has been around now for 20 years or so, which in the scheme of the overall industry is still quite new and something that continues to become more and more in demand. In Chapter 3, "Executive Support—Stop Now!" we will discuss the PMO cycle where the need for PMOs demand comes in stages and is hot and demanding for a period, and then slows down and PMOs are not used again for some time. So, as PMO Manager, this becomes something that you will deal with in this role. Get used to it and learn to work in this kind of environment.

PMOs were created to track work being done across different organizations within a company. When large technical projects are designed, such as the NASA space program, the demand for management across projects is evident and therefore the use of a PMO makes sense. This created the necessity for PMOs that spread from NASA to many other organizations across the different industries. When the introduction of project management software, use as Microsoft ® Project, planning and tracking project related data across different organizations became much more possible and much easier for PMO Managers to track and report on project data. With this newfound ability, came the creation of PMOs in support of the entire enterprise.

PMOs, today, show up in almost every industry, ranging from software to construction, and each industry has unique characteristics based on their own specific needs. A construction PMO, for example, might have to work with the press and, therefore, will tend to be much more mature and rigorous in their processes than say a PMO in the software industry. So, as PMO Manager, you will adapt your PMO specifically to your industry; however, the general characteristics will typically be the same. As you read through the book, consider the different PMOs that are used across each industry and update or enhance your PMO where applicable.

Summary

In this chapter, we covered a brief overview of the history of project management to give you an understanding of how the demand for PMOs came into existence. It started with basic project management needed when hunting for food, to the huge and complex programs seen today at NASA. As PMO Manager, you should understand the history and understand the evolution of where and how we got to where we are today so that you have the context and knowledge to successfully drive your organization.

Chapter Review Answers:

1. Yes, from planning your weekend activities, to large-scale construction efforts, you should treat everything like a project.

2. It is estimated that the construction of the Passage Tomb at Newgrange would have taken more than 20 years with resources of at least 300 men.

3. The Passage Tomb, located in Newgrange, Ireland was the first major building.

4. The Gantt chart, also known as a bar chart, provides a graphic representation of a schedule for planning and controlling work, and recording progress toward project stages.

5. PMOs were created to track projects across organizations. When large technical projects were designed, such as the NASA space program, the demand for management across projects was evident. This created the necessity for PMOs.

Chapter 3

Executive Support—Stop Now!

Questions you should be able to answer after reading this chapter:

1. What is the PMO Cycle?

2. Why is it important for PMO Managers to be constantly selling and marketing the PMO?

3. What is the average shelf life of a PMO Manager?

4. What are three of the five main areas executives tend to focus on in their organizations?

5. What are three standard PMO value questions?

One of the key components required for creating and implementing a Project Management Office (PMO) is the backing and support from your senior management and executive staff. As PMO Manager, your success in the organization depends on whether you have your management's support. PMOs come and go based on the support, or lack of support, from executives. It happens all the time. One of the first things that companies will cut when times are tough is the PMO. Many industry executives say things along the lines of, **"Project Management Offices are nothing but overhead; they never do any real work."** It is a strange phenomenon that companies tend to cut PMOs over other, less efficient, internal groups. The PMO becomes the "default" organization that executives choose to eliminate when looking to reduce costs. However, what generally occurs when the PMO is eliminated is that the PMO structure goes away, but the Program and Project Managers usually stay with the company, performing the same role, just somewhere else in the organization.

Executives understand the need for the project management skill set for every project, but what executives often feel they don't need is that big, old, centralized organization that is creating unnecessary processes and standards. Therefore, they assume that cutting the PMO won't be a problem or have any negative impact. It happens all the time. I call this the **"the PMO cycle,"** as shown in **Figure 3.1 PMO Cycle**, below. The cycle begins with the start of a new PMO; it is fully functional, everything is going well, and the PMO Manager can do no wrong. Then, something happens and an executive abruptly shuts down the PMO. Sometime later, executives move around in the company, or some major problems arise on a high-profile project, and someone decides that a PMO can solve the problems. A new PMO starts up. Something happens again, executives change, or something goes wrong, and someone shuts down the PMO. This cycle continues and continues in organizations for years. It happens all the time across companies. If you have not seen it yet, you will soon enough. Have a look at the PMO cycle.

Figure 3.1 PMO Cycle

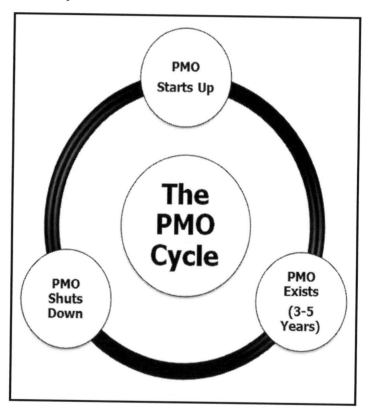

With the PMO cycle in mind, PMO Managers should always be prepared for the possibility that their PMO might be shut down. It is the reality of this role, which PMO

Managers must live with, that executives might shut down the PMO. Sometimes, the PMO is shut down for valid business reasons, while other times the reasons seem random. This is something you just have to live with. Seasoned PMO Managers have been dealing with this for years. Therefore, part of your job as PMO Manager is to prevent your PMO from being shut down. By constantly showing executives, management, customers, and anyone who will listen, the value of your PMO will go a long way in keeping your PMO running for many years.

Part of the PMO Manager's role is selling the value of the PMO. By continually selling and marketing your PMO, it might not be the first on the chopping block the next time the company hits troubled times. Think about the various surveys and data that show PMOs have roughly a 1–3 year shelf life and, therefore, PMO Managers tend to have the same shelf life at that particular company. This does not have to be the case, though, and it is your job to control it and control how long your PMO lasts at your company. Reality check, though, PMOs tend to be executive pet projects and tend to stay around as long as the supporting executive stays. Executives themselves typically remain in the same position for 3–5 years at a single company, so if you have an executive who supports your PMO one day, then decides to leave the next, your PMO might be in jeopardy and in trouble. A PMO can persist for many years with no need to be shut down. More often than not, political reasons are behind why a PMO is shut down. As along as the PMO Manager continues to refine and improve the PMO, and change and adapt based on business or organization changes, a PMO can continue to thrive. PMO Managers must be diligent about showing the value of the PMO. They should understand company politics and steer the PMO in the same direction as the business is moving to keep the PMO fresh, relevant, and continuing to provide value.

Bill's Thoughts:

I have managed large PMOs and have been involved with PMOs for many years. The whole PMO concept is amazing and is often confused by so many people. Some people call PMOs a single person doing one thing, others call PMOs what they are: organizations that drive either portfolio/program or project management best practices and standards. Regardless of what it is and how it is being done at your company, my thoughts are that you have to market and educate to everyone the value that the PMO brings. Maybe this is specific to the software industry, but if your management or senior leadership doesn't know what you do, or they don't perceive your PMO as adding value, you are in for one hell of a long battle by having to continually justify and fight for the PMO's existence. Spend the time to create your marketing/educating material, and ensure that you have, and continue to have, management on your side.

What are executives looking for in a PMO and why is the PMO the cut first when times get tough? What don't executives see in the PMO today, that makes them not value it? There are hundreds of answers to these questions, and of course there is no right or wrong answer, but as PMO Manager, you should be continually thinking about these questions and determining what you are doing in your PMO and how you are responding to them. PMO Managers should ensure that the PMO proves valuable and aligns with the company's future direction at all times. And if the PMO goes off course, the PMO Manager needs to steer it back on course as soon as possible.

The value of a PMO is a long debated subject and something the PMO Manager needs to stay on top of at all times. Ask the following questions when checking the value of your PMO and how it relates to the company goals:

- Does the PMO increase the probability of meeting the company's goals?
- Are there clear links in the PMO to the company's executive strategies?
- How is the PMO's performance measured? Do these measurements improve the project's performance?
- How is the PMO perceived in the organization?
- What level does the PMO Manager report to in the organization's structure?
- What level is the PMO in the organization?
- Does the PMO affect the bottom line? If so, by how much?
- Do executives see the benefits of having a PMO?
- Are Program Managers and Project Managers more efficient and effective because of the PMO?
- Are projects on schedule and on budget because of the PMO best practices?

Tips & Best Practices:

A successful PMO must have executive support. PMOs without executive support will have nothing but trouble!

These are some standard questions that PMO Managers face and must be able to answer when their executives ask and challenge the validity of the PMO. It's important that you are knowledgeable about and have solid data to back your answers; otherwise, you might find your PMO on the chopping block.

When PMO Managers struggle with their executives, it is a best practice to focus on how the PMO is specifically helping that executive's group or his/her pet projects. In doing this, they will see firsthand the value that the PMO and its processes are bring to them specifically. Executives tend to focus on the following areas when inquiring about pet projects:

- Forecast accuracy—Are project dates and budgets being accurately forecasted?
- Go-live date accuracy—Are projects hitting their go-live dates?
- User acceptance—How many users accept and are satisfied with the project results?
- Quality measurements—What kind of quality problems did projects have after going into production?
- Metrics, metrics, and more metrics—How are the projects performing against the organization's metrics?

Executives regard these simple, but effective, project management questions as a way to get clarity and help them track and support their projects and efforts, so when working with the executives make sure you can provide answers and know what is going on with their specific efforts. In other cases, when there is a lot of executive support around the PMO, and the PMO is supporting executive's pet projects and the PMO is missing something like formal dashboards or reporting mechanisms, it is amazing how quickly money is freed up to create real-time dashboards. This allows executives real time data updates on how their pet projects are progress. By using dashboards, executives have the ability to generate project data and create project metrics for their groups. There is much more information about Dashboards, with a sample, in Chapter 11, "PMO Reporting". Refer to that chapter for more details. As PMO Manager, when your executive team provides money and support for capturing and reporting specific project management areas, it is a very good place to be in and, at least for a while, your PMO should be relatively safe from that chopping block. Remember, though, don't get too comfortable.

Summary

It is interesting that companies today shut down PMOs without the full understanding of what that decision actually means to the company. Executives and senior staff have an ongoing perception that a PMO is overhead and that by shutting it down means nothing more than re-assigning some resources to other parts of the organization and getting rid of the PMO Manager. It happens all the time, and it is something that you, as PMO Manager, need to be ready for and expect it may happen. Make sure you are continually marketing and selling your PMO to management. It is an important part of your role. If you do not regularly make the time to market your PMO and voice what your Program and Project Managers are doing to your executives and your customers, expect to be in a spot where a shutdown is possible. Never has the time been so right than now, when you are starting to build and implement a PMO, where you should also focus on how you will market and educate your executive staff about the value that a PMO brings to your organization.

You can't **"stop now"** because you have been hired to build a PMO, but it is in your best interest to make sure you continue to market the value and sell the importance along the way. Regularly marketing, educating, and selling your PMO will go a long way in gaining valuable executive and customer support when building and maintaining a PMO.

Chapter Review Answers:

1. PMO starts up, PMO shuts down, and then the cycle restarts.

2. By continually selling and marketing your PMO, it might prevent it from being the first on the chopping block the next time the company hits troubled times. Of course, marketing and selling is not the only course of action, the Programs and Projects have to delivery as well.

3. The average shelf-life of a PMO Manager is one-three years.

4. Executives focus on: forecast accuracy, go-live data accuracy, and quality measurements.

5. PMO value questions include: Does PMO increase the probability of meeting company goals? Is there a clear link between the PMO and the company's executive strategies? Does the PMO affect the bottom line?

Part Two

Chapter 4

How to Build a PMO

Questions you should be able to answer after reading this chapter:

1. What are the three areas PMO Managers should focus on when assessing a PMO?

2. What are the three process methodologies used in most PMOs today?

3. Why is it important to think about different methodologies?

4. Where does the project management methodology sit with respect to other methodologies?

5. Why is it important for the PMO Manager to have a background in the three process methodologies?

When developing a Project Management Office (PMO), you are likely to hear a number of different thoughts and opinions about what you should do first and where you need to focus your time. Understand, there is no right or wrong way to build a PMO, but there is a structured and organized way of doing it, and there is an unstructured and random way of doing it. Ask yourself, which approach do you think is best?

The approach outlined in this book is one of the structured methods that you can use to increase your chance of success. It will not guarantee your success; however, it will increase your chances and give you the foundation you need to establish your PMO. There are many different methods you can use; this is just one recommended method, but not the only one. An important distinction to remember as you read this book is that you do not need to implement everything you read, but you should at least consider the various suggestions and tips, and then determine which of those would work for your PMO. Some suggestions will work and some will not.

There are many factors that influence how you build or enhance a PMO. Some executives might put huge pressure on you to create a component of the PMO sooner rather than later; whereas, some might have a hot button they want resolved right away and expect you to fulfill it with your PMO. However, if you are starting from scratch and have the ability to build your PMO the way you see fit, it is a best practice to do so in a structural and methodological way and build it slowly. This, of course, implies the caveat that your organization and management layer support you building it deliberately and logically. If, however, management wants you to hurriedly build a PMO, the end result will be a PMO that will be very painful to operate on a day-to-day basis. Try to avoid such hasty situations. If management is putting a huge amount of pressure on you to put implement certain components, get some structure around just those areas first and let the other components of the PMO wait until the hot-button areas from management are implemented and working properly. Then, build the remaining components. Crawl, walk, run...crawl, walk run.... This is an important concept when doing anything, but especially building a PMO.

One of the areas covered in the first chapter that is important and relevant to use now as you start building or enhancing your PMO is to ensure that you capture and track your major PMO build decisions in the provided **Table 1.1 PMO Build Decision Chart**. This table will be an incredible asset to you through the PMO build process, so keep it handy and remember to track everything as you go. You will need the table again when you start the implementation process.

Lastly, before we get started building your new PMO, or even enhancing an existing PMO, you must consider the following few key factors throughout the whole build process:

Resources —Resources are going to be critical to the success of your PMO. Relationships with management and team members, and customer expectations, are all critical when building or enhancing a PMO. As you build your new PMO, continue to focus on what you are doing from a "people perspective" and consider resources throughout this PMO process.

Procedures —Building a PMO means building and implementing many processes and procedures, so as we walk through the build or enhancement process, keep these two in mind. Are there too many or too few procedures, are people trained on the new procedures, do people need more training on the procedures? Too many procedures and processes can make or break PMOs, so make sure to continually think about them as you build or enhance the PMO.

Infrastructure —The concept of "infrastructure" will generally correspond to both software tools and people tools. Infrastructure can be used for a variety of things, such as training as well, so it is not just about tools. It is about the whole infrastructure around you. A weekly status report is a tool. Microsoft® Project 2010 is also a tool. The combinations of all your tools, all your training, I consider an infrastructure. Throughout this process, think about all the infrastructure components (including tools) that are required when building or enhancing a PMO.

We will continue to address resources, procedures, and infrastructure throughout the build or enhancement stages. Write them down somewhere and keep them at the forefront of your mind continually.

Okay, it is now time to get started. One of the best practices for building a PMO is to treat the process like one big project. Therefore, you should do what you expect your Project Managers to do: create a project schedule for all the tasks required to build and implement a PMO. What a cool idea to track your progress, run reports, and give your management team an ongoing status of how the PMO build or enhancement process is progressing! **Figure 4.1 PMO Build Schedule**, below, outlines the high-level steps for creating a PMO project schedule. In the following PMO project schedule example, you see that there are only seven high-level steps for building or enhancing a PMO. That is it, only seven steps and you have a working PMO. If only it were that simple.

Figure 4.1 PMO Build Schedule

Task Name	Resource Names
-PMO Build Schedule	PMO Manager
+Step 1 - Grow PMO Manager Skills - Ongoing Activity	PMO Manager
+Step 2 - Obtain Executive Support (Chapter 3)	PMO Manager
+Step 3 - Assessment Period (Chapter 4)	PMO Manager
+Step 4 - Recommendation Period	PMO Manager
+Step 5 - Design & Build or Enhance Period (Chapter 5 - 12)	PMO Manager
+Step 6 – Implementation PMO Deliverables/Processes Period (Chapter 13)	PMO Manager
+Step 7 - Refine, Enhance and Grow Period (Chapter 14 - Chapter 16)	PMO Manager
+Step 8 - Celebrate Period	PMO Manager
PMO Built & Implemented - Time to Mature and Grow - PMO Project Complete	PMO Manager

Wait. Why is there an eighth step in the schedule when there are only supposed to be seven? Step 8 is probably the most important step: the Celebrate Period. This is the time you, as PMO Manager, dedicate to celebrating and letting your PMO team know that you appreciate the great work they have done managing and executing projects. This can be an event such as a PMO offsite day or a meeting where the focus and appreciation is on the PMO team members. As PMO Manager, it is a best practice to take your team members offsite or away from their day-to-day jobs to work on team bonding and show your appreciation to them. Most of the year, the PMO team members are busy managing their projects and rarely come together with the other members of the PMO. The Celebrate Period step is the one day a year generally (it can be more) where the team can celebrate, interact, and enjoy each other's company.

Bill's Thoughts:

The Celebrate Period step has been something that I have done in my last couple PMOs and they have been incredible for boosting morale, sharing stories, appreciating good work and celebrating the successes of the PMO. I cannot stress how powerful this day is for PMO team members and I highly recommend everyone takes this best practice very seriously and implements it in their own organizations.

We will reference the PMO Build Schedule throughout this book by showing sample rows and the high-level steps for that particular task in building a PMO. It will give you an idea of the task deliverables to create in each area of the PMO. The PMO Build Schedule will be a helpful to use as a high-level guide as you go through the PMO build and implementation processes. The full PMO Build Schedule (.mpp file or Excel ® file) is a companion guide to this book and can be found on the book's web site http://pmotacticalguide.com. It is a companion guide only because all the contents in the PMO Build Schedule are already in the book, and by using it, you would save time re-typing the contents. You certainly do not have to use this PMO Build Schedule, it is optional, but highly recommended.

PMO Build Schedule Breakdown

In addition to Step 8: Celebrate Period, there are seven main steps in the PMO Build Schedule to complete prior to celebrating, let us look at each of those areas now:

Step 1: Grow PMO Manager Skills

This is your time to grow and learn about PMOs and ramp yourself up and get trained in areas around portfolio, program, and project management that you are unfamiliar with and will need in this role. It is 100% fine if you do not know everything about PMOs when you start, nobody does, so use this time in the schedule to ramp up and learn as much as possible.

Step 2: Obtain Executive Support

This is critical and something we covered earlier in the book. It is self-explanatory, really, but you need executive support before you can go forward in building and implementing a PMO. Full stop. You will notice that it is also the second task in the PMO Build Schedule and that executive support actually drives the execution of the other six steps in the schedule. Meaning, you cannot go any further if you do not have full executive support.

Step 3: Assessment Period

This is the time when you determine whether there is an existing PMO in the company, and if there is, you spend time reviewing assessing that PMO. Some PMO Managers come into an existing PMO, and some have the luxury of building one from scratch. In either case, you need to assess what is happening from a portfolio, program, or project management perspective. As PMO Manager, you must perform a complete assessment of the organization within company where the PMO sits and then the PMO itself if there is one; otherwise, you will hamper your chances of being successful at running your

PMO because you might not have all the information you need. Spend the time and do a proper assessment; your management has hired you for a reason, so you need to do a proper job assessing and understanding everything. The end result of the assessment period will be the creation of a PMO Recommendation Report that eventually (Step 4 – Recommendation Period) you will present to your management team to discuss the state of the existing organization, the state of the existing PMO if there is one. This report will then be helpful input for tactical PMO implementation phase.

When assessing existing PMO environments, PMO Managers should focus on assessing the following areas:

1. PMO environment
2. PMO organization structure and existing head count
3. Current PMO portfolio of work
4. PMO budget and financial process
5. PMO problem areas and areas that are doing well
6. PMO maturity model
7. PMO methodologies
8. PMO tool set
9. PMO reports
10. PMO training and education components

Step 4: Recommendation Period

This is the time in the build schedule that you present your formal PMO recommendations to management. This is where you present PMO Recommendation Report and discuss your findings. These recommendations will span the different areas you noted were working or not working during the assessment period. For example, if you are building a new PMO and you assess that the projects in the company are not following any sort of methodology, your recommendation would be to create a project management methodology.

Step 5: Build or Enhance Period

This is the time in build schedule to create and build the PMO processes, deliverables, training, and so on. However, you cannot jump into building those areas without first spending some time designing the various components before you build them. It is like any project you build, you initially spend time designing and then getting feedback before you begin building. It is a best practice for all PMO Managers to follow this same process when building a PMO (Design then Build). The time frame for the initial design phase will vary from PMO Manager to PMO Manager and company to company especially when you consider the experience of the PMO Manager. If a PMO Manager has built PMOs before, then the design phase will be much quicker. It is important to have a good design in place before you start building and randomly implementing processes in your PMO.

If you are coming into an organization where there is already and existing PMO, then it is highly unlikely you will be building anything new immediately, but you will be more enhancing what is already in place. The same logic and processes apply, you just will be enhancing, not building.

Step 6: Implementation PMO Deliverables/Processes Period

This is the time in the build schedule where you start to implement the processes created during the build on enhancement phase. The implementation process will be ongoing and at a pace that is acceptable by the organization. Organizations cannot change too quickly, so you as PMO Manager will have to allow for that when rolling out any new processes. As PMO Manager, you can create a number of new materials, but do not expect that you must release them as quickly as you create them. The organizational change management component for rolling out PMO processes and procedures needs careful consideration about how it might affect the company.

Step 7: Refine and Enhance (all items in Step 5) Period

This the time in the build schedule where you continue to refine and enhance all of the PMO foundation items you created in Step 5. If you are creating a PMO for the first time, so you will go through pilot periods where you create processes or material first, and then pilot them in a couple groups to ensure they work. This pilot period gives you the time to refine what you have built so that it works across the company.

As you progress through the book, you will also progress through the PMO Build Schedule so that by the end of the book, you will have created a PMO for your organization. By completing that process, your PMO is set up in a structured and organized fashion, which will give you a much better chance of success. There will be more information about the PMO Build Schedule later in the book.

Now that you understand the basic steps and you're ready to start on them, let's now move to one of the first things that most PMO Managers write when creating their PMOs: mission and vision statements. Let us look at them now.

PMO Mission and Vision Statements

Every PMO needs a mission and vision statement. It is important to establish a mission and vision to drive the foundation of your PMO. Every PMO has them, yours will too. When you create your mission and vision statements, you need to believe in them and practice them daily. PMO Managers who do not believe in their mission and vision statements tend to be unsuccessful. Every company has mission and vision statements, and your PMO's mission and vision statements should align with the company's overall statements as well. Sometimes there is not a clean delineation between the company's and the PMO's mission and vision statements, but there should be some common elements in each. Having those common elements will make for much easier conversations with your management layer and will keep the direction of your PMO and the company's direction going the same way. There are thousands of different iterations of PMO mission and vision statements, and it is a best practice to choose one that you are most comfortable with for your PMO. Then, if necessary, make adjustments to it until you believe it and can stand behind it. As PMO Manager, you will spend a lot of time in your day-to-day job marketing these two statements, so embrace both the mission and the vision of your PMO and stand behind them whenever possible. Let us spend some time now looking at some common PMO mission statements.

Sample PMO mission statements:

The Project Management Organization (PMO) will provide our customers with high quality project management execution. We will work effectively to help our customers on an ongoing bases.

The Project Management Office (PMO) leads and manages the portfolio of software and business process improvement projects. The PMO is responsible for selecting, and managing project resources to ensure that projects are aligned with strategic goals of the company.

The Project Management Office (PMO) implements and supports project management methodology to enable our organization to deliver projects faster, cheaper, and with the highest of quality in everything we do.

As these examples show, mission statements do not need to be complex or difficult to understand, they can actually be brief and still be effective. It is important that the mission statement for your PMO is something that you and your PMO staff members can rally around and stand behind for the statement to be effective.

Sample PMO vision statements:

To be a PMO that drives value across our portfolio, program, and project management. We want our Project Management office to set the standards across the company and use the best practices and procedures defined in the industry.

Promote best practice standards and methodologies into a project management discipline that advances the core vision and mission of the company.

To drive excellence in the management and delivery of projects.

Like mission statements, vision statements can also be brief while still being effective. Remember, when vision statements are long-winded they quickly lose their effectiveness. It also puts executives and PMO staff in a position of not understanding the vision statement which can lead to big problems when you start to market your PMO to executives, customers, or team members and you don't really understand it.

PMO Value Drivers and KPI's

When creating and building a PMO, one of the key focal points is to create a series of PMO value drivers. These value drivers are areas that you will focus on to help drive the creation and implementation of your PMO. It is a PMO best practice to use PMO value drivers for major categories, such as portfolio management, governance, and people management. When creating PMO value drivers, it is also important to think about Key Performance Indicators (KPI's) for your PMO. There are hundreds of different KPIs that PMO Managers use to drive their organizations—some of these will be company-specific, while others will be program- or project-specific. As a rule, there are some industry-standard KPIs that you can use in your PMO, such as:

- Delivery timeliness—number of days delayed (actual versus planned)
- Consistency of project management practices
- Budget accuracy—cost versus budget

The list can go on and on, and as the PMO matures, more metrics and KPIs can be added that align to your management/customers' expectations. However, adding too many metrics too early when building your PMO can be an issue. Try to avoid using too many metrics in the beginning. It is a best practice to keep it very simple to start with and only work with three–four KPIs at the most, and then add more KPIs as the PMO matures. Starting with a few and socializing those will give you a goal and path to work towards as you expand and grow your PMO.

There are many different opinions on what an effective KPI looks like in PMOs today. Some opinions were founded based on personal options and some were founded on industry best practices. Here are some important considerations when creating KPIs for your PMO:

- Make sure every KPI is goal-oriented.
- Look how to use KPIs as inputs to PMO Performance decisions
- Allow KPIs for all areas of the PMO, such as portfolio, program, and project management.
- Continually monitor and control KPIs; however, make formal updates only once per year.

Watch for more information about how we use KPIs later in Chapter 14.

PMO Budget

There is never a great time in the PMO build process to ask for a budget for your PMO because management tends to avoid budget talks whenever possible, but you are definitely going to need resources to build your PMO. You can use existing employees, or you might decide to use vendor staff. In either case, you will need some budget. It is still early in the process, so you might have to stagger your budget requests based on first building the PMO, and then making a second budget request when implementing the PMO. This way, you can break up the costs by moving some costs to later in the process. The initial budget request will be for support staff to help you build the PMO, and the second budget request will be for tools, software, training, and so on during the implementation phase.

The budgeting process will be very specific to your company, so you will have to understand any company specific processes first before officially asking for budget for your PMO. Let us look at some of the details around what you would need for a budget when first building a PMO. These include:

High-level budget requirements for the PMO build stage:

- PMO Manager wage (your wage)
- PMO support staff to help your administer the PMO creation.
- PMO vendors to help you build various components of the PMO, such as a Project Management Methodology, Change Control process...etc.
- Some PMO staff – Program Managers, Project Managers...etc.

- **High-level budget requirements for the PMO implementation stage:**

- Portfolio, program, and project manager wages
- Software, tools training, and yearly licensing
- PMO Dashboards software or development costs
- Project Management Institute® (PMI) training (for example, PMP®, PgMP®, and so on)
- More PMO staff – Program Managers, Project Managers...etc.

Both budget requirement areas will vary completely, and you might be fortunate enough to be in a situation where budget is not an issue, but that is rare in most companies. As PMO Manager, jump on the budget request early and stay on top of it. Your success in building a world-class PMO is dependent on whether you have a management team that supports you and provides you enough budget to bring in the right resources and build the PMO that is right for your company. You are going to have to drive this budget process for your PMO and stay on top of it yearly, as the budget process tends to be a yearly event. As soon as you get your PMO in place and it is meeting management and customer expectations, you should have very few issues retaining your budget allowance year after year. If your PMO is not doing well, your PMO budget requests will be more difficult to obtain and justification will be that much harder.

Process Methodology Groups: The Big Three + One

After selecting your KPIs, the next PMO area in which to focus on are the process methodologies. The three industry standard process methodologies are: portfolio management, program management, and project management. Most traditional PMOs use a combination of all three, but some do not. Therefore, choosing which process methodology, or combination, to use is not a straightforward decision. You will need to ask your management team and customer base for direction because this is not a decision you can make alone. Will this be a traditional PMO with portfolio management, program management, and project management all in a single organization? Alternatively, will it be a portfolio management PMO? A program management PMO? A project management PMO? So many combinations can be used. You need to balance your decision with the type of PMO. We will talk about different PMO types later in the book, but for now, think about the concepts of a supporting portfolio PMO, a directive project PMO, a coaching PMO, and so on as they related to the different process groups (Portfolio, Program, Project) that you will also want in your PMO. The different variations can be confusing to anyone, but they are broken down in later chapters, so hang in there.

To get you thinking about what your PMO might include, see **Figure 4.2 Four P's of PMOs**. The figure shows the three process methodologies surrounded by the PMO. You can see that all of these have relationships, starting with "Portfolio" and then moving to "Program" and finally to "Project" as this also represents the standard PMI structure. As a reminder, the PMI processes start with portfolio management, and then broken down into program management, and then is further broken down into individual project management.

Figure 4.2 The Four P's of the PMO Lifecycle PMO Lifecycle

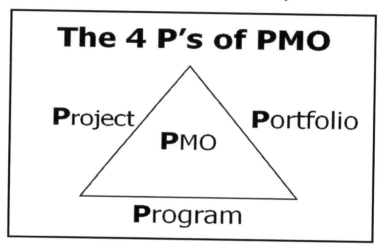

Now, let's break down each process methodology so that you understand them enough to know which to include in your PMO. Alternatively, when evaluating an existing PMO, it is also good to know these methodologies as well so you can evaluate how they are already being used. However, before we go do that, there is one thing to mention and that is the 4th P in the PMO. It is the PMO itself. Don't forget, that the PMO is the overarching organization that holds the other 3P's together. Make sense, that's how we get the 4 P's in the PMO Lifecycle. You can have Portfolio Management done in an organization by itself, or you can have Project Management done by itself, but having a centralized PMO ties everything together nicely and keeps standards and consistency across Portfolio, Program and Project execution.

It is important to spend some time reviewing some of the industry standard definitions for each process methodology, let's do that now.

Portfolio Management —A collection of projects or programs, and other work, that are grouped together to facilitate effective management of that work to meet strategic business objectives. The projects or programs in the portfolio might not necessarily be interdependent or directly related. Portfolio management is the centralized management of one or more portfolios; it includes identifying, prioritizing, authorizing, managing, and controlling projects and programs to achieve strategic business objectives. Portfolio management extends beyond the support of projects and program investments because of the constant ongoing balance and interaction among programs and projects and programs within the portfolio.

It is important to understand portfolio management in detail to determine whether you will need to include the methodology in your new PMO. **Figure 4.3 Portfolio Management** outlines a typical portfolio management structure.

Figure 4.3 Portfolio Management

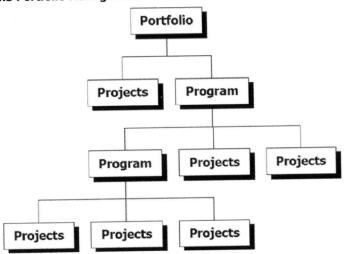

In the figure above, the portfolio is the first logical grouping of the projects and programs within the company. Portfolios can have multiple levels of hierarchy beneath them, with the second level being either projects or programs. At the third level, you could have multiple programs or projects. The most important aspect of building your portfolio structure is to understand that you can never have a top-level project and a second-level program.

When you think about building a portfolio process, you do not need to reinvent the wheel. PMI has an existing portfolio progress that should already work, to some degree, at your company. Undoubtedly, you will need to make adjustments for your company, but at least it is a place to start. You might find that your company does not use portfolio management, so your PMO might not need a full-blown implementation. Chapter 8, "Portfolio Management," is dedicated to discussing the portfolio management methodology in detail. Not only will you learn the importance of this area, but also you will learn how to incorporate the portfolio management methodology in your PMO.

Program Management—A "program" is a group of related projects that is managed in a coordinated way to obtain benefits and control that are not possible when managed individually. Programs include an element of ongoing work and might include elements or related work outside the scope of discrete projects in the program.

Companies use the term "program" in a wide variety of ways. Sometimes, program means simply an initiative or promotional campaign. However, it is the term "program" that often causes confusion with people because of the different ways people use that term in some companies. There are some companies that uses titles like Program Manager, Functional Analyst, or even Report Analyst interchangeably, which causes great confusion. Especially, during the tactical day-to-day execution of a project or a major program where the program manager is not doing the PMI defined Program Manager role but acting like a functional analyst. As PMO Manager, you should align the taxonomy correctly with industry standards, when applicable, to save confusion and keep everything as simple as possible. If it is not possible to follow industry standard terminology, that is okay, you just need to be aware of how you are using the term "program" in your company. A best practice, though, is to use industry standard terminology.

Figure 4.4 Program Management shows a standard program management structure used by most companies and is one that you should adopt as you build your PMO. Programs have an interesting characteristic in that they can align with both programs and projects, which in some cases when there is second-level Programs they have their own set of projects. Therefore, in the figure 4.4, you will see a top-level program that has both a second-level projects and a second-level program aligned to it. The second-level program has three third-level projects aligned to it.

Figure 4.4 Program Management

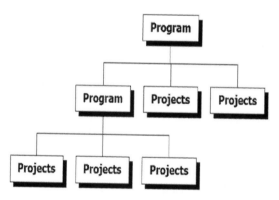

As PMO Manager, analyze which type of environment you have and align your program structure to this figure; it makes the most sense and aligns nicely with PMI. In doing so, you will keep everything standardized and easily understood by a Project Management Professional® (PMP). Later in this book, Chapter 9, "Program Management Methodology," this describes how you should incorporate the program management methodology in your PMO.

Project Management—A temporary endeavor to create a unique product, service or result. Therefore, project management is the management of a project. The third level in **Figure 4.5 Project Management**, below, and the last process methodology, is project management. At the point of needing and building a PMO, the core function of the PMO will most likely be project management. Project management is the foundation of most PMOs and is something that new PMO Managers must consider as one of the most important areas when establishing and driving their PMO.

Figure 4.5 Project Management shows the industry-standard project management structure. Project Managers can have as few as one project, (especially if it is a large effort) or could manage multiple smaller projects all at the same time. There is no maximum number of projects for an individual Project Manager to have, and that number will depend on many factors and frankly the skills sets of the individual. The whole ratio for Project Managers-to-projects conversation is an interesting one and something that all PMO Managers will face and have to work out for their PMOs. Normally, PMO Managers again depending on size will use a 3:1 ratio for projects to project managers. Therefore, each project manager can manage three projects at a single time and still be successful. This ratio calculation has worked for many PMO Managers across different companies.

Figure 4.5 Project Management

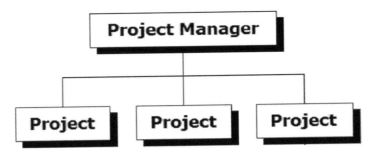

Project management will be the foundation of your PMO and your job as a new PMO Manager is to make sure it has the highest level of focus. There are always new and better ways to improve the project management skills of your individual Project Managers and, as PMO Manager, your role is to drive those improvements for your organization. The project management industry is continually changing and, as PMO Manager, you need to adapt to those changes and continue to drive new and improved ways of doing project management into your PMO. It is up to you to adapt to industry changes and keep improving your employees.

Later in this book, we will go into each process methodology in much more detail to help you understand the basic principles for establishing each one in your own PMO. For now, it is important to understand the basic concepts of each methodology so you can start to think about how each might work with your PMO.

Differences in Process Methodologies

Not only is it important to understand the differences among the three process methodologies: portfolio management, program management, and project management, it is especially important to understand the difference between program management and project management. You would be very surprised how many large companies do not have the basic understanding, and how it makes for a very difficult and confusing work environment. There are large companies out there that use the title Program Manager for highly skilled people who are not fulfilling that role. These individuals would be more appropriately titled, Functional Analysts, Architects, or even Software Testers, but due to the lack of discipline from a project management perspective at these companies, or more aptly, a lack of PMI compliance or acceptance, the company has chosen to use the title Program Manager incorrectly from a PMI perspective. However, when a company has an individual who is actually performing program management (in the purest sense of the title), that person is also called a Program Manager. You can imagine just how confusing that would be day-to-day for the individuals working in the different program manager roles at the same company.

The expectations put on an individual with the title Program Manager are that the individual performs a specific role. If the individual does not have the skills, desire, or background to complete that role, there needs to be some discussions and fact-finding as to whether the individual is actually performing the duties of a Program Manager. It is important you and your staff are clear about their roles and responsibilities at all times and if the person is not doing the work of Program Management, then do not give them that title.

Table 4.1 Portfolio, Program, and Project Manager Roles provides clarity and guidance for PMO Managers to understand the differences about each process methodology role.

Table 4.1 Portfolio, Program, and Project Manager Roles

Role:	Responsibilities:	Notes:
Portfolio Manager	Responsible for company's end-to-end project portfolio. For much more information about portfolio management, see Chapter 8, "Portfolio Management Methodology," later in this book.	Generally, this role does not perform program management or project management duties.
Program Manager	Responsible for company's programs. Can have one or many programs, but the role has complete end-to-end responsibilities for the entire program. For much more information about program management, see Chapter 9,	Does not perform portfolio management and will do limited project management

Role:	Responsibilities:	Notes:
	"Program Management Methodology," later in this book.	duties. Will often have a team of Project Managers working for them who drive the projects in the portfolio.
Project Manager	Responsible for company's projects. Can have one or many projects, but responsible for tactical delivery of a project or many projects. For much more information about project management, see Chapter 10, "Project Management Methodology," later in this book.	Does not perform portfolio or program management duties. This person owns all-up project delivery.

As PMO Manager, it is important that you understand the three process methodology roles and that you build methodologies, various processes, and best practices for each role. Every company and PMO structure is going to be different, but make sure that you are thinking about these three roles as part of the initial building of your PMO. In later chapters, the book goes into great depth on each of these three different process methodologies giving you the foundation you need to understand them well.

PMI Compliance

The project management industry needs compliance. Your PMO needs compliance. When thinking about establishing PMO compliance measurements, across the three different process methodologies (portfolio, program, and project management) think about ensuring that your PMO employees are following the industry-standard methods established by PMI whenever possible. Using PMI as the standard, it would make perfect sense for you to use the same terminology and definitions defined by PMI whenever possible. As PMO Manager, you need to drive PMI-type compliance in your PMO because you can run into trouble if you deviate from that compliance and your employees do not follow any kind of standards or processes. Most companies try to stick as close as possible to PMI compliance standards, while other companies go completely off the rail and do not track closely to PMI compliance standards at all. When companies do not follow PMI compliance standards, they make it very difficult to hire outside resources who do have PMI backgrounds. Those companies end up explaining, "how their company does it" and defending their non-industry standard way they do it. In those cases, it is likely that the company will lose credibility and cause employees a lot of confusion along the way and often quick turnaround right out of the company.

As PMO Manager, most of your employees, unless they are administrative in nature, will fall into the three main process methodologies (portfolio, program, and project management); therefore, you should expect them to follow the processes and procedures you establish when defining those methodologies. The project management industry lends itself very well to creating standard processes and procedures, and then documenting them in user guides, manuals, or playbooks for team members to follow. Later in this book, we go over in great detail each process methodology (portfolio, program, and project) that you, as PMO Manager, will be able to use in your PMO and offer to your employees. Remember the importance of your staff using the standard processes you create with them and try to prevent them from recreating any new processes without your knowledge. When Program/Project Managers go off on their own and skip process and procedures, or manage the projects the way they want to manage them, it is much more difficult for you to help them when they end up needing your help. When you are called in, you will need to figure out what is going on with the project first, and figure out what processes they are using so you know where to start helping them. It can be a real problem, and you will be at a huge disadvantage when trying to come in and quickly help them out and you have no idea they are using different processes or procedures that you have never heard of. This is not a situation you ever want to be in with your team members or your management or especially in front of your customers. You can lose credibility very fast when you are ramping up on something in front of a number of people because one of your employees decided to use a non-standard process and not let you know about it until you are in a position where you need to help them.

When discussing the three process methodologies (Portfolio, Program and Project), it is so important that you, the PMO Manager, understand them well and that you know the difference between those processes and development methodologies. Being clear and deliberate about those differences will help you run a more efficient PMO mainly because you will be able to call out the differences to those who are confused. It is amazing that so many people do not understand the differences between a process methodology and a software development methodology as an example.

Let us spend some time now looking at those differences.

Differences in Industry Methodologies

One of the important components of being a successful PMO Manager is to understand the different methodologies available to your PMO, better than anyone else in the organization. Then, with that knowledge, being able to shape those methodologies to ensure they meet the needs of your management team, customers, and your team members. PMO Managers who do not understand the methodologies can continually struggle in their role, get frustrated, and sometimes just not know how to move things forward. If, as PMO Manager, you are uncomfortable with, or do not understand, the methodologies within your PMO, or you do not understand the company's methodologies that are related to your PMO, a best practice is to immediately sign-up for training or self-study and ramp-up on the methodologies by whatever means possible. It can almost be guaranteed that you will be asked the following three questions repeatedly while in this role and therefore you must have a clear understanding of the process methodologies and the development or manufacturing methodologies in your company.

1. Which methodology are you using in your PMO?
2. Explain the methodology you're using in detail?
3. How does project management play a part in the development or manufacturing methodology you are using? Is there a difference?

That is one of the main reasons why we are covering methodologies in this chapter, because of the amount of times you will be asked about methodologies and answering those three questions. Prepare for them now, because these questions are coming!

In the software industry, and for those of you who are running a software PMO, you will encounter many people who question project management methodologies and software methodologies and how they differ. It is interesting to note that the software industry is one of the only industries where project management is questioned about its validity. It is often heard from software companies that they can "do without the overhead" of project management. This would simply never happen in construction; it is unheard of not to have a Project Manager on a construction project and, therefore, the methodology is never in question. Project management in software is still relatively new and therefore it is continually challenged. It will take time, but one day software project management will be recognized as important as construction project management and software companies will be supportive and not question the value of Project Managers as they do today.

The reason why the value of project management is so important and why the questions continue to arise is due to the lack of understanding about project management methodologies and what a Project Manager does to make them so valuable on a project. Let us move now to the different methodologies across some of the bigger industries just to understand what they are and how Project Managers play a role. Just understanding the different methodologies is good, and then it is quite easy to see where Project Managers actually fit. Having this information will enable you to have smarter and more informed conversations around the role of Project Managers (especially in the software industry), and should put your management, stakeholders, and customers at ease when you propose that all projects have a Project Manager assigned to them. For those in industries other than software, this is good information for you to know as well, on what your software PMO Manager counterparts are facing. You never know, you might find yourself in an industry like software that does not value project management as much, so this information is helpful as well.

Industry Methodologies

As you can imagine, the business world is a very complex environment and there are many industries working every day to accomplish something. It could be building a plane, a house, a bridge, anything, but regardless of the industry, each will have its own methodology or process they follow to create whatever it is they are creating. It is those methodologies, or formal processes, that also require a form of project management within them. As PMO Manager, you need to understand and help shape the methodology used in your company as it is used across these different methodologies. It is also your responsibility to understand where to adjust the methodology, or where to reduce or add tasks, all while driving what is right for the customers and project team members. It is a balance that you will juggle throughout this role, so understanding different industry methodologies will be very beneficial.

Tips & Best Practices

Regardless of which industry you are in, as PMO Manager, it is important to know your industry's methodology well.

Construction Industry

The construction industry has a number of variations of their standard methodology, but the main phases include the following examples:

- Programming, schematic design, design development, construction documents, bidding, construction, occupancy
- Project conception, scope clarity, estimating, procurement bidding and contract negotiations, engineering, construction, closeout
- Planning, tender, contract awarding, buying, construction
- Concept, charter, real estate, planning, design, estimation, bid, award, notice to proceed, construction

As you can see in the construction industry, there are many different variations of how construction projects work, and there really is not one correct way over another, there are just different flavors. If you are a PMO Manager for a construction project, your company will be using a construction process and through your training (including schooling) and personal experience in the field, you will know these phases inside and out and will be able to help the project teams where applicable.

Pharmaceutical Industry

The pharmaceutical industry has a number of variations of their standard methodology, but the main phases include the following examples.

- Research and production, pharmaceutical engineering, quality control, industrial production of an active substance, industrial production of a pharmaceutical product
- Pharmaceutical development, technology transfer, product manufacturing, product discontinuation
- Pharmaceutical process
  - Develop a validation protocol, an operating procedure or a validation master plan for the validation
  - For a specific validation project, define owners and responsibilities

- Develop a validation project plan
- Define the application, purpose and scope of the method
- Define the performance parameters and acceptance criteria
- Define validation experiments
- Verify relevant performance characteristics of equipment
- Qualify materials, (e.g., standards and reagents for purity, accurate amounts and sufficient stability)
- Perform pre-validation experiments
- Adjust method parameters or/and acceptance criteria, if necessary
- Perform full internal (and external) validation experiments
- Develop SOPs for executing the method in the routine
- Define criteria for revalidation
- Define type and frequency of system suitability tests and/or analytical quality control (AQC) checks for the routine
- Document validation experiments and results in the validation report

As you can see in the pharmaceutical industry, there are also different variations of the manufacturing process and, as PMO Manager in that industry, your schooling and years of experience in the field should give you the background and foundation to know how to drive these projects forward and make the appropriate trade-off decisions. You do not just fall into a PMO Manager role in the pharmaceutical industry. This is another industry where nobody questions the Project Manager role.

Manufacturing Industry

The manufacturing industry has a number of variations of their standard methodology, but the main phases include the following examples:

- Car Manufacturing Process
    - Chassis
    - Car body
    - Painting
    - Internal car integration
    - Attaching the body to the chassis
    - Finishing items such as tires, battery, gas and antifreeze

- Airplane Manufacturing Process
    - Determine market requirements and objectives
    - Determine regulatory requirements
    - Establish airplane requirements and objectives
    - Conduct design studies to match technology and design to meet requirements and objectives (there can be trade off—e.g., weight might be increased to meet range and noise requirements)
    - Design the product (airplane)
    - Build airplane
    - Test airplane

- Deliver airplane

The manufacturing industry also has a number of different variations within its lifecycle and each is very specific to the type of product being produced. As for the car example, that process is just the manufacturing process and putting the car together; it does not call out the steps of design or prototyping, and so on. Each phase is critical in creating a car, just much earlier in the process. The auto and airplane industries are more examples of where the Project Manager plays an important role in the process as well and there is usually little to no question about the use of Project Managers across those industries.

Information Technology Industry – Software Projects

The information technology industry (software industry) has a number of variations of their standard methodology, but the main phases include the following examples:

Waterfall/Traditional:

- Initiation, requirements, design, development, test, acceptance, release

Scrum/Agile:

- Initiation, business requirements, architecture and design, development, testing, delivery, and product feedback

In the software industry, there are some variations of the two standard methodologies for delivering software applications and products. Becoming a PMO Manager is often much easier than in any other industry; because people do "fall" into the role and do not necessarily have methodology or project management expertise. Putting people who are not capable of performing the PMO Manager role, can negatively affect and harm the programs and projects they are involved in.

What you will see in each of the methodologies (construction, software, and manufacturing) is that they are very different in nature and that none of them specifically call out project management activities as a main part of their processes. Each methodology is very specific about how to create a particular product or item, but there is no special call out as to how the Project Manager manages the project along the way.

Why is that? Have you thought about why project management processes are missing? Project management is simply an overlying process that sits on top of each methodology, and without the project management processes (and someone doing it), the product (or tangible item) can go off track (late), over budget, or does not provide the expected value to the customer. Without someone steering the boat, the boat will crash.

Bill's Thoughts:

I cannot stress enough to you as PMO Manager how much you will live and breathe "the value of project managers" conversation during the course of a work day, especially if you are a software PMO Manager. I have worked across two countries on hundreds of projects and I cannot count the number of times I have been asked to justify the role of Project Manager. This topic is near and dear to my heart and therefore I want you all to really understand how important it is to your success and the success of your project management team. If they do not feel like you support them, you will not be successful. Not many other managers/leaders of different organizations have to fight the way PMO Managers have to fight for project management and trust me knowing the various project management and development or manufacturing methodologies inside and out will definitely help you win the battle.

Let us spend some time now and review the project management methodology based on PMI, and go over the various stages of that process.

Project Management Methodology/Life Cycle:

The project management methodology/lifecycle includes the following stages and processes:

- Initiation, Planning, Executing , Monitoring and Controlling, Closing

Tips & Best Practices

Some people call project management a process while others call it a methodology. The take-away is to recognize that project management is different from the other development or manufacturing methodologies. You do not see, for example, design, develop, and test in the project management methodology because that is specific to a software methodology only, not a project management methodology.

As noted, the project management process is very different in the construction, software, and manufacturing industries. The different industries focus on producing their product, or item. Have you ever thought about why or how PMI became so popular and how the *PMBOK® Guide* became so widely adopted and accepted across the different industries? What happened to make PMI standards accepted in construction, manufacturing, and so on and not as accepted in software? Why did methodologies across construction, and manufacturing industries not change their steps or processes to formally include project management within the methodology itself? For example, why does the car manufacturing process, not include planning, chassis, planning, create car body, planning, painting and so on, where the planning process (from the project management methodology) would fall between every formal step of the manufacturing methodology? If that were the case, the car manufacturing process would look like this:

- **Car Manufacturing Process**
- **Planning**
- Chassis
- **Planning**
- Car Body
- **Planning**
- Painting
- **Planning**
- Internal car integration
- **Planning**
- Attaching the body with the chassis
- **Planning**
- Finishing items such as tires, battery, gas and antifreeze

Imagine how much longer it would take to produce a car! That would just be crazy and never happen because the added cost and time to the car manufacturing process would be passed onto consumers and we would never be able to afford the cars! It would take forever to get a car out of the manufacturing phase. It certainly would not make sense to add six separate planning steps into the car process. Project Managers certainly plan throughout the every process it is not just specific to one step at a time. Planning once instead of six times makes so much more sense, thereby saving time, money, and reducing any rework. However, an interesting question arises— just because the planning process is not specifically called out in the original car manufacturing process, does that mean no planning is being done? Do you think the big car manufacturing companies do not plan how they manufacture their cars? Clearly, they do, and clearly, they use very strict and rigorous project management best practices all while not formally adding "planning" to each methodology step at each phase, but adding it on top of the methodology, which is how project management should be applied and therefore you need project managers to drive this efforts.

So why do you think that is? As PMO Manager, regardless of the industry you are in, these are the types of thought leadership questions and answers you need to have and be able to converse with your staff, management, and your customers.

The answer to why industries never formally change their methodologies to add the project management methodology is simple really, none of the industries **"had"** to change anything. They figured out a way to adopt the project management methodologies as a process that sits on top of what they were already doing and, therefore, could continue to be successful without adding any additional steps. Clearly, construction did it, the car manufacturers did it, and the software industry did it, but reluctantly. The software industry is much slower to adopt and accept the project management methodology. As PMO Manager, you are in the perfect role to enforce the project management methodology and prove to the software industry how valuable Project Managers are to the execution and success of projects.

Now that we covered and explained how project management sits on top of the different methodologies, who among you cares? Why should you care? Why should a PMO Manager who is running a large PMO at an automobile plant care about how project management methodologies work within different industries? Well, it is an interesting question and you may not necessarily care, but as practitioners in the project management industry, you should care and you should know how project management works regardless of your industry. You do not have to be masters of this information, but you should be knowledgeable. Having this knowledge and understanding of the methodology of your industry well, will help you make better decisions when you need to adjust the methodology. Knowing the problems your PMO Manager counterparts in other industries are facing is also interesting and maybe you can offer suggestions, provide best practices, or help them out if they reach out to you. Just think about the next PMI meeting you attend—you are not just sitting with people who are in software or construction, you are sitting among people across many different industries and, therefore, you should expand your thinking and learn about the challenges other folks are facing and if possible help them. Additionally, you never know when you might be in that industry yourself and this information gives you knowledge of what you could be up against if you do wander over. It is unlikely you will go from being a software PMO Manager to a manufacturing PMO Manager, but you never know, stranger things have happened!

Why else is it important? Well, it is important because if your industry is anything like software, the role of Project Manager is always in question and part of your job will be to continually protect your Project Managers and justify their role in your organization and on projects. If you have a team of Project Managers working for you, and they do not have any support, or your management team continues to question their value, you are going to have some unhappy people who will eventually go to a different organization or company.

Frankly, this is so important for you to think about these different methodologies and to recognize and be aware of these differences as you perform your day-to-day role. The PMO Manager role and the difference that role plays in software industry compared to how it works in other industries such as manufacturing is very different and good to know.

Another major area of confusion is the misunderstanding that the project management methodology and the software methodology are the same thing. **They are not**! You would not believe how many times those in the software industry say they are performing project management because they are creating the deliverables required by the software methodology. If you create a software project schedule are you project managing? Creating the deliverables around project management and actually managing and leading the project are two different things.

As PMO Manager, and especially in the software industry, it is so important for you to call out the differences between the project management methodology and the software development methodology to everyone who will listen. Management, your stakeholders, and customers need to know that completing a software deliverable called a "risk plan," for example, does not constitute project management. It is not project management because all the other things that are associated with that risk plan (for more information, see Chapter 10, "Project Management Methodology," later in this book) are much better aligned to the role of Project Manager than simply filling out the deliverable. The same applies for project schedules, issues lists, budget spreadsheets, resourcing, and so on. They are all needed as part of the project management methodology, but not project management.

As PMO Manager, you have a huge role to protect the project management discipline and the responsibility to your Project Managers working for you who may need help in understanding the different methodologies as well. Actually, you will have a number of different expectations put on you in the role of PMO Manager. These expectations will be from your management, your customers, your employees...etc. Each will have different needs and wants from you and so, it is a good time to look at some of those expectations and specifically qualifications now.

PMO MANAGER QUALIFICATIONS/EXPECTATIONS

It is important to understand some of the expectations that you will be dealing with working as a PMO Manager, especially as you may be new to the role. There might be expectations from your management of what you will be doing in your day-to-day role that you may not be aware of and getting everyone on the same page is important. Also, if you are in the management role now and you are hiring a PMO Manager, then these qualifications and expectations are important to consider during the hiring process.

PMO Managers must have a number of different qualifications to be successful running a large PMO. There is no question that each company will have their unique challenges and expectations for their PMO Manager. However, here is a list of qualifications common across the PMO Manager role regardless of the company.

The first and most obvious qualification is that you need to live and breathe the project management industry. That means, at the minimum, you understand portfolio, program, and project management. You are required to have the background in one or more of these roles. You do not have to be an expert in any one of them, but you have to care enough to learn about them if you do not know them, and you have to want to know more about the ones you do not know that well. You need to take this responsibility of learning the methodologies very seriously when building your PMO. As PMO Manager, the moves you make, the things you say, and how well you market your PMO will factor into how successful you are in this position. Here are some key components of your PMO Manager role:

- **Helper**—You will be asked to step in and help your Project Managers drive components of their projects. You will be asked to help in a variety of areas, just expect it in this role.
- **Advisor**—Acting as an advisor is going to be critical for a PMO Manager. Advising Project Managers how to manage their projects, advising customers on how their projects are tracking, or advising executives on the state of the PMO are all key responsibilities you will take on.
- **Teacher/Mentor/Coach**—Teaching is going to be an area in which, as PMO Manager, your Portfolio, Program and Project Managers will look to you to help them with continually. As PMO Manager, ensure you are well versed in all areas of portfolio, program and project management, because your PMO staff members are going to need some coaching somewhere in the life of their projects.
- **Facilitator**—The role of facilitator will come up often for you, and you will need to be comfortable in this role. You will be facilitating a number of PMO training sessions, PMO review sessions, and other activities, and you will need to be comfortable in this role.

- **Audit/Quality Function**—The auditing function as PMO Manager will either take a portion or a majority of your role, and you will need to decide this based on the PMO type you create, as well as how important you believe it is in the success of your PMO. I believe there is a balance and, as a PMO Manager, you will need to be comfortable doing some auditing as part of your day-to-day role.
- **Strategic Planner**—PMO Managers are constantly balancing their strategic work with their tactical work and, as PMO Manager, you will be constantly looking at the strategic direction of the company, as well as the direction of your PMO, and shifting where applicable.
- **HR Manager**—PMO Managers who have direct staff will also have a component of being an HR Manager as well. You will have to hire, fire, give performance reviews, and more.

Finally, the last and probably the most important role for a PMO Manager, is to be a respected Portfolio Manager, Program Manager, or a Project Manager. If you do not have a background in any of these three areas and you are unable to tactically help your employees on their troubled projects, you run into some credibility issues with them very quickly. That is, when they turn to you to help them on project and you do not have the skills to help them, they end up in a spot where they do not know who to turn to for help and support. Your success in this PMO Manager role will be in question and, in the long term, this could be difficult to overcome. They will not end up using you for anything and your role becomes diminished. This is also true for any PMO employee who needs help. You need to have the skills and ability to help anyone in your organization. Of course, this is not always possible, and you can't be a master in every area, so that's why you should at least know the basics of project management at a minimum and work on portfolio and program management or other areas of your PMO that you are not as familiar with later on.

Tips & Best Practices

Successful PMO Managers have the ability to be jack-of-all-trades and are able to float from strategic to tactical thinking effortlessly. However, it will not come easily, so do not expect that it will.

Summary

The building or enhancing of a PMO is going to vary from company to company and industry to industry; however, this book is going to give you the foundation to help you start. This chapter is focused on areas to giving you the foundation only, but read on because you need much more information to start building or enhancing your PMO than what we covered here in this chapter. The areas we covered, such as creating mission and vision statements, PMO value drivers, and KPIs are all critical to defining the direction you are going to take your PMO. Finally, we discussed the principles and definitions outlined in portfolio, program, and project management and that those principles and definitions are industry standards and something that every PMO Manager should utilize in their PMOs. Do not reinvent the wheel and come up with new PMO processes and procedures that are different then industry standards, as it is not cost effective and it will slow down your ability to show the value of your PMO to your management and customers quickly. You can also quickly lose credibility as a PMO Manager, if you are proposing non-industry standard processes that nobody is familiar with and have not been tried and tested in the industry.

It is also very important to understand how the methodology used in your industry recognizes the discipline of project management. Some industries, such as construction or manufacturing, have no issues with the role of Project Manager, while other industries, such as the software industry, continually struggle with defining the Project Manager role. Your role as PMO Manager is to recognize the value of project management and speak to the differences and the value proposition that Project Managers bring to projects. Ensure that you continually talk about the project management discipline, and recognize and acknowledge it as a required role for every project. In doing so, you can help move the project management profession forward across all industries.

PMO Build Decisions:

1. Write your PMO mission statement

2. Write your PMO vision statement

3. Decide your PMO value drivers and KPIs

4. Decide your PMO budget amounts

5. Decide how close you will match and align to PMI

Chapter Review Answers:

1. There are many areas to focus on during the PMO assessment period but the top three include: PMO environment, PMO organization structure, and the current PMO portfolio of work.

2. The three process methodologies are: portfolio management, program management, and project management.

3. The process methodologies are fundamentally different. PMO Managers must understand the complexities of each methodology. For example, a pure portfolio management methodology is completely different than a project management methodology when it comes to the tactical, day-to-day execution.

4. The project management methodology is the lowest point. Meaning, at the top of the structure is portfolio management, followed by program management, followed by project management. Project management is the lowest tactical point in execution.

5. PMO Managers should have experience with each methodology for the greatest chance of success in this role. Having some knowledge and background in each space allows PMO Managers to understand trade-off

decisions and make priority calls, but most importantly, lets them draw upon their own experiences to help them find solutions.

Chapter 5

PMO Models

Figure 5.1 PMO Build Schedule – PMO Models

Task Name	Resource Names
Step 5 - Design & Build or Enhance Period (Chapter 5 - 12)	**PMO Manager**
Design PMO	**PMO Manager**
Design PMO Core Components	**PMO Manager**
Build PMO	**PMO Manager**
Create PMO Business Management Area on Centralized Repository Site (Sections to create are documented in Implementation Phase)	PMO Manager
- Create PMO Core Components	**PMO Manager**
Create PMO Mission Statement	PMO Manager
Create PMO Vision Statement	PMO Manager
Create PMO Value and KPI's	PMO Manager
Create your PMO Budget	PMO Manager
-Create PMO Model (Chapter 5)	**PMO Manager**
Document PMO Build Decisions	PMO Manager
Review different PMO Models (Support, Directive, Coaching)	PMO Manager
Determine which of the 4's of PMOs to use for your organization	PMO Manager
-Create PMO Maturity Model	**PMO Manager**
Select PMO Categories for PMO Maturity Model	PMO Manager
Review PMO Measurement System	PMO Manager
Create PMO Service Offerings	PMO Manager

Questions you should be able to answer after reading this chapter:

1. Name three types of PMO models.

2. Name the three most common types of PMO models.

3. Why is it important for PMO Managers to understand all of the models?

4. How many measurements are in Dr. Kerzner's Project Management Maturity Model?

5. What are two factors to consider when selecting a PMO model?

When starting to build your PMO, one of your first tasks is to decide which PMO model to use. This decision is one of the most strategic and difficult decisions to make. It is important to understand that there are many different PMO models used today, and there is not one model that will fit every company exactly. As PMO Manager, you ultimately should select the PMO model you want to use for your PMO by selecting the most applicable parts from the various models for your organization. After you determine which PMO model you think is best, you will then have to sell that model to your management team, customers, and PMO employees, so they also believe it is the right model for your company. Your goal by marketing and selling the PMO model is to have it accepted and ultimately adopted for use. Remember, in Chapter 3, "Executive Support—Stop Now!" when we covered the importance of having executive support? Well, that support is critically important when selecting and implementing a PMO model. In this chapter, we cover the different PMO models and give you information so that you can work with your management team, customers, and PMO employees to select the right model for your organization. There are a number of factors to consider during the selection process, which we will examine as we cover the different models in more detail and ultimately select which one will work best for your PMO. When selecting the PMO model, it is a best practice to choose an existing industry standard PMO model (for example, a supportive model) as the foundation, and then adjust that model to meet the unique needs for your industry and your company. Remember the saying, "crawl, walk, run?" Well, that concept is very applicable to selecting and designing a PMO model and it is highly recommended that you adopt that notion throughout this process.

Why is selecting a PMO model so important? Why is having a PMO model in general so critical to how you develop and eventually implement your PMO? These are great questions to consider, but let's first go over some specifics about why deciding which model to use is important and how that decision will drive what you, as PMO Manager, do on a daily basis.

Finally, remember that you will design the different components of your PMO model before you build and then implement it. Remember, design it first, test that design, tweak where necessary, and then build and implement. Keep the concept of designing at the forefront of your mind for every PMO component (not just the PMO Models). Let's look into PMO models now.

Choosing the Right PMO Model

PMO Managers who are responsible for choosing the PMO model for their company are actually in a very difficult position, because choosing one PMO model over another can have huge consequences on how long you, the PMO Manager, and your PMO last in the company. There are many factors as to why one PMO model works over another and PMO Managers need to balance those factors and ultimately decide on the PMO model to use. Some of the company's environmental factors to consider when choosing a PMO model include the following:

- How much budget is there for PMO staff? How well is the PMO funded?
- What is the history of PMOs in the company—what has previously worked or failed?
- What is the maturity level of portfolio, program, and project management in the company?
- What are the biggest pain points in portfolio, program, and project management currently in the company?
- What are the PMO Manager's capabilities—your own background and experience will play a role in what you and your management will decide to use.
- Will company politics interfere with selecting the right model?
- Which PMO model does your leadership/management team want to use?
- What model do your PMO employees want to use? Which models have they already used before?
- At what level of the organization does the PMO sit? For example, does it report to the CIO level, VP level, Director level?
- What is your industry?
- Are there other PMOs in your company today? If so, does this PMO report to an Enterprise PMO?

These are just some of the important questions that you must research and ask yourself before choosing or suggesting a PMO model for your company. Be very careful about the PMO model you choose because there are many different decisions and directions you will take your PMO based on the model you select. In the end, you will have to decide which PMO model to suggest to your management team to then finalize that decision together. In some cases, all you can do is suggest, your management team will have the ultimate decision on the PMO model.

Over time, and after the PMO has proven its value and the programs and projects are consistently and repeatedly delivering results, you can start making changes to the PMO model. These changes should be made to increase company effectiveness, not just for the sake of making changes. That is a very common practice for PMO Managers where they make changes to the initial PMO model after they can see growth and maturity in the company and in the PMO itself. One of the biggest problems that PMO Managers face when selecting one PMO model over another is just that—they select one model over another and assume the model is set in stone. It happens all the time. It shouldn't, but it does. PMO Managers are under so much pressure to build the PMO and start showing value that they make rash decisions, such as choosing the easiest and quickest PMO model just to get the PMO going. It might not even be the right PMO model for the company. Generally, rash PMO model decisions will hurt the effectiveness of the PMO down the line. Some PMO Managers tend to think that they can only use one model or another, when in fact, it is highly recommended, and a best practice, to take the best pieces from many models and fit them into a model that is right for the company. Most PMO Managers do not even consider that tactic. PMO Managers **do not have to choose one PMO model over another**, they just don't, and when they do (for a variety of reasons why) it often leads to their early demise as PMO Manager. Let's try and prevent that from happening to you; you need to go out there and research every PMO model so you can pick the best parts from each model to use in your PMO. Just like selecting the best players for a basketball game, you select the best parts from various PMO models and incorporate them in your PMO.

Industry PMO Models

There are many different PMO models used across the industry. As PMO Manager, it can be difficult to know exactly which model is the right one for your company. It can even be difficult to choose a starting model because there are so many choices, and so many variations and considerations to those choices. This is why selecting the best parts from each model is the best method when choosing a PMO model. If, however, you are in a PMO already and have an existing PMO model, still spend the time to review the different PMO models in this chapter anyway because maybe the current model was right at one time, but is no longer working or effective. It is quite possible you can pick up a trick or two in the different PMO models below that you can turn around and use in your PMO today.

Let us spend some time now and look at the following PMO models:

Supportive PMO—The supportive PMO model generally provides support in the form of on-demand expertise, templates, best practices, access to information, and expertise on projects. This PMO model works in a company where projects are loosely controlled—management deems project rigor and enforcement unnecessary—and emphasis is on supporting the Program and Project managers.

Controlling PMO—In companies where there is a desire to "rein in" the activities, processes, procedures, and documentation, you should use a controlling PMO model. Not only does the controlling PMO provide support, it also requires that PMO employees adhere to the rigor and processes established by the PMO. Requirements might include adoption of specific methodologies, templates, forms, conformance to governance, and application of other PMO-controlled sets of rules. Additionally, PMO employees might need to pass regular reviews of their efforts (programs/projects) by the PMO Manager or delegate to ensure they are adhering to those standard processes.

Directive PMO—The directive PMO model goes beyond control and actually "takes over" either the programs or projects by providing experienced resources to manage them. When the PMO takes on new efforts (programs/projects), the PMO Manager assigns highly professional PMO employees to them. This injects a great deal of professionalism into the different efforts and, because each PMO employee originates and reports to the directive PMO, it guarantees a high level of consistency of practice across all efforts.

Managing PMO—The managing PMO model focuses more on governing programs and projects and tends to be heavy on training, standardized processes and procedures, and centralized reporting. This PMO model receives a lot of management support, which helps PMO employees' job satisfaction by removing obstacles and challenges from their efforts.

Consulting/Supporting/Coaching PMO—The consulting/supporting/coaching PMO model focuses on mentoring and coaching PMO employees and their project teams. This model offers many best practices, processes, and procedures as helpful resources to project teams. The consulting/supporting/coaching PMO model often has very successful mentoring or coaching programs in place that often last for years. Training programs for both Program and Project Managers tend to range from PM 101 to PM 301 level courses. The PMO Manager for this PMO model shares project management best practices across multiple functional areas. This PMO Manager also spends time looking at where the project management industry is heading.

Project Repository PMO—The project repository PMO model has a large centralized repository of templates, methodologies, standards, procedures, tools, and best practices available for use by the PMO employees, including project teams. For example, in this model, the PMO Manager should be consistently looking for new templates, testing existing templates, and refining and working with project teams to ensure the templates are effective. The PMO Manager would be doing that same process of evaluating, testing, and refining for everything in the repository such as tools, standards, best practices...etc.

Enterprise PMO—The enterprise PMO model typically oversees the programs and projects across the whole enterprise. The previous PMO models mentioned tend to be company-based and are not always recommended for working across the enterprise. A common characteristic that enterprise PMO models have across most companies is that their departmental PMO Managers report to them formally, or on the dotted line. A formal relationship has the PMO Manager sitting in a departmental PMO and formally reporting to the Enterprise PMO Manager. An informal relationship has the departmental PMO Manager reporting status and PMO items to the Enterprise PMO Manager, but the departmental PMO Manager will formally report to a functional manager. The other common thing about Enterprise PMOs is that they can have multiple PMOs reporting to them, so there can be a Finance PMO, IT PMO, Marketing PMO and in almost all cases, those different departmental PMOs will roll up and report to the Enterprise PMO.

Other PMOs out there include **center of excellence PMOs, managerial PMOs, and delivery PMOs** as well. You can do our own research and look deeper into any of those PMO models to understand exactly which components will work and not work for your PMO. As noted, often there will be bits and pieces from the various PMO models that you can incorporate in your PMO. Remember, the reason for choosing bits and pieces of the different PMO models is because there is no PMO or company that is exactly the same. For example, you cannot have an enterprise PMO model in one company and that same enterprise PMO model work at a different company. It is just not possible, and the PMO Manager who thinks they can take one PMO model from one company to another company and not change anything is definitely set up to fail.

Bill's Thoughts:

Choosing the correct PMO model is critical and was something I was lucky to have been able to choose when I was building and implemented my PMOs. The PMO model that you select will never be cut and dry; your PMO model will never be just "controlling," "supportive," or "directive." Your PMO model will have flavors from each model, for sure, but it must have a dominate characteristic. Based on my personality, my PMOs were directive-based with some supportive characteristics. In both of my PMOs, I started with the supportive PMO, moved to the controlling PMO, and ended up with a directive PMO. I would recommend that you choose one PMO model (such as the controlling PMO) as your starting point, and as you grow your PMO, your model will also grow and mature.

Four P's of PMOs

Before any final decisions on the PMO model can be made, the PMO Manager must decide on which process methodologies are going to be part of the PMO as well. Remember earlier, we covered the three process methodologies: portfolio, program, and project? Well, we did that because those methodologies and the choice of which one of them (and maybe it is all of them) are you going to use in your PMO is a critical decision point in the PMO model you choose as well. There is an intersection between the PMO process methodologies and the PMO Model choice and it would look similar to **Table 5.1 PMO Model and Process Methodologies** where, as PMO Manager, you decide & document which PMO model and process methodology you are going to use. For example, as you can see in this table, there are some PMO models where portfolio management is not relevant, and in others where it is. The same logic applies to the program management; there are some types of models where program management is much more relevant than for other models. Use this table as a guide; there are too many combinations of PMO models and process methodologies to show. You will see, though, in the table that most PMOs do include project management across every PMO model. However, that does not always have to be the case. You can certainly have PMOs that are simply portfolio PMOs and do not include a program or project management component. The value of this table, especially when building the PMO, is that it gets you, the PMO Manager, thinking about the various combinations of models and process methodologies so that you can ask the right questions to determine which combination is right for your situation. Ultimately, the end result is to determine the combination that works for your PMO, or to review an existing PMO and determine if the existing combination is effective.

Table 5.1 PMO Model and Process Methodologies

PMO Model / Process Methodology			
PMO Model	**Portfolio**	**Program**	**Project**
Supportive	Yes	Yes	Yes
Controlling	Yes	Yes	Yes
Directive		Yes	Yes
Managing	Yes		Yes
Consulting		Yes	Yes
Project Repository			Yes
Enterprise PMO	Yes	Yes	Yes
Center of Excellence		Yes	Yes
Managerial			Yes
Delivery	Yes	Yes	Yes

Again, use this table as a guide only; it is **not a recommendation** of what you should use in your PMO, as there are many variations and considerations that only you will know about your company and your management and customers that will drive the final PMO model and process methodology decision.

Choosing the PMO Model for an Existing PMO

As PMO Manager, you might be coming into an existing PMO. It happens all the time, as you get into the PMO and start looking around, it is very likely that you find that the existing PMO needs some adjustments in order to make it more successful. Oftentimes, the existing PMO might not be using the right PMO model, and it is your role to determine the issues with the existing model, and then make the recommendations on how the PMO model would change to improve its overall effectiveness. When determining the PMO model for an existing PMO, you should already know the different models in the industry very well, and then use that knowledge when assessing the current PMO to determine any enhancement areas. Comparing the different PMO models to the existing PMO model gives you an advantage because you know what you are working with in the existing model and what it may or may not be missing. By understanding the different industry PMO models already, you may see very quickly that you are working with a supportive PMO or a directive PMO, so you can notify management where some potential problems are and what changes can be made to turn the existing PMO around and make it more effective.

Before you offer suggestions or changes to an existing model, though, make sure you grasp the current situation and identify problem areas. You can always make improvements and changes to an existing model, but make sure there is no question that the changes you make, focus on fixing the problem areas. Company politics can be one of the biggest problem areas, and those types of issues can be challenging to resolve and might have nothing to do with the existing PMO model.

When assessing the existing PMO model, you might find that the existing model is a supportive PMO; you also see that it's failing badly, programs and projects are all over budget and nothing is hitting their schedules, frankly everything is a mess. In those cases, instead of adding components to the existing PMO, you might recommend moving the PMO to a completely different PMO model—one that prevents or slows down some of the issues from occurring. This is why it is so important to understand the differences in the PMO models, and why one model might be more effective than another model, when you run into situations like this one.

As PMO Manager, you need to know these models well, grasp, and understand PMO models thoroughly—especially when you are walking into an existing PMO and you have to be ready to field questions as to why the current model is worse than the one you are proposing. Be ready and prepared for that challenge right away because, quite often, if you have been called in and assigned as the new PMO Manager, there were clearly problems and valid reasons why they needed you and something was most likely wrong with the current PMO. One of the first things on your list to do is figure out what went wrong with the existing PMO and what needs improving. Spend time with the management team, customers, and the PMO employees to find out those reasons before making any PMO model changes or recommendations.

To better your knowledge, spend time and do research on the Internet, read books on the subject, and get as familiar as you can with the industry PMO models and, as indicated earlier, make sure you understand the different process methodologies as well. Understanding both will be critical to your success as PMO Manager. You also owe it to yourself and your organization to know both of these topics well and better than the rest of the employees in the company, especially as PMO Manager.

Bill's Thoughts:

I have always been thrilled and love digging into PMO models and knowing what different companies do in their PMOs. It is so interesting to review, for example, how manufacturing runs their PMOs, how software does it, and so on. Just spending a little time looking at what works and doesn't work enables you to be much more valuable to your company and make smarter decisions about what changes to make to an existing PMOs or what to add when building a new PMO. I highly recommend, if you are serious about being a PMO Manager, that you spend the time and understand the different models in the industry.

Considerations for Selecting the PMO Model

The PMO model and maturity measurements system that you choose are going to dictate how you, as PMO Manager, drive your PMO on a daily basis. If you run a supportive PMO, for example, your daily activities will consist of tactically being involved in projects from a supportive perspective—offering consulting advice, suggesting templates and processes, and doing what you can to support the project in a real hands-on manner. On the other hand, running an enterprise PMO, for example, you probably won't get in the depths of any one particular program or project, but could tend to be working across multiple departmental PMOs and keeping all the statuses aligned and providing management reporting. These are just two examples of the kinds of scenarios you can run into by making one PMO model selection over another. So consider, what your strengths are as well in this PMO model selection process. You certainly want to be in a role that plays to your strengths and if you are in a situation where you can select the PMO model, it should be a model where you can provide the most value to the organization as well. Consider that in this PMO model selection.

When selecting a PMO model, you should think about some of the following considerations.

Management Opinions/Recommendations—Your management team is going to have a huge influence on the PMO model you end up choosing. It is very common for strong management teams to force a desired PMO model choice.

Office Politics—plays a role in the PMO model that you choose. Typically, office politics will force a PMO model choice that is the least impactful to the overall company. This is just another factor, but sometimes the hardest one to deal with during this process.

Staffing—The PMO model you choose will also help define your staffing model and the types of personnel needed for your PMO. For example, if you have a supportive or consulting PMO, you, as PMO Manager, will want to staff your PMO with trainers, teachers, or consultants who have the ability to train and teach the Portfolio, Program and Project Managers. If you have a directive PMO, you will want to hire and staff your PMO with industry experts who are looking for the latest trends and best practices to direct or guide your PMO employees. We talk about staffing in a later chapter, but understanding how PMO staff is used for one particular PMO model over another PMO model is definitely going to be important in this selection process. As you read and understand the different PMO models, keep an eye to how staffing is handled in the different models.

Methodology— Process methodologies (portfolio, program, and project) are integral as well in the PMO model selection process. For example, if your PMO model is coaching and you only have project management as your process methodology, then everything you do in your PMO will be around coaching and improving project management methodology. All training sessions, tools, standards, and best practices will only focus on project management and nothing else. In this scenario, it is much easier to run a PMO, especially when there is on one thing only to focus on. It is rarely the case where the PMO has just one process methodology, but it happens and so understand that the process methodology selection plays an important role in your PMO model decision as well.

Budget—The availability of budget also plays a role in the PMO model selection process. Budget is actually a very interesting dynamic in running a PMO because there are different budgeting models that companies use to fund their PMOs. The budget conversation will be very important for you and your management team to have early in the PMO building process. In doing so, both of you understand exactly how much budget there is for the PMO. In some cases, management might decide on a model where you charge back the expenses of having a PMO employee on an active programs or projects to the organization that they are in running the effort. In other cases, management might decide to fund the PMO separately, you, as PMO Manager, will then have complete control of the budget from a centralized fund, and you lend out your PMO employees to the different efforts across multiple organizations. There are several different budget models, and a very important conversation to have with your management team as early as possible in the PMO build process and definitely again during the PMO Model selection.

In the end, you will have five main factors that you, as PMO Manager, will face when choosing the final PMO model for your company. Make sure that you are aware of these considerations and have as much information as possible to make this critical decision.

PMO Maturity Model

Regardless of the PMO model that you choose, your next focus will be building a PMO maturity model. The PMO maturity model is a measurement model for your PMO. The PMO maturity model shows management how well the PMO is executing. If you are enhancing an existing PMO, document the existing maturity model and look for areas that are working well and not so well. Most existing PMOs will have some sort of maturity model in place already and, as PMO Manager, you need to review it, study the merits of the model, and consider it carefully before you recommend or suggest changes to it. You might not have any history with this PMO, so you could be making some early assumptions that might not be true. That is a bad spot for any PMO Manager.

Having a PMO maturity model is a great way to measure the effectiveness of your PMO and gives you the ability to understand what and where to focus to improve the PMO. Every company uses a form of measurement to determine how well things are progressing and your PMO will be no different. Actually, this is a great way to prevent your management or your customers from scrutinizing your PMO, by implementing a measurement model when first building your PMO, so you have the relevant data to provide them on how well the PMO efforts (programs/projects) are performing. By doing this, this should reduce any concerns that your management or your customers will have around the effectiveness of your PMO. You to be in a place where you can have real conversations with them around how well the PMO is performing and looking at real data to prove its effectiveness. It is an important part of a PMO Manager's job to drive their organizations at the tactical, day-to-day level by having measurement models in place and showing data to management and customers on how the PMO is performing. If it is performing well, than you and your management can talk about making things better, if there are issues, then the data will show you were to focus to improve those areas.

The maturity model provides PMO Managers with the foundation of their PMO. The maturity model is based on categories and measurement scores. These categories are applicable to your industry and your company specifically. Most companies will not have the same categories or the same number of categories. This is for the PMO Manager and their management team to determine together when building or enhancing a PMO.

One of the key components of a PMO maturity model is to have a measurement system. This system allows PMO Managers the mechanism to score the different categories within their PMO. Dr. Harold Kerzner's Project Management Maturity Model is industry leading and can be used as a measurement system for your PMO maturity model. For more information about Dr. Harold Kerzner's model, search the Internet or read his countless best-selling project management books. There is no sense in creating your own measurement system when Dr. Kerzner has already created one. His model is the industry standard model for measuring project management maturity, not necessarily PMO maturity, but we are going to cover how it will work for both. It is highly recommended that you use the Kerzner's project management maturity model as your measurement system for your PMO maturity model.

However, there is one difference in how you are going to use the PMO maturity model than how Dr. Kerzner suggests using it. Instead of assessing your PMO at a single level (level 1-5), look at your PMO as having different levels of maturity across the different categories you select for your maturity model (i.e. Tools). This is a different perspective from how Dr. Kerzner sees it, but in doing so, you are able to mature components of your PMO at different rates. This is what happens in the real world of PMOs. Using this approach allows your PMO to have different assessment scoring ratings across multiple different categories. Having the different categories gives your PMO the possibility of being at different levels for each category. Does that make sense? For example, say you have a Metrics/Repository/Knowledge category and you assessed it at a level 2, and you have a Tools category and you assessed that at a level 1, and then you have an Organization/People category that you assessed at a level 2. Thus, you have three different scores across the three different categories. That's amazing and gives you so much flexibility. You no longer make the same mistake that almost every other PMO Manager in the world makes and that is rate your PMO at one level only. Long gone are the days when PMO Managers say, "My PMO is at a level 3." Nope, you can say it is at a level 1 for Tools, a level 3 for Process, and a 2 Organization/People. By taking this approach, your PMO maturity model gives you more flexibility and gives you a very different way to drive your PMO. The flexibility is amazing. Does that make sense, it is pretty easy to understand! If you use Dr. Kerzner's project management maturity model only, then you end up with rating your PMO at only one level at a time. That may be fine in some cases, but it will limit your flexibility in the long run and your ability to measure the different categories with different scores. Using Dr. Kerzner's Project Management Maturity model as the only method to rate your PMO maturity, you also lose the ability to be at different levels across different categories and, hence, lose your ability to track at a much more granular level because you are tracking across one category not multiple categories. Using the multiple categories and rating each category is definitely a best practice that PMO Managers should adopt in their PMOs.

It is important to note that Dr. Kerzner's Project Management Maturity model is primary for project management maturity, not PMO maturity. The way we have applied Dr. Kerzner's model in this example is a bit out of context to how and what it was originally intended. Because Dr. Kerzner's model is an industry standard and is widely accepted to apply toward project management maturity, it is still a best practice, we just found a different and creative way of using it for assessing the PMO maturity as well. As PMO Manager, you will find that having that flexibility and different ratings across the different categories will be very beneficial.

Figure 5.2 PMO Maturity Model Using Four Categories shows a PMO maturity model that uses four categories against Dr. Kerzner's five-level measurement model. In this figure, you will see each category and you will see Dr. Kerzner's measurement system applied to each category. These scores represent "future state" and "current state" for each category. The "future state" is shown in light gray and the "current state" in dark gray. Another best practice and something that I have used in the past is to actually document the accomplishments you did in your PMO for each category and list them to the right of the measurement scores. It is important to show what you accomplished in your PMO to warrant those scores.

Figure 5.2 PMO Maturity Model Using Four Categories

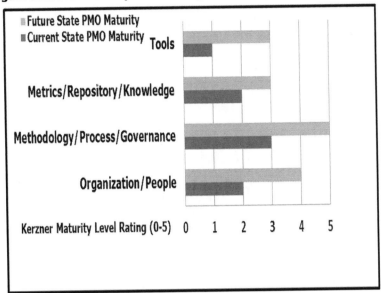

What do you think? Make sense? This PMO maturity model applies to any PMO and uses industry standard ratings (Kerzner model). Using this approach is highly recommended and a best practice to implement within your new PMO. It is such an important way to establish and set up your PMO, and a great model to track maturity.

PMO Maturity Categories

Creating and selecting the appropriate categories from the PMO model for your PMO will depend on many different factors and considerations. It would be almost impossible to give a complete list of categories for every company, because every company is so different. However, to get you started, here are some sample categories that you could use that may or may not work. They include:

- Tools/Infrastructure
- People or Resources
- Methodology
- Process
- Governance

As PMO Manager, make sure you are driving this PMO category selection process with your PMO employees, management and your customers. As a group, you all have to determine which categories make sense for your PMO. Do not just pick categories for the sake of picking categories because you will be applying measurements to each category and the more categories you have, the more you potentially get measured. There are many different approaches to creating and understanding which categories to use for your PMO. Organizational factors, politics, management opinion, and overall project management maturity will all play vital roles in deciding the categories to use for your PMO. The following key questions should be considered when developing your own set of categories for your PMO:

- What do Project Managers need in order to perform their jobs?
- What organizational factors or processes drive the categories of your PMO? Possibilities include: Sarbanes-Oxley, portfolio management, and auditing.
- What are the key areas the leadership team or your customers want the PMO to drive?
- What categories do your PMO employees feel are necessary?

The different questions and scenarios are company-focused and, therefore, it is impossible to have a right or wrong number of categories, you just have to be smart about picking your categories and understand that there is a measurement component for each. If you need a number, then it is recommended to use four or five categories at the most, and a minimum of three. If you have too many categories in your PMO, it can get too complicated and almost impossible to move the scoring measurements forward against every one of them. If you only have one or two categories, the lack of categories can result in a weak PMO structure. Achieving the right balance in the number of categories and how much measurement you want to do in your PMO is ultimately up to you, the PMO Manager.

PMO Maturity Scoring

As you gathered from **Figure 5.2 PMO Maturity Model Using Four Categories**, it is easy to adopt this PMO maturity model to fit any PMO. However, it is very important that, as PMO Manager, you are able to control and change the number of categories that work for your company. It is also important that you **do not change the industry-standard** Project Management Maturity Model created by Dr. Harold Kerzner. By not following Dr. Kerzner's Project Management Maturity model, you could lose credibility or add unneeded complexity that causes confusion in this measurement process.

Bill's Thoughts:

The PMO maturity model will help you tremendously if you decide to implement it in your PMO. Using this model will give you so much flexibility and will allow you to have a much better conversation with your leadership and management team that would not be possible if you were using a single-number maturity model (i.e. PMO is rated at level 2). I can't stress enough that you will constantly be rated and questioned on the value your PMO is providing, and where you are heading and taking the PMO into the future. Using this PMO maturity model (with the 5 point scoring system) enables you to drive those conversations at such a detailed and tactical level and have real data to support how well the PMO is performing in the different categories. I love this model; I have used it for years now and it is really something you should consider adopting as well in your PMO.

In **Figure 5.3 DR. Kerzner's PM Measurement Model**, you will see the standard definitions for the five levels of measurement maturity. This model very nicely defines the scale to which you measure your different categories in your PMO maturity model. Adding additional measurements to this scale complicates the model and is not recommended. Abstain from adding to this model at all costs. Using an industry-standard maturity model gives your PMO credibility and allows you to track to established standards. Adding more or reducing from the model takes you outside of the norm and might invalidate the whole model. This is not something you want to occur in your PMO; you want everyone to understand and adopt the standard model. You also want to use the fact that it is a standard across the industry as a good reason why you are choosing to use in your own PMO and not reinventing something from scratch.

Figure 5.3 Dr. Kerzner's PM Measurement Model

(1) Ad-Hoc	(2) Planned	(3) Managed	(4) Integrated	(5) Sustained
Common Language: In this level, the organization knows the need and value of basic project management terminology	**Common Processes:** The organization matures and recognizes that common processes must be developed so that one project's successes and lessons learned can be applied to the next project	**Singular Methodology:** The organization sees the synergy from multiple process methodologies and finalizes a single project management model	**Benchmarking:** The organization views project management as a means to become more competitive. So, the company decides to benchmark "best in class" or "best in industry" practices to improve its singular project management model	**Continuous Improvement:** In this level, the organization continues to evaluate best project management practices and uses this information to enhance its singular methodology or project management business model

As we look at the different industry PMO maturity models and Dr. Kerzner's standard measurement model categories (ad-hoc, planned, managed, integrated, and sustained), it is important that you create the right maturity model for your PMO and that you score your maturity fairly and with an eye toward continual improvement.

Scoring your PMO categories too low might set expectations with management or your PMO employees that might be difficult to turn around, and setting the score too high can set different expectations and bring its own challenges. A score that is higher than it should be is going to look like there is a level of maturity that is simply not there. That can falsely represent the actual maturity level of the PMO and management might expect more than the PMO is capable of providing.

Regardless of which PMO maturity model you use, selecting the right categories at the beginning of defining the maturity model is very important, although can be changed later. The maturity models can change and adapt over time, but at the beginning, make sure to select the most relevant categories to your company and your industry. Then look to adopt and change the categories if you need to down the line. As PMO Manager, you should focus on where and how the maturity model is working first, and look to adjust it and make enhancements ongoing. At least once a year you should be re-addressing the PMO maturity model, and make any adjustments or changes at that time. Too many changes cause instability in the PMO and no ability to take real measurements of how well the PMO is progressing. Once a year, however, is enough time to evaluate how everything is working and make corrections where needed.

Running a PMO without a maturity model can leave you struggling and with no process in place to measure, how well everything is going. It would be difficult to know where to improve the PMO or where to back off because the PMO is operating at a level that is acceptable to management and the customers. That is such a key point, when you are using the Kerzner maturity model across the different categories, you can see where there may be categories that have high scores and you decide that you are not going to try to mature those categories anymore. For example, you can have a Tools category at a level 4 maturity, and you and your management decide 4 is mature enough for tools, so you make the decision to no longer focus on maturity your PMO tools. What your PMO employees have and are using for tools are working well enough, and no further investment in tools is required. In this case, you made the choice that PMO tools do not need to move to a level 5 maturity and the PMO can still execute successfully.

Creating PMO Service Offerings

As you have now probably spent a number of hours working with management and customers about which PMO model to choose, it is now time to decide which services you will offer based on that model. Many service offers are simple to define after you have the PMO model in place. Many decisions you make around which services to offer will partially depend on your company's industry, and company type as well, so it is important to understand those factors in creating service offerings for your PMO. Your own background and experience will also play a role in determining the service offerings as well, but those will be second to the needs of your company and industry. I.e. if you are a long time project management trainer or come from the consulting world where you managed projects, then there could be some service offerings that your PMO can have that are tailored to that background.

Typical service offerings:

- Create and maintain a centralized repository for project information (repository model)

- Project management training (supportive/coaching model)

- Creation of project management best practices (supportive/coaching model)

- Program/project auditing (directive model)

These are just some of the multiple service offerings that you, as PMO Manager, must define after nailing down your PMO model. A complete list of service offerings would almost be impossible to provide to anyone because of the vast amount of industries, difference in companies, and management opinions. However, the take-away for PMO Managers is to define the initial service offerings for your PMO and build the PMO roles and responsibilities staffing model using those service offerings as a contributor to that process. We are going to talk more about service offerings in the next chapter, when we go over staffing for your PMO. We also cover service offerings again in the PMO Roles & Responsibilities Staffing Model Matrix that ties PMO staff to service offerings.

Bill's Thoughts:

Do not forget to create a list of service offerings at the time you build your PMO. Many PMO Managers forget to create this list and start PMOs with no idea what to do next. Also, do not underestimate the amount of time it will take to create a list of service offerings and to get their buyoff and approval from management. Spend the time to document and create a list of service offerings, which will provide you the path to building the right PMO for your organization. In the two PMOs I built, this is exactly what I did and it allowed me to have very high-level and strategic conversations with my management team and customers, and very tactical conversations with the PMO team members about how we were going to run the organization.

Creating and documenting your service offerings is an important step in building and implementing your PMO, and it is highly recommended. These offerings set the foundation for how you will operate your PMO and what you are going to offer to your customers.

Summary

When summarizing the PMO model selection process, it can't be stressed enough the importance of this decision. On one hand, you have to have a model in place to drive your PMO forward, but on the other hand whatever model you pick, it is not going to be the sole model for your PMO because you are going to have bits and parts from many different models. Remember, there are seven different (ten total, you need to research three of them for more detail) PMO models documented in this chapter and you, as PMO Manager, would be very wise to take parts of the different models and create your PMO based on the areas that work for your company. Do not get stuck having to choose one model over another model because you can end up not being able to use components that your organization needs that were not part of the original model. For example, if you use a directive PMO model only, and your Project Managers are desperate for coaching and mentoring, which is not a component of the directive model, your chances of running a successful PMO might be limited. Another example would be if you use a coaching PMO model and your yearly budget for your Project Managers are funded by project budgets, you will not have the budget to bring in coaches even though that is the basis of your whole model; thereby, setting you up for failure. In this example, any outside experts you bring in will be an overhead tax to your project's budget, so think about that impact to the budget or the fact that there could be no budget for coaches. You can quickly go over budget if you miss planning for that overhead in this case coaches because that is the PMO model you are driving. That kind of scenario is exactly why knowing your PMO budget and how your PMO employees are paid for each year are important considerations in this process.

PMO Build Decisions:

1. Decide which P's to use in your PMO.

2. Decide on the initial PMO model you will use.

3. Decide which categories you will use for your maturity model.

4. Decide which measurement framework you will use for your maturity model.

5. Decide which service offerings will be part of your PMO.

Chapter Review Answers:

1. Three types of PMO models are: supportive, controlling, consulting/supportive/coaching PMOs.

2. Three most common PMO models are: supportive, controlling, directive.

3. PMO Managers must understand which components will work and which won't work for their PMO. Understanding only one model will pave the way for how the PMO Manager drives the PMO. Without understanding the other models,

the PMO Manager might try to force-fit their limited knowledge into their organization, which may or may work.

4. Dr. Kerzner's project management maturity model includes five measurements (Ad-Hoc, Planned, Managed, Integrated, and Sustained).

5. There are many, but two are: management opinion and methodology (portfolio, program, or project).

Chapter 6

PMO Staffing Models

Figure 6.1 PMO Build Schedule – PMO Staffing Models

Task Name	Resource Names
PMO Build Schedule	**PMO Manager**
+Step 1 - Grow PMO Manager Skills - Ongoing Activity	**PMO Manager**
+Step 2 - Obtain Executive Support (Chapter 3)	**PMO Manager**
+Step 3 - Assessment Period (Chapter 4)	**PMO Manager**
+Step 4 - Recommendation Period	**PMO Manager**
+Step 5 - Design & Build or Enhance Period (Chapter 5 - 12)	**PMO Manager**
Design PMO	**PMO Manager**
+Design PMO Core Components	**PMO Manager**
-Build PMO	**PMO Manager**
Create PMO Business Management Area on Centralized Repository Site (Sections to create are documented in Implementation Phase)	PMO Manager
+Create PMO Core Components	**PMO Manager**
+Create PMO Model (Chapter 5)	**PMO Manager**
+Create PMO Maturity Model	**PMO Manager**
-Create PMO Staffing Model (Chapter 6)	**PMO Manager**
Create a PMO Roles and Responsibilities Staffing Model RACI	PMO Manager
Create a PMO Organization Model	PMO Manager
Create a PMO Career Path, moving through Project Coordinator, Project Manager, Program Manager, Portfolio Manager	PMO Manager
Document PMO Build Decisions	PMO Manager

Questions you should be able to answer after reading this chapter:

1. Describe the value of the PMO Roles and Responsibilities Staffing Model RACI.

2. What are three common PMO employee qualifications?

3. When would you hire a permanent employee over a vendor or contractor? Do having vendors and contractors make sense for some projects?

4. Name three typical PMO roles

5. What is the value of creating a PMO organization chart?

The PMO staffing model that you use will depend on many different factors, some that you can control, and some that you cannot control. These factors will vary from industry to industry and from company to company. However, the great thing about PMO staffing models and your role, as PMO Manager, is that it is in your hands to create and define exactly what your staffing needs are for your organization. It is repeatedly heard that people are running PMOs on their own, which is simply not a long-term recipe for success. Actually, it would be very challenging for anyone to run a PMO alone without some sort of support or administrative help. If you are in that position now, there are some recommendations later in this chapter for you to review and consider.

It is interesting that management can be supportive of PMOs, hire you as the PMO Manager, but then not give you the staff to support it. PMOs tend to be one of the few organizations in which management expects one person to work alone and be successful. This is a work environment that, as PMO Manager, you should be prepared for and know how to handle if you are ever in this position. Frankly, this typically happens because the concept of using a PMO is still new to companies, and therefore, management is unwilling to sink a lot of money into an organization that they aren't confident will help the overall company be successful. Unlike human resources or the finance organization, your PMO and role as PMO Manager is to make sure that you are showing "quick wins" continually and that you are perceived as helping the company and adding value. This is turn will help you, by allowing you to hire your PMO staff and build your staffing model.

There are many factors to consider when determining which staffing model is right for your organization, and probably the biggest consideration is the PMO model. We just covered the different PMO models in Chapter 5, "PMO Models," and one of your decision points was to choose the PMO model for your organization. Now, you will use that PMO model to help determine the staff you need to hire for your PMO. Actually, the PMO model you chose should give you the insight into the type of staff you need to hire. For example, questions like do you need to use permanent company employees, or can you get away with using contractors or vendors. In a supportive PMO, for example, hiring a number of highly skilled contractors to "support" or "guide" your employees in program or project execution is scenario where you would consider both the PMO model and the staffing decision as input. In the supportive example, contractors are preferable to hiring permanent employees who are put in the position of having to "support" other employees, which often does not turn out that well.

Previously, we covered the importance of resources, procedures, and infrastructure; and if you think about it, the PMO staffing model is all about the people (resources). When you have the right people in the roles, where they are most experienced and most comfortable, it is paramount for your success as PMO Manager. Your resources are the backbone of the organization and without them happy and fully committed to the role, you will struggle to be successful. Often, the PMO Manager is also the functional manager to the PMO employees, which adds another dynamic to consider when staffing your PMO. If you are the functional manager, you act and behave differently than you would if you were managing vendors or contractors. As you enter the PMO staffing model process, think about how important each resource is to your success and build yourself a team that you are proud of and that will take you into the future.

Finally, remember that you should design your staffing model and staffing plan before you start hiring your employees and vendors or contractors. This chapter will take you down the path to understanding all the different aspects of managing PMO employees and various vendors or contractors, but do not forget to run the staffing model by your management team for approval and to make sure you have the budget to cover the PMO staff that you require. Do not just rush out and start hiring people, get your approvals first.

Let us start looking into PMO staffing models now and determine how to go about hiring the right talent for your organization.

Building PMO Staffing Model

When selecting the right PMO staffing model, there are some factors to consider that are common to most PMOs.

One of the first considerations you should take into account when starting to think about staffing your PMO is your PMO model. Is your PMO model supportive, directive, controlling, or consulting? The PMO model you chose will drive the skill sets needed in for your organization. After deciding which PMO model to use, the next step is to set up the organization structure within that model. This is an important step because it is very possible, for example, to be using a supportive PMO model and have a number of different groups focused on different areas of that model. Therefore, you would need different staff for those different focus areas. For example, you could hire someone who is an expert at using Microsoft® Project to teach and mentor your Project Managers on using Microsoft® Project, and in your same organization, you could hire a methodology expert to train your Project Managers on methodologies. The Microsoft® Project expert and the methodology expert would most likely be two people with very different backgrounds, but both needed in your supportive PMO model. Does that make sense? Understanding your PMO roles is a big component in understanding the staffing needs of your organization.

One of the simplest and fastest ways to establish the staffing needs for your PMO is to create a **PMO Roles and Responsibilities Staffing Model (RACI)**. When you understand this process and how it works, you will quickly see how valuable it is. You should already be familiar with the RACI model from your previous project work; PMO RACI is not that much different because the fundamentals of how to use the model are the same. The only exception is that this RACI will be comprised of your PMO service offerings and will map to the individual PMO roles needed to provide those services. For example, you could have a service offering, "Provide yearly PMO funding" where you have a role, such as a "PMO Executive," mapped in your PMO staffing RACI to that offering. Therefore, essentially, you are assigning the PMO Executive the task of providing you with the PMO budget for the year. Understanding the staff you need for your PMO will highly depend on the services your PMO will provide. This RACI is a tool to use to understand your PMO from a services and staffing perspective and will provide insight to holes that you have from a services perspective, or from a role/individual perspective. In either case, it is a win-win situation to know what is missing so that you can easily fill it if needed. You might reach a point where the services that your PMO offers are nice but unnecessary, and if you do not have an individual to fill the role, then you can cut it from your PMO. Maybe add it back at a later date. This is simply your choice and it is better to cut something earlier than later in the process. Creating the PMO staffing RACI is an important process to go through with your management team and customers to make sure you set expectations of the services that the PMO will offer and their associated roles. By doing this, you should also expect that your management team and customers are supporting your resource decisions from the start. In most cases, this mapping exercise (between the services offered by the PMO and the roles) also becomes an important component in any PMO marketing you do. Sometimes, as PMO Manager you need to market and make people understand why you are bringing in resources and what services they will be working on within your PMO.

In Chapter 5, "PMO Models," we talked about developing specific PMO services, and now with those services documented, you can attempt to align them to the roles and resources needed in your PMO. Let us look at **Figure 6.2. PMO Roles and Responsibilities Staffing Model RACI**, below, which illustrates the expected roles of individuals across the top of the RACI and the different PMO services, by group, down the left side of the RACI. The intersection cell between the services and the individual required to fill that role are completed with the standard R, A, C, I assignments; and is the same process and no different from how all RACIs work on projects today.

Figure 6.2 PMO Roles and Responsibilities Staffing Model RACI

PMO Roles and Responsibilities Staffing Model RACI PMO Type: _____ Responsibility Definitions: R- Responsible A - Accountable C - Consult I - Inform	PMO Executive Leader:	PMO Stakeholder(s):	PMO Manager:	PMO Administrator/Coordinators:	Portfolio Manager:	Program Manager:	Project Manager:	Methodology Specialist:	PMO Trainers
Provide Executive Support for PMO									
Provide PMO Leadership	A	R	R		C	C	I	I	I
Provide PMO Goals and Missions	A	R	R		C	C	I	I	I
Provide PMO Funding	A	R	R		C	C	I	I	I
Provide Leadership and Drive PMO									
Drive day to day operations of the PMO	R	R	A,R	R	C	C	I	I	I
Hire, Retain and Mentor to PMO Staff	R	R	A,R	R	C	C	I	I	I
Drive PMO Budget and financial Decisions	R	R	A,R	R	C	C	I	I	I
...									
...									
Provide Portfolio Management Services for PMO									
Drive Organization Portfolio Process	I	I	R	R	A,R	C	I	I	I
Drive Portfolio Budget Process	I	I	R	R	A,R	C	I	I	I
Drive yearly Planning session	I	I	R	R	A,R	C	I	I	I
Provide Program Management Services for PMO									
Drive Program Management Processes for Org's Programs	I	I	R	R	C	A,R	R	I	I
Drive Program Budget Process	I	I	R	R	C	A,R	R	I	I
Drive Program Staffing Process	I	I	R	R	C	A,R	R	I	I

This sample **PMO Roles and Responsibilities Staffing Model RACI** is an excellent tool to understand the mapping between the services offered by your PMO and staff needed to fill those services. By completing each of the major groupings (for example, Provide Executive Support for PMO), and then the services within that group (for example, Provide PMO Leadership), and then adding the type of commitment in the intersecting cell, you will have completed the RACI for your PMO and will have taken a huge step in defining your PMO staffing requirements. This is such an important task for you, as PMO Manager, to create for your organization because it is going to set the foundation for your PMO services and the roles that you need. The PMO staffing RACI is something that the PMO Manager is responsible for creating themselves along with the support of their executives, customers, and if they exist PMO employees. This RACI requires the background knowledge of the company's organizational politics, knowledge of specific PMO requirements, and direction on the different services that the PMO will offer, all of which are discussions that are held between management and the PMO Manager, and occasionally some or limited PMO employees.

If you are evaluating an existing PMO, one of the first things you can do to understand the current services that the PMO offers, is to complete the same type of RACI for that

PMO. This will ground you on the services the existing PMO offers and will highlight the areas where that PMO may be short on staff or not offering a particular service. This is a smart way to approach creating a new PMO or reviewing an existing PMO.

As the PMO progresses and time moves on, one of the best practices for PMO Managers to follow is to continue to update the PMO RACI and, as any new PMO services are introduced, they are added to the RACI and the appropriate staff is hired, or found internally, to provide the service. When first creating a PMO, there are a lot of unknowns and areas that are unclear, so really, the only method of keeping the RACI accurate is to refine and update it as things make more sense and mature.

PMO Staffing Qualifications

One of the common challenges that PMO Managers will face when completing the staffing model is defining the roles and services for each staff member. The required skill sets will differ from role to role, but there are some key qualifications that PMO staff members should have that you should look for when you're hiring your PMO team. The qualifications are going to differ dramatically from role to role but, as PMO Manager, you need to make sure you are looking for common characteristics for your PMO staff members.

Common PMO team member qualifications and skills include, but are not limited to:

- PMI certification across program and project management, specifically. Certification is especially important for the Program and Project Managers in the group.
- Industry experience in your organization's industry.
- Formal PMO experience and using standard PMO tools and processes.
- Strong process and analytical skills tied with sharp decision-making abilities.
- Strong customer service skills with a focus on listening to the customer.
- Proven ability to work well in a fast-paced and ever-changing environment.
- Strong methodology background and experience.
- Specific experience in that particular role, which might seem obvious, but is definitely something to consider and look for when hiring individuals.
- Strong communication skills.

Another area where you can find qualifications for PMO employees, is to query the various job sites by searching for "PMO". It is amazing how common the PMO roles are and how the job characteristics are similar across the project management industry. The job qualifications include, but are not limited to, the following:

- Bachelor's degree in Business Administration, Computer Science, Information Systems, Management Information Systems, Project Management, or equivalent experience required.

- 10+ years' program management process and practical experience required, which might include software development and design, professional services consulting, and/or program management.
- 8+ years' experience managing implementations of large-scale projects, multi-disciplined, cross-functional and highly visible projects/programs, responsible for multi-million dollar budgets and a team.
- Must have excellent, accurate, and effective oral and written communication skills as well as positive, customer-focused interpersonal skills and attitude.
- Must be able to work both independently and as a team, within the PMO, IT delivery teams, and with business partners.
- Must be able to use the Microsoft® Office suite of applications, including advanced use of Microsoft Excel.
- Ability to analyze data and connect the dots, making recommendations to management and the project teams in a timely manner.
- Thorough understanding of project management in an information technology environment.
- Experience performing project management activities within a large, complex program preferred.
- Experience creating and managing detailed project, program, and/or portfolio financial data and performing the analysis necessary.

There is not a huge difference between the common PMO team member qualifications and skills and any list obtained from the different job sites, besides specificity to the job in particular. As PMO Manager, this list of qualifications gives you a great starting point for hiring the right people for your organization.

PMO Employees—Working with Employees who are not assigned or selected by you

In some cases, PMO Managers do not get to pick and choose who works for them and like any other organization they can be left with some employees who are not a good fit or who do not want to work there. Especially, if you are a new PMO Manager, and you are taking over an existing PMO, you might inherit PMO employees who are not happy and who do not want to work in the organization. This happens all the time, and as PMO Manager this is something you need to prepare for. Luckily, most functional managers deal with the same situation in their organizations as well, so you should be able to work with them and with your human resources team to put a plan in place to move the individual out of your organization or out of the company. Every company is going to handle these types of situations using different processes and procedures, so it is a good idea to collaborate with your human resources team to determine how the process works in your company. It is so important as PMO Manager to have a team of employees and contractors that want to be there and are invested in your success, and making the PMO that they work in successful as well.

Permanent Employees vs. Vendors or Contractors— What makes sense?

One of the challenges that PMO Managers face when defining their staffing models is to determine which roles should be staffed with employees and which roles should be staffed with vendors or contractors (employees outside of the company). This is a common question for PMO Managers as people come and go in the organization. This can be a difficult decision to make and depends on a number of factors, such as:

- What is the organization's PMO model? Directive, controlling, supportive?
- Does the project contain company secrets or exclusive information?
- Are there issues with contractors or vendors seeing budget information for the project?
- Is it a long-term project that will span multiple years and would be too risky to give to a vendor or contractor?
- Does the role require in-depth knowledge of the company?
- Are there political issues going on within organization that a contractor or vendor would not be successful navigating through?
- Is the project time-based, which includes specific deliverables?
- Do you need a level of expertise for the project that is not available with an employee?

These are just some of the questions that you need to think about when filling out your PMO staffing model. There are definitely conversations that need to occur before selecting the type of resource (employee/contractor/vendor) for the role as well. Sometimes, it does not matter whether you fill the role with a contractor, vendor, or an employee just because of the nature of the role, while other times it clearly does matter. Many different people have said that a vendor should fill the Project Manager role because he or she can be a neutral third party in managing the effort and will not let company politics get in the way of performing the role. If you think about it, a good place to start building hiring PMO staff would be to use vendors or contractors as Project Managers. There is certainly a good track record of this working across many organizations that use the vendor model for Project Managers and they tend to be very successful so it is a model you should consider as well.

Bill's Thoughts:

I have been lucky to have built a strong community of vendor and contractor Project Managers who I have used in my PMOs for several years. I have made an effort to build relationships with both the vendor and contractor Project Managers and with several different consulting agencies. Having a relationship with the consulting agencies and with the individual vendors and contractors at those companies is beneficial because it gives me a network of contacts who I can call upon when needed. Building a network of vendors, contractors, and consulting agencies is a good best practice for any PMO Manager.

Permanent Employee Management—PMO Career Path

In some cases, the PMO Manager is actually the functional manager of the PMO employees, and in those cases, the functional responsibilities of the company will drive many different responsibilities of the PMO Manager. The following are some company-specific functional manager tasks that are common to any functional manager, not just PMO Managers. These activities can include:

- **Performance Management Activities**—Performing yearly performance management reviews on employees, such as giving promotions, writing performance documentation, and highlighting and monitoring course corrections.
- **Employee Training**—Providing employee training and making sure employees are taking the standard and company mandatory training, such as procurement and HR training.
- **Employee Hiring and Dismissal**—Hiring and firing all direct employees in the organization.
- **Employees' Personal Administration Management**—Administering vacation days, time off, sick leaves, and so on. There is whole level of administration around employees that managers are responsible for at most companies.
- **Career Growth**—Growing and shaping employees into future leaders of the company.

There are other managerial responsibilities for which functional managers are responsible, but are company-specific. As a PMO Manager, who also has functional responsibility for company employees, make sure you are trained in those responsibilities and that you take the time to care for and support your employees.

PMO Career Growth

As noted, one of the components of being a functional manager is to work with each employee and determine how to grow each of them into future leaders and help them each progress through their careers at a respectable rate—a rate that is both acceptable to the company and to the employee. Employees will move on very quickly if they do not feel supported or they do not see a clear path for career growth. This is so important for PMO Managers as well because employees in the project management field often do move around quickly and can generally be portable from company to company, with ease.

So, as PMO Manager, you want to make sure you are working closely with your employees and showing them a career path and the typical timeframe it takes to move from position to position. PMI has done an excellent job of defining some minimum qualifications for project management professionals to follow when looking to receive certifications. **Figure 6.3 PMO/PMI Certification Career Path** shows a very good career path for any PMO Manager to use in their organization and with their employees on career discussions. This career model also aligns with current certification requirements from PMI and, therefore, PMO employees will see the different certifications available and the time requirements for those different certifications. In this model, you will also see the time requirements for the main roles of most PMOs. The four main roles of a PMO range from Project Coordinator to Portfolio Manager, and the recommended years of experience that are associated with each role is also shown.

For example, project professionals with 1–3 years' experience should stay in the Project Coordinator role in most PMOs.

Figure 6.3 PMO/PMI Certification Career Path

The great thing about this career path diagram is that your employees can see both their career paths and how their careers align to the industry standard PMI. As you work with each employee, depending on their years of experience and current certifications, this model gives you a great tool to have meaningful career conversations with them.

Vendor and Contractor Management

Many PMO Managers struggle when it comes to understanding the process for managing vendor and contractor staff. Vendors and contractors are key members of PMOs and therefore, it is important to have a structured and organized approach to managing them. It can be risky adding vendors and contractors to your program and project teams, so make sure you handle each vendor and contractor in a standard and repeatable manner. Earlier in the chapter, I mentioned the importance of PMO Managers establishing relationships with company-approved consulting agencies. By doing so, you can get the best possible candidates, better rates, and a long-term relationship with companies that will be beneficial for years to come.

There are different ways to use vendors and contractors in PMOs today, ranging from hiring them as staff augmentation, to hiring full vendor teams to work the whole project. Your PMO might experience every one of these vendor models, so be aware of them and prepare for them in your PMO.

The following are some areas that PMO Managers should focus on when working and dealing with vendors and contractors in their organization:

- **SOWs and Purchase Orders -** It is important that PMO Managers have a standard statement of work (SOW) template that matches the company's requirements and that is aligned to the procurement process.

- **Hold vendors and contractors to the same bar as employees**—It is important that vendors and contractors are treated the same way from a program and project execution perspective. Your company might have rules around what vendors or contractors can participate in (for example, no company training, no company sponsored morale events, and so on), but around execution, everyone is rated the same.

- **Watch PO Spending**—Depending on how your PO is set up, you, as PMO Manager, need a process to approve timesheets and POs before letting the vendor company bill your company. Figure that process out quickly, because you are responsible to know what is being spent and if a contractor spends too much too early and needs to be let go, it can have a huge impact on the program or project.

- **Vendors and contractors are people too**—It is very difficult for your vendors and contractors to be successful if you have them fill roles where they need to make decisions or drive efforts and they have no authority or respect. This is very common in companies that tend not to treat the vendors and contractors with much respect, which often leaves them frustrated and ready to move on.

- **Manage and control roll-off dates**—One of the key areas PMO Managers need to watch closely is when vendors and contractors are planning or scheduled to roll off a project. If the role is for an ongoing need, make sure you have plans in place to back-fill that vendor or contractor with an employee or another vendor or contractor so there is no impact to program and project execution.

- **Performance Manage Tightly**—One of the key things the PMO Manager can do with their vendors and contractors is to tightly and continually manage their performance. Vendors tend to have a high bar and therefore they should be performing at a higher level with greater success. You often pay a lot more for a vendor than you do for a permanent employee, so you expect more from a vendor because you are paying more.

Typical PMO Roles

Part of creating the **PMO Roles and Responsibilities Staffing Model RACI** is to define the typical roles and individuals needed in the PMO. Luckily, some of the common roles and individuals needed are provided in the following list:

- PMO Manager
- PMO Director

- PMO Vice President
- Administrative Assistant to PMO
- PMO Project Coordinators—you can have more than one of these individuals.
- Portfolio Manager
- Program Manager—you can have more than one of these individuals. The number of Program Managers you hire will depend on the number of programs in the PMO.
- Project Manager—you can have more than one of these individuals. The number of Project Managers you hire will depend on the number of projects in the PMO.
- PMO Methodology Mentors
- PMO Reporting Analysts
- PMO Dashboard Team—including Developers or Analysts
- PMO Resource Managers—you can have more than one of these individuals. This will largely depend on the size of the PMO.
- PMO Finance Managers
- PMO Trainers—this role tends to have more than one individual; however, the role is usually a vendor or a contractor resource and not necessarily an employee.

When defining this list for your organization, it is important to get these roles into an Organization model to show and talk to people about what the organizational structure will look like when resources are hired and in their roles. **Figure 6.4 PMO Organization Model**, below, provides a view of a standard structure of the typical roles in most PMOs. As PMO Manager, you would create this organizational structure during the time you are creating the **PMO Roles and Responsibilities Staffing Model RACI** to ensure that you have the different roles accounted for in your PMO. The tools will work together very nicely.

Figure 6.4 PMO Organization Model

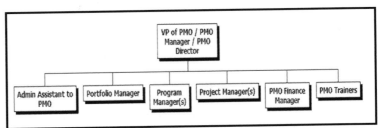

This is just a simple example of what a typical PMO organization structure might look like and what your organization's operating model might look like when you are ready to fill those roles. The other important aspect of having a view like this is that you are able to see where you can move people or roles under other roles, for the most efficient operating model. Visually, this is a good tool for understanding what the organization structure is going to look like and where people fit in the structure. It is much more difficult to explain who reports to who and various reporting relationships without a model like this.

Tips & Best Practices

Build your PMO organization model when you are building your PMO Roles and Responsibilities Staffing Model RACI because you will often make staffing decisions based on discussions you have when creating the RACI.

PMO Project Coordinator Role

One of the common roles across many PMOs is the Project Coordinator role, which puts junior-level Project Managers in a PMO to assist the various roles in the organization. These individuals tend to be right out of college and have little work experience in the project management industry. The Project Coordinator works with the Project Manager to help successfully drive projects and complete the administrative overhead of managing projects. Project Coordinators work as assistants to the PMO Manager and are not usually left alone to manage efforts themselves. They help with administrative tasks, such as training, hiring, and so on. The premise behind the Project Coordinator role is to have it filled by someone new to the project management industry who is looking for an opportunity to come into the industry to grow and learn on the job while not costing the company a lot of money. This Project Coordinator role to the individual filling it, and the company itself, is a win-win for everyone. There has been many Project Coordinators that have become successful Project Managers.

Bill's Thoughts:

The Project Coordinator role is something that I have used in a couple PMOs now, and I'm very proud of the process I established and set up. I was lucky in my hiring and worked with good companies that gave me junior and low-cost applicants who were dedicated to project management and willing to learn on the job. I would highly recommend PMO Managers to consider hiring Project Coordinators to help grow young and inexperienced project management types and to give them a shot in the industry.

Project Coordinator qualifications and skills include, but are not limited to:

- University or college graduate.
- A keen interest in project management, such as becoming a Certified Associate in Project Management (CAPM)® and eventually a PMP.
- Industry experience in your organization's industry. For example, a software person should have worked in software before.
- Real-life work experience in the business world. You don't want to hire people who have no experience in the business world at all, but depending on where and how you are going to use the Project Coordinator, it might be an option.

- Formal PMO experience and using standard PMO tools and processes.
- Understanding project environment, scope, goals, deliverables, budget.
- PMO reporting experience.

One of the things that you will see right away when reviewing these qualifications is that the individual filling them will likely be very young; therefore, your expectations of this person shouldn't be that high. It would be unfair to put a person in a role who has little to no project management experience and expect him or her to drive a large, complex project. Instead, the right thing to do would be to put this person on a complex project supporting the Project Manager, thereby, allowing him or her to learn how to manage a project from that Project Manager. As PMO Manager, you should check in and regularly connect with the Project Coordinator to ensure that he or she is learning and growing. You also need to check with the Project Manager to ensure that he or she is getting the expected level of assistance from the Project Coordinator. The other consideration when hiring someone at this experience level is that you can expect the rate of pay to be very low. Rates and compensation will vary depending on a number of factors, and as PMO Manager, you will need to negotiate them with the consulting agency or your human resources department. In all, the Project Coordinator role has been very successful, and I highly recommend PMO Managers take full advantage of this role in their organization.

PMO New Hire Onboarding Guide

After analyzing and understanding the various qualifications and staffing requirements for your PMO, one of the best practices PMO Managers can do for their employees, vendors, or contractors when bringing them into the organization is to create a PMO onboarding guide. Most new employees are confused and unsure of exactly what to do during the first couple of days/weeks, so an onboarding guide will help get them up and running in no time. The onboarding guide does not need to be formal, but it should cover some of the following areas:

- Company security information
- Company parking pass
- Company email and network access
- Company computer and software guidelines
- PMO marketing materials—including the PMO mission and vision statements
- PMO centralized repository home page
- PMO training and process links
- PMO methodologies
- PMO centralized status reporting
- Engineering methodologies
- PMO vacation or out-of-office calendar
- Program/project transition guides

The onboarding guide is a best practice and highly recommended for any PMO. As PMO Manager, it is your responsibility to create an onboarding guide for your PMO or give it to a PMO employee as an extra assignment. This is something that will take little time to create and will certainly add tremendous value to your organization and to anyone new starting your organization looking for some of these routine and common startup items.

Going It Alone—PMO's of One

One of the current industry trends is that companies are creating PMOs with only one person. These are called "PMO's of one." Companies are going with PMO's of one when they want to have a PMO, but don't exactly know what to do with it yet, so they don't want to spend a lot of money by fully staffing it until it proves itself. When speaking to the PMO Managers in these situations, most feel the weight of the world on their shoulders and feel like they are being set up to fail. PMO Managers need some help to allow them to be successful and they cannot be successful running a PMO alone. Some PMO Managers have used a staffing model where they would "borrow" time from Project Managers. In most cases, this did not work out well because they would continually hear from those same Project Managers that because the PMO work was not part of their full time job or part of their yearly performance responsibilities, the "extra" PMO work they were being asked to do would be much lower in priority than their actual job. Some of the PMO Managers struggle with where to start building their PMO's processes/procedures, and so on, so therefore need the help of extra employees if for anything to bounce off ideas or to get some help running stuff past. The "PMO of one" concept is actually a very bad idea and a trend we need to stop sooner than later. As PMO Manager, you need to work with your management team to make sure you are not put in this situation, and if you are in it, the expectations of what you can deliver need adjusting. Large PMOs with various PMO employees can do some great work and create many deliverables, while a single individual in a PMO can accomplish very little. Sometimes, PMO Managers are put in that type of situation, though, and if you are, the following suggestions should at least make it easier and help you be successful:

- Obtain some contractor support. Even if you can hire some college students who have recently graduated, some of them will be begging for a shot in the industry. These individuals can come cheap and offer some amazing help to your organization.
- Select the correct PMO model for your staffing model. For example, if you have no staff, which appears to be your situation here, your PMO model can be supportive (but limited), or directive (but limited). The "limited" conditions are due to you, the PMO Manager, having only so much time in a day to provide support, coaching, or mentoring. Therefore, you will be limited in scope on what you can accomplish. The same argument applies to the directive PMO model, if your PMO is about directing and ensuring your Program and Project Managers follow certain standards, your ability to do auditing or checking on how well the program or project teams are using those standards will also be limited. Again, you will not have enough time to track and enforce everyone across all programs and projects.
- Look for mentoring opportunities within your organization. There are often people who want to become a Project Manager and who are willing to learn by performing project management related tasks just for the experience. Those individuals work well in this scenario, but be careful as well, because they may not have a lot of project management experience, which could impact the projects they are working on.

- Ask your management team for help. Remember, a successful PMO requires the management team's support, and if you are running your PMO alone, this is the perfect opportunity to ask for help.

Bill's Thoughts:

It is so important to build relationships with local consulting agencies that will provide you with quality PMO resources. I have established relationships with local consulting agencies that know exactly what I need and what I am looking for in PMO staff. From Portfolio Managers to Project Coordinators, if you are working with 2-3 main agencies that know your requirements and know exactly the type of people you want in your PMO, it will be much quicker to get the people you need. How important is that when your top Project Manager just left your highest priority project and you have nobody available to replace him or her?

Summary

As we wrap-up the PMO staffing model chapter, you should realize that building a large PMO team is quite a complicated task if you don't have a process in place to do so in an organized fashion you will struggle. As PMO Manager, start the process by completing the **PMO Roles and Responsibilities Staffing Model RACI**, as this will give you a good head start on the PMO services that you will offer and which roles you will need to perform those services. The RACI mapping exercise will also expose any glaring holes in either your services or in your staff (those who are unqualified to perform the services) and will give you the data you need to request those resources with your HR team and management. As PMO Manager, take real caution and care in hiring your PMO team because, in some cases, they can be with you for many years and a bad hire can have a negative long-lasting impact. Just as much as a good hire can have a positive impact, a bad hire can hurt and destroy your creditability. Make sure you take the time and effort when creating a good, solid set of qualifications and standards that will act as your minimum bar for hiring people in your organization. If you create this qualification list, use it to make smart hiring decisions. Otherwise, settling for lesser-qualified people might be okay in some circumstances, but understand that you are taking a risk that could impact your PMO.

PMO Build Decisions:

1. Decide on roles and which services offerings will be in your PMO.

2. Decide on which roles initially will be in your PMO.

3. Decide on the qualifications for your PMO staff.

4. Decide whether you will hire vendors, contractors, and/or employees, for your PMO roles.

5. Decide which roles are most suitable for vendors and contractors and which roles employees must fill.

6. Decide if you will approach your management team for a PMO Coordinator role to help you build and administer the PMO.

Chapter Review Answers:

1. The PMO Roles and Responsibilities Staffing Model RACI describe PMO service offerings and the roles needed to provide those offerings. The RACI is extremely valuable for understanding how to staff your PMO.

2. PMO employee qualifications include: industry experience, customer service skills, and communication skills.

3. When deciding to hire a permanent employee over a vendor or contractor some considerations to ruminate include: Does the project contain company secrets or exclusive information? Are there issues with contractors or vendors seeing budget information for the project? Does the role require in-depth company knowledge?

4. Typical PMO roles include PMO Manager, PMO Director, and PMO Project Coordinator.

5. Organization charts provide a view into the organization's operating model and helps you recognize where staff is needed.

Chapter 7

PMO Training

Figure 7.1 PMO Build Schedule - PMO Training

Task Name	Resource Names
Step 5 - Design & Build or Enhance Period (Chapter 5 - 12)	**PMO Manager**
Design PMO	**PMO Manager**
Design PMO Core Components	**PMO Manager**
Build PMO	**PMO Manager**
Create PMO Business Management Area on Centralized Repository Site (Sections to create are documented in Implementation Phase)	PMO Manager
+Create PMO Core Components	**PMO Manager**
+Create PMO Model (Chapter 5)	**PMO Manager**
+Create PMO Maturity Model	**PMO Manager**
+Create PMO Staffing Model (Chapter 6)	**PMO Manager**
-Create PMO Training (Chapter 7)	PMO Manager
Determine PMO Training Opportunities	PMO Manager
Review PMO Training Tips and Best Practices	PMO Manager
Review PMO Training Pitfalls and Areas to Avoid	PMO Manager
+Creating a Mentor Program	**PMO Manager**
+Create a PMO Buddy System	**PMO Manager**
PMO Training - Other Opportunities	PMO Manager
Document PMO Build Decisions	PMO Manager
PMO Training Complete	PMO Manager

Questions you should be able to answer after reading this chapter:

1. What is the difference between a PMO mentoring program and a PMO Buddy System?

2. Why is it important to have a program or project management methodology for the PMO mentoring program?

3. What are two PMO mentor qualifications? Why is it important to have qualifications for PMO mentors?

4. What are three PMO Buddy System guidelines?

5. How often do you review and reevaluate the PMO Buddy System?

One of the areas that PMO Managers should focus on when building their PMOs is employee training and education. Your role is to ensure that your PMO employees and program and project teams have the necessary skills to perform their jobs. It is also important to keep your own training and skills current. Look for shared training experiences in which both you and your employees can participate. Examples such as attending conferences or taking outside training are great ways to keep you, the PMO Manager, and your PMO employees current and to keep everyone's skills fresh.

There are actually a number of different considerations when thinking about the type of training needed for your PMO. These considerations include: existing skill sets of the PMO team members, soft skills training, staffing model, available budget, and the use of in-house presentations compared to formal training events. PMO training and education can come in a number of different formats and not everything has to cost a lot of money or be a formal process. You can have brown-bag meetings or informal lunch-hour meetings that are just as effective as paying money to send employees to formal training classes.

One of the considerations when thinking about PMO training and education is the makeup of the PMO from a staffing model perspective. Depending on the various services your PMO offers and groups and individuals who provide those offerings, training can range from subjects on how to hold project kickoff meetings, to engineering methodology deep-dive meetings, and everything in between. As PMO Manager, consider the staffing model when thinking about the training programs and materials that you are developing because if you do not offer the full range to your organization, you will likely leave people out. They may in turn think that their group is not important, which would not be your intention. There is definitely a lot to consider when you think about setting up training for your organization.

Earlier in the book, we talked about the three key processes to think about when building your PMO: resources, procedures, and infrastructure. When you think about training and education for your PMO, you are actually considering two of those areas: resources and infrastructure (i.e. tools). Come to think about it, procedures and processes could be included as well, but let's keep it simple for now. It is important to be constantly testing and understanding how those areas factor into how you build your PMO because it makes you consider those three areas every time you need to make a different PMO build decision. For example, when you are building your PMO training and education components, think about each resource and what impact training has on them. Think about how many hours you expect them to take this year in training. Do they have the training necessary to do their jobs? Your resources play a huge role in building the training components of your PMO, so make sure you factored in each resource and the impact on them when considering the PMO training you will offer.

One of the best practices in the industry that we will tackle in this chapter is the creation of a PMO mentoring program, or a less formal, PMO Buddy System. Both of these programs are integral to building a PMO and are areas that are important when considering the different PMO training and education options. These programs do not include specific training classes or presentations, but they do provide ongoing education and learning opportunities for PMO employees. Finally, the PMO model you chose also plays a big role in the types of training and education offered by your PMO. Think about a supportive PMO and the type of training it would include compared to a directive PMO and its training. When selecting the PMO model, PMO Managers will have to adapt the various course offerings based on the model they chose.

Let us move now into PMO training and walk through some of the areas to think about when establishing training for your organization, and then we will look specifically at creating a mentoring program or a PMO Buddy System for your organization.

PMO Training and Education

As PMO Manager, one of the toughest decisions around PMO training and education is when to start. There is actually no right or wrong time to start PMO training; training your employees should be the foundation of everything you do. Every time you roll out something new or introduce a change to a process, as PMO Manager, it is your responsibility to market those changes and train everyone. Actually, this is really a good thing because it gives you the constant ability to get in front of management and your team members and teach them something new. This is an excellent way to keep your presentation skills polished and continue to grow and mature your PMO. You should embrace and be continually active in this process.

Why is PMO training so important? The answer is simple, because any time you roll out a process (or if you roll out a software product), your employees are going to look to you for training. Therefore, it is important that you are giving your employees the information they need to use the processes or tools that allow them to do their jobs more efficiently. Actually, you will end up losing credibility fast if you roll out a process or a tool and do not provide support, in the form of training, to the team using it. In chapter 12, we will go into detail about piloting and using an evaluation process when rolling out tools and processes within your PMO.

Because there is never a good time to implement training, let us start now and go over some of the areas to think about when implementing training and education in your PMO.

PMO Training Opportunities

- **PMI Certifications**—We all know that PMI has a number of different certifications and, as PMO Manager, it should one of your main focuses to ensure that your employees are trained using industry standard processes. You should be working with each team member and ensuring that they are getting PMI training when possible. PMI offers the following certifications:
    - Certified Associate in Project Management (CAPM)®
    - Project Management Professional (PMP)®
    - Program Management Professional (PgMP)®
    - PMI Agile Certified Practitioner (PMI-ACP)®
    - PMI Risk Management Professional (PMI-RMP)®
    - PMI Scheduling Professional (PMI-SP)®
- **PMO Processes/Procedures**—Every process rollout must have associated training materials. Even if the training is 1:1 or an informal brown-bag meeting, every process must have some sort of training associated with it. This process includes governance, change requests, lessons learned, and so on. It is a best practice to ensure that any PMO process has the associated formal or informal training.

- **PMO Model Training**—Think about the various types of training you would have in your PMO if you are using a supportive-only PMO, or if you are using a directive PMO. In a directive PMO, you might train your PMO members about the auditing process and how their work will be audited, where supportive PMO training might focus heavily on process and tools training. The PMO model you selected will determine the types and the different training opportunities for your PMO team members.
- **PMO Tools & Software**—Every tool must have associated training materials. Sometimes, this material will be part of a software package; other times, it will be third-party vendors specializing in that software product.
- **Portfolio Management Methodology**—In reviewing the portfolio management processes, there is specific training associated to portfolio management that is required in PMOs with this discipline. Portfolio planning process, for example, would be an area where the Portfolio Manager would host a brown-bag training event.
- **Program & Project Management Methodology**—In reviewing both program and project management methodologies, there are specific processes and controls within each that require training. The training will be unique to program and project management that would not be applicable to the portfolio process. For example, financial management and tracking at the program and project level might be different from what you would do at the portfolio level. Within the program and project space, there are specific training courses that your PMO should offer as well.
- **Development or Engineering Methodology**—Depending on your industry, it makes sense to offer the specific development or engineering methodology training for the projects that your PMO supports. For example, in software PMOs, having Waterfall Development or Agile Development methodology training might be applicable. In manufacturing PMOs, having engineering methodology training would be applicable.
- **PMO Employee Soft Skill Training**—Soft skills training, such as team leadership, communications, and team building training, is as important as tools and procedure/process training. Focus on which soft skills each employee requires and focus on getting him or her that training.
- **Training Opportunities Tied to PMO Employee Career Path**—As PMO Manager with functional management responsibilities, you will want to ensure that you focus the training opportunities with the career path of your employees. When you have functional accountabilities for your PMO employees, look for where each employee is heading in his or her career, and allow them to take training that helps them achieve their career goals.

Tips & Best Practices

When setting up training for your Program and Project Managers ensure you get a broad enough audience for running your pilot programs; do not limit this to just PMO employees.

PMO Recommended Skills Training

As PMO Manager, and in some cases as a functional manager to your PMO employees, it is a best practice to have a minimum set of critical skills training for each PMO employee (employees and contractors). The training applies to the top four roles in the PMO: Portfolio Managers, Program Managers, Project Managers, and Project Coordinators. The recommended soft skills pertain to all roles, while the hard skills are catered to the particular role. For example, work breakdown training for a Program Manager would be the same training and concepts taught to Project Managers. Their roles force their focus to be different, but the concepts remain the same.

The critical training is divided into hard skills and soft skills, each being critical to the success of the person in this role.

Critical Soft Skills Training:

- Leadership Training
- Team Management Training
- Project Communication Training
- Presentation Skills Training
- Conflict Resolution Training
- Influencing Without Authority Training
- Coaching and Mentoring Training

Critical Hard Skills Training:

- Overview of Project Management
- Advanced Project Management
- Project Planning
- Project Communications
- Developing Work Breakdown Structures
- Project Estimating
- Project Scheduling (including tool training, such as Microsoft Project®)
- Project Risk Management
- Project Shutdown
- Critical Chain Method
- PMI Training

PMO Training Tips and Best Practices

As PMO Manager, you role is to implement training in your PMO while not impacting the execution of the programs and projects in your organization. Therefore, you have to be a bit creative when thinking about the training that you are offering and how to least impact your team members, while trying to improve their skills sets and mature your organization. Here are some of the best practices in the industry and, as PMO Manager you should be looking to adopt these wherever possible.

- Schedule PMO lunch-hour brown-bag events whenever possible to provide peer training for best practices and standard processes across portfolio, program, and project management areas.

- Schedule PMO staff meetings on a biweekly cadence, you should use the occasional staff meeting to offer specific PMO training.

- Use PMO staff to provide and present training material. When you use your own employees, you cut costs and give them experience presenting the work that they are doing with other members of the team.

- Use the PMO mentoring programs and buddy systems.

- Ensure your content can provide enough information for anyone with their PMP certification to obtain PDUs. People with their certification are always looking for ways to obtain additional PDUs, so if you can provide it, that will be looked upon very positive and you may end up getting more people coming to your training events. PMI has a category that PMO Managers can take advantage of when offering training and your Program Managers and Project managers will appreciate it.

PMO Training—Mistakes to Avoid

There are some traps you want to avoid when rolling out training for your PMO. These mistakes and pitfalls include:

- Not providing budget to PMO employees for training.
- Limiting who can go to project conferences, based on seniority.
- Not including vendors or contractors in PMO training events. Remember, contractors often turn into employees, and you want everyone working in the PMO to have the same training opportunities and be working and doing things the same wherever possible.
- Using training budget for "other" more important things, such as project overruns. Imagine if you heard management is cancelling all PMO training and taking back the training budget because Bob's project is over budget and they need to take the training money to cover Bob's overruns. That is a morale killer and PMO Managers need to avoid it at all costs or suffer with some unhappy employees.
- Using up training budget at the end of the year. Providing training just to waste or use up any remaining budget available does not do anyone any

good, and in most cases, the training goes to waste and the budget is not well spent.

As PMO Manager, you have the ability to establish two very good programs that will give your employees the ability to obtain training from mentors or others in the PMO. One of the best practices for PMO Manager to take advantage of is creating and formulizing two specific programs: the PMO Mentor Program and the PMO Buddy System.

Let us spend time now and review both programs.

PMO Mentoring Program

One of the most important things a PMO Manager can do for their PMO team members is to create and build a mentoring program, or a less formal, buddy system. PMO Managers should focus on creating these programs early in the building of the PMO so it is part of the foundation and becomes part of the DNA of the PMO. In doing so, as the PMO matures, the mentoring program grows as well. Mentoring programs are an integral part of your PMO and provide an ongoing support and mentoring mechanism for your PMO employees. There are surveys and data that prove that PMOs that have mentoring programs in place have much more success around program and project execution than PMOs that do not. Mentoring programs provides a win-win situation for everyone (mentor and mentee) and rarely do these programs result in a negative impact to the PMO.

When establishing a PMO mentoring program, one of the best practices is to look around for any existing company mentoring programs and take any best practices or processes that are applicable. That just makes sense, but you would be surprised how many PMO Managers try to create their own versions of mentoring programs from scratch because they think that their PMO is different. Take what is already working in those existing programs and adjust it for your specific PMO needs. There is no sense creating a mentoring program from scratch when there are established programs in place, just because the program is not focused for PMO employees. The way most mentoring programs are set up at companies tend to be for all employees, not specific roles such as (Program or Project Managers) and therefore, as PMO Manager, creating a mentoring program just for your PMO employees makes perfect sense and is really a good practice. It makes perfect sense to create a specific mentoring program for your PMO employees that focuses on improving their project-specific skill sets. In doing so, you, as PMO Manager, can control the processes/procedures, and how the program is run from start to finish. This also gives you a lot of control to make changes where necessary and the ability to add the participation in the program directly to your PMO employees' workload/activities (commitments) for the year. Normally, when you add this type of mentoring program to their work activities, your employees become engaged and excited about the program, which leads to more involvement and more participation.

When PMO Managers establish mentoring programs, they provide employees with opportunities and chances to solve leadership challenges or developmental issues that they might be struggling with in their programs and projects. There are many times during the course of program or project execution that employees struggle or find they don't have anyone to turn to for support or help, and sometimes they don't like to turn to you, the PMO Manager, because they are afraid it will negatively impact them. Providing a mentoring program or a buddy system will eliminate that completely and will give employees different people to bounce ideas off of so they will not feel like they will be looked on negatively by management.

It is important that, as PMO Manager, you have ensured that your management team is supportive and adopts the concept of the mentoring program for it truly to be successful. There will certainly be situations that come up when running a program like this that will require management support, and having their support at the beginning of this program is highly recommended. For example, the mentoring system, or even the buddy system, can be done relatively cheaply, but could have some associated costs such as web cameras, for example, if the two employees are not in the same building or in the same country. Without management support, even buying some low-cost web cameras could be challenging, thus negatively impacting the program.

Before we go into how to create a PMO mentoring program, let us talk about the two different mentoring programs available to PMO Managers: a PMO Mentor Program or a PMO Buddy System.

PMO Mentoring Program—A company- or organization-wide sponsored program that is formal, with guidelines and processes for everyone in the program to follow. These programs tend to be ongoing with formal checkpoints at the year mark. The PMO Mentor Program is usually a subset of the formal mentor program offered by the company by may also be a standalone system.

PMO Buddy System—An informal system where PMO team members (contractors or employees) are paired up or "become buddies" with other PMO team members—generally for a year—to share ideas, assist one another, bounce ideas off one another, and generally be a go-to person for the other. PMO Buddy Systems are much less formal and do not have a lot of rules and regulations around the process.

In most organizations, there is usually room for either program, you just need to figure out which one will work for your PMO. In some cases, if you are building a PMO, you might just want to create an informal "buddy system" to get it started and get your employees involved and engaged in the process, formalizing and adding more rigor or structure as things progress. Then as things mature, you can introduce a much more structured PMO Mentoring program.

Bill's Thoughts:

I have created two different mentoring systems in my PMOs and I have found them to be extremely valuable and well worth the effort to establish for any PMO Manager. My advice would be to keep it simple and make sure that you constantly checking and refining the program to ensure it is working and providing value. Nothing is worse than a program that is not working or providing value because it just becomes overhead and something that everyone ignores.

Let us move now to creating your own PMO mentoring program.

Creating a PMO Mentoring Program

There are a number of key deliverables needed to start the PMO Mentor Program. In **Table 7.1 PMO Mentoring Initiation Tasks,** it documents the various processes and deliverables needed to kick off this program.

Table 7.1 PMO Mentor Program Initiation Tasks

#	Deliverable	Notes
1.	Executive support for the mentoring program.	It is important to have support from the leadership team for possible funding requests in the future for the mentor program.
2.	Mentor program goals and objectives outlined and documented.	It is important to have clear goals and objectives outlined before introducing the mentor program to the organization. Spend time to create goals and objectives for the mentoring program.
3.	Clearly delineated PMO team members job descriptions and responsibilities for the various levels of both Program Managers and Project Managers.	It important to have a job description, or at least a list of job duties, for every role in the mentoring program. This allows mentors to have something to work with to aid and direct their mentees in the program. Without it, there is no consistency on how the mentor and mentee relationship will work.
4.	A program and project management methodology that drive programs and projects in the organization.	Having the program and project methodology in place is a lot like having the job duties listed. The methodology will provide an aid for the mentor to work with the mentee to see actual work deliverables for their projects. Having a methodology in place will also allow for some very meaningful conversations between the mentor and mentee.
5.	An established program and project auditing process.	The mentor and mentee should use this audit process to have dialog between the two and it can help grow the skills of the mentee by

#	Deliverable	Notes
		understanding what they have and have not done on their efforts.
6.	The mentoring process is outlined with clear expectations for how someone would enter or exit the program.	It is important that expectations are clear between the mentor and the mentee before starting and leaving the program. It is important to remember that people join the mentoring programs for many reasons, and it is not fair for people to come in and out of the program randomly. Everyone should agree to the conditions established at the beginning of the program and stick with their agreements through the process.
7.	Clearly defined timeframes for the mentoring programs. Best practice is creating it for a one-year period.	It is a best practice to establish mentor and mentee relationships for a one-year period. After that period, everyone reviews the relationships again to determine if they are working.
8.	Clearly document commitments for both the mentor and the mentee.	Defining the "rules" and "expectations" for the mentor and the mentee are important because it sets the expectations and guidelines for both parties so they will each know what is ahead for them so they can then determine if want to be part of the mentor program.
9.	Create PM mentor meeting guidelines and expectations guide.	This one page document will guide the conversations between the mentor and mentee during their meetings. If anything, it becomes a conversation starter between the two individuals around what they should cover in their meetings.
10.	Create mentor qualifications document.	It is important for employees to understand that not everyone can be a mentor; there are specific

#	Deliverable	Notes
		qualifications to become a mentor.
11.	Create a PM mentor enrollment process.	This can be a simple website or an email alias, but you should have a process that employees use to sign up to take part in this program.
12.	Establish a feedback process.	This process can be very simple to start, but it is important when kicking off a program like this that you are getting feedback and listening to what is working and not working in the program.

PMO Mentor Qualifications

Not everyone is capable or qualified to be a mentor, so one of the first things that PMO Managers must do before rolling out a PMO Mentor Program is establish some basic guidelines for employees who want to be mentors. At the minimum, consider the following qualifications for defining who can be a mentor in your PMO Mentor Program:

- Ability to mentor individuals
- Ability to mentor project teams
- Analyzes project deliverables
- Analyzes project processes and defines, when necessary, changes or enhancements to the process
- Understands the program management methodology (for program mentors)
- Understands the project management methodology (for project mentors)
- Coaching skills
- Consulting skills

As PMO Manager, you must take these qualifications very seriously because putting someone in the spot (even for a pilot program) who is not qualified to be a mentor can do more damage than good for both employees (mentor and mentee).

PMO Mentoring Program Guidelines

Anytime you establish a new program for employees—and before they get involved or want to participate—they will want to know what they are getting into, so it is important to document some guidelines and parameters. It is best practice and recommended to go with the following guidelines, at a minimum:

- Time investment should be monthly, with a maximum of two hours. Mentor and mentees should plan for two one-hour meetings, per month.

- Mentor and mentee should both strive to complete one or two goals, at the most, during this relationship. Trying to accomplish more than two goals can be very difficult and might lead to failure.
- Both mentor and mentee are required to be engaged and active during the course of their involvement in this program. Everyone is busy and people must be flexible with their time; entering into this program requires a certain time commitment.
- Both mentor and mentee should be flexible and understand that relationships take time to develop and the relationship might not always be great at the very beginning. Remember most relationships tend to go through the "storming, norming, forming" phases when they start.
- The mentee cannot expect that the mentor has all the answers or is the subject matter expert in all areas, but the mentee can expect that the mentor will be willing to help the mentee whenever possible.

PMO Mentoring Program—Time for a Pilot Program

After creating the initial deliverables for the PM mentoring program and establishing the rules for becoming a mentor, it is time to try a pilot program using a limited number of employees in the organization. The time period for the pilot program should be no more than six months, with mentor and mentee meetings occurring monthly. Regardless of the size of the organization, big or small, use a very small group of people to try out the PMO mentoring program. Do not attempt a large rollout of the process too early; there will be a lot of excitement and people will want to be involved, but resist rolling it out to a large group of employees in the beginning. Actually, you will have more chances of success if you roll it out slowly and make enhancements as it matures.

In **Table 7.2 PMO Mentoring Program Startup Steps** outlines the steps to start a PMO mentoring program. It is not necessarily a complicated process and following the steps should get you started down the right path for this program. As PMO Manager, you might need to make changes to these steps for your program, but these steps should give you a great starting point.

Table 7.2 PMO Mentoring Program Startup Steps

1.	Schedule and gather interested PMO employees for the PMO Mentoring Kickoff Meeting. Employees can be working in any role, but should be of "like" roles. For example, try to keep your Project Managers together, your Program Managers together, and so on. However, as noted, people join mentoring programs for different reasons, so pair "like" roles when possible.
2.	Provide employees with the deliverables you created in Table **7.1 PMO Mentoring Program Initiation Tasks**, such as: The PMO Mentoring Program Goals and Objectives document. The PMO Mentoring Program Mentor and Mentee Commitments

	document.
	The PMO Mentor Time Commitment Expectations document. For the pilot program, this timeframe can be flexible and not binding.
	The list of job descriptions, job duties, program and project methodology deliverables, and job aids.
	A two-week check-in meeting invitation for all parties.
	A one-month check-in meeting invitation for all parties.
3.	Establish the roles for each individual in the PMO mentoring program. This should be done with all members during the initial kickoff meeting; however, the qualifications to be a mentor have already been put to use and your pilot program already includes individuals who are qualified to be mentors in the organization. During the pilot program, it is important to have employees in one role only; an employee should not be a mentor and a mentee at the same time.
4.	Let the employees start the process. Don't get in the way when they meet, let the process take hold with the pilot team members.
5.	During the two-week check-in meeting, encourage everyone to talk about what is working and what is not working. Take good notes, make necessary changes to the program, and let the employees continue in the program.
6.	During the one-month check-in meeting, encourage everyone to talk about what has been working and not working since making the changes suggested at the two-week checkpoint meeting. Listen and make additional changes that will enhance the program. Tell the pilot team members that they will meet again at the end of three months.
7.	Between the one-month and the three-month check-in meetings, it is important as PMO Manager to check in individually with the pilot team members to ensure they are getting what they are expecting out of the mentoring relationships they have. At this point, hold off on making changes to the program unless necessary. Sometimes, it takes time for things to work themselves out.
8.	At the three-month point check-in meeting listen to how things are going from each team member. Make changes where necessary, as you have done previously, but make only slight changes, as the program should be quickly maturing and becoming very valuable to the employees. Tell the pilot team members that they will meet again at the end of another three months, which will be at the six-month point and the end of the pilot

	program.
9.	At the six-month check-in meeting, call an end to the pilot program and finalize the PMO Mentor Program. At this point, make any last minutes changes and get the program ready for official roll out.
10.	Official rollout process begins. This is when you open the PMO mentoring program to all members of your PMO. Have new team members follow the same process to sign up as the pilot team members followed and roll out your new program.

Advanced Tips and PMO Mentoring Program Concepts

PMO mentoring programs come in many shapes and sizes. The process we just created was assigning "like" roles to work together in a mentor/mentee relationship. This relationship gives the employees an opportunity to share ideas, bounce problems off each other, act as sounding boards, and so on. It is a great starting point for any new PMO; however, there are other types of mentoring programs as well. If you have an existing PMO, or have a mentoring program in place already and want to enhance your program, here are some ideas and tips for creating some different types of mentoring programs. Here are some examples:

Coaching Mentoring Program— In this program, the mentor is actually a coach and applies coaching techniques to their mentees. This is a formal coach/employee relationship and needs to be staffed with "coaches" who have experience with coaching relationships and who are very senior individuals. The PM coach guides their mentors and tends to try to find the solution and take ownership and responsibility in the outcomes alongside the mentor. Their job is to coach and guide their mentees to discover solutions and complete the work themselves, but the mentors in this situation often gets caught up and want to get more involved.

Subject Matter Experts Mentoring Program— In this program, the mentors are actually subject matter experts on a program or project related item. For example, your mentors might be Microsoft Project® experts or planning experts, it can be anything as long as it is program or project related. The process for establishing this PMO Mentor Program is a "one-to-many" relationship for the mentor and mentees where the mentor has multiple mentees at the same time. In this type of program, it is more of a trainer/trainee relationship compared to the traditional mentor/mentee relationship. The only difference is that the mentor would provide more hands-on support to the mentee and the mentor would be expected to spend more time and train the mentee in all of the details. The expectations for both the mentor and mentee would be to keep the focus on one subject area only, and if there is a need for a different type of relationship by either party, then this type of PMO mentoring program might not be as effective as possible for these individuals. As PMO Manager, this program is worth trying if you have a number of subject matter expert employees in your PMO who have time and are willing to share their knowledge and expertise in the different areas.

PMO Buddy System

PMO Managers have another way of creating a PMO mentoring program that does not necessarily have a lot of formality or a ton of processes/procedures behind it. This type of program is perfect when the PMO is just starting out or when there is not a lot of executive support and you, as PMO Manager, want to simply get the program started. This type of program is called the **"PMO Buddy System"** and tends to have very few rules or restrictions; it is much less formal than an official PMO mentoring program. The PMO Buddy System pairs "like" roles together to act in a mentor/mentor type of role where no one person is the lead or takes on the leadership position. The simple process of pairing employees who share the same type of role gives them each someone who they can talk to, share concerns with, bounce ideas off of, and act as a sounding board about their projects.

Bill's Thoughts:

I have used a "PMO Buddy System" before and it worked wonderfully. I used it in two different companies and because it was informal, it was accepted more readily. The concept of informally putting Project Managers together to help one another and bounce ideas off each other was extremely valuable. It was surprising how the employees embraced the idea and liked having a PMO team member who they were "buddies" with and could ask for help from and share project war stories. I highly recommend this approach if a more formal program would not work in your organization.

Some other areas where the PMO Buddy System works well is where the two "buddies" (employees) take a very active interest in each other's projects and participate in calls, meetings, and become a neutral third party on the buddy's projects where he or she is there to support the other person in whatever possible. When this happens, it is a good sign that the program is working for those individuals.

PMO Buddy System Guidelines—There are very limited rules and regulations in the PMO Buddy System, which is why the program works so well in some organizations. As PMO Manager, you are going to have to judge which rules you need to follow in your organization; however, it is best practice to keep as few rules as possible, but there has to be at least some guidelines.

These guidelines for the PMO Buddy System include:

- PMO buddies commit to the program for a certain amount of time. The PMO Buddy System should continue for a minimum of three months before relationships are reviewed and it is determined whether the relationship should continue.
- PMO buddies share ideas, suggestions, and best practices whenever possible.
- PMO buddies commit to 1–2 "buddy" meetings, monthly, to share ideas and connect with each other.
- PMO buddies commit to being open and honest with both their "employee buddy" and management on whether the relationship is working, sooner

rather than later, and will not continue the relationship if it is not beneficial for both parties.

- Neither "employee buddy" is obligated to take on the leadership role in the relationship. Each individual should approach the relationship informally, but with a caring and a friendly attitude.

Table 7.3 PMO Buddy System Startup Steps outlines the less formal process and steps to get you started in setting up the PMO Buddy System program. Note that some of the steps are identical or similar to starting the official PMO mentoring program. However, one of the biggest differences is that you will not necessarily pilot this buddy system; instead, you will go ahead and start the system and enhance it along the way.

Table 7.3 PMO Buddy System Startup Steps

1.	Schedule and gather interested PMO employees for the PMO Buddy System Kickoff Meeting. Employees can be working in any role, but should be of "like" roles. For example, try to keep your Project Managers together, your Program Managers together, and so on. However, as noted, people join mentoring programs for different reasons, so pair "like" roles when possible. Provide employees with the guidelines established for the program. Refer to the guidelines established earlier.
2.	Establish buddy relationships between the employees. As PMO Manager, you role is to pair the individual employees and make sure everyone involved in the pilot has a "buddy." Try to keep "like" roles together, but because this is an informal process, it can be fun to mix it up and not necessary have project managers just with project managers. Pair up program managers and project managers as "employee buddies" that pairing can also work and be beneficial for both parties.
3.	Let the employees start the process. Do not get in the way when they meet, let the process take hold with the team members. Less is more in this program.
4.	During the two-week check-in meeting, encourage everyone to talk about what is working and what is not working. Take good notes, make necessary changes to the program, and let the employees continue in the program.
5.	During the one-month check-in meeting, encourage everyone to talk about what is working and not working since making the changes suggested at the two-week checkpoint meeting. Listen and make additional changes where necessary.

6.	Between the one-month and the three-month check-in meetings, it is important as PMO Manager to check in individually with the team members to ensure they are getting what they are expecting out of the mentoring relationships they have. At this point, hold off on making changes to the program unless necessary. Sometimes, it takes time for things to work themselves out.
7.	At the six-month period, the PMO Buddy System should be considered up and running and an integral part of your organization.
8.	After a year, reevaluate the PMO Buddy System and make necessary changes.

Summary

One of the key areas that PMO Managers can focus on for their employees is on PMO training and education programs. Training not only keeps employees improving and increasing their skills, but it also shows your employees that their career growth is important to you and that you care about their future. When PMO Managers ignore or leave training and education as an afterthought, employees feel left out or as if their manager is not interested in their careers.

Creating mentoring programs, such as the PMO Mentoring Program, or the less formal PMO Buddy System, is a PMO best practice that many successful PMO Managers have employed for years. Mentoring programs will continue to drive the maturity of the PMO employees and drive camaraderie and team spirit within your organization. These programs will raise the skills of your PMO employees and give everyone involved other people and places to turn to for help or assistance with their program or project problems. Often, employees, for one reason or another, do not like to go directly to their managers for help, so by offering a sounding board or a peer for your employees to work with directly, you help them improve their skills and the skills of the overall organization.

As PMO Manager, it is in your hands to create or ignore the PMO mentoring program. As you build your PMO, think about the value mentoring will bring and how beneficial a formal or even informal type of program is to your employees and your organization.

PMO Build Decisions:

1. Decide the PMO training that you will create as the initial training offerings for your PMO.

2. Decide which program (PMO Mentor Program or PMO Buddy System) you will create in your PMO—or initially, will you decide not to use a mentoring program?

3. Decide what in-house training you will establish for your PMO and how you will deliver the training sessions?

4. Decide which roles in your PMO should be part of the mentoring program or PMO Buddy System?

5. Determine from management how much budget is available for creating these two different programs?

Chapter Review Answers:

1. The PMO Mentoring Program is formal; whereas, the PMO Buddy System is less formal and not as structured.

2. Methodologies help mentors guide and direct mentees in following the tasks and deliverables within the methodology. Methodologies provide a guide and help mentor and mentee be on the same page.

3. PMO mentors should be able to mentor individuals and project teams and should have strong coaching skills. As PMO Manager, take these qualifications seriously because assigning a mentor who is unqualified (even for a pilot program) can do more damage than good for both players (mentor and mentee).

4. PMO buddies share ideas, suggestions, and best practices whenever possible. PMO buddies should commit to 1–2 "buddy" meetings, per month.

5. You should review and reevaluate your PMO Buddy System yearly.

Chapter 8

Portfolio Management Methodology

Figure 8.1 PMO Build Schedule - Portfolio Management Methodology

Task Name	Resource Names
Step 5 - Design & Build or Enhance Period (Chapter 5 - 12)	**PMO Manager**
Design PMO	**PMO Manager**
Design PMO Core Components	**PMO Manager**
Build PMO	**PMO Manager**
Create PMO Business Management Area on Centralized Repository Site (Sections to create are documented in Implementation Phase)	PMO Manager
+Create PMO Core Components	**PMO Manager**
+Create PMO Model (Chapter 5)	**PMO Manager**
+Create PMO Maturity Model	**PMO Manager**
+Create PMO Staffing Model (Chapter 6)	**PMO Manager**
+Create PMO Training (Chapter 7)	PMO Manager
+Create Process Methodology Areas (Chapters 8-10 - where applicable)	**PMO Manager**
- Create or Enhance Portfolio Management Methodology (Chapter 8)	**Portfolio Manager**
+Initiation	**Portfolio Manager**
+Planning	**Portfolio Manager**
+Executing & Controlling	**Portfolio Manager**
+Closing	**Portfolio Manager**

Questions you should be able to answer after reading this chapter:

1. Why is portfolio management so important to an organization?

2. What role does a PMO Manager play in the Portfolio Planning Process?

3. How does collecting "lessons learned" during portfolio planning help?

4. What are the main steps of portfolio management?

5. Why is the Portfolio Execution Process broken down into two areas?

There are many different components of portfolio management and every organization will tackle the process differently based on a number of factors. Ultimately, companies perform portfolio management to balance the challenges of making decisions about investment priorities and aligning those programs and projects while still balancing the risks and tradeoffs against performance. It is so important that there is a link between an organization's strategies and projects to ensure alignment. PMOs play a huge role in this process by keeping everything aligned and working together.

Portfolio management is made up of many different areas, such as governance, project selection, management pain points, financials, pair-wise comparison methods, and so on. In most companies, the PMO Manager needs to consider where and how portfolio management is utilized. Sometimes portfolio management is not done in the PMO, and therefore the PMO Manager will not have say on how it is utilized, but will need to be tightly aligned to how it functions regardless. Oddly enough, some companies do not involve the PMO Manager, which can often lead to huge holes and consequences in the program and project execution downstream. In some companies, formal portfolio management processes are not needed. Those companies apply portfolio management, but with a lot less structure or rigor. Not all companies can afford a large-scale portfolio management processes. For example, in small companies, or companies that are still growing their project management maturity, the portfolio management process can be quite simple, which is okay because of where they are in their maturity. Not every company is mature in portfolio management, program management or even project management. What you find is that most small to midsize companies are very immature in how they handle portfolio management. This is okay because companies do not always need mature portfolio management, but they do need to be aware of the consequences of not having it and what the impacts are on the execution of Programs and Projects. As PMO Manager, regardless of whether you are working at a large company, mid-size company, or have been hired at a small company, it is your responsibility to keep a handle on this process and drive it (even the simplest version) using solid processes and best practices.

In most PMOs, the portfolio management processes generally play some sort of role; in some cases, it can be very formal and in other cases informal. In some PMOs, the PMO Managers are very activate in the portfolio management process and are involved in daily activities. Portfolio Managers need to make decisions for the programs and projects during the planning cycle and continue to be active with those same programs and projects in the execution phase. In other PMOs, the PMO Managers receive a list or a spreadsheet with the list of program and project names and are told to "execute" this body of work. Nothing more, nothing less, they must jump in and make it happen. These are two very real, very different processes where both companies have their own way of handling portfolio management. It is also clear that there are two different maturity levels as well at these two companies. It is a best practice and highly recommended to make Portfolio management, at its core, be part of your PMO.

Another area that PMO Managers need to consider is the PMO model (supportive, controlling, directive, and so on) when determining where and how portfolio management will work within their PMO. If you have a fully supportive PMO, then the role that the PMO employees play in portfolio management is a supporting role; they have no real stake in the execution of the portfolio management process. If the PMO model is directive, then the PMO Manager might hire a Portfolio Manager who reports through the PMO structure, and drives and directs the Portfolio process. As PMO Manager, think about how portfolio management will play a role in your organization and make the appropriate changes and updates based on where it lands. This is something to consider as you begin to understand the portfolio management processes better and how those processes will work within your PMO model. Alternatively, you might find that portfolio management processes do not align well to your PMO at all, and so what happens in that case? What happens to the whole portfolio management processes if it does not align to your PMO, but it is still part of your responsibilities? That can be challenging for any PMO Manager and something that when selecting your PMO model, a large part of the consideration process.

Earlier in the book, we talked about the three key processes to think about when building your PMO: resources, procedures, and infrastructure. When you think about portfolio management, you focus on all three processes. When you think about your resources, you will need to decide on whether you will hire a Portfolio Manager or whether the PMO Manager will take on the these portfolio responsibilities in addition to their PMO role. Also, when considering your different resources for your PMO, think about all the people involved in portfolio creation and execution. Portfolio management has a number of processes and tools associated, so it is important to think about those as we move through creating and growing your portfolio management methodology for your organization.

Finally, remember that there is a design component to building a portfolio management methodology in your organization. The specific parameters and nuances of your company (e.g. Regulatory considerations) will drive exactly how you will use portfolio management, so consider designing this methodology first with all those different company considerations, and then once you are sure it matches your organization, you can actually develop the portfolio processes. Take the time to know your organization's different nuances so you can determine the right components to build for your portfolio management methodology. If you company for example is small or mid-sized, you many not utilize and not feel like you have to implement a huge portfolio management process, but a smaller scale version will work just fine. Implementing a full blown portfolio management methodology, with all the structure and all the formality in a company that is not ready for it will not likely be successful and you may end up being frustrated by the processes and cause negative impact on you and your PMO.

Let us move now to learning about portfolio management methodology and processes.

Portfolio Management Breakdown

Portfolio management—A collection of programs or projects and other work that is grouped together to facilitate effective management of that work to meet strategic business objectives. The portfolio of programs or projects do not have to be interdependent or directly related. Portfolio management is the centralized management of one or more portfolios; it includes identifying, prioritizing, authorizing, managing, and controlling programs and their projects to achieve strategic business objectives. The main function of portfolio management is to assist management with funneling, analyzing, and determining where to invest. This type of work will carry over from year to year and will be an integral part of the company's processes.

To help you understand portfolio management, let us start with a diagram because it is often easier to explain in pictures than it is in words. **Figure 8.2 Six Strategic Steps in the Creation of Portfolio Management** shows the typical six-step process that many organizations use in their strategic planning sessions. It is also a good representation of where portfolio management stands in the hierarchy of the company's strategic process. In most companies, there is a vision that sets the guiding principles for that company, and from that vision they develop one or many strategies. That strategy will drive operational planning, and that planning process generates the portfolio that the company will execute for the year. From a portfolio management perspective, you can take two paths: you can establish and create a series of programs that have individual projects, or you can create individual projects without the programs. That is where many companies will differ and, as PMO Manager, you need to know because this will be the foundation for how you create your portfolio management processes within your PMO. It is very important that you do not underestimate how complex this simple diagram really is and how it is done in most companies, and then in your company. At the highest level, this diagram is very close and strategically correct, but in the end, though, each company will tackle this differently. Companies base how they do their portfolio management processes based on these different areas: complexity, industry, management, or executive direction. Every company should include these six steps they just may have a seventh or eighth step as well. On the other hand, a company might re-order the steps in a different order, but fundamentally, **Figure 8.2 Six Strategic Steps in the Creation of Portfolio Management** is applicable and correct for every company implementing portfolio management. What they should not do is change the portfolio, program, and project hierarchy as shown in the last three arrows of this diagram. It would be strange if they did that and would raise alarms to individuals and practitioners who understand industry standards and, therefore, would question the validity of the hierarchy. If you run into this case in your PMO and you see the management team suggesting a different hierarchy, show them this diagram and explain how the project management industry works. Walk them through the process to ensure they follow what the industry is already doing as closely as possible. The portfolio, program, and project structure should not change from company to company without some unique circumstances or industry considerations that make it applicable to do so.

Figure 8.2 Six Strategic & Tactical Steps in the Creation of Portfolio Management

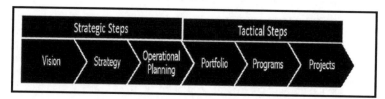

Note: The industry standard hierarchy is portfolio → program → project structure. Think very carefully before you make any structural changes to this for your PMO, and if you do, consider the downstream impacts of that change.

Now that you've seen the six strategic & tactical steps for how many companies run this process, let's focus just on portfolio management to better understand what and how much you should use for your PMO.

There are a couple different paths a PMO Manager can take with portfolio management and these paths will differ based on the maturity of your company. Because the focus of this book is to provide you with as much information as possible to build a successful PMO, let's assume that your company is relatively mature and has given you the authority and the ability to implement a solid portfolio management process. Now, the caveat to this whole chapter is that one phrase above, **"the maturity of your company,"** which will make a huge difference in how much you are able to do in this role. I have seen cases where the PMO Manager has nothing or very little to do with the planning and portfolio process, so consider that as you go through this chapter and consider what you realistically can and cannot implement. You may have the best intentions to put the most rigorous process in place, which is great, but if your company is not mature enough—or if they are just starting with a formal portfolio process—you might not be able to implement a lot. Therefore, your role is to balance what is being done, what you see needs to be done, and then recommend the best approach to management. Companies work much better using the crawl, walk, and run theory, than they do when they just start running. It never works to start out running; companies cannot seem to change fast enough and putting a full-scale portfolio management process in a very immature company would be considered running. Your role is to understand that balance and work to put in a portfolio management process that the company can accept and grow with into the future. This is a good time to understand exactly what a dedicated Portfolio Manager does because as PMO Manager if you are unable able to hire a dedicated Portfolio Manager, these are some responsibilities you are going to take on yourself. Otherwise, if you can, look for assigning these roles and responsibilities to your dedicated Portfolio Manager role.

Roles and Responsibilities of a Portfolio Manager

The industry has some common roles and responsibilities for the Portfolio Manager and, as PMO Manager, your knowledge of these are important because you will generally be the person hiring the portfolio manager for your organization. As noted above, the portfolio management discipline might fall under you and you have to hire someone to do the role, or you might end up performing the role yourself. This is often the case, many companies simply cannot afford the funding for both a Portfolio Manager and a PMO Manager, and so they often decide to combine the roles; thus, saving money by not separating the roles. Most of the time, the reason for this (as noted above), is due to the lack of maturity in portfolio management at the company and management feels that it makes sense to combine the two roles. In most cases, this never works out well, but companies sometimes have to learn this important lesson the hard way. Expect, as PMO Manager, that you will have some of these portfolio tasks assigned to you. However, if you are in the position to hire a Portfolio Manager, here are some of the roles and responsibilities of the role. This can differ from company to company, but most of them will apply. These include, but are not limited to, the following:

- Drive the portfolio management process
- Monitor the portfolio and its alignment with the company or organizational goals
- Establish and maintain a framework or methodology for portfolio management in the organization
- Perform portfolio optimization
- Drive capacity planning and resource allocations
- Drive portfolio selection
- Drive portfolio prioritization
- Monitor and report performance of all components of the portfolio, including financial and value via KPIs
- Drive portfolio analysis
- Produce and distribute performance reviews and performance monitoring reports
- Regularly make investment presentations to executive or management team

These are just some of the many different roles and responsibilities of Portfolio Managers. Look for someone who can meet these qualifications when establishing and building your PMO. This list is a great starting point for you when hiring a Portfolio Manager and you can apply these qualifications right directly into your job description for posting the role.

One of the key responsibilities outlined for Portfolio Managers is driving the portfolio management process. That process or methodology is also an industry standard and it is best practice and highly recommended that you, as PMO Manager, stay as close to industry standards wherever possible. Let us look at what the industry defines as a portfolio management process.

The portfolio management process group, as defined by PMI, includes the following characteristics:

- Portfolio Initiating Process
- Portfolio Planning Process
- Portfolio Executing Process

- Portfolio Controlling Process
- Portfolio Closing Process

These processes are the same across portfolio, program, and project management and are adopted by most PMO Managers in the industry. As PMO Manager, when building your PMO, you should stick to defining and creating the same methodology as the industry uses, just adjust that methodology to what makes sense for your organization. Below, you will find the required portfolio deliverables for each of these processes, but your role is to understand how to implement them in your organization.

Before we get into the methodology, one thing PMO Managers (or Portfolio Managers) need to understand is the portfolio planning process in their organizations. In some cases, this process can be very basic, in others, it can be very sophisticated, and in others, non-existent. Earlier, I mentioned that your company was mature in some processes, so therefore let us assume that it does not have a Portfolio Planning Process in place today, but you've been asked to figure out what the industry is doing and come up with a process for your organization. For the sake of this book, this is going to make the most sense and, as PMO Manager, it is important to understand too that this whole area might not be anywhere in your purview or responsibility. Therefore, let us walk through the generic Portfolio Lifecycle Process to give you want you need to implement them in your organization. If you are lucky and your company has a mature portfolio management process already in place, that is great and rare, and then it should be easy for you to figure out how to plug into that process. Most companies do not have a Portfolio Management process at all, or have very immature processes, so staring with something gets you on the right track and set up for success.

Let spend some time now and look at the various Portfolio Life Cycle processes for more information on managing and driving your portfolio.

Portfolio Life Cycle Processes

The portfolio management process will differ from company to company, organization to organization, depending on number of factors. However, as noted, it is important to follow the same parameters and concepts of the down-stream processes (program management and project management) to provide layer-to-layer consistency in the organization. For PMO Managers building PMOs and setting up methodologies and processes, using a consistent model gives your employees and others a standard and consistent framework that will keep things consistent across the different disciplines. Consistency is important and can often be a saving grace when Portfolio Managers, Program Managers or Project Managers are unsure how to move forward in their respective areas, following the process steps usually gets them on the right path.

Many organizations handle portfolio management very differently and there are a number of ways that organizations drive their portfolios depending on many different factors, such as management input, organization maturity, portfolio budgets, industry, and so on. There is no right way or wrong way of performing portfolio management there are just different ways. In the project management industry, portfolio management is still so new to many companies. Therefore, you often see them struggling to follow this process correctly from year to year. Actually, due to how complex the portfolio process is, and can get, companies tend to muddle through it year over year and, in the end, complete it one way or another, but that is not to say there is not a lot of re-work and wasted effort occurring along the way. Unfortunately, while portfolio management continues to grow and companies mature in the process, they will continue to struggle until they become more mature and processes are internally ironed out and working smoothly. As PMO Manager, you make sure you are active in portfolio management, grow your own skills, and grow the maturity of your company's processes in this area.

PMO Managers need to remember that even if portfolio management at a company is new and still maturing, you will still have your management team or executives that will have opinions on how they want their portfolios executed or what they want to work on for the upcoming year. Sometimes, what they ask for and the reality of what the organizations can handle is not aligned. Some executives or leadership team members have very strong opinions on the setup and running of their portfolios, while other executives could care very little as long as the work is occurring and the organization is running effectively. As PMO Manager, know where your management team is at and how structured and formal they want things to run and have a conversation with them if there is misalignment. Many times there is a balance that you must strike with the management team to continue to move the portfolio forward through the year.

This chapter is about taking industry standard portfolio management processes and learning how to adjust them for your organization. As noted earlier, it is a best practice to take the foundation of anything and then update it where necessary for your own needs. It is so much better than starting from scratch and gives you something to work from with this or any other process. Remember, there is no one-size-fits-all portfolio management methodology.

Let us move now into the Portfolio Initiating Process and learn some of the key steps and processes to kick-off your portfolio correctly.

Portfolio Initiating Process

Kicking off a portfolio is one of the most important phases in the portfolio management process. If you kick it off successfully, it is going to give you a much better chance of success. The portfolio process is the key to establishing and defining work for the organization. When this process is botched or done half-heartedly, there is a huge negative impact to everyone in the organization. This is an important process to do correctly and in a timely manner. Ensure you are working with your executives, customers, and stakeholders and obtaining their approval and support along the way. As PMO Manager, you typically drive and own this process, so how well this process is run is your responsibility. You must also ensure that you keep the program and project team members engaged along the way to ensure alignment and commitment among everyone—especially because they are the people actually performing the work of the portfolio throughout the year.

Table 8.2 Portfolio Initiation Process focuses on the specific portfolio deliverables in the initiation process. This is an extremely busy time for any Portfolio Manager because of all the work required during this phase. The following minimum set of portfolio management deliverables for most organizations falls to the Portfolio Manager (or his or her team) to create during the Portfolio Initiation Process.

Table 8.2 Portfolio Initiation Process

#	Task	Notes
1.	Develop a portfolio management document control system	This document control system can vary from software to software such as (Microsoft® Project Server or UMT Project Essentials 2010 ®). Regardless of where information is stored, as PMO Manager, it is your responsibility to establish a central location available and accessible to anyone needing portfolio information.
2.	Determine portfolio scope	One of the most important aspects of kicking off the portfolio is to determine the scope. Portfolio Managers work with management, stakeholders, and leaders to determine the scope of the portfolio process.
3.	Create the portfolio charter document	This document contains the fundamentals of scope, objectives, constraints, assumptions, communications, budget, and so on. This document follows the same characteristics of the program and project charter documents.

#	Task	Notes
4.	Develop portfolio metrics/dashboards	A couple key tools that Portfolio Managers require are dashboards and metrics. For more information about metrics and dashboard, see Chapter 14, "PMO Measurements and Performance Tracking" later in the book to learn much more about metrics.
5.	Develop a portfolio management team, including the selection of the Portfolio Leader/Manager	Gather and obtain resources to drive the organization's portfolio. The Portfolio Manager might be the PMO Manager or might be someone else.
6.	Develop a roles and responsibilities document	Create a RACI document for every role and person in the portfolio. This document will bring to light any missing people from roles.
7.	Develop a portfolio review board process	This is an important step to ensure that you have a board coming together, making decisions, and helping the portfolio process move forward.
8.	Develop a portfolio Work Breakdown Structure (WBS)	This WBS documents and organizes the portfolio, program, and project structure.
9.	Hold the portfolio kickoff meeting	This meeting formally begins the organization's portfolio of work.
10.	Develop any applicable training plans on process or tools implemented in this phase	It is important that training plans and materials are created for any new processes or tools created during this phase.

Further Considerations

Portfolio Managers have many things to consider when creating and kicking off the initial portfolio of work for the organization. Here is a list of considerations and areas for the Portfolio Manager to think about during the Portfolio Initiation Process:

Strategic plan—The company's strategic plan is very important to understand during the Portfolio Initiating Process. As PMO Manager, you are ultimately accountable for driving your organization toward the strategic direction of the company. Make sure you have a copy of your company's strategic plan, study it, pass it among others in your group, and use it to help shape your portfolio in your organization. Regardless of what is in your PMO plan, you might need to change direction and realign with the strategic plan if there are misalignments.

Program and project selection methods—This is a very important component of the process and consists of a systematic approach to analyzing the proposed project. The evaluation process can be formal or informal and usually consists of the following:

- Feasibility analysis—Either a formal study or a simple group brainstorming session.
- Cost-benefit analysis—This compares the expected or predicted project costs and benefits.

As PMO Manager, you should be driving the processes and procedures around the program and project selection method. It is best practice for companies to make this a very formal process and a requirement that every program and project that lands in the portfolio has gone through this rigorous process and is reconfirmed every year. You should be very active in the program and project selection process even if you are not formally part of it—you need to know which programs and projects end up in your portfolio. You also want to ensure that you are aware of how the selected programs align to the company's strategic direction because multiple times through the course of the year, you will end up defending (or at least explaining) how the efforts align to the strategic plan. Another best practice to implement is putting a feasibility study process in place to provide management with more information and to help them select the right program and project mix. Feasibility studies can weed out programs and projects that are of little value long before they make it to the selection process. We cover much more on the selection process later in this chapter in the Portfolio Planning Process.

Techniques, such as NPV or ROI—The definition of net present value (NPV) is the difference between the present value of the cash inflow and the present value of the cash outflow. Generally, this technique analyzes the profitability of a project. The NPV analysis is sensitive to the reliability of the future cash inflow that a project will yield. Return on investment (ROI) is a performance measure that evaluates the efficiency of an investment compares the efficiency of a number of different investments. To calculate ROI, the benefit of an investment is divided by the cost of the investment, where the results are expressed as a percentage or a ratio.

From a PMO Manager's perspective, it is important to know the NPV or the ROI for the projects within your portfolio. With this knowledge, you can make the right trade-off decisions as well as balance those projects with the strategic direction of the company. If you see a project with a low ROI, for example, and it appears there is no alignment with the strategic plan of the company, you can recommend to not go forward with that project or, at a minimum, you can determine a different portfolio where it would fit in your PMO.

Executive Oversight—There are so many areas where executive oversight can be very beneficial during this process. As PMO Manager, it is important to consider how to use your executives at this time. One area is in resource conflict during the initial program and project scoping phase where high-level executive oversight can help resolve resource conflicts between projects. This oversight incorporates formal sourcing strategies to determine the skill sets needed for each project and the best source of resources. Use your executives wisely and they will help you be successful in this early process—not using them or keeping them out of the loop could cause some serious issues.

Portfolio Project Mix—The mix of programs and projects within your portfolio depends on a number of factors that may or may not be in your direct control, but is something that you need to be aware of and manage closely. As you review the projects that are in your portfolio, look at the feasibility analysis and review it against the strategic direction of the company. Your role is to review the selected programs and projects and to question or challenge their selection if you see areas where the alignment is unclear. As PMO Manager, you will do a year's worth of reporting and explaining of your programs and projects so you need to ensure that the mix is balanced and in line with the current company and management direction.

Organizational Politics—When defining the yearly programs and projects mix, politics can radically change which efforts will get the green light to go forward and which ones will be rejected. Politics comes into play at every level, in every organization and sometimes plays a role in which programs and projects end up in the yearly portfolio. As PMO Manager, be aware of politics during the selection process; your awareness and ability to adapt is a good starting point in helping you be successful in this process.

Programs or projects from previous years not yet realizing their expected value—There are often programs that, during the course of the year, for one reason or other do not attain their expected value. Therefore, at this juncture, management determines whether to keep these projects going or shut them down. This is usually a year-over-year process. In any case, consider these programs and projects during the portfolio process because, often, the expected value of these programs and projects span over multiple years so they are automatically added to the next year's portfolio list.

Executive Pet Projects—In almost every organization, executives have their own pet projects. It is a best practice for the PMO Manager or the Portfolio Manager to watch for these efforts to come to light in the Portfolio Initiation Process. It is wise to determine where the funding will come from, who will work on them and any associated timeframes. Allocating funding and being aware of pet projects early in the process prevents any surprises down the line and allows for adequate planning of these efforts.

To conclude the Portfolio Initiation Process, the items documented in **Table 8.2 Portfolio Initiation Process**, above, will give you a great starting point for your organization to kick off the portfolio management process. The tools and deliverables noted in that table are the foundational items and the minimum to complete for driving a successful Portfolio Initiation Process.

Tips & Best Practices

Every company needs a vision and PMO Managers should be aware of that vision to help make and drive strategic decisions.

Portfolio Planning Process

The Portfolio Planning Process helps management and executives prioritize multiple projects by applying a set of principles based on strategic and financial objectives of the company. This process is often time consuming and a complex. PMO Managers or Portfolio Managers must ensure they balance the understanding of the project's potential returns, potential value, and risk exposure against project delivery while determining the right program and project mix for the organization. It is no easy task and therefore working through the processes and deliverables in the Portfolio Planning Process outlined below provides the right steps in ensuring your company goes through this process successfully. Just like an investment portfolio, the goal of this process is to find the proper balance in the portfolio to maximize returns and minimize risk while keeping things on track across budget, value, time, and customer satisfaction.

Portfolio Planning Process

The Portfolio Planning Process is very complicated with many variables and factors; most companies struggle to do well with this at all. The companies that do a great job have very formal processes in place, address it yearly, and are constantly balancing and moving priorities based on the needs of the business, the industry, and the economy. This is certainly not an easy process to accomplish for a company and it is critical that senior management and customers all support and are heavily involved in this process.

How do companies do their internal planning process? What do they do to get their plan of record established and set for the year? As PMO Manager, you are going to have to know this well and may play a very critical role in this process. Even if you are not, you will end up owning the results of the process, so it is in your best interest to learn it and know it well.

Let us spend time and look at what the Portfolio Planning Process looks like today in some companies, so that maybe you can take some ideas and concepts and apply them to your company.

Portfolio Planning Overview

Introduction

Portfolio planning is the process of translating the organization's high-level strategy into a ready-to-execute portfolio of projects, taking into account characteristics such as the organization's cost and resource constraints, risk appetite, and so on.

And, in a more straight-forward terminology: it's about transforming a set of unstructured, unfiltered, sometimes incoherent, portfolio of ideas into a set of well-defined projects. Each project has its own set of milestones, deliverables, and benefits that are directly linked to the organization's KPIs, which will ultimately deliver the organization's strategy.

Although it seems like stating the obvious, the whole "raison d'etre" of a portfolio of projects is to deliver the organization's strategy; and the only way to measure the success of a project—and a portfolio—is by assessing its contribution to the organization's KPIs. We cover KPIs in more detail in Chapter 14, "PMO Measurements and Performance Tracking," so please review that chapter for more information about KPIs.

Therefore, the main objective of the Portfolio Planning Process is to ensure that the organization is "**Doing the Right Things**" to deliver its strategy, such as selecting the best sub-set of projects to deliver the strategic KPIs, given existing constraints—before it focuses its energy on "Doing Things Right" —ensuring that projects are being delivered on time, on budget, and on scope.

Figure 8.3 Doing the Right Things Right Chart illustrates the combination of the two: "Doing the Right Things Right."

Figure 8.3 Doing the Right Things Right Chart

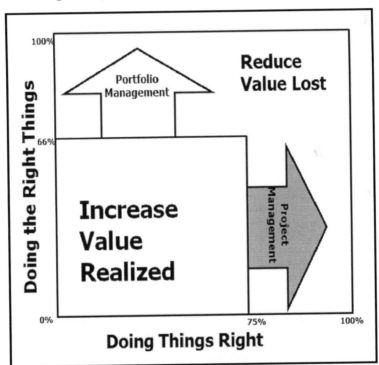

The sad truth is that most organizations fail to follow this approach and end up with projects that, even though they might be executed brilliantly, have no impact on the way the organization is achieving its strategy. Therefore, only a combination of the macro and the micro of portfolio planning (as shown in **Figure 8.3 Doing the Right Things Right Chart**)—doing the right things (the portfolio management discipline)

and doing them right (the project management discipline)—will increase the probability of having a portfolio that will deliver the organization's strategy.

The planning process consists of three steps: **1) Create**, where ideas are gathered, sorted, and translated into projects; **2) Select**, where projects are prioritized and optimized against cost and resource constraints to identify the best sub-set of projects to deliver the organization's strategy; and **3) Plan**, where resources are assigned and the projects, together with their projected benefits, are sequenced. Only when these three stages have been completed successfully can the organization move on to the final step: **Manage**, where the projects are launched and the benefits they deliver are tracked.

The PMO Role

The PMO has a crucial role in ensuring that the Portfolio Planning Process is executed successfully. In essence, the PMO is the "responsible adult," guiding a bunch of executives who, at times, behave as unruly teenagers, and providing them with sound, objective advice. To do so, it needs to have the right mix of resources, procedures, and infrastructure in place and should enjoy the appropriate level of support from senior management. But first and foremost, it needs to ensure that the whole framework is not viewed as just a fancy theory. It should be viewed at a practical level—in other words, eliminate the "it's a nice theory, but in real life..." approach.

Resources

To begin, facilitating this process requires assertive, skilled and experienced individuals who cannot only manage the end-to-end planning framework, guiding the projects through their gate-based approval process, but who can also provide a sounding board and act as quality assurance. These individuals must be able to challenge project sponsors and stakeholders when the information provided does not meet the required standards. The PMO Manager is also responsible for opening any bottlenecks that result from slow response and should, therefore, have the right level of mandate that will enable him or her to do so.

Procedures

The PMO processes that oversee the planning phase should be clear, simple, and well-defined. And, where possible, they should be designed in consultation with stakeholders. If the process chart ends up looking like an overflowing spaghetti bowl, then the probability of the right projects getting through it is obviously very low. In addition, stakeholders will have less difficulty buying into a process they helped design and understand, rather than one that requires them to be rocket scientists.

The PMO is responsible for ensuring that best practices around PMO processes are continuously identified, shared, and implemented and that user feedback is gathered and acted upon. As part of this, the PMO will ensure that all stakeholders—including project sponsors, project managers, and so on—go through dedicated training to familiarize themselves with these processes and their associated reporting requirements.

Infrastructure

The PMO role is to identify and deploy the tool that will best meet the project and portfolio management maturity, current and planned, of the organization. There are a variety of software products on the market that can be deployed to support the Portfolio Planning Process and the governance around it. Although a tool is only as good as the process it supports, not having a tool at all is not really an option: users are more apt to accept a process, any process, that is delivered with a software tool than one that is described with a slide deck and flipcharts.

The following sections describe the details and practical implications of the three steps of the Portfolio Planning Process: create, select and plan, culminating in manage, and the role the PMO plays in each one.

Create: From Idea to Project

Introduction

"And the Portfolio was without form, and void," (Genesis 1:2... well, almost) is a good way to describe the starting point of the Portfolio Planning Process: a plethora of ideas that originate from different parts of the organization. Some with a price tag in the hundreds of millions of dollars, and some in the tens of thousands; some that address real business needs and some that were thought of only after a long night out drinking with the team.

The "create" phase is basically the filter, in the form of the project-approval process, through which ideas must pass. These ideas must be evaluated as to their contribution to the organization and their existence (and in some cases their sponsors' existence) justified, before they are allowed to join the organization's project portfolio.

The main benefit of a structured, step-by-step approval process—one that uses a standard, consistent business-case template—is that all ideas, without exception, must go through the same evaluation process in order to become projects. It basically erases the back-door option of adding projects to a portfolio "because I said so" or because it is someone's pet project. Following the process allows the organization to compare apples to apples, using the same criteria making an educated decision regarding the probability (or promise) of success and the benefits, it will deliver.

The project approval process usually takes place ahead of the annual budget planning exercise, in order to provide management with the financial requirements for delivering the organization's project portfolio for the coming year. In certain situations—unexpected change in market circumstances, re-prioritization of strategy, and so on—the process might be deployed on an ad-hoc basis as well.

The role of the PMO is to facilitate the approval process and to ensure that the right information is available at the right time, with the right quality, to the right stakeholder.

As the owners of the process, the PMO should also ensure that all stakeholders are clear about how it works, what is expected of them, and how to deal with any bottlenecks that might appear along the way as a result of, say, an approver who pushed approval-related email to the bottom of his or her pile.

The Project Approval Process

The first step in the project approval process requires a centralized repository where ideas can be logged using a basic template. This template can include fields such as the project name, which problem it is intending to resolve, and how it is planning to resolve them—in other words, the project's name, objectives and approach.

The PMO then acts as the initial reviewer of the ideas and decides which ones should move ahead to the next step in the process. In each step, additional information is entered and reviewed by a pre-defined list of stakeholders. Moving to the next step only occurs after the approver is satisfied that the information received is sufficient and of the right quality.

Examples of this information, added in the different steps, include:

- Project name, scope and objectives
- Areas of business impacted by the project
- Business drivers that the project will contribute to (in order to define the strategic alignment of the project with the overall goals of the organization)
- Cost and benefits (both financial—expected revenue increase and the project's NPV—and non-financial, such as customer and employee satisfaction)
- Risk assessment divided into categories, such as technology, third party, operational, and so on
- High-level resource requirements

Some of these steps (see **Figure 8.4 Project Approval Process Example**) can also be defined as gateways, which require the reviewers to decide whether they are satisfied with the information and business rationale presented to them so far, which leads to one of three decisions:

- **Go**—The project, which, at this stage, is actually an idea, not a project, can move to the next step in the approval process.
- **No Go**—There is not enough justification to take this idea forward (in other words, the project has no business case).
- **Need more information**—There is not enough information to make a decision.

- **Figure 8.4 Project Approval Process Example** shows a typical workflow for approving projects—from the initial idea to the final approval (or rejection).

Figure 8.4 Project Approval Process Example

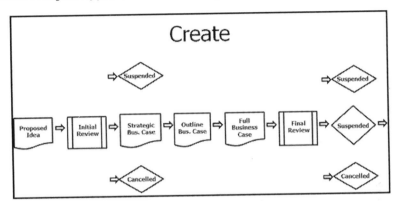

Obviously, the project approval process is not a one-size-fits-all kind of process. Different types of projects require different levels of detail and approval workflows; some organizations might argue that approving a $100,000 project should follow a less stringent process than approving a $5 million dollar one. Others will say that the steps for signing off on a pure IT project, such as an upgrade to the email system, should be different from a pure business project, such as setting up an office in a new country. Whatever the case might be, all of these projects need approval only after fulfilling the specific project approval requirements.

After all of the ideas have passed through the project approval process filter, the organization is left with a comprehensive list of the projects that need to be implemented in order to deliver its strategy for the coming years. This does not mean that all approved projects will automatically be implemented; the next steps in the Portfolio Planning Process—namely, selection and planning—will have to take place before the final list can be determined. However, you will need to somehow convince stakeholders that not all projects are equal—some are worth more than others—in other words, you need to find a mechanism for prioritizing projects.

Evaluating Projects

A word of warning: the following section deals mainly with the theory and best practices of deciding which projects are worth investing in. Justifiably or not, the terms "theory" and "best practices" carry bad connotations. In itself, this isn't a good enough excuse to avoid them and go for Plan B, which usually consists of a shouting match to determine which projects will take the top prize.

The PMO Manager, as the facilitator of the whole process, is therefore responsible for obtaining the buy-in of stakeholders by communicating its benefits and by ensuring clear and simple execution. Anything less will almost guarantee the failure of a long-term adoption of these practices.

Evaluation Criteria

To be able to prioritize the project portfolio and decide which should win a share of the organization's resources, it is necessary to develop a criteria for comparing them against each other. In some cases, especially where the number of projects is relatively small, projects can be prioritized based on the knowledge of senior managers (although, this "knowledge" is more of an intuition, or gut feeling, than a scientific formula). In other cases, where the number of projects is large, a uniform, consistent set of criteria (one or more) is required.

The criteria forms a mandatory part of the business case template and should provide a detailed description of how to calculate the evaluation criteria in order to ensure that all contributors are using the same step-by-step methodology and parameters. Obviously, most project sponsors will claim that their projects meet the highest levels of each criteria, hoping that this will push them to the top of the priority list. Therefore, it is essential for the PMO Manager to oversee this process and review the results with great care and push back where necessary, rather than accept a project as-is.

The three main types of criteria used by organizations to prioritize and compare projects are:

1. **Financial Value**—Such as net present value (NPV) or the return on investment (ROI) of a project. This is basically, a financial projection of the future net returns of the project—either in actual figures (NPV) or as a ratio of the original investment. This projection requires information such as:
   - Project cost
   - Cost of capital (such as a discount rate)
   - Project life time
   - Projected annual incoming cash flow (the combined financial value of all project benefits, per year)

2. **Strategic Value**—Also known as the strategic alignment indicator, this value represents the level of alignment that a project—and a portfolio—has with the organization's strategy. More specifically, this is the weighted average of the strength of the link between the project's benefits (financial and non-financial) and the organization's objectives and KPIs. The information required for calculating the strategic value includes (there are more details in the following section):
   - The organization's prioritized objectives
   - KPIs and target KPIs, per objective
   - The list of benefits for each project, measured in the same units as the KPIs
   - The type of link (for example, strong, moderate, and so on) between each project and the set of objectives

3. **Risk score**—A weighted indicator of the risk profile of a project across different risk categories. This can be calculated using the following information:
   - Weighted risk categories, such as technology risk, third-party risk, dependency risk, and so on

- A set of questions for each category to assess the level of risk it poses to the project
- A scoring mechanism to calculate the category risk and the overall project risk

The calculation of the financial criteria and risk score are relatively straight-forward and can be built into the business case template using a projected financial benefits table and a risk questionnaire. The strategic value criteria, however, require a preliminary process to be followed and will therefore be discussed in more detail below.

Calculating the Strategic Value

To define the project's strategic value, it is necessary to take a step back and to remind ourselves that first and foremost, the outcome of each and every project should be to support the implementation of the organization's strategy. The issue is: how can we tell that this is indeed the case?

This is where the concept of portfolio alignment comes into play. Basically, the alignment of the project portfolio with the organization's strategy ensures that projects that support the organization's top priorities are moved to the top of the list. To generate a prioritized list of projects, the organization must have a well-defined prioritized list of objectives and a framework for linking the projects' benefits to the objectives' KPIs.

This process is described in more detail later in this chapter.

Defining Objectives

To begin with, the strategy of the organization needs to be properly reflected in its overall objectives. (Note that the term "organization" is only used for simplicity and can be replaced by other terms such as division, region, or even a program.) These objectives must be specific in scope, action-oriented, able to serve as high-level goals for an individual project, and should ideally have been agreed upon through a consensus approach by as wide a group of senior managers and stakeholders as realistically possible.

Objectives are typically categorized into three areas: demand management (for example, market share, sales effectiveness, increased revenue), supply management (for example, operational efficiency, customer responsiveness) or support services (for example, infrastructure efficiency, regulatory requirements). Most importantly, however, objectives need to be measurable: each one should have a set of one or more KPIs which, along with their defined targets, enable decision makers to monitor and control the successful delivery of the objectives in real terms.

Effective KPIs must be relevant to their associated objective, specific, readily measurable by the organization, realistic and achievable, and contain a time element.

Tips & Best Practices

For more information about KPIs, see Chapter 9, "Program Management Methodology."

Prioritizing Objectives

After the objectives have been agreed upon and the KPIs defined, they need to be prioritized. Despite what a few senior managers will tell you, not all objectives have the same importance. For example, after analyzing market conditions, an organization may decide to focus its efforts (and initiate projects) to reduce its cost base rather than increase its revenues; therefore, objectives such as "improve efficiency" or "reduce costs" are prioritized over "increase revenues" or "improve market share."

Therefore, the prioritization process is used to determine the relative importance of the objectives and to calculate their priority. One way of doing that prioritization is to use the Pairwise Comparison method, which ranks the objectives in pairs against one another in order to generate these values. This exercise should ideally be conducted in a group session because it has the added advantage of creating transparency and achieving consensus among decision makers by forcing them to choose and explain their priorities. This exercise also can help deal with a culture of "the one who shouts the most gets his way" and ideally should minimize the number of "blood on the wall" sessions, although, it will never eliminate them...

In these Pairwise Comparison group sessions, participants are asked to vote on the priority of each pair by answering the question "how strongly is objective X more or less important than objective Y?" The answers range from "extremely more" through" extremely less." Voters are encouraged to avoid the "equally important" answer as much as possible. When the vote is too close, additional discussion takes place to clarify the position of each side before a second vote.

A few tools are available in the market (for example, Microsoft Enterprise Project Management Solutions (EPM)) for modeling this process and generating the prioritization vector, which assigns a normalized value to each objective to reflect its relative importance vs. the other objectives.

The objectives prioritization process requires interaction with the highest level of stakeholders in the organization in order to get their input for defining the objectives and the KPIs, and for prioritizing them. This interaction might not prove to be an easy one, especially if senior managers cannot reach agreement on the priorities of the organization. The PMO Manager has a crucial role in guiding stakeholders through this process, ensuring the objectives are well defined, and preparing and facilitating the group sessions. In addition, the PMO Manager should record the outcome of the sessions to allow it to serve as input for the next steps in the process, which is to prepare and present reports that analyze the findings.

Linking Projects to Objectives

We have now reached a point where we have a set of prioritized and measurable objectives on one side, and a set of projects on the other. The question is: how do we link these two lists? More specifically, is there a way to link them that reflects the type of support each project provides to the objectives as a whole. Finding this link will help us to generate a list of prioritized projects.

This is where the business case template becomes essential. As part of the project approval process, project initiators need to detail the benefits that their project will deliver, along with the estimated time frame for realizing those benefits. The benefits can be financial or non-financial, direct or indirect; however, in order to link them to the KPIs, it is essential to describe the benefits using the same units of measurement as the KPIs. In other words, if a project delivers benefits that cannot be shown to support any KPI, it has no justification and should probably be cancelled (exceptions to this case are sometimes regulatory projects; although, it can be argued that regulatory KPIs should be part of the organization's objectives as well).

The link between project benefits and objectives' KPIs can be defined as binary (meaning, yes or no); however, as with many things in life, this is not necessarily a black or white type of situation, but rather shades of grey. Therefore, a more accurate representation of this link—one that answers the question, "how strongly does this project support this objective?"—can be achieved by defining several levels, such as low, moderate, strong, and extreme. Converting these levels into numbers, and taking into account the weights of each objective (as defined in the objectives prioritization step above), will generate the required result: a list of prioritized projects, each one with its own indicator, the strategic value.

Combining Criteria

To summarize the prioritization step—projects can be prioritized using different criteria, the most common being financial, strategic, and risk. However, one can also combine these criteria to create what might be argued a more accurate one (if accuracy is the right term for what is, in essence, a qualitative approach), as it allows for a decision to be made that takes into account all available information. To do so, it is necessary to bring the different criteria into a single frame of reference by normalizing the values associated with each project and assigning a weight to each criterion, according to the example in the table below. **Table 8.1 Evaluation Criteria** shows an example of three projects with different evaluation criteria values, together with the combined and weighted score.

Table 8.1 Evaluation Criteria

Project	NPV ($000)	Risk score	Normalized NPV (50%)	Normalized strategic value (30%)	Normalized risk score (20%)	Combined score
A	5,000	75%	0.5	0.35	0.375	0.43
B	4,000	85%	0.4	0.45	0.425	0.42
C	1,000	40%	0.1	0.2	0.2	0.15

The information required to calculate these figures is obtained as part of the project approval process. It is the PMO's role to ensure that the appropriate templates, definitions, and parameters are available to the relevant contributors and that the information entered into them is of the right quality. After the PMO Manager has satisfied itself that all the projects that have made it thus far have passed all gates and have the appropriate information, the decision-making process can shift from being a project-focused process to being a portfolio-focused one.

Changing Priorities

The beauty of the prioritization framework is not only in generating a list of prioritized projects, but also in its ability to change these priorities every time a change in the market requires the organization to change its own priorities.

Say, for example, that the market unexpectedly takes a turn for the worse and the organization needs to quickly assess its options. Reprioritizing the objectives to be in line with the new market conditions will immediately result in the projects that are linked to these objectives to be reprioritized as well; the outcome will be a portfolio that is better positioned to deal with the new situation. Furthermore, the PMO does not have to wait for market events to occur; nothing is stopping it from running multiple "what if" scenarios and assessing the sensitivity of the portfolio to different events. That way, when one of these scenarios turns out to be real, quick decisions can be made in terms of which projects should be put on hold, which new ones should be launched, where should the resourcing focus be, and so on.

Select: Optimizing the Portfolio

Creating a portfolio view for all the projects in the organization is a luxury that up until a few years ago was considered too complicated to achieve, at best; and a waste of time, at worst. However, incorporating selected components from disciplines such as Harry Markowitz's portfolio theory and linear programming into ubiquitous software tools has paid back handsomely by allowing decision makers to have full transparency of both the current state of their projects as well as the impact their decisions will have on the future state of the organization's strategy and KPIs.

The previous step has created a prioritized list of projects, each one with its own normalized priority indicator. However, until we agree on the budget that will be allocated to this portfolio, and how to divide it between the projects, at this stage, this list is no more than a wish list. As such, if we add up the costs of all these wishes and go cup-in-hand to the decision makers, in nine out of ten cases, they will question our sanity and send us back to the drawing board with firm instructions to come back with a more sensible number.

After the total budget has been agreed upon, it's time to find a way to distribute it among the projects we believe are the most eligible. There are multiple ways of doing that: allocating budget down the priority list until it runs out, setting aside funds for the "must do" projects (usually regulatory ones) first, or using the ratio between the evaluation criteria (be it financial, strategic, risk or a combination of them) and cost to determine which will we get the most bang for the buck.

Most portfolio management software tools available today support one or more of these methods; a combination of them is recommended as the most practical approach, using linear programming to maximize the evaluation criteria while using the project cost (or any other parameter for that matter, such as resource requirements or even risk) as the constraint. The outcome is an optimized project portfolio—a sub set of the original wish list—with the highest combined value for the evaluation criteria that can be achieved for the agreed budget.

It is important to remember, however, that this optimized portfolio does not necessarily include the projects with the individual highest evaluation criteria value; rather, it proposes those with the highest ratio between this value and the project's cost.

However, this is not necessarily the end solution. The example above optimized the portfolio using one type of evaluation criteria—strategic, financial, risk or a combination of both—as the optimization criteria. By running these criteria in parallel, the organization can compare various portfolios that deliver towards individual criteria, or a combination of them.

Figure 8.5 Portfolio Selection Under Multiple Criteria, below, illustrates a portfolio that is being optimized against a cost constraint using three different criteria: financial value (FV), strategic value (SV), and risk (C1).

Figure 8.5 Portfolio Selection Under Multiple Criteria

Portfolio	Status	Cost	NPV	FTE	Risk	Strat. value	Advisor FV	SV	CI
New Financial Planning Software	Go	1000	970	7	47	0.119041			
Customer Self-Serv (VRU/Internet)	Go	970	600	5	20	0.075893			
Competitive Analysis Unit	Hold	750	120	3	25	0.066517			
CRM-Segmentation Discovery and Mg	Kill	2200	750	3	50	0.061999			
COLI Plan Administration System	Go	1250	120	5	12	0.061408			
Future Builders/Money in Motion	Go	600	230	7	23	0.060862			
Enhanced Telephony Self-Serv	Hold	610	610	3	10	0.050316			
Service Delivery Project	Go	1230	230	4	25	0.049852			
Training	Kill	670	120	5	29	0.048871			
Automated Common Remitter	Go	2910	610	5	5	0.040609			
Customer and prospect Optimizer	Go	1250	250	3	20	0.033670			
Management Reports	Go	1250	250	11	11	0.031832			
Open New Offices	Kill	2200	200	15	15	0.026902			
Windows 2000	Delay	3555	700	9	9	0.026369			
Field Growth Initiative	Hold	1700	555	4	35	0.022364			
Campain/Targeting Support	Hold	2673	673	5	17	0.019792			
Virtual Wholesaler	Delay	2960	960	14	14	0.018629			
CRM-Workstation Infrastructure	Go	1555	555	4	4	0.017322			
CRM-Message Center	Kill	600	600	2	60	0.016760			
Implementation Assistant	Hold	1531	484	8	8	0.016517			
Virtual Report Center	Kill	484	198	2	19	0.016517			

What is now apparent is that different optimization scenarios result in different portfolios comprising different projects. Sound confusing? Not necessarily: the rule for selection should be straightforward. If a project has been selected by all of the three criteria, it should be implemented. It makes sense strategically, it has a good financial return, and the risk is acceptable. On the other hand, if a project has been excluded in all three criteria, it should most likely be rejected (unless, of course, it is a regulatory project or the CEO's pet project). This leaves 10-15% of the projects that made it through one or two criteria, but failed the third one. This "grey area" is where management should focus most of its attention.

The challenge is to use this additional intelligence to decide on the final mix of projects in the portfolio. Why should a specific project be selected? Is there some reason that has not been factored into the analysis yet? Should NPV or risk considerations outweigh the suggested solution if strategic value is optimized? Answering these questions facilitates the final kill/hold/go decision on whether to include a project in the final portfolio.

As in the previous steps, the PMO Manager plays the role of a facilitator and proactive sounding board throughout this process. In addition to gathering, preparing, and presenting the data to decision makers, the PMO Manager should act as objective intermediary to ensure that the decision making process is impartial and that no executive can bully other colleagues into accepting his or her point of view.

The portfolio level analysis—unlike a project-by-project one—allows for multiple scenarios to be reviewed. Different cost levels can be used as constraints and the impact of the different portfolios on the delivery of the strategy, or part of it, can be analyzed. For example, a certain level of investment is able to support a portfolio that is more strategically aligned—that is, better delivers the strategy of the organization— while a different level can support a portfolio that delivers better financial returns. The

PMO Manager needs to record the outcome of these discussions as well as the decision making process that led to it and ensure that the outcome is acted upon.

Plan: Allocating Resources and Sequencing Projects

Introduction

Now that the budget has been secured and distributed among the programs and projects, and the final project list has been agreed on, you should be ready to move into the implementation phase, right? Not so fast, unfortunately. Having the budget in place does not yet mean that the organization has the appropriate resources to deliver the projects. Or, maybe the total number of resources looks fine, but when you look into the details you realize that the skill mix is not right. For example, you might have too many C++ Developers and not enough testers or too many Project Managers and not enough Business Analysts. And no, hiring the missing resources is not always an option—market conditions and the organization's onboarding capacity are just two factors that stand in the way of doing that (good luck with finding and onboarding 20 Project Managers in two months in a buyers-only market). Therefore, the last stage in the Portfolio Planning Process is to create a delivery roadmap for the optimal portfolio, which was identified in the "select" phase, by confirming the portfolio's "deliverability" in terms of available vs. required resources.

The assumption is that by this stage, Project Managers have been assigned to each project and detailed project and resource plans have been created. As a side note, it's important to remember that this requires a list of generic skill types so that the Project Managers can select from it when they prepare the resource plans—something that the human resources department should provide, but isn't always readily available.

Resource Allocation Issues

Most project sponsors expect—demand would be a more accurate term actually—that their projects are implemented as soon as the budget has been agreed upon. This, of course, is a recipe for a planning nightmare, where a huge up-front demand for project resources—Project Managers, Business Analysts, Developers, and so on—is followed by a steep decline once the projects are reaching the end of their life cycle. These peaks and troughs in resource utilization are quite wasteful. Therefore, the objective of the planning phase is to ensure efficient allocation of resources throughout the life cycle of the portfolio in order to minimize these peaks and troughs. Since the alternative is a never-ending cycle of recruitment drives followed by on-the-bench idle time (or worse), this is an objective worth fighting for.

After detailed resource plans have been created for all projects, the demand side can be calculated by adding up all resource requirements, per skill type, per time unit (for example, per month). This can then be matched against the supply side—the total number of resources (or full-time equivalent (FTEs)) available in the organization, per skill type, for the same time unit (again, another project for the human resources department). Additional granularity can be achieved by distinguishing, for example, between permanent employees and contractors, secondary vs. primary skills, and so on.

The resulting chart (an example of which can be seen in **Figure 8.6 Resource Supply vs. Demand Summary—Shortages (highlighted) and Surpluses (un-highlighted)** shows the shortages and surpluses for each skill type and allows the PMO to shift project start dates, taking into account inter-project dependencies, in order to optimize resource utilization throughout the portfolio's life cycle.

Figure 8.6: Resource Supply vs. Demand Summary – Shortages (highlighted) and Surpluses (un-highlighted)

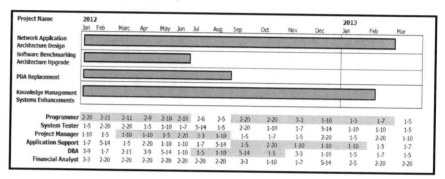

Project Name	2012 Jan	Feb	Marc	Apr	May	Jun	Jul	Aug	Sep	Oct	Nov	Dec	2013 Jan	Feb	Mar
Programmer	2-20	2-21	2-11	2-9	2-10	2-10	2-6	2-5	2-20	2-20	3-3	1-10	1-5	1-7	1-5
System Tester	1-5	2-20	2-20	1-5	1-10	1-7	5-14	1-5	2-20	1-10	1-7	5-14	1-10	1-10	1-5
Project Manager	1-10	1-5	1-10	1-10	1-5	2-20	3-3	1-10	1-5	1-7	1-5	2-20	1-5	2-20	1-10
Application Support	1-7	5-14	1-5	2-20	1-10	1-10	1-7	5-14	1-5	2-20	1-10	1-10	1-10	1-5	1-7
DBA	3-9	1-7	2-11	3-9	5-14	1-10	1-5	1-10	5-14	1-5	3-3	1-10	1-5	1-7	1-5
Financial Analyst	3-3	2-20	2-20	2-20	2-20	2-20	2-20	2-20	3-3	1-10	1-7	5-14	2-5	2-20	2-20

It is important to remember that the aim is not to reach the 12th degree of accuracy in calculating the resource profile, but rather to build a high-level view of the areas, and timeframes where the organization will face resourcing issues. A shortage of 0.3 FTEs of a Project Manager for two months, for example, can probably be addressed by assigning the tasks to another Project Manager; but a shortage of five Business Analysts for, say, three months, can have a profound effect on the organization's ability to meet its deadlines.

Benefits Realization Timeline

One last impact to consider when shifting and re-shifting the projects' timelines is the changes it has on the benefits realization timeline. By definition, each project has made it to this stage because it has benefits that will, presumably, contribute to the organization's strategy. These benefits will not be delivered on the exact same day when the project is delivered, but rather over a timeline of one or more years following the project's completion. This timeline moves each time a milestone is changed, and eventually affects the timeline for delivering the organization's target KPIs. This milestones/benefits link is often ignored either because it was not established in the first place, or because exposing it has sensitive political implications. Nevertheless, the implications of changes in project timelines need to be transparent and clear to all decision makers.

The PMO

As in the previous steps, the PMO Manager acts as the main quality assurance and review function throughout the Portfolio Planning Process. Accuracy is key here, but in addition to ensuring that the correct data is being used, the PMO Manager is also responsible for generating the resource profile reports and for analyzing potential resource scenarios before they are submitted for review and acted upon by senior management. Shifting multiple projects back and forth to identify the optimal utilization will generate a large number of portfolio timelines—it is useful to focus on no more than four or five scenarios because anything more might impact the long-term motivation of the analysts. Issues, such as when resources should be recruited or trained, how many of them of them to hire, and with what skills, are only some examples of what the PMO Manager needs to tackle. Others include maintaining the benefits realization timeline and ensuring the link with the projects' milestones is transparent.

The bad news is that any organization committed to optimizing its performance faces a myriad of options and always will be forced to make difficult choices. The good news, however, is that a holistic approach and a structured decision-making framework help eliminate the bad options and highlight the right decisions.

Most organizations that go through growth (planned or unplanned) are required to shift their approach to project and resource planning from a single project approach (where the "one who shouts the most" gets his or her way) to a consolidated, transparent, portfolio approach where projects are judged based on their financial and strategic fit and the impact of the portfolio, as a whole, can be assessed.

The key to the success of this shift is in communicating the benefits it delivers to the organization and to the Project Managers and in utilizing a phased approach—never a big bang—in rolling it out and adopting it.

A framework for Portfolio Planning Process focuses senior management's decision-making process on the portfolio that delivers the mix of project benefits that brings the greatest financial and strategic value to the organization.

The PMO is the only organizational unit that can ensure the success of this framework. Being the only body that is fully dedicated to overseeing the delivery of the portfolio, its responsibilities do not only include providing full transparency around this process, but also ensuring that a fit-for-purpose framework exists in the first place. When building this framework, the PMO Manager would be wise to remember:

- **Keep it simple-** Do not over-engineer the processes. Take baby steps while implementing it and use the concept of early-adopter groups to obtain buy-in and incorporate feedback into the next steps of the implementation.
- **This is a change project-** Manage it as one to ensure users have a chance to provide feedback at every stage. Executive support is also crucial and should be seen by everybody, rather than being the usual "we support you 100%" behind-the-scenes lip service.
- **Communication is key-** Regular meetings, status email, simple and clear reports, newsletter and brown-bag lunches help obtain and maintain the users' buy-in through the process of building the framework.

When the framework is in place, the create, select, and plan processes are good to go.

To summarize the main concepts discussed in this section:

- Doing the right projects is as important as doing the projects right.
- A delivered project—even though it may be on time, on scope, and even under-budget—does not equal a successful project because it might have no contribution to the organization's KPIs.
- Find your common currency. Having such a currency enables the organization to compare and prioritize the projects and minimize the risk of shouting matches. This currency can be financial (NPV or ROI), strategic alignment, a risk measure, or a weighted combination of them.
- The only relevant project benefits are the ones that contribute to achieving organizational objectives and can be linked to the organization's KPIs. Projects without these links are suspected pet projects and their sponsors should be sent for further training.
- Decisions to select, change, or end a project must be made at the portfolio level; this is the only view where managers can see and understand the impact on the organization's performance.
- A fully-funded project does not necessarily mean a delivered project. Detailed resource analysis needs to be performed to assess whether there are enough resources, of the right skill set, at the right time, to deliver it.
- Developing a benefits realization timeline and creating the milestone/benefits link is a tough challenge; however, this should not be used as an excuse for not doing it at all.

"And The PMO saw everything that he had made, and, behold, it was very good." (Genesis 1:31almost).

Let's move now into looking at **Table 8.3 Portfolio Planning Process** which focuses PMO Managers (or Portfolio Managers) on the complexity of portfolio planning. This process is very complex and there are tremendous amounts of items that are required for planning a portfolio. As previously noted, portfolio management is still quite immature in the industry and, due to that fact, many companies do not tackle portfolio planning in a structured manner, which brings even bigger problems and issues during the Portfolio Executing Process of programs and projects.

Table 8.3 Portfolio Planning Process

#	Task	Notes
1.	Develop a portfolio management plan	This is the main document that describes how you will run your portfolio in your organization. Make sure to include any processes or procedures required to plan and execute the portfolio of work for the organization. The Portfolio Planning Process occurs once a year; however, the execution occurs year-round. The Portfolio management plan should include both areas.
2.	Develop the portfolio scope	The portfolio scope planning process determines and defines the scope of the portfolio. This process is the foundation work that the organization will perform for the year. As PMO Manager, you have the responsibility of understanding and selecting how the programs and projects become part of the portfolio. Therefore, it is important to be active in this process. Part of the scope definition process supports the process of breaking down the types of projects the organization will include in the portfolio. This process includes determining which projects fall within scope while balancing resources and their assignments. As PMO Manager, this is your area of responsibility because the results of this scope process fall into your other area of responsibility, which is portfolio execution. It is very important that you are active in this process, drive this process, and understand the programs and projects that end up in your portfolio of work for the year.
3.	Develop portfolio items and deliverables	Part of planning the portfolio of work is creating some of the portfolio items and deliverables. PMO Managers should understand that this planning phase is a great time to start executing some of the initial portfolio deliverables.
4.	Develop a portfolio	The portfolio project schedule development process identifies the activities to produce the

#	Task	Notes
	schedule	various portfolio deliverables and, secondly and more importantly, to schedule all programs and projects that make up the portfolio. As PMO Manager, you should be fully involved in the schedule creation process and aware of both the activities to produce the deliverables and timeframes of the programs and projects. Even if there is a separate Portfolio Manager working in that role, PMO Managers must also be part of this process. To create the portfolio schedule, there are some scheduling tasks that you must complete, such as: • Understand and analyze the different dependencies in the program and project schedules. The goal is to understand any dependencies between them and report those dependencies to the Program Managers and Project Managers, and then to watch and track their efforts. • Perform the duration estimating process so you understand the estimated number of work periods to complete all the programs and projects in the portfolio. This is an important process in the portfolio management process because it is literally the first chance where you can look broadly across and understand how long these work activities will take and how long, from a time perspective. This process helps create roadmaps, staffing and resource decisions, budgeting, and so on. • Develop and analyze the portfolio resource model. As you are developing the portfolio schedule and analyzing the various program and project resources, use the same information in the portfolio schedule. Any resources needed for

#	Task	Notes
		portfolio work also need to be included in this process. It is important to use project scheduling software to develop the portfolio schedules. Software tools such as Microsoft® Project, Oracle® Primavera, or any of the other different scheduling programs on the market will work as well. You will be able to show your resources, portfolio costs, timelines, and resources assignments very easily. **Note:** If you have the ability to put all program and project schedules into a project server environment, it is highly recommended. Tracking and reporting program and project dependencies will be much easier. When developing a portfolio schedule, use the same best practice techniques as you use when developing regular program and project schedules.
5.	Develop a portfolio Work Breakdown Structure (WBS)	The portfolio schedule development process is important to get as accurate as possible so that when you create the portfolio WBS, it shows you all the programs and projects in your portfolio. A portfolio WBS is a very important communication tool and something, as PMO Manager, you should be creating and providing status on a continual basis throughout the planning and executing of your portfolio. The portfolio WBS has all the programs and projects for your organization listed, including the associated deliverables for driving the portfolio.

#	Task	Notes
6.	Develop a portfolio selection process	Develop a process for selecting the programs and projects approved for the year. This process will be very different from company to company but, as PMO Manager, you need to drive this process for your organization. The best time to create it is during the Portfolio Planning Process.
7.	Develop portfolio communications plan	This plan is a critical tool for PMO Managers for communicating portfolio activities, costs, status, and any other areas that management or customers have deemed important. The structure of the portfolio communication plan will vary from organization to organization, but should focus on what your stakeholders and management need in addition to the basic foundation items, schedule, costs, resources, issues, and so on.
9.	Develop a portfolio procurement plan	This plan documents the process and procedures to obtain resources within the organization. The plan should include, at the minimum, the following areas: Procurement terms Procurement schedule Procurement administration Roles and responsibilities Budget and cost information Requisition steps Selection steps The key to this plan is to document and outline the steps to obtain any resources not currently available in the organization needed to drive the portfolio work. The procurement process is documented in the planning phase in order to have people in place and available

#	Task	Notes
		for the execution process.
9.	Develop a portfolio resource plan	This plan defines the resources (human and otherwise) needed for the proposed programs and projects within the portfolio. PMO Managers must have a good handle on the resources required for their portfolio and can make tradeoff decisions on where to load resources based on the needs and requirements of the programs and projects. PMO Managers should be part of the planning processes so they can also work closely with the company's employees, or with local vendors, to obtain resources for the portfolio of work.
10.	Develop a portfolio cost estimate	The portfolio cost estimating process develops a cost estimate for all resources needed for the portfolio. The goal is to create an estimate before starting any work on the portfolio to ensure that there is enough program and project budget available and to be able to plan accordingly if there is not. When making management aware of the cost estimates to complete the portfolio work, and they feel it is too expensive, provide them options to trade off what to include and not include in the portfolio.
		Note: It is a best practice to get an all-up portfolio estimate in place and in front of the leadership team so you do not end up starting too early and having to cancel due to lack of funding.
		The portfolio estimate drives the cost budgeting process. The budgeting process is the act of establishing priorities and makes the budget decisions about where to allocate monies across the programs and projects. As PMO Manager, you are required to work alongside your leadership team and your finance team and allocate the budget to every program and project in your portfolio.
		Note: Major decisions, such as how much

#	Task	Notes
		budget accuracy does the project team need to adhere to (e.g. +-10%) is important to understand when performing this budget process. The budget accuracy rate (for example, +- 50%) is needed because it is that extra percentage, in dollars, you should add to your budget for contingency funds. This will give the programs and projects a budget buffer in case any risks or unexpected problems occur and affect the costs of the programs and projects. The extra monies allows the Project Managers to accept these Risk events and keep everything on track if they need to use it (for example, if the project falls behind schedule and they need to hire additional resources to catch up there is money available to obtain those resources.)
11.	Develop a portfolio quality plan	This plan documents the quality standards and the process the team uses to manage and monitor quality. As PMO Manager, you need to understand the different components of the portfolio processes and ensure that everyone is applying the highest level of quality possible. Portfolio quality management plans include basically the same components of a project or program management plan, focusing on these top areas: Quality management process Quality assurance process Quality control process Quality audits/auditing
12.	Develop a portfolio organization structure	The portfolio organizational structure documents the roles required to execute the portfolio. This process is important because it defines the organization structure of the programs and projects in the organization. This process does not change that much year

#	Task	Notes
		over year, but could depending on company strategy, direction, and executive desires. PMO Managers provide opinions during this process on who should work on which programs and projects and who should report to whom in those various structures. It is important to be active in this process so that you can direct program and project assignments. These assignments can be important in the success or the failure of the project. Part of creating the organization structure might include adding resources that are not already available or part of the organization. Often, for example, portfolio staff come and come and go usually more often than staff on programs and projects would, so there might be opportunities through the year to directly hire members of the portfolio management team. The portfolio employees tend to roll off when portfolio planning is complete. As PMO Manager, in most cases, the portfolio management staff report to you directly and you need to determine the roles and responsibilities required for that team. In smaller organizations, or where there is limited budget, the PMO Manager and the Portfolio Manager are one in the same person. Other times, you will be responsible for hiring all the staff for the portfolio work, so handling this process will be an important part of your role. You will also need to pay attention to the pulse on staffing across your programs and projects, so be aware of that workload as well, and hire additional staff if your team members are feeling overwhelmed or overworked.
13.	Develop a portfolio issue management plan	This plan outlines how to document, store and process issues about the portfolio.
14.	Develop a portfolio	This plan outlines how to document, store,

#	Task	Notes
	risk management plan	and process risks about the portfolio.
15.	Develop a portfolio change management plan and process	This plan includes the process and procedures for making changes to the portfolio. These changes can range from adding new programs and projects, adding or removing funding, or making priority changes. As PMO Manager, having a change control process across portfolios, programs, and projects are critical to the success of driving these distinct areas, so it is in your best interest to establish these processes for your organization and keep the Change control process the same where possible.

Further Considerations

Due to the complexity of this planning process, there are many areas for PMO Managers and Portfolio Managers to consider. Review these areas, and then determine if they are applicable to your planning process and your organization.

Portfolio Plan Items:

Organizational policies—Every company is full of different organizational policies that drive how one thing or another occurs in the different functions and departments. In the Portfolio Planning Process, it too is forced to deal with different organizational polices and, as the PMO manager, you should focus very closely on the policies that are most applicable to this area. Sample polices around portfolio planning might include financial management, vendor sourcing, and marketing polices. Each could be important in the planning process and it is important that you take some time and learn these polices, adjust your processes and be flexible through the process.

Portfolio management information system (PMIS)—One of the main things the industry has learned over the last several years is the use of a PMIS for managing the organization's portfolio. The amount of time and headache that you will save by using a PMIS is priceless and critical in the planning process. There are many software tools for portfolio management, such as:

- IBM® Rational® Portfolio Manager
- Microsoft Dynamics® CRM
- Microsoft® Project Server

- UMT Project Essentials
- Planview®

For a more complete list of tools, see Chapter 12, "PMO Tools and Processes".

Each of these tools has their own unique features as well as advantages and disadvantages. There is no recommendation of one tool over another, but what is important with these tools is how you can use them in building your PMO. There will be a couple main features to look for with portfolio management software tools, at the minimum, look for these features:

- Customized fields for portfolio management change control
- Reporting and charting capabilities
- Centralized access
- Outlook integration
- Strong security features

These software features are critical and it is strongly suggested to not purchase any portfolio management software unless it can handle these very basic functions. As PMO Manager, it is also your responsibility to create processes and procedures for each of these functions within your portfolio management area of your PMO. If you do not have formal processes in place, it will certainly hurt your chances of being successful. It could also lead to you having huge issues controlling your portfolio.

Business goals—One of the key components of the planning process is for you to understand your businesses goals. Understanding these goals will help you create your portfolio for the year. The business goals are in the controls section of the planning process and that is due to the business goals being something that could shape the portfolio for the year. For example, if one of your business's goals is to increase sales, and there is not a single project in your portfolio that will help increase sales, that is a problem and it is your job to raise that concern to management. Every PMO Manager should take the time, understand the business goals, to help them understand the year's portfolio of work that is based on those business goals. It is a lost opportunity if you ignore the business goals or if you are not seeing the relevance of how those business goals are aligned to the programs and projects of your portfolio.

Portfolio plan—One of the key outputs of the planning process is the development of a portfolio plan. The portfolio plan is actually very simple; it is the list of programs and projects for the organization to work on for the year. Most portfolios are reviewed each year and, therefore, the process would be where the organization re-reviews the program and project mix to make sure everything is still valid. Other components of the portfolio plan include the financials, ROI, and business value.

Organizational internal planning process—Every company that drives large programs and projects will have some form of internal process around the planning cycle of the company. At some companies, it is a very complex and formal process that takes literally months to get though, while at other companies, it is informal and has little to no structure. The size and type of company often dictates how formal the organization completes the planning process. In larger companies, the planning process is much more formal than in smaller or mid-size companies. In most cases, as PMO Manager, you must get involved and understand this process end-to-end so that you can play a role in it and be a contributor to the process. Being involved in this process early, and throughout, allows you to make better decisions and tradeoffs when you are in the Portfolio Executing Process.

Executives informal decisions—One of the considerations to consider during this planning process is the informal decisions that executives or management make about what is in and out of scope, from a program and project perspective. This happens a lot and, as PMO Manager, you need to react and adjust to these decisions and inform management of the impact their decisions have.

Internal planning tools (organization-specific)—PMO Managers should also consider internal planning tools during the planning process. These tools often align to different processes in the planning process (such as resource tools, financial tools, and so on) and are critical in the overall success of the planning cycle. This is just something to think about and look for as you drive the planning process because there might be some additional ramp up or time associated to using the tools that adds even more time in the planning cycle.

Budget restraints and holdbacks—One of the common areas that PMO Managers deal with in the planning process are holdbacks and budget restraints. When organizations have specific financial requirements and holdback requirements, PMO Managers should consider this part of the process and adjust where applicable. It would be a good idea to ask about these restraints or holdbacks early in the process, before finalizing anything.

Internal planning documents—A common output of the planning process is a set of internal planning documents for use with management and the executive teams. These documents will be very helpful in documenting the various planning components, decisions, action items, and so on. You should actively look for these types of documents in the planning cycle and complete the ones that are most applicable. That keeps you in the loop and an active part of the planning process.

Scope Planning Process Items:

Portfolio Charter—This document states the objectives, scope, constraints, and risks involved in managing and driving a portfolio. It is highly recommended that when creating the document that you start with defining and documenting the basic objectives first, and then add scope, risks, and constraints, and then any other areas as applicable. There are many examples of portfolio charter templates available as good starting points.

Cost/Benefit analysis—This evaluation appraises, assesses, or makes a case for a program or project and determines the cost-benefit ratio. This well-used process helps management understand these aspects for each project and allows them to make decisions on whether to go forward or cancel projects based on the analysis. Having this information for each project also allows management to make trade off decisions when needed.

Tips& Best Practices

Portfolio initiation decisions can drive how you run your organization and can play a big role in the Portfolio Planning process. Be careful and think through the long-term issues of making decisions in the initiation phase and how that impacts decisions in the planning phase.

Organization constraints—The constraints of an organization will vary from company to company. During the scope planning process, knowledge of these constraints is important to understand. Every organization will have constraints one-way or other and, as PMO Manager, understanding these constraints is important. Constraints can vary from SOX compliance to budget or regulatory issues, and each can play a factor in the planning process.

Portfolio scope initiation—The output of the scope planning process is a list of the programs and projects to be included in the portfolio.

Organization boundaries—Organization boundaries can play a role in the planning process. If the PMO drives the planning process, or the finance team drives it, then, as PMO Manager, you need to factor in the different organizations and the requirements of those organizations during this process. One organization might do things differently than another organization, so it is important to recognize the boundaries as you drive the process.

Program and project lists—Through the planning process the biggest take-away deliverable is the list of proposed programs and projects that will make up the year's portfolio.

Budget—The budget is definitely a control device that is used during the planning process. The budget might not be final yet, but it is going to drive how much scope will be possible.

Executive control—One of the other control points to utilize during the planning process is executive oversight or control. Executives should be active during the planning cycle to ensure the planning team is selecting the right programs and projects for their organization's portfolio.

Portfolio Scope Definition Items:

Portfolio scope description—The portfolio scope helps determine which projects should fall in and out of the portfolio. For example, if the portfolio scope definition says that all projects must be information technology projects, any projects that are not in information technology are not considered part of the portfolio. This is quite possible when you are working in a large Enterprise Portfolio Management Office (EPMO) environment where there are multiple portfolios and having these types of definitions is beneficial because it allows for greater refinement and determination of where programs and projects fit in the different portfolios. As PMO Manager, you could end up with multiple portfolios, so be aware of this definitions and alignments of programs and projects is important. It is a great way for filtering your programs and projects into the different portfolios.

Business planning process—This process is very important for PMO Managers to be aware of and involved in from the beginning. The business planning process can be complex and, if not done correctly, PMO Managers can be left holding a mess to try to execute. The suggested programs and projects might not be in alignment with the direction of the organization and, therefore, if they end up in the portfolio for next year, they could be very difficult to manage. As PMO Manager, stay active and involved as much as possible in the planning process because you will end up with the list of programs and projects to execute through the year.

Budget line items established with executive oversight—Many organizations will require executive oversight and control on each budget line item for each program and project in your portfolio. This is a process that you, as PMO Manager, should embrace and drive for your organization. This will be quite different in every organization, but if yours is one where executives want this kind of visibility, definitely take the time and drive this exposure and review process with them.

List of strategic projects—One of the outputs of this process is a list of strategic projects, by programs and projects within the organization. By having a consolidated list, you, as PMO Manager, will know exactly what is going to be part of your portfolio for the year. It is highly recommended that you spend the time and drive this strategic program and project list. It is so important that you are a critical part of this process from beginning to end.

Project selection type process—One of the areas to consider in this process is how the company decides which types of projects to include in their portfolio for the year. For example, what happens when construction companies need to replace large software systems or financial systems and there is not necessarily an IT shop? Well, because they are a construction company and not a software company, through their internal processes, they might decide not to select this project as one they will do internally, but instead put this in the outsource category and have an outside company update the software system. They might not have skilled IT staff that knows an IT development methodology well enough to drive this type of project. The project selection process would reject the project (because it is not a construction effort) and put this type of project through a different approval process in the company. This is one of the many types of examples of projects going through the selection process that then gets filtered out and put into a different process altogether.

Existing resource expertise in organization for types of project (for example, a software company will not take on a construction project)—This connects with the project selection type process because it aligns to selecting the projects where the company has the most skill sets. Construction companies do not tend to put software Project Managers onto construction projects, and vice versa. The existing company's resource pool have a specific skill sets and, therefore, would be successful in performing those types of projects. As PMO Manager, it is important to have a resource pool, understand everyone's skill set, and assign them to the appropriate type of project.

Portfolio Project Schedule Activity Items:

Scope statements—Are the phrases that refer to the activity that occurs during the early phases of planning when the team is still defining the processes around what the portfolio of work should provide. For example: 1) The scope of this effort will be to add a new financial system. 2) The financial system will include vendor and contractor expenses. 3) The financial system will work in a global environment. These three statements include all the additional "scope" for the financial system and are examples of scope statements. Look for these statements and document them as part of the planning process.

These statements are good to understand because having this knowledge of the various statements help define the various activities needed to occur in the projects. As PMO Manager, you can work with individual program and project teams to ensure they are incorporating these statements into work deliverables, or at least considering them in their work efforts.

Analysis or integrated activities—The process of understanding, in detail, the integrated activities across the programs and projects in your portfolio allows you to help drive your portfolio more efficiently. As you can imagine, in large portfolios, there are areas where various project activities come together (for example, buying hardware) so that you can compile the common tasks and coordinate them to occur at the same time. Performing this kind of analysis to look across the different programs and projects could prevent projects from duplicating efforts and spending additional time or dollars. It helps everyone be more efficient. As PMO Manager, you are in the prime position to do this kind of work across your portfolio and everyone benefits from your analysis.

Management review—The PMO Manager drives the management review and continues to provide management the visibility and exposure to various project activities. One of the outputs of analyzing any activity that integrates across projects (for example, buying hardware) will be to provide management the level of exposure and granularity that they might be looking for across the portfolio. It will certainly let them know that the programs are working in a coordinated manner, which is usually a good thing for productivity of the organization.

Past project schedules—Past projects schedules are incredible at assisting in obtaining and determining the activities for your portfolios. Most Project Managers organize their project schedules by larger process groups and pull activities from those process groups across multiple projects. Having those activities within the project schedule helps define the work tasks needed to drive your portfolio of programs and projects if the work efforts remain generally the same from year to year. As PMO Manager, you need to be involved throughout the life of programs and projects so you are familiar with those activities and can assist your program or project managers as to whether those same activities are needed on their efforts. In your role, you should be very active in reviewing project schedules and understanding different components of the projects in your portfolio of work. Pure Portfolio Managers will not necessary have this visibility or might not need it, but as PMO Manager, you certainly will because time and time again, you will be asked to step in and help your program and project managers. You should see some familiarity among projects, especially if they are using the same development and project management methodologies.

Organization's project management methodology deliverables—Most organizations, without realizing it, have project management methodologies in place that they use to drive their projects. These methodologies, and the various deliverables, are important in understanding the activity definitions for each project and should be considered during this process. When defining project activities, having knowledge of project management methodologies is important to consider.

Organization's software development methodology deliverables—Every company that delivers software has a process they follow to develop that software. These methodologies, such as Agile or Waterfall, or combination of both, help teams deliver software by using a standard approach with a series of activities. When defining projects, it is important to understand these activities in the different methodologies so you are aware of what happens during the life of the project.

Project scheduling tool—A software tool, such as Microsoft® Project, or some of the other various scheduling tool, is important to use in the activity definition process. Using an automated tool provides you with a better ability to view every project activities and determine the various dependencies between activities in the project. Doing this without using a software tool would be time consuming and make it easy to miss activities or critical dependencies.

Dependencies between activities—One of the key control points during this process, and when defining the activities to occur on a project, is to determine the dependencies between the activities and to understand if you are missing or leaving something out. If you are not thoroughly reviewing each activity, it is much easier to miss something and possibly leave out activities that are key to the success of the project.

Project's activities list—One of the final outputs of this process is to complete a project activity list. This list helps everyone know the activities of the projects, which helps set budget allocations, timeframes, resource requirements, and so on.

Portfolio schedule—Is the schedule that displays the beginning and ending dates for the Programs and Projects in the portfolio. When working across a portfolio, it is best practice to use month(s) as your timeline for your programs and projects. The portfolio schedule allows you to determine very early your dependencies between the various projects. Creating a very high-level portfolio schedule, similar to **Figure 8.7 Example of a Portfolio Schedule**, provides a great starting point for having direct conversations with people running the programs and projects and have them talk about the different dependencies, if any, among the efforts. In this example, you will see the dotted line on the Portfolio schedule, that line represents the date the Portfolio schedule is created and where the programs and projects fall according to today's date. In this example, you can see two projects have already completed and two projects are still very active. Using this dotted line gives great perspective in where you are today, and the various dates of the different efforts in your portfolio.

Figure 8.7 Example of a Portfolio Schedule

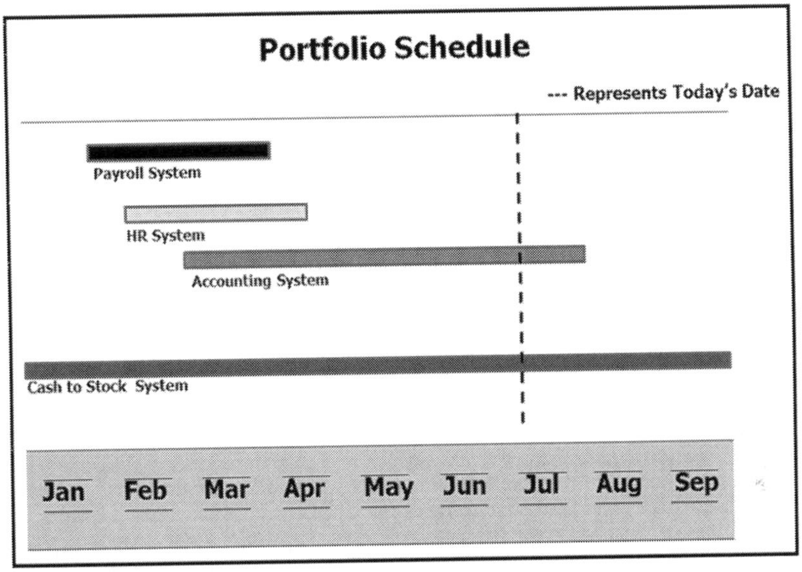

Tips & Best Practices

Portfolio planning is important. Planning anything is critical to drive success. Over-planning anything is not necessarily a good thing because you can take too long to complete it, but over-planning is better than not enough planning.

Precedence diagramming methods—This a tool for scheduling activities in a project schedule. This method uses boxes (better known as "nodes") and connects them with arrows (showing dependencies). This method of diagraming is not as popular as it once was, but in reality, it is very important for Project Managers to perform on their schedules. As PMO Manager, when reviewing the portfolio schedule and the various projects on that schedule, you should understand the sequencing of the project's tasks within your portfolio. It is a best practice for PMO Managers to create a Precedence Diagram for their programs and projects in their portfolio and document the order and the connection points between them. **Figure 8.8 Precedence Diagram** shows an example of a project's precedence diagram.

Figure 8.8 Precedence Diagram

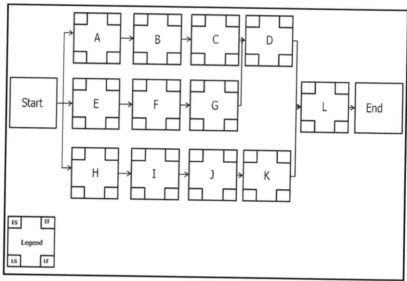

It is not important now to go into all the details and the processes around how to do the precedence diagramming technique. There are many resources on the internet and training courses you can take to show you how. The main purpose of showing you the diagram here is for PMO Managers to understand the process themselves so they can help their Project Managers if they need it or build one themselves for their Portfolios. It is a great tool you can use when looking for sequencing and whether there are any dependencies among programs and projects your portfolio.

Schedules of all projects within the scope of the portfolio—This is a key control point for this process because the schedules have work activities and dependencies within them and, therefore, are the main source for the dependency analysis process. The PMO Manager should strive toward having a good understanding of each schedule and each dependency, when possible. This information will drive the process analysis and determine where dependencies exist.

Automated work breakdown structure reporting tool—The use of an automated WBS tool is critical to the dependency analysis. It is a much easier process for the PMO Manager to track project task dependencies using software. One tool that works directly with Microsoft® Project, for example, is WBS Chart Pro™. This is an amazing tool that is highly recommended for PMO Managers, Portfolio, Program and Project Managers. Everyone that is using a project schedule in one form or another should use WBS Chart Pro™. It is definitely a best practice to do project task dependency analysis with a tool than with pen on paper. As PMO Manager, make sure you understand the software tools so you are able to assist your Program and Project Managers when needed.

Resource requirements—Understanding the resource requirements duration-estimating process is critical because you need to know who and what is required to do the project work. For example, think about needing a crane for a construction project. Knowing that you need a crane first, and then gets you asking questions such as how long you will need the crane, how long you will need a crane operator, how much budget do you need to rent the crane, and so on. All valuable questions that could not be asked if you did not understand thoroughly your resource requirements for your portfolio.

Identified risks—Understanding the adherent portfolio risks during the duration estimating process is important for you, the PMO Manager, because it allows you very early in the process to plan for these potential risk events and to reduce the risks from occurring. There is no chance of preventing them all, but knowing the possible risk events allows you to put monies aside, change policies, and basically track the possible events before they occur. During this duration estimating process, knowing the possible risks also allows you to add time in the schedule in case they do occur.

Program Manager and Project Manager reviews—One of the key processes that PMO Managers can ensure they complete is the review of the project's duration estimates for all programs and projects in the portfolio. Having the Program Managers and Project Managers actively engaged in this process and ensuring they understand when and how long a task will take provides them valuable insight into driving their respective programs and projects. PMO Managers also need to be involved in this so that they have a broader and wider view of all durations across the whole portfolio.

Basis of estimates—One of the more important outputs of the duration estimating process is to understand the basis of the estimates for each of the activities in the programs and project schedules. PMO Managers, during this process, should question and get facts around the duration estimates and it is definitely a best practice to question the task lengths to ensure that there is no padding going on with the estimates. On the other hand, the PMO Manager should be looking to ensure that the teams actually have enough time to complete the tasks. PMO Managers should be looking at all task durations with both these lenses.

Expert judgment—One of the biggest considerations when performing duration estimating is obtaining the estimates from the experts or the people performing the work. Getting expert judgment is going to the source that has done the work before, or who will end up doing the work, and getting the estimates for the task. If you have resources that are not assigned to perform the task and or offering or suggesting time estimates on how long to complete the task, it can be problematic and should be avoided when possible. It is highly recommended that, as PMO Manager, that you turn to your experts (in most cases, the assigned resource) to provide the estimates for the task, not anyone else.

Historical project performance—One of the key components of driving and understanding project estimates is the past performance of the project teams. If you have teams that have continued to hit the estimates on their projects, obtaining estimates for task durations from those teams is less risky than getting task estimates from project teams that continually go late or struggle to complete their projects on time. This is an important to understand the past performance of project teams and make sure you are using creditable resources who have proven capability to provide you with the task duration estimates.

Resource management tool (MS Project/Primavera)—The resource management process is one that you must track by using software such as Microsoft® Project, Oracle® Primavera, or even Microsoft Excel. Doing resource management leveling and capacity allocation without software is so much more difficult, time consuming, and easy to make mistakes. Microsoft® Project, for example, is set up very nicely for resource management. Once you have the data in the software tool, you can do so much with it and make many changes and choices with little effort. From a portfolio perspective, having a centralized tool for resource management allows PMO Managers to move resources, review program and project assignments, and spread resources across the portfolio evenly.

Portfolio Schedule Development Items:

Portfolio network diagram—This diagrams works like a project network diagram and its purpose is to depict the sequence in which the elements are to be completed. The diagram displays the sequence of tasks, summary tasks, milestone deliverables, and external projects, in some cases.

Figure 8.9 Portfolio Network Diagram shows an example of a typical portfolio network diagram and, as you review the diagram, you will see some very interesting characteristics that are important when creating this diagram for your own portfolio. Some items to consider during this process are to ensure you carry the three main characteristics (at a minimum) in every box on the diagram. These items include: program name, project name, and project duration. These three simple items tell a lot about this portfolio and are important when creating this network diagram. The arrows and lines on the diagram are very important to display because they provide the person reviewing the diagram the order in which to execute the programs and projects in the portfolio. Including the expected durations in the boxes provides the expected timeframes for the work. One can start to map the work of the portfolio across roadmaps making it easier to determine resource needs, timeframes, and budget needs.

Figure 8.9 Portfolio Network Diagram

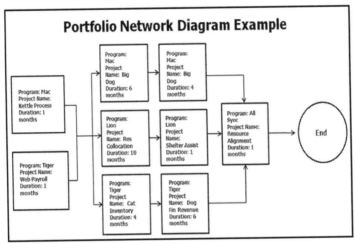

It is a best practice for PMO Managers to create portfolio network diagrams for their portfolios. Just looking at this example, you can quickly see how valuable this tool is from a communication perspective and how valuable it will be for management or leadership teams to understand and clearly see the expected timeframes of all the programs and projects in the portfolio.

Resource pool description—One of the advantages to creating a resource pool is to document the various resources required on the programs and projects. Having this information during the development of your portfolio schedule is critical because it allows you to document and understand the resources you need for the portfolio. In some cases, where you need to obtain resources that are not internal, such as vendors or contractors, having the resource pool gives early visibility into those needed resources. For example, if you need a crane for a construction project, you want to document the need for that crane in your resource pool so the Portfolio Manager or PMO Manager who is developing the portfolio schedule can estimate the appropriate amount time in the schedule to go through the process of renting that crane. PMO Managers should be taking a hard look at each of the project schedule's resources and ensuring they are documented in the resource pool. In many cases, companies have templates that Project Managers can use to complete a resource pool, but even if there is no template in place, it is just a list of all the resources you need for your programs and projects and therefore quite easy for anyone to create.

Figure 8.10 Resource Pool Description shows an example of a typical resource pool description, but again, it can vary from company to company. As you can see, it is a very simple tool, but when you add all the resources needed, the timeframe for how long the resource is required, it becomes a very good tool for understanding the resource needs for your programs and projects within your portfolio. Take each resource pool description for each program or project and review them all across the whole portfolio to see who and what resources you need for your efforts. This becomes a very powerful planning tool for Portfolio and PMO Managers.

Figure 8.10 Resource Pool Description

Project Name:												
Prepared by:												
Department Name:												
Cost Center Code:												
Date:												
PROJECT PERIODS (Time Fame Resource Needed (H/D/W/M)) (Shade in periods of resource Required)												
Resource #	Needed Resources	1	2	3	4	5	6	7	8	9	10	
Example	Crane											
1	[Specify resources]											
2												
3												
4												
5												
6												
7												
8												
9												
10												
11												
12												
Other Resource Concerns/Issues:												

Duration Compression—The process of shortening a project's completion period without reducing scope, but often results in higher costs. There are two well-known techniques for performing this process to meet hard dates or other schedule parameters outlined by stakeholders. The two techniques include: fast tracking and crashing. We'll go into details for both of these techniques for your review. As PMO Manager, when you are developing the portfolio schedule, these two techniques might be an important part of the process you follow. For example, if your portfolio is projected to go too long or you are asked for financial reasons to bring in your programs or projects because you don't have enough budget, these techniques can be very valuable.

Fast tracking
Fast tracking a project schedule involves the process of looking at the schedule and assessing when it is practical to do work in parallel instead of sequentially completing the activities. It is a best practice to apply this process when the project activities are somewhat independent of each other. This process overlaps activities on projects. Most projects execute tasks in sequential order, but this is done differently with the fast tracking process. In fast tracking, you end up doing both tasks at the same time, but

you just cannot finish them at the same time; that process will continue to be sequential.

Some things you need to watch for during the fast tracking process includes rework where the team is going over the same thing (software code, for example) multiple times. When you fast track, you have an increased chance that something is not done properly, or missed, and needs redoing.

The project management industry calls the second technique crashing.

Crashing

Crashing a project schedule involves analysis of cost and schedule trade-offs to obtain the maximum duration compression (shortening of the project schedule without changing the scope), with the least amount of cost. This technique is not usually very popular with Project Managers because it deviates from the original schedule set at the beginning of the project.

This process is not always the most feasible option for your project because it can often result in increased project costs and the hiring of additional resources (which costs more money). The general rule is if you are crashing a schedule to look for items on your critical path that have little to no impact on the project's budget. That may or may not be possible. Although there are risks involved with duration compression, the ultimate goal is to bring a project back on track and end up with an improved, shorter duration.

Resource requirement updates—This output process simply updates and ensures that any resource requirements through this portfolio schedule development process are updated and known to the customers and management. PMO Managers must take an active role in understanding the resources (people and equipment) required to execute the portfolio.

Expert judgment and project management software are important in other areas above, but are also important considerations in the schedule development process. Having experts around building schedules by using project management software best practices and techniques will go a long way in developing and driving solid project schedules and increasing the chance of running successful projects.

Portfolio Resource Planning Items:

Resource capacity description—The input for this resource planning process is used to analyze a resource's availability, capacity, and utilization across the various programs and projects in the portfolio. As PMO Manager, you need to ensure you are balancing your resources, understanding their skill sets, and assigning them appropriately to prevent burnout.

Management judgment—Management strategy plays a big role in the resource planning process for your portfolio. When planning and possibly assigning resources to your portfolio, management will have their opinion about who they want or do not want for their different projects. Every company is the same in that regard, and most management teams will tell you which resources you can and cannot use. As PMO Manager, you should be aware of these concerns and make the appropriate adjustments to your resource plans.

Portfolio resource constraints—Often, PMO Managers have resource challenges and constraints that they have to deal with during the planning process. It is quite common to have resource challenges that include issues around skill sets, availability, motivation, and time constraints. In every case, the PMO Manager will need to schedule around these challenges to ensure their portfolio is staffed appropriately.

Resource allocation strategy—Resource allocation strategies are going to vary from company to company, manager to manager, and maybe in some cases, industry to industry. Meaning, the construction industry might handle resource allocation very differently than the software industry. Other considerations might include something like the critical chain, developed by Eliyahu Goldratt, where the process takes multi-tasking out of the equation altogether and uses single processing as the allocation method. Your role as PMO Manager is to understand your company's resource allocation strategies, as well as to understand your leadership team's direction, and staff your programs and project's within your portfolio according to those parameters. It is a best practice and highly recommended that your management team signs off and approves your final resource allocation across your portfolio.

Required skills to perform the work of the portfolio—One of key components of any PMO Manager is to understand the skills required to perform the work of the portfolio. If the work requires you to have Electricians and you only have Plumbers available, then it is important during this resource planning process to get the right resources available, in time, to perform the work. PMO Managers can expect to drive this resource planning process for their organization and have a skills database that has each resource available to make the correct assignments based on the skills sets required.

Resource plan—A resource plan is also another important input to the resource planning process. It is difficult to understand the different resources and their current work allocations to programs and projects and assign them to anything new during the planning process without a resource plan.

Fully loaded resource sheet—A fully loaded resource sheet is one of the important outputs of this process. In the resource sheet, you have all resource assignments across the organization and the timeframes noted to these assignments. Most of the information, if done in a software product should be very easy to report on to your management.

Portfolio Cost Estimating Items:

Program and project cost estimates—The most important component of the cost estimating process is to gather the appropriate costs and estimates of each program and project in the portfolio. This process will differ per company, and the biggest difference to consider is the percent of accuracy expected when creating these cost estimates. Some companies in the planning phase actually use a plus/-minus accuracy of 100%. Meaning, the estimate can cost up to 100% more than the estimate provided.

Programs and projects need some flexibility in their estimates to allow for risks and other unknown factors, but giving them 100% is not realistic and ends up not being an estimate at all. PMO Managers should drive estimate accuracy between 50–75% on their programs and projects, at a minimum. There are factors that could reduce that accuracy but make sure you have a target and don't accept a plus/minus of 100% estimate.

Tips & Best Practices

Understanding your portfolio costs is so important to get in front of your leadership team early and often. The leadership team will want an ongoing view of how your portfolio is execution from a cost and schedule perspective.

Resource rates—As you build and plan your portfolio, one of the common things you will run into is the different resource rates. Resources can be humans or equipment, and often PMO Managers make the mistake of ensuring that there is allocation of dollars on programs and projects for the staff, but then fall short and do not include machine or hardware costs until it is too late in the project. In the cost estimating process, resource rates are important to know in the planning process to ensure there is enough allocation of budget for *all* resources required in the portfolio. One of the areas where PMO Managers can get some breaks and negotiate better deals for their resources is if they work with a smaller number of contract companies, build relationships with them, and become a repeat customer. When you spread the work across too many companies, you lose that repeat business and usually will have a much harder time getting price breaks for your resources.

Tips & Best Practices

Resource rates vary depending on so many different factors. I recommend that you work with a limited set of companies so you can get the best rates possible for your organization.

Financial estimating tools and techniques—The financial team often has a number of tools and techniques available for you to control the portfolio. As PMO Manager, take the time and learn these tools for financial tracking and ensure your Portfolio Manager is utilizing these tools as well.

Organizational finance policies and procedures—The financial estimating process is going to be very important and a very big part of most PMO Manager's day-to-day responsibilities as they drive their portfolios. So, in the process of creating the cost estimate of the portfolio, as PMO Manager, take the time and learn the financial processes of your company. Understand the tools and processes available to you to control the finances of your portfolio because these tools will make reporting and tracking much easier. Many companies handle their financial processing using different methods and processes, but as PMO Manager, if you do need to create PMO program and project specific financial processes or procedures, make sure they align as closely as possible to the overall company's financial processes.

Portfolio forecast of expenditures—One of the reasons for completing the cost estimating process is to develop a forecast for all the portfolio costs and expenditures. Having this information available to your management and leadership team provides the forecast for the portfolio of work and sets expectations or ranges to what kind of budget the portfolio will require.

Cost management policies—Another result of this process is the creation or updating of policies around cost management for the portfolio. Depending on the different resources and configuration of the portfolio, updating the policies around cost management will be important. As PMO Manager, ensure you engrain the cost management policies to everyone working on your programs and projects in your portfolio. There can be no exceptions, people need to know this process well and should understand how to manage costs. This is where you can put on brown bag training sessions, create webinars, or other training materials, whatever it takes to ensure that everyone understands these new cost management policies.

Resource allocation sheet—This sheet will be an incredible input for this process because it covers all the resources, their allocations and, therefore, their associated costs. In most cases, resource rates are within the resource allocation sheet so, as PMO Manager, you have this one sheet to help you estimate the costs for your programs and projects in your portfolio.

Portfolio estimates for all programs and projects—Part of the output of this process is a complete list of all estimates for all programs and projects in the portfolio. As PMO Manager, you send this master planning sheet to executives for approval of the year's portfolio, and then you own the execution of all programs and projects on the list.

Portfolio Cost Budgeting Process Items:

Cost estimates—The cost estimates obtained earlier in this process is a critical input to the cost budgeting process. The cost estimates drive the allocation of dollars to the programs and projects for this process. As PMO Manager, your role is to understand and validate the cost estimates, and then set the final allocations. If you get a cost estimate, but cannot stand behind the data, it would be wrong for you to allocate final budget dollars based on those estimates. You can also be in the position of not providing enough dollars to other programs and projects that do have better data and can stand behind what they are asking for their efforts.

Portfolio project schedules—The portfolio project schedules are critical in the cost budget process because they define the work items and work timelines to allocate the budget. When project schedules are fully resource loaded and fully cost loaded, they provide the total costs of the project directly within the schedules. Besides allocating additional monies for risks, overages, or buffers, each project schedule when they are fully cost loaded, will provide the right allocation of budget amounts to get the work done for that project.

Product development methodologies—The product development methodology plays a very important role in allocating budget to the programs and projects. For example, in software projects, if you choose to use an Agile methodology compared to a Waterfall methodology, the project life cycle can actually be much shorter, and therefore the projects can cost less. It is not always the case, but it could happen. When in reality what usually happens is because project schedules are shorter in Agile, you often have to add more resources and then costs expands making Agile projects more expensive in some cases than a Waterfall project. The resources bill at 100% on an Agile project compared to 50% or less on Waterfall project. So, as PMO Manager, think about which methodology you are using, (for example, software, manufacturing or construction) and research and determine how that methodology is going to factor in to the overall project budget allocations.

Organizational financial goals—Every organization has their own set of financial goals and these goals act as control points to allocate budget to the programs and projects in the portfolio. For example, if an organization has specific limits, such as a maximum on budget amounts, it is a best practice to raise these goals during the budgeting process so that everyone stays aligned with them. It happens all the time where programs and projects get a maximum amount of dollars assigned to them, per fiscal year, regardless of what they need, and then have to work within those budget constraints. As PMO Manager, focus on understanding all financial controls when making budget allocations, or working with management to make budget allocations, to ensure you follow in line with the process.

Budget baseline—The output of this budgeting process is the creation of the budget baseline. This budget baseline establishes the program and project allocations for the year. In most cases, there are opportunities to adjust the budget during reallocation/restatement periods, but that tends to only be at certain times during a year; and programs and projects should be working towards what they were allocated for a budget on an ongoing bases.

There are generally four times a year when project teams look at their program and project budgets for changes or updates based on how the team is performing towards the budget at that point in time. As PMO Manager, you might be responsible for controlling and driving this restatement process alongside of your Finance Manager. You might also be responsible for tracking budget baselines and the changes to that baseline throughout the year and reporting to your management team. Watch this closely, generally budget and dollar allocations are often very political and very important for you to stay on top of throughout the year.

Statement of priorities—The end of the budget allocation process also brings the creation of a statement of priorities, which is the official list of priorities for the organization. In this case, it is often a prioritized list of the programs and projects in the official plan of record for the year. This list is important because it allows priority calls, direction setting and an understanding of what is the most important program to the organization. As the year progresses, it is best practice for PMO Managers to market and publicize this list and review the list throughout the year to ensure the priorities have not changed. Programs at the beginning of the year might not have the same priority at the end of the year and therefore the list would need updating.

In each of these cases, management priorities, organizational politics, the resource allocation sheet, and program and project budget allocations (all covered above) all play a valuable role in the cost budgeting process. As PMO Manager, consider the importance of each of these in this process.

Portfolio Quality Planning Items:

Product development methodologies—The product development methodology is an important part of the quality planning process because it has components within it that incorporate quality checkpoints to ensure the product is of high quality. As PMO Manager, your role is to ensure that the teams are using these quality points through the life of the programs and projects and keeping quality as a high priority.

Enterprise quality policies—Through the planning processes, one of the controls that planning teams use are various policies that organizations have in place to control quality. Most organizations have quality policies in place that drive the standards to which teams build the product, building, application, and so on. This could range from a variety of different things (the number of bugs in software code, for example) and in most cases, project teams need to adhere to these policies throughout the life of the project. It is important for PMO Managers to follow up, checking, and keeping project teams on task to adhere to the quality policies.

Quality management strategy—One of the outputs of the quality planning process is to determine how to manage quality throughout the portfolio. An output to this process is a quality management plan document. As companies mature, this document gets updated for the particular program or project, rather than creating something new every time. The quality management plan documents the process for the PMO Manager to track and manage quality checkpoints for the programs and projects in the portfolio. As PMO Manager, you need to be active in understanding and driving quality across your programs and projects, so get involved, stay involved, and make sure your program and project teams are delivering the highest quality possible.

Project management methodology—Covered in Chapter 10, the "Project Management Methodology" and plays an important role in ensuring that project teams execute on quality checkpoints throughout their projects.

Portfolio Organizational Planning Process Items:

Staffing requirements—The staffing requirements for each program or project are an important input to this planning process because the basis of this document is to define the types of staff, skill sets, and timeframes needed for each program or project. The staffing requirements list is really an important part of this planning process and would be hard to perform without it. As PMO Manager, watch this list closely because it defines the roles and skill sets that you might be lacking in the portfolio and, therefore, you could be responsible for hiring the people/resources to fill the roles.

Human resource practices—When defining the organization to execute your portfolio of work, it is important to establish rules and policies for your staff. Most companies establish a number of human resource practices and, as PMO Manager, you must ensure you are adhering to those policies and practices at all times. These human resource policies include areas such as hours of work per week, overtime rules, equal employment opportunities, and so on.

Role and responsibilities assignments—An output of this process is the final assignments of resources (staff and other resources) to the programs and projects within the portfolio. This is such a valuable list to help you understand the staff needed to execute the portfolio. It also provides you with a view into which staff you can roll off or move to other areas of the company. In the case of vendors, for example, you can use this list as a roll-off notification list and let the vendor go, when applicable.

Staffing management plan—This document defines how to use resources and for how long, the skill sets required, specific policies and procedures to handle and manage those staff members, and so on. It is an important output to this process and, as PMO Manager, it is important that you understand the staffing management plans for your organization. In some organizations, there can be multiple staffing plans; whereas, others might just have one. Nonetheless, it is an important tool for this process.

Expert judgment—A key input to this process is your expert judgment about who works well and not so well together. As PMO Manager, you have the opportunity to work with many different people and many different teams, so your opinion about which people should work together will be valuable to share during this process. Every organization has strong performers and not so strong performers, and as you are selecting and building project teams, it is an important process to have the strongest team members working together to build the strongest teams possible.

Historical team dynamics—Historically you also know which teams work the best together and which teams tend to struggle. During the planning process, it is a perfect time to look at lower performing teams and make staffing adjustments. This is the best time in the year to do this because teams are not yet settled, so making these changes now is the least impactful.

Project scheduling tool and various staffing reports—One of the tools you will use during the organizational planning process is a project scheduling tool and the staffing and resource reports available with that tool. As we mentioned up to this point, most of this information already exists in the software; therefore, when making organizational changes or staffing decisions, use the various software applications and reports available to you for this process.

Portfolio Staff Acquisition Planning Items:

Staffing management plan—This plan will be a huge asset to the staffing acquisition process because it defines the resources and skills needed and available for the programs and projects and also specifies where there are still openings. As PMO Manager in charge of staffing for your programs and projects, you are required to understand the staffing requirements for each program and project. You need this plan to determine which skills and resources to hire. You are often part of the roll-off process as well and, therefore, are responsible for reducing the workforce, when applicable.

Procurement processes—Large organizations tend to have procurement processes in place and procurement teams to ensure that staff follow the processes and procedures to obtain staff and resources for their programs and projects. Even small companies have rules around hiring vendors or obtaining resources and ensuring that company employees are following the right processes through the procurement process. As PMO Manager, you need to be aware of these processes and ensure you do not break rules when hiring resources for your programs and projects. Be aware and watch these policies closely; they often change and could get you and your company into trouble if you're not careful.

Recruitment policies—Like the procurement process described above, companies large and small should have rules around obtaining resources that, as PMO Manager, you need to follow when hiring resources for the organization. As part of this process, recruitment policies act as controls to establish rules for you to follow. These resource types can be direct employees, vendors, temporary staff or other resources. In most cases, there are different types of rules around the different types of resources you are hiring.

Portfolio staff acquisition plans—The main output of this process is a plan for hiring resources required to execute the plan of record for the portfolio. This plan documents skill sets, timeframes, resource types, and so on. As PMO Manager, consider this as your marching orders and the plan you need to execute and hire the required resources. This is a good process to follow because you can then take the acquisition plan, work with various vendors (remember, use a small set of vendors), and develop a strategy to hire the best resources to fill the openings.

Existing SOWs/POs with vendor staff—One consideration to factor in when hiring, or even reducing, your work force is the existing contracts or POs already in place with your staff. It is important that you do not break contracts or human resource practices during this process. A best practice for PMO Managers is to ensure that vendors POs, for example, are complete prior to this process even starting. That way, if there are staff reductions, there is no complexity around reducing the vendor staff. The timing can be worked around quite easily by reducing the timeframes for vendors from one-year contracts to six-month contracts and having the POs close as you start the planning cycle.

Budget restrictions—Every company has budget restrictions of one form or another; one consideration of the staffing acquisition process is to factor in those restrictions. Restrictions can vary from company to company and, as PMO Manager, you need to completely understand them and work within those restrictions through this process.

Portfolio Communications Planning Items:

Portfolio communications plan—This plan is a very important document that is used throughout the Portfolio Planning Process, and then used through the Portfolio Executing Process. It is beneficial for everyone involved in the planning process to be updated and informed with the latest status and information.

Stakeholder analysis—From a communications perspective, it is important that you drive the communication needs of your stakeholders. Understand what your stakeholders want from a communications perspective, and then continue to provide that communication throughout the Portfolio Planning Process and the Portfolio Executing Process. During planning process, your stakeholders will be continually interested in what is occurring and how things are progressing, so communications during this process is important.

Portfolio Issue Management Planning Items:

Portfolio issue management plan—This plan is important to track and drive throughout the portfolio planning process because management will want to stay on top of the issues and do what needs to done to prevent issues from side tracking the programs and projects. As PMO Manager, it is important to track, record, and communicate portfolio issues during the Portfolio Planning Process and the Portfolio Execution Process. You must ensure that you keep everyone aware of the issues and get the help you need to close them off as soon as possible.

Portfolio Risk Management Planning Items:

Stakeholder risk tolerance—During the risk planning process, one of the key components to being successful is to understand how much risk your stakeholders are willing to take on their programs and projects in the portfolio. Having that knowledge lets you know which risk items can be avoided, which must be accepted, and which ones should be transferred. Work with your stakeholders early in the Portfolio Planning Process to ensure that you understand their risk tolerance and run your Portfolio Planning Process according to their tolerance levels.

Organization's risk tolerance—Part of preparing the portfolio risk management plan is understanding how much risk tolerance the organization is willing to take. Sometimes, the stakeholder risk tolerance and the organization's risk tolerances are quite different. Knowing this ahead of time allows you to make future decisions much easier. For example, if the organization has a low-risk tolerance for budgeting, decisions around budgeting will be considered more carefully due to the organizations sensitivity in that area.

To conclude the Portfolio Planning Process, it is easy to see that this is a very busy and important component of the portfolio management life cycle. The Portfolio Planning Process is one of the most time-consuming processes; however, in reality, it tends to get very little time assigned to it during the course of driving your portfolio work. The Portfolio Planning Process tends to be much like the planning processes in the program management and project management lifecycles; it gets very little of management's attention and is often overlooked unless the PMO Manager continues to keep it top of mind and ensure that the Portfolio, Program, and Project Managers do so as well. However, like Program Management and Project Management, it is important not to overlook Portfolio planning as well, and not to skip any of the deliverables outlined in **Table 8.3 Portfolio Planning Process.** The deliverables in that table will help you run the portfolio process more effectively and give you greater chance of success.

Tips & Best Practices

Plan your portfolio. Spend the time, explain to management how important it is to plan your portfolio. Take the time and do it. Lack of planning, will certainly hurt your execution phases.

Portfolio Executing Process and Portfolio Controlling Process

There are two main phases of the Portfolio Executing Process and the Portfolio Controlling Process for PMO Manager to drive. These include defining the portfolio work for the organization (the programs and projects selection process) and the work of actually executing the approved programs and projects. When reviewing these two books of work as different entities, PMO Managers can focus on successfully completing the planning work first, and then shift to the execution phases when the program and project work begins. Often, the initial planning process occurs during the course of the year prior to the new year and, therefore, is ready when the new year rolls around. For example, some companies use January as the start of the new year; all of the planning work for the year occurred three to four months prior to January. In this example, the organization's planning work started in September and finished at the end of December, so the program and project teams started executing in January. Other companies you July as the start of their new year, and therefore, during the March or April timeframes, those companies will be deep into locking their programs and projects for the upcoming year. Regardless of when the start of the year is, the companies all have roughly a three to four month period prior to complete the planning process.

As PMO Manager, one thing you will find is that it is almost impossible to separate the Portfolio Executing Process from the Portfolio Controlling Process. This theory is the same for program management and project management, so it is best practice for PMO Managers to combine the two phases here in portfolio management and in the following "Program Management Methodology" and "Project Management Methodology" chapters as well. The biggest reason and it is mentioned later in those chapters as well, is the question on how would anyone execute something without having some level of controls processes in place already? Realistically, it is almost impossible across portfolio, program, and project management to draw a line between executing and controlling the work, therefore it was intention put together for that reason. This is also the exact same reason that Portfolio, Program, and Project Monitoring processes do not get called out specifically throughout this book. Think about that realistically, can you execute or control something without monitoring it? PMI likes to use monitoring and controlling together, I feel like PMO Managers should align executing and controlling together and monitor become part of the DNA of the PMO, Portfolio, Program and Project Managers roles. You will apply this same rationale with Program and Project Management as you enter those chapters later in the book.

The Portfolio Executing Process and Portfolio Controlling Process of the portfolio management process is very exciting, very busy, and incredibly time consuming. The PMO Manager's role during both processes is to guide and watch the execution of multiple programs and projects in the organization. Status reporting, communications, budget management, quality assurance, governance, and stakeholder and management reporting all become part of the daily responsibilities of the PMO Manager, and Portfolio Manager (if there is a dedicated one) during these phases. In large organizations, PMO

Managers hire dedicated Portfolio Managers (as noted above) who drive the execution and controlling processes for Portfolio on behalf of the organization. Let us move now into some of the minimum key deliverables that the PMO Manager or Portfolio Manager is responsible for during these processes.

Table 8.4 Portfolio Executing Process and Portfolio Controlling Process: Planning Process focuses on the various activities and areas that the PMO Manager, or the Portfolio Manager, should monitor and drive during the execution of the portfolio process. During these processes, this is where the work of the Portfolio occurs and there it is also where most of the opportunities for changes to the programs and projects occur as well. The PMO Manager and Portfolio Manager need to watch for and track those changes closely to ensure there is no negative impacts to the programs or projects.

Because the execution process is broken down into two areas: the Portfolio Planning Process and the Portfolio Executing Process, it made sense to create two separate tables as well.

Table 8.4, Portfolio Executing Process and Portfolio Controlling Process: Planning Process

#	Task	Notes
1.	Update portfolio scope	During the planning process, and while you are building the scope for the portfolio, there is a continual process of updating and changing scope. It is important at this point to ensure you use the change request process, especially if the scope is locked and the stakeholders have already agreed to it.
2.	Update and report on project metrics and dashboards	During the planning work, it is important to update customers and management with the various metrics and dashboards on how the planning work is progressing.
3.	Hold weekly planning working sessions	It is important during the planning work that you meet weekly and ensure that you are connected and driving the planning activities. It is important that, as PMO Manager you drive this work, keep the groups together, and continue the ongoing communications.
4.	Implement a portfolio change control process	Implementing a change control process here keeps the planning work on track and all changes needing approval before being accepted.

#	Task	Notes
5.	Hold monthly reviews with customers and management	Holding monthly meetings to report on how the progress of the planning activities is proceeding is an important step in keeping people connected and updated on status.
6.	Prepare a weekly status report on planning activities	This is important to ensure that stakeholders, customers, management, and team members are aligned and updated with the latest status.
7.	Develop applicable training plans on process or tools implemented during this phase	It is important that training plans and materials are created for any new processes or tools created during this phase.

Table 8.5 Portfolio Executing Process and Portfolio Controlling Process: Execution Process focuses on the various activities for the PMO Manager, or the Portfolio Manager, to monitor and drive during the portfolio execution. The goal of the work in this phase represents complete work of the portfolio. As PMO Manager, your role was to originally create the portfolio of work during the planning phase, and now your role is focused on executing the portfolio. Your role becomes more about guiding and monitoring your program and project teams to ensure that everything is executing to plan.

Table 8.5 Portfolio Executing Process and Portfolio Controlling Process: Execution Process

#	Task	Notes
1.	Update the portfolio management plan as to how you are actually driving the portfolio	Update the portfolio management plan as necessary after the list of programs and projects have been established and defined for the organization. There are areas that can change between the planning and execution phases, so updates might be necessary.
2.	Update the portfolio scope, if applicable	During the planning process, the portfolio scope can change, so it is important to update the scope to its most current level.
3.	Update and report on the portfolio schedule	This work includes pulling together the latest program and project schedules and reporting to stakeholders and management the overall

#	Task	Notes
		schedule.
4.	Update and track finances, weekly	One of the most important components of portfolio management is tracking finances for the organization. When tracking weekly, the limited overhead can expose how program and project teams are forecasting (over or under); therefore, exposing the latest finance happenings. If you leave reporting to only monthly, you lose three weeks' worth of business and project decisions. That is just a bad practice and not recommended.
5.	Update "lessons learned" information	One of the key components of portfolio management is to capture "lessons learned" throughout portfolio execution. As the programs and projects are executing, collecting this information feeds very nicely into planning next year's portfolio. There is nothing more important than keeping this information updated and current so that you can report the findings at the end and include them in the next planning cycle. Without this information (collected weekly), you lose a wealth of knowledge. This is often difficult to reproduce if you end up needing it.
6.	Perform communication check with customers, leaders, and appropriate stakeholders	Communications through the Portfolio Execution Process is important and something that is extremely valuable. It is best practice to do this reporting weekly, but formally at a meeting with customers and management monthly. The Monthly Business Review (MBR) is a very common way of bringing together all components of the portfolio and letting everyone understand exactly where the portfolio is tracking.
7.	Update and implement a change control process	The Portfolio Executing & Controlling process is absolutely the largest area for programs and projects changes and problems to occur; thus, requiring a solid portfolio change control process.

#	Task	Notes
8.	Update and implement a quality management process	During the execution and controlling of the portfolio, quality management is utilized most of the time in the individual programs and projects. However, as PMO Manager, your involvement and role in this process is important. Your knowledge of quality issues across all programs and projects, and being able to share that information with other areas is very valuable and could prevent program and project teams from running into their own quality issues. As PMO Manager, you are in a unique position to look across the organization and share quality information—more than most individuals in the organization, so it is your responsibility to share where applicable.
9.	Update and implement risk and issue tracking	As PMO Manager, look across the various programs and projects in your portfolio and track risks and issues. The programs and projects have their own risk and issue tracking; however, the risks and issues that occur might not impact the portfolio. It is the "portfolio impacting" risks and issues that need the right level of visibility and tracking and you need to report them to your management chain and stakeholders when applicable.
10.	Develop any applicable training plans on process or tools implemented during this phase	It is important that training plans and materials are created for any new processes or tools created during this phase.

To conclude the Portfolio Executing Process and the Portfolio Controlling Process of portfolio management, your role is to continually watch and drive both of these areas across all programs and projects in the portfolio. Make sure, though, that you leave the tactical execution of the programs and projects to the individual teams and stay out of the execution unless you are needed. Your role is more of an overarching role where your focus is reporting status and ensuring Program Managers and Project Managers are getting what they need to drive forward and be successful.

Portfolio Closing Process

The Portfolio Closing Process is a unique process in that it might not ever happen in your organization. Or, if it does, it "closes" for the year, not permanently. In some cases, portfolios shut down permanently, but that's a rare event and occurs when there are just a couple unique situations, such as a company's strategic change of direction, stakeholders change, or some other major company event that is portfolio impacting. However, at most companies, the portfolio management process occurs yearly and does not usually end. This is such a unique component of the portfolio process that everyone needs to understand because when there is not necessarily an end in sight, you treat the driving of the portfolio differently with a longer view of the work. The only other process like the portfolio management process that also does not necessarily shut down is the program management process. The project management process definitely shuts down and has specific tasks to close down a project.

With a portfolio's process not necessarily closing in the traditional way, the work necessary for the PMO Managers tends to be a little more limited and not that difficult. However, that is not to say that this process is not important; actually, the exact opposite is the case. Closing the portfolio (when it does occur) calls for careful handling by the PMO Manager or the Portfolio Manager. This is because most of the work at this time is administrative, such as contract closing, team member reassignments, PO closing, and financial management, which occurs so rarely that things are often missed. Actually, making mistakes, or not closing a portfolio correctly, can lead to the company continuing to pay invoices when work is complete, resources not being reallocated to new programs or projects, and documents going unsigned and unapproved while most of the old team members have moved on. Take the time and close the portfolio correctly to allow you and your team to move onto new areas in the organization knowing you finished and closed off the portfolio correctly.

Table 8.6 Portfolio Closing Process focuses the PMO Manager or the Portfolio Manager on closing the portfolio from an administrative perspective, moving resources to different programs or projects, and closing down all documentation.

Table 8.6 Portfolio Closing Process

#	Task	Notes
1.	Close and approve all procurement documents	These documents include SOW documents, POs, contracts, and any document needed to purchase resources in the company. This is going to vary greatly from company to company so make sure you work with your finance department and close off the documents where applicable.
2.	Develop acceptance	Create the formal acceptance documents and determine the process to obtain approvals before

#	Task	Notes
	documents and associated acceptance approval process	actually requiring them. This process can be time consuming from a portfolio perspective and something PMO Managers must ensure they stay on top of during the closing process.
3.	Hold "lessons learned/post-mortem" meeting	It is highly recommended to collect "lessons learned" during the life of the portfolio; however, at the end of the portfolio there needs to be a final session where the portfolio team and customers talk about the portfolio.
4.	Close out all portfolio documents	This process is one where everything is closed, shutdown and wrapped up. There should be no resources left, documents should be closed and backed up, and the project shutdown occurs.

To conclude the Portfolio Closing Process, it is important to understand how to close the portfolio properly and ensure things are in order before moving on. Stay focused on crossing the T's and dotting the I's to ensure that the organization is not liable or there are no loose ends leftover. There is nothing worse than leaving a PO open, not reassigning staff, or leaving the company open for lawsuits because you forgot to complete something during this closing process.

The Portfolio Closing Process is a rare event in most companies, so do not worry too much about the tactical parts of this process or having everything documented in **Table 8.6 Portfolio Closing Process**, above. Companies will generally have the closing process be the same across each portfolio and, frankly, most of the time when you do go through it, it will most likely be the first time for the company as well. It is such a rare event for most companies because portfolios usually continue for many years.

Summary

To conclude the portfolio management process, we have covered a tremendous amount of tactical deliverables that, as PMO Manager, you have the due diligence to review and determine whether they are applicable to your organization. Not all of the deliverables across the various life cycle processes (Portfolio Planning Process, Portfolio Executing Process, and so on) will be applicable, but as PMO Manager, you need to determine which ones are for your organization. Having too much information is better than not having enough, so let the various tables guide you in what you should look for during the portfolio process. You are the judge on where rigor and structure is best required in your organization, but too little and you will have problems, and too much, you lose flexibility.

As you review each table in this chapter, and in future chapters, regard them as best practices and minimum deliverables required for that area of the life cycle. Just taking some of these deliverables and applying in your organization is most likely going to put your organization in a more mature state than they are today and will increase your chances of success.

The portfolio management process (some call it "the planning process") ranges greatly and, as PMO Manager, your role is to figure out where you fit in this process and how you can add value. In some companies, this will be a big part of your PMO and you will be responsible for a lot. In other cases, it will be outside of your PMO and your role is limited. In all cases though, as PMO Manager, you tend to get the execution side of the portfolio, so being involved during the planning makes sense and is highly recommended. It is so much tougher to be handed a program or project list and be told to "go execute" it. It happens more times than it should, so if it does happen to you and you are not in the portfolio planning process like you should be, don't worry because there is a lot of great information and processes in the "Program Management Methodology" and "Project Management Methodology" chapters that you can use to be successful.

Some companies have taken to software products to drive their portfolio management processes; this is something that, as PMO Manager, you should be involved with the selection and purchasing for your organization, if possible. There are many portfolio management software products on the market and you have a huge opportunity to be a valuable resource in this process. Imagine you are driving it for the organization, entering the data, working with your stakeholders and customers, and reporting on the data throughout the planning process, and then again during the execution process. You would be extremely valuable to the organization if that were your role and, as PMO Manager, you are in the perfect position to take on that role on for your company.

Finally, whatever the process is, whatever your role will be, companies usually have a lot of maturing to do in portfolio management, and the industry as a whole is still quite young. With the deliverables outlined in the tables and what we covered in this chapter, you are definitely in a good spot and have a good chance of getting your organization through the "planning" and "executing and controlling" processes.

PMO Build Decisions:

1. Decide whether any of the "further considerations" noted earlier in planning phase you will utilize in how you execute your portfolio.

2. Decide the role the PMO will play in the Portfolio Planning process? Heavily involved, or handed a list of programs and projects to go execute.

3. Decide if you will hire a separate Portfolio Manager, or will the role be shared with the PMO Manager role?

4. Will the portfolio management methodology be used in the organization?

5. Will portfolio management fall under the PMO, or outside?

6.   Which tools will you use to manage the portfolio?

Chapter Review Answers:

1.   Ultimately, companies perform portfolio management to balance the challenges of making decisions about investment priorities and align programs and projects while balancing the risks and tradeoffs against performance.

2.   PMO Managers play a major role in the Portfolio Planning Process if they act as Portfolio Manager. If he or she is not a Portfolio Manager, he or she still needs to be active in the entire process.

3.   Collecting "lessons-learned" information throughout the Portfolio Planning Process helps teams and individuals learn and grow for the next planning cycle. The experiences they encounter in one cycle can help them grow in the next cycle.

4.   The main steps in portfolio management are: initiating, planning, executing, controlling, and closing.

5.   The Portfolio Execution Process includes defining the portfolio work for the organization (the program and project selection process) and the work on the approved programs and projects.

Chapter 9

Program Management Methodology

Figure 9.1 PMO Build Schedule - Program Management

Task Name	Resource Names
Step 5 - Design & Build or Enhance Period (Chapter 5 - 12)	**PMO Manager**
+Design PMO	**PMO Manager**
+ Design PMO Core Components	**PMO Manager**
-Build PMO	**PMO Manager**
Create PMO Business Management Area on Centralized Repository Site (Sections to create are documented in Implementation Phase)	PMO Manager
+Create PMO Core Components	**PMO Manager**
+Create PMO Model (Chapter 5)	**PMO Manager**
+Create PMO Maturity Model	**PMO Manager**
+Create PMO Staffing Model (Chapter 6)	**PMO Manager**
+Create PMO Training (Chapter 7)	PMO Manager
+Create Process Methodology Areas (Chapters 8-10 - where applicable)	**PMO Manager**
+ Create or Enhance Portfolio Management Methodology (Chapter 8)	**Portfolio Manager**
+Create or Enhance Program Management Methodology (Chapter 9)	**Program Manager**
+Initiation	**Program Manager**
+Planning	**Program Manager**
+Executing & Controlling	**Program Manager**
+Closing	**Program Manager**
Document PMO Build Decisions	PMO Manager
Program Management Methodology Complete	PMO Manager

Questions you should be able to answer after reading this chapter:

1. What are three high-level responsibilities of Program Managers?

2. Where do program knowledge areas play a role in program management?

3. What are the three focus areas of the program life cycle?

4. What are the three steps in the Benefit Management Process?

5. What is a program management oversight table?

One of the important components of successful PMOs is the use of a program management methodology. As PMO Manager, one of your main responsibilities is to drive and maintain the components of the program management methodology in your organization. There are many different program management methodologies used today, the most popular being from the PMI. PMI's book, *The Standard for Program Management,* outlines the main components of a typical program management methodology and guides Program Managers through managing their programs at a very high level. PMI's book is an excellent reference for concepts and areas around Program Management that you may be looking to understand at the high level, but it lacks the tactical aspect and the focus about how to manage your program, which is what this chapter will provide. Programs are unique in nature and have their own definitions. How you run your program might be very different from how another Program Manager runs his or her program, but the main concepts are the same and that is what is important when establishing a program management methodology within your PMO.

From the project industry perspective, many define programs as the process of managing several related projects, with the intention of improving an organization's performance. This definition is widely accepted in the project industry and is the foundation as to how you run your program(s) in your PMO. PMO Managers are responsible for making sure the PMO has established definitions for both programs and projects and that they are separate and understood well by everyone.

One of the unique things to consider when establishing the program management methodology, and something that Program Managers will run into with their programs that is unique to programs and not projects, is that programs often go on for years and years and can appear to be never ending. Projects, however, are unique in that they have a start date and an end date; whereas, a program might not ever have an end date. Larger programs, such as the ones in leading car manufacturers or airplane manufacturers can go on for many years and continue to do so as long as they are successful. This is an interesting concept to understand when it comes to building and driving a program management methodology because one of the program life cycle components is closing, and in some cases, the Program Manager may never make it to that closing phase. In some cases, the Program Manager who is starting a new program will never hit the closing phase, for a variety of reasons. As PMO Manager, consider the closing component when staffing and working with your Program

Managers to ensure that they have a long-term mindset and that they are not rushing to close programs, which many Programs Managers fall into the trap of doing in their efforts. Especially, if they came from being a Project Manager where closing down a project is a large part of their role.

The same logic can be applied to initiating a program. At one time, every program went through the initiation phase, which could have been many years ago, or last week. However, not every Program Manager on a program will necessarily go through the initiation phase. For example, the Program Manager on a single program today, depending on the size of the program, might not have been the same Program Manager who initiated the program. Often times, programs that go on for many years have cycled through multiple Program Managers. As previously mentioned about the closing process, just because one Program Manager initiates a program, the same person does not need to close the program. That person can move to something new and the program will still be okay. As you enter the program initiation phase section below, this section provides a helpful checklist of tasks and deliverables for establishing your program. Even if the program is well underway, the initiation process checklist is something you can use for your existing program to see if you are covering various areas and highlight areas you are missing. You could be missing something important. Think about those two unique areas, initiation, and closing, as you work your way through this chapter.

Bill's Thoughts:

I have managed large programs over my career at several different organizations and it is no easy task. I have run into many different scenarios where I could have used tactical help and had someone walk me through the different stages of my programs and what to do to manage some of the areas. When you are managing programs, you are often so caught up in managing all the issues and fires that you often cannot see everything as clear as an outsider looking in. As PMO Manager, your Program Managers are going to lean on you to help them through some of the more difficult areas of their programs, and I can't stress how important it is for you to bring fresh eyes and help your Program Managers be successful. You can look at the different areas of the program and see where they need help and offer guidance where necessary. Rolling up your sleeves and getting your hands dirty to help your Program Managers where they need it will prove to be very valuable.

This chapter will walk you through the Program Manager roles and responsibilities. This chapter covers the program management methodology taken from PMI and from real-world best practices. Much like Chapter 8, "Portfolio Management Methodology," or Chapter 10, "Project Management Methodology," the goal of this chapter is for you, the PMO Manager, to work with your Program Managers and create the various deliverables and tasks to apply to their programs today. The details outlined in this chapter are the basics for establishing and driving a program in your organization, regardless of the type of program, the fundamentals are here to help you be successful. The caveat is that there is no possible way to capture every unique aspect of your organization or your particular industry, but applying the best practices and creating the deliverables provided in this chapter will help you get started and moving in the right direction.

When considering how program management will work in your organization, think about the PMO model that you selected. As discussed in Chapter 8, "Portfolio Management Methodology," the same considerations are valid for program management. Think about where and how Program Management will fit within whatever model you select.

Keeping with the common theme of considering resources, procedures, and infrastructure as we continue building the PMO, the program management methodology closely matches the same concepts as the portfolio management methodology and project management methodology. As with the portfolio management methodology, the program management methodology also maps to resources, procedures, and tools in the same manner. Therefore you should think of them the say way and when you think about program management in the same way. The same scenarios work with the program management methodology as with the portfolio management and project management methodologies. Make sure to consider resources, procedures, and infrastructure throughout this chapter when you build your program management methodology.

As we covered in Chapter 8, "Portfolio Management Methodology," there will definitely be a design component to ensuring you select the right components for the program management methodology that match your industry, company, and specific requirements for your industry. The program methodology is a framework; it is not meant for complete adoption. Spend the time to understand program management, and then adopt the components that work for your organization.

Let us move now into the program management methodology and focus on building the right methodology for your organization.

Program Management

So far, in Chapter 8, "Portfolio Management Methodology," we established a portfolio management methodology and we covered what Portfolio Managers do in PMOs. Our focus now is on program management, the next important phase in the PMO build process. The PMO Build process calls for PMO Managers to develop a program management methodology and to do so it starts by first understanding what is in a Program Management Methodology and then second, applying that methodology onto the programs in the organization.

There are hundreds of different organizations and hundreds of different program and project types; it would be impossible for one book to cover every angle for everything needed in program management. This chapter certainly won't be able to do that either, but what it will do is walk you through some basics of program management. This chapter will lead you from what you learned in the previous chapter, "Portfolio Management Methodology," to the next chapter, "Project Management Methodology." The combination of chapters 8, 9, and 10 will help you build and implement an effective PMO because they include the three biggest characteristics that are required in most PMOs.

What is Program Management?

Program management is the centralized, coordinated, management of a program. That is it. It is that simple. Program management is managing everything within a program, and managing it from inception through the life cycle, including the closing process. Programs, unlike projects, can continue for many years and technically might never end. Although at some point, they usually end. Airplane manufacturers have major programs that will continue for years, but will eventually end because a different plane down the road will replace the current program. The other aspect of managing and driving a program is to ensure the team is achieving the overall strategic benefits and its objectives that were defined and approved by the customers during the initial process. It is so important for Program Managers to understand the program management life cycle first. Second, Program Managers need to understand what the program is trying to achieve for the customer. Understanding the overall goal of the program allows the Program Manager to make trade-off decisions and guide any Project Managers driving projects that are part of the program, into making different project-level decisions or changes as well. By not understanding the overall goal of the program, Program Managers blindly lead their programs.

Another way to look at program management is the same way you view project management, but with bigger scope, a broader view of everything, and much less technical or deep understanding of any one project within the program. This is commonly called the "umbrella" role where one person (the Program Manager) oversees everything in the program. Like an umbrella covering 1–2 people, a Program Manager covers everything in the program. Another way to look at it is to say a

Program Manager can manage a program with ten individual projects and will understand a little information about each of one of those projects. The Program Manager generally won't understand anything too deeply about each project (especially if there is several in their program), but he or she will know the scope, schedule, budget, and the top one or two risks. However, a Project Manager can generally manage 3–4 projects at one time and will be expected to have a very deep understanding of each. The Project Manager is expected to have a deep understanding of not only scope and schedule, but budget and every issue, risk, and every team member concern. Do you see the difference among the Program Manager and Project Manager roles and why it is so important to distinguish them? As PMO Manager, it is important that you make the decisions about who your Program Managers are (look broad, not deep) and who your Project Managers are (look deep, but not necessarily broad) as you staff and resource your PMO. Making these types of hiring and resource decisions can make or break a program and an individual project; therefore, you need to pick your staff very carefully and put the right people in the appropriate roles.

Who are Program Managers?

Program Managers have to be good Project Managers. As PMO Manager, you should believe that to be the case as well. It is going to help you decide who to choose for your Program Manager roles if you believe that they need to be good project managers. The selected Program Managers must have the fundamentals of what Project Managers do to run a project down pat to be able to apply those same skills to running a program. Remember, look broad, not deep, but have the skills to go deep if you had too. Program Managers, without that level of experience or background in project management, tend to struggle when managing their programs. If you have a poor Project Manager, there is a good chance that same person will be a poor Program Manager as well because those two jobs are so closely aligned and the skill sets are essentially the same. One difference is that a Program Manager needs to think broader than a Project Manager, but essentially the skill sets are the same; therefore, the transition for a great performing Project Manager would be easy and actually a best practice career path PMO Managers should consider adopting. Program Managers need the foundation and experience that Project Managers have by managing projects and applying the same logic to managing programs.

High-level Responsibilities of Program Managers
Program Managers must monitor and drive the following high-level responsibilities across all projects in the program:

- Project communications
- Project scope
- Project interdependencies
- Project risks
- Project issues
- Project finances

- Project quality
- Project resources
- Project procurement activities

As you can see, the high-level responsibilities align nicely to the project management knowledge areas defined by PMI, which is exactly where PMO Managers want their Program Managers to focus their programs and associated projects. Having Program Managers, focus on these areas will better the chances for successful delivery at the project level. It also gives the Program Manager and the Project Manager key components of the project to focus on together.

Tips & Best Practices

Every program consists of at least two or more projects; otherwise, it is just a big project.

Hiring Program Managers

What are some of the roles and responsibilities for a Program Manager, and what are some of the qualifications and characteristics that you should look for when hiring a Program Manager for your organization? The following list covers some of the qualifications and characteristics you should look for when hiring a Program Manager:

- Drive program management process
- Monitor the program and make sure it aligns with company or organizational goals
- Monitor program management activities of individual Program Managers
- Monitor project management activities of individual Project Managers
- Drive organization planning
- Drive benefits management
- Drive program governance
- Drive customer and stakeholder satisfaction
- Drive program communications
- Monitor and drive management approval
- Drive program management methodology, including enhancements and improvement opportunities

All of the qualifications and requirements are important when selecting the right individual for the Program Manager role within your organization. In every case, Program Managers must understand and drive the program management lifecycle as they manage the programs.

Project Managers Are Not Program Managers

A superstar Project Manager does not mean that he or she will be a superstar Program Manager. As we just covered, it is important that Program Managers look much broader than Project Managers, who work on individual projects, so it is no guarantee that a positive transition from Project Manager to Program Manager is possible. As PMO Manager, do not fall into the trap of assuming that a good Project Manager will naturally fit into that broader, more strategic role. We noted this briefly earlier, and it is important to cover again because it is that important. When poor Project Managers are promoted and put into a Program Manager role (and this happens), they often quickly fail after a short time in the new role. This is because he or she never had the skills to be an effective Project Manager and therefore was unable to make the successful transition to Program Manager. If someone struggles managing projects and does not have the basics of project management down, then asking him or her to work in a broader role without that project management foundation is going to be problem. With that being said, if someone is a successful Project Manager, he or she may not necessarily be a successful Program Manager, but that person would at least have a good head start. A successful Project Manager knows what triggers to pull, what levers to move, so when moving into the more broader Program Manager role he or she should be able to adapt to that role as well, taking the past project management experience into account when making decisions as a Program Manager.

Program Management Life Cycle

As we saw in Chapter 8, "Portfolio Management Methodology," portfolios and programs each have their own life cycle and methodology, and understanding them is important to building and implementing a PMO. The program management life cycle is very different from the portfolio life cycle and aligns closer with the project management life cycle, which we will examine in Chapter 10, "Project Management Methodology." There is actually very little difference between the program management life cycle and the project management life cycle. The differences tend to be around what the Program Manager does in the PMI nine knowledge areas compared to what the Project Manager does in those same knowledge areas. Remember, look broad, not deep when you are a Program Manager.

Program Managers have some unique aspects to their roles, different from Portfolio Managers and Project Managers. They include, but are not limited to, the following:

- Benefit management
- Program governance
- Stakeholder management

These three areas are very specific and accepted by the industry as key components of program management and thus, the Program Manager role. Rarely will you see a Project Manager responsible for those three areas, but you will probably see the Portfolio Manager responsible for those areas. Often, companies will merge the Portfolio Manager role and the Program Manager role into a single role. It is a best practice to keep them separate for simplicity purposes, but understand that some companies, for a variety of reasons, combine the two roles. In building your new PMO, or enhancing an existing one, look at what you are doing across those two roles and if possible keep them separate.

Let us spend some time now and look into each of the three areas of benefit management, program governance, and stakeholder management.

Benefit Management

One of the toughest components of a Program Manager's role is tracking and realizing benefits across the program. No other role in a program has the responsibility of identifying, defining, formalizing, and tracking a program's benefits. This includes tangible and intangible benefits and ongoing tracking to determine whether the program is realizing those benefits. In recent years, companies (generally large companies) have hired individuals trained in Six Sigma who have become key team members in programs to help Program Managers realize the benefits of their programs.

Bill's Thoughts:

In my career, I have seen benefits management done a million different ways, and in most cases, it was rarely successful. As PMO Manager, my advice to you is to get someone working for you or with you who is going to be a driver and who can get you your benefit information for your programs. Finding someone to work with the customers and ask the right questions about what they want out of the program is extremely important and not easy. The benefit management process is not a straightforward process; it is an art and a science. It requires someone with knowledge of the financial discipline and someone that has a Six Sigma background. Having those two resources working directly in your PMO and alongside your Program Managers would be very beneficial and help ensure the right benefits are being captured from the customers, thus given you a better chance of success on your programs.

There are three main processes in benefits management that Program Managers must follow in their programs. As PMO Manager, one of your responsibilities is to help your Program Managers through these processes. Because this effort involves multiple stakeholders, keeping this process on track can be challenging.

The benefits management process consists of the following steps:

Step 1 - Value Identification

Value identification generally occurs at the inception of the program. Every program and associated project(s) strives to improve a certain outcome or to produce some value. This can vary widely from company to company and industry to industry. The program's value identification is either established by the project visionary (the person requesting the program), someone in the benefiting organization, or by the project team member. Here are two top sources for the value identification step:

- Collaborate with the business stakeholders on identifying the negative impact of the current status and the positive impact on the desired status of the effort in question (the project)

- The Business Cases Analysis document is traditionally the document that identifies the initial estimation of the problem statement and desired benefits.

Step – 2 Value Analysis

The value analysis is when you need your Quality Lead the most. The industry uses nine widely known methods to estimate value. Quality Leads familiar with value methodologies can easily provide advice on the most suitable method for each scenario. It is crucial to follow the lead of a knowledgeable Quality Lead who can provide vital help in optimizing your measuring plan to be statistically sufficient, with minimum cost and work disruptions. **Here are two thoughts to consider in this step:**

- It is one layer deeper than the high-level value tags identified in the previous step. It involves testing the hypothesis that the value identified is influenced by the drivers, levers, or causals targeted by the program.
- Identify value metrics: there are two likely scenarios a Program Manager might encounter in this step:
  - Metrics relative to the value are already defined and are a standard organizational or business unit scorecard member.
  - Metrics are not established and hence, your best bet is collaborating with your Quality Lead to choose relevant metrics that meet the ten criteria of a great KPI.

Step 3 - Value Planning—Creation of a Business Value Realization Material

The program owner frequently collaborates with business groups or financial planning to construct and finalize the plan. The project team leads this process to obtain final buyoff from all stakeholders involved in the project.

The value assumptions, KPIs, measurement plans, and list of accountable or responsible individuals are in the Business Value Realization Book (BVR), or a structured Microsoft® Excel template that contains distinct tabs detailing the following items:

- Problem statement behind the program
- A measure of the magnitude of the problem statement
- An evidence of the strategic or organizational alignment of the program
- A list of applicable KPIs, their alignment to the existing scorecard of the organization, and their baseline and forecasted values
- Any assumptions, calculations, or formulas leading to the value
- A calculation of the ROI, NPV, or any other financial metric that is standard for the particular organization

The efforts focused on the delivery of the BVR book is primarily focused on:

- Establishing KPI/metric measurement plan
- Establishing baseline values for relevant KPIs or metrics
- Establishing a forecasted target for KPIs
- Incorporating value into the program plan

216

Recently, the value process is becoming a key component of established PMOs and an embedded discipline in the project industry. The Program Managers are evolving from just mere program coach into a value guardian, where he or she is becoming a whistle blower any time the forecasted or realized value is questionable and the program's success could be in jeopardy. Many times, that concept, or term "whistle blower," has a negative connotation; however, as PMO Manager, you need to encourage your Program Managers to look out for and expose when the situation arises on their programs. It does not have to be negative, but can be looked upon as actually quite positive and dong the right thing for the company.

We will cover KPI metrics and measurements plans later in Chapter 14, "PMO Measurements and Performance Tracking."

In addition to the traditional cost and delivery tracking, and along the same lines as the PMO active in value realization, the typical Program Manager might be responsible for reporting on the following components in their programs:

- Value realization reports
- Monitoring different components
- Updating and maintaining the benefits register
- Reporting and communicating the benefits realized through various communication channels about the program
- Value transition
- Consolidating or coordinating value
- Transferring ongoing ownership of the value process to the permanent organization

Tips & Best Practices

Finding and involving someone who has a background in benefits management and KPIs is a welcome addition to the program management team and any PMO.

When the program is still in the envisioning phase, it is the responsibility of the Program Manager to investigate the program's value. Working on a program that does not have a clearly defined value proposition can be very ominous, especially as the final milestones of the program near. As PMO Manager, your role is to work very closely with your Program Managers to make sure they know the value of their programs and that their customers and leadership understand and agree to that stated value. When the proper attention is placed on measuring the "problem statement" that triggered the decision to invest in a solution (regardless of whether it is a program, product, an IT effort, or a service), it pays dividends later on in the life cycle. Avoiding that work, or randomly making the decision to invest, can have huge consequences down the line when the project team has delivered the project to the customer and the end-result did not provide the value the customer expected it to provide.

Selecting and understanding the business value process is not easy and it is definitely not the sole responsibility of a Program Manager, or even a PMO Manager. You definitely need to understand it, but there is no expectation that you must do it yourself or without the help of a Six Sigma expert. Having experts or certified Six Sigma Black Belts on your program teams will definitely give you the skill sets required on the team to drive the capturing and recording of the programs benefits. Here are some important guidelines and considerations a Program Manager should keep in mind while addressing the benefits management and business value process:

- Value process effectiveness—The value process does not need to be complex; it needs to be understood by the stakeholders so they endorse it, that's all. Complex value processes and formulas make it a lot harder for leadership to buy-in fully when deciding upon the business value proposal. There is the old saying, "keep it simple, stupid" and that applies nicely to this value process.
- Value process needs to be economical—If the process gets too complex, it will likely become very hard and expensive to execute from a cost and resources standpoint. Having a knowledgeable or financial resource who is certified in Six Sigma can be key to establishing a rigorous business value plan with optimized and minimized resources. It is important to avoid compromising any statistical rigor while trying to keep the resources optimized to an affordable level with the business and IT organizations involved.
- The value process must be credible—The tools, methodology, and measurement plans need to be compliant to known statistical disciplines, financial rules, and heuristics while maintaining simplicity. This way, trust becomes easy to establish and commitment and adherence to the business value plan becomes a highly likely outcome of the effort.
- The value process focuses on the program effort—Credibility is at stake when the Program Manager ignores to identify the program percentage contribution to the total value realized by the business unit. Many teams ignore taking into consideration the holistic dynamics involved in producing the total value and might, due to lack of knowledge of proper techniques or for the sake of over-simplicity, overlook the "% contribution" conversation and oversize the forecasted program promised value.
- The value process should be "balanced scorecard" compliant—Program Managers focus too often on financial benefits and might ignore the intangibles realized by the program. Some programs focus solely on those intangibles, including high-level corporate strategic goals that might be hard to rate, rank, or measure. This might drive some behavior around exaggerating the tangible gains to justify a program that might have a greater focus on the intangible, but might have a significant long-term benefit (including financial benefits) to the company. So, for example, efforts that are focused on employee satisfaction with IT infrastructure might end up with an artificially inflated efficiency "soft-dollar" estimate, ignoring the actual hard dollar cost which results from good employee attrition. Many studies concluded that poorly executed process tools significantly contributes to employee decision to quit the company out of frustration. This costs the company money in

repeated hiring, training, and paying for the mistakes or lost opportunities of an undertrained workforce.

- How do we isolate the effect of the IT program? -There are two commonly used approaches to that question:
    - **Control groups**: where a particular region, group, branch of the organization, or a customer segment receives the product or service while the other (or others) remain unchanged, using the old product, process or tool. The difference in the performance metric identified at the inception of the effort between the two groups should be a leading indicator to the value realized in broader or full adoption or launch.
    - **Trend lines**: largely a forecast model, which Microsoft Excel is perfect for using to create forecasts of the future performance without the program in question adopted. This methodology, given its simplicity, can indicate a good range for the baseline future performance of the organization or the product without adoption. The development team or senior stakeholders can use the projected baseline to set a reasonable target that matches the capabilities of the program or its designed breakthrough. As adoption occurs, while monitoring the KPI and the delta between the baselines determined by the trend line, the actual performance values realized are translated into the final value realized by the business unit.

It is the prime responsibility of the program owner to be directly involved in:

- Measuring the magnitude of the problem—generic statements or unfounded estimates (guestimates) are not rigorous enough methods to convince upper management to commit funds and person hours.
- Establishing a business value model, be it ROI, (the most preferable method in the IT world today), NPV, or another model that gets an independent review by quality and finance personnel to check the assumptions, robustness, and the value chain story is recommended.
- Assigning unbiased quality and finance personnel who act as customer advocates and who draft the measurement plan for the KPIs or the value levers involved. Have them schedule periodic meetings to stay on top of and report the vital signs of how value is tracking.
- Reporting on how the program team is delivering on value and highlighting any changes in schedule that mandate a revision of the value realization and any relative scope changes that could temporarily or permanently affect the promised value of the program.

Common Benefits Management Calculations

There are three increasingly popular metrics value calculations commonly adopted by many of the top 500 companies around the world used to calculate benefits management calculations. These include:

Formula 1: ROI - ROI, or Return on Investment, a Percentage, ROI % = Benefits − Costs / Costs X 100

Formula 2: Benefits to Cost Ratio - Benefits to Cost Ratio = Benefits / Costs

Formula 3: Payback Period - Payback Period = Total Costs/Annual Savings

One of the tools to manage benefits is the program benefits register table. **Table 9.1 Program Benefits Register Table** provides an example. This is a standard program management form for managing and communicating benefits information. It is highly recommend that you use this table, or a variation of this table, for tracking and reporting benefits information for the program. It is important for you, the PMO Manager, to review every program benefits register table across your organization to ensure that your Program Managers are tracking and keeping benefits at the forefront of their role, as well as understanding the details and the expected benefits for each program. Some companies have their own version of the program benefits register table while others will have nothing, so this form is a great starting point. If you have a Six Sigma expert on the program, make sure he or she also approves and uses this form as well.

Table 9.1 Program Benefits Register Table

Description	Link to Objective (s)	Accountability /Owner of Benefit	Stakeholder	Baseline	Target	Approach /Method

There is certainly a lot of work in the benefits management section that Program Managers must complete as part of program management. These processes are going to differ slightly from company to company; however, the context of the benefits management process is what is important to understand. It is also important for you, as PMO Manager, to spend time in the benefit management process and make sure your

Program Managers are driving value into their programs and eventually down to their projects. These types of discussions when you focus on driving value for Program Managers are much more relevant these days to your business customers and are starting to be a different dimension in your Program and Project Manager's tool boxes. This is compared to the scope, schedule, budget, triple constraint conversations that was once top-of-mind and the only tradeoffs Program and Project Managers had (and used) to make on their efforts.

Program Governance

Program governance is the process of "governing" resources, procedures, and services through program leadership. As PMO Manager, you ensure that your Program Managers understand some standard definitions and roles of the program governance process. Governance processes are very different from company to company, some are very formal and structured while some companies are more informal. As PMO Manager, you should understand what your organization will allow and is willing to accept from a governance formality perspective. Putting a very formal program governance structure in place in a company that is unstructured could fail badly. However, if you have a formal organization with many processes in place, then having a governance structure will likely be very positive and go over well. It is a balance and something that you, as PMO Manager, need to understand before you suggest putting in a governance process for programs within your PMO. Luckily, if the company has a PMO (and they have hired you), there is a good chance that the company will allow a structured governance process and you should be able to move forward with it. Even a formal company with many processes will want the governance structure to begin with baby steps and slowly increment how much structure goes in from the start. A governance structure certainly can begin with limited structure, and then grow as the program matures so that the customers and executives can accept the processes and see how this new structure is benefiting the program and associated projects.

Role of Program Governance

One of the easiest ways to understand program governance is to understand part of the role it plays in a program and across an organization. The following list provides some typical rules around the role of program governance:

- Perform governance at the program level, not the project level (if the project is part of a program). The exception being, if the project is a standalone effort, it will have its own governance process. Otherwise, it is part of a larger overall program.
- Governance will include both strategic and tactical aspects.
- Governance process manages both tangible (money) and intangible (strategy) assets.
- Governance process contains formal escalation processes. This allows projects to have a path to executives for support, direction, and clearing roadblocks.
- Ensure that your governance processes clearly document roles and responsibilities for customers, team members, and executives.

Even a basic program governance structure is better than no governance structure. By having even the simplest structure in place, you can always grow and mature that structure later as the PMO matures or as the organization matures in Program Management.

Tips & Best Practices

The program governance process will vary from company to company, but the biggest thing PMO Managers should worry about is actually having a governance process.

At a high level, the program governance process should include the following activities:

- **Control** the program's scope, contingency funds, and overall value of the individual projects through the life of the program.
- Define the "desired business outcomes" (end state), benefits, and value. Define the business measures of success and overall value proposition of the program while ensuring that the customers approve and sign off on those outcomes.
- **Develop** the organization's project delivery process. This includes the continual building and enhancing of its ability to deliver more complex and challenging projects, with the focus of coming in on time and on budget while generating the maximum value for the customer.
- **Establish** the basis for project governance, approval, and measurement process with the customers. This includes defining roles and accountabilities, policies and standards, and associated processes within the program.
- **Evaluate** project proposals within the program to select those that are the best investment of funds and limited resources and that are within the organization's capability and capacity to deliver.
- **Enable** through resourcing of projects the harnessing and managing of business needs through the provisioning of the governance resources, where applicable.
- **Monitor** the project's progress, stakeholder's commitment and engagement, results achieved, and the leading indicators of success. Where applicable, monitor failure points so that project teams can learn, going forward, what not to do in order to be more successful.
- **Measure** the outputs, outcomes, benefits and value against both the plan and measurable expectations of the customers, executives, and team members

You will also need to control the tactical components of the governance process as well. Some of the tactical activities include:

- Outline and document the relationships between all internal and external groups involved in the project.
- Document and identify all stakeholders who are interested in the project.

- Describe the proper flow of information regarding the project to all stakeholders via a formal communications plan.
- Ensure the appropriate review of issues (important enough for stakeholder review) encountered within each project are handled within the governance process.
- Ensure that customers and management provide approval for individual projects at each major milestone (for example, design complete, and architecture complete).
- Define a process to assess the compliance of the completed project to its original objectives.
- Create a process for assigning Project Managers to projects in the program.
- Establish and approve the program's roles and responsibilities. This includes ensuring that within the individual project that clear roles and responsibilities is also established.
- Create an overall program schedule that spans all individual projects and their various stages from initiation through deployment.
- Create a program-level status reporting process that includes providing upward status to the stakeholders and management team for ongoing visibility.
- Provide a central document repository for the program and links to individual projects within the program.
- Provide a centralized process for the management and resolution of issues and risks that arise during program execution.
- Ensure that the project management methodology has its own process for issue and risk management, outlined in the next chapter.
- Create a centralized process for managing independencies across all projects in the program.
- Create a centralized process for managing finances across all projects in the program. A program-level financial report is expected to be communicated throughout the program life cycle.
- Create a process for evaluating quality issues across all projects in the program. Some projects will have their own unique and specific quality management functions; however, program governance should include quality oversight.
- Create a centralized process for resource management across the program and the individual projects in the program. This process should include attracting, obtaining, and releasing project team members for both program and projects, when applicable.

There is definitely a lot of information about what a Program Manager does when running a program governance program. One of the areas of governance that is important to cover is what the governance body does in a program. When pulling together a team of executives, customers, and team members to make up a governance body, what are the expectations of that body? The expectations of the program governance body include:

- Develop the right plan.

- Execute and manage risks to the plan.
- Improve project delivery (both speed and quality).
- Secure benefits.

It is also important to cover what a governance body does, but you need to understand "how" the governance body works and what the key areas are that they are looking at during the program execution.

Figure 9.2 Program Governance Body—How It Works breaks down some of the key success factors, as well as some critical questions that a governance body will review to change the direction, one way or another, for a program.

Figure 9.2 Program Governance Body—How It Works

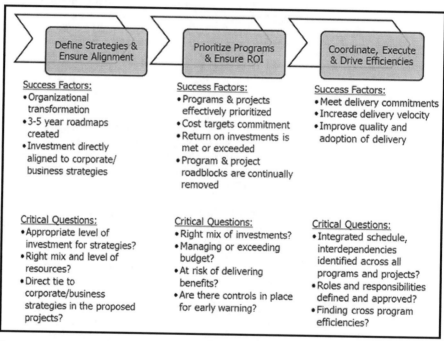

As you can see in the figure, there are several different considerations, but only three major areas. Those areas include: defining strategies and aligning those strategies to the direction of the organization; prioritizing and making priority calls to ensure that you are obtaining the highest level of ROI possible; and the coordination and driving of efficiencies as an ongoing function that the governance bodies are performing throughout the life of the program. These efficiencies cross many different boundaries from project team delivery, program and project costs, project adoption, and various quality components. Each of these three major areas plays a major role in how governance bodies play critical roles in programs and projects through initiation to deployment.

As PMO Manager, make sure your Program Managers are driving a governance structure for their programs and that their governance structure closely aligns to what you have established as the standard process for your PMO. There is nothing worse than Program Managers on your team creating governance structures that do not aligned to your PMO guidelines. If that does happen, it is best to take the Program Manager aside and determine why they are not using the standard processes. Having common structures and formats in place within a PMO, helps drive commonality between programs, makes everyone more efficient. We have covered some key components about how to create a program governance structure focusing on both what it is, from a high-level, to tactically "how" a governance body works. This gives you, the PMO Manager, necessary information to establish a program governance structure in your organization and define the roles and responsibilities of both your Program Managers and your customers and executives who will participate and be part of that governance process.

Stakeholder Management

One of the keys to being a successful Program Manager is how well one manages his or her program's stakeholders, customers, or anyone involved in the program. Stakeholder relationships can make or break a Program Manager. Time and time again, when Program Managers have good solid relationships with their stakeholders, they have a much better chance of succeeding at driving their programs. Program Managers who struggle with relationships, or tend not to focus on relationships, tend to struggle with their programs. Clearly, this is not always the case, but something PMO Managers have seen for many years. The Program Managers who figure out how important relationships are to their overall success in their programs and to their careers, in general, tend to be much more successful than those who do not bother building relationships at all. As PMO Manager, one of your roles is to continue to check in with your Program Managers to ensure that they are focusing on stakeholder management and, where possible, to help them work through any issues or concerns to allow for the best possible relationships between the Program Managers and their stakeholders. You can really play a big role in this process and help your Program Managers be successful if you believe in it yourself.

Tips & Best Practices

The stakeholder management process is critically important; an unhappy stakeholder makes for a very long program that becomes much tougher to be successful.

Stakeholder Analysis

One of the key components of stakeholder management is to determine very early in the initiation of the program who the stakeholders are and what influence they have on the program. Analyze and determine the interests of the various stakeholders in your program by focusing on interests, expectations, and the influence an individual stakeholder can have on a program. This is not a difficult process at all, but can be time consuming based on how many stakeholders you have and how big the program is in the organization. To help Program Managers with this process, it is important they have the right mindset and they are thinking of some key questions.

Stakeholder Analysis Questions

1. Who has the ultimate power to make decisions and change the direction of the program?

2. Who are the interested parties for the program?

3. How do the parties interact or work together?

4. Do the parties work together effectively?

5. What level of interest do these stakeholders have on the program?

The list of stakeholder analysis questions can go on and on, but these five key questions should get you thinking about your stakeholders in a different way and in a different light. Thinking about the stakeholders using these initial questions give Program Managers a good start in the stakeholder analysis process. Larger, more complex programs, tend to have more stakeholders, which make this process more time consuming to complete, so having these questions is very helpful.

Bill's Thoughts:

In my first book, Project Management Communications Bible, I took a great deal of time stressing the importance of project communications and the impact it has on the customers and stakeholders. I talk in the book about how to ensure that Project Managers sit down with their customers and talk about what they need for status from the project. My thoughts on stakeholder management are really the same points that I wrote and elude to in my first book, and they are applicable to mention again: if you don't have satisfied stakeholders, and they are not "managed" appropriately, your program will have a good chance of failing and everyone, and I mean everyone, will be unhappy.

Another way to help with the stakeholder analysis process is to capture the stakeholder information in a stakeholder register. This tool is introduced by PMI in Chapter 10, "Project Communications Management," in their book, *A Guide to the Project Management Body of Knowledge (PMBOK® Guide, 4e)* as part of a project's overall management strategy. This is a brilliant tool and something very useful for Program Managers and Project Managers alike to use for their programs and projects, respectively. **Table 9.2 Stakeholder Register** is a very simple version and provides Program Managers the basic information to capture about each stakeholder and can be expanded or enhanced for the needs of the program. Program Managers might want to stay aligned to what their Project Managers are using for the stakeholder register in case there is a need to combine the information in the future.

Table 9.2 Stakeholder Register

ID	Stakeholder Name	Role in Project	Contact Information	Major Project Needs	Influence	Notes
1	Sam Smith	CEO	SSmith@email.com	On Time	2	N/A
2	Bob Jones	CIO	Bjones@email.com	Scope Accomplished	1	Hit scope
3	Mary Taylor	CFO	Mtaylor@email.com	On Budget	2	Hit Budget
4	Sally Holt	CTO	Sholt@email.com	No Tech Problems	1	N/A

Understanding Your Stakeholders

One of the key reasons for capturing stakeholder information is to use that information throughout the life of the program. It makes little sense to spend the time and capture the information if you are not going to use it to understand and work effectively with your stakeholders.

Understanding each stakeholder is very challenging, but having a good register is going to help you better understand what your stakeholders are all about, but that does not solve everything. It is going to take time to build individual relationships with the key stakeholders or with the key stakeholder's representatives. In some cases, stakeholders will promote key staff members on their teams to represent them on projects.

To understand your stakeholders is to understand how they might affect you on the project. Will they support you, will they fight you, or just what will your relationship be with your stakeholders? You could have good relationships with some stakeholders and not so good relationships with others. That is going to happen, but experienced Program Managers still know how to work those relationships so everyone in the end wins and the program runs successfully. Stakeholder management is very difficult and something Program Managers need to manage very tightly.

Program Managers have an opportunity to build great relationships with their program's stakeholders through the life of the program by performing some very basic stakeholder analysis. These activities include:

Communication—A Program Manager who spends his or her time communicating with the stakeholder and ensuring that the stakeholder is getting the information needed to make program-level decisions is going to build great credibility with stakeholders. Ongoing communication is a key to a Program Manager's success; therefore, stakeholder communication is an important part of that process.

Leadership—A Program Manager with strong leadership skills is going to instill a level of confidence with stakeholders that will help build solid relationships. A Program Manager with these skills will set direction, drive strategy, and build credibility that will make a positive impact on stakeholders. Leadership skills are a key to a Program Manager's success and something that PMO Managers should look for when hiring them.

Collaboration—One of the key functions of a successful Program Manager is being a strong collaborator with stakeholders and team members. Strong collaboration is going to give stakeholders the sense that the Program Manager is working for them and with their best interests in mind. Someone who is closed off or unwilling to work closely with everyone in the program will quickly turn off a stakeholder and will have a much more difficult time being successful.

As PMO Manager, one of your roles is to assist your Program Managers in the stakeholder management process as they actively manage their individual programs. By walking your Program Managers through some of the fundamentals discussed in this section, you set them up to have much better relationships with their stakeholders, which in turn helps them deliver their programs with a greater chance of success. It is also important to understand that there are very difficult stakeholders who can be difficult to please regardless of what you try or how hard you try to connect with them. This is where your Program Managers need your help the most and where you might need to help smooth relationships and drive communications between the individuals. Do not underestimate that by giving some of your time to focus on this and help your Program Managers will go a long way in helping them be successful.

Program Management Process Groups & Knowledge Areas

The program management life cycle is very simple by nature, but can be very difficult to execute. Larger programs, especially, can be very complex and go on for many years. With larger programs, it is often very difficult to have oversight and coverage across a large number of projects while keeping everything under control and running smoothly. That is why it is important for the Program Managers to have solid backgrounds in project management so they can apply those same skills at the program level. One of the key differences is the Program Manager will look horizontally across all the projects in the programs; whereas, the Project Manager will go vertical (deep) into the multiple projects he or she is managing.

The program management process includes the processes and procedures to manage all aspects of the program and its associated projects. The industry definition is, "this being the process of managing several related projects." The specific details of management include benefits, deliverables, resources, budgets, governance, and so on. Each area that is applicable for most programs, across most companies, is documented in this chapter.

Tips & Best Practices

Ensure you drive your programs using these life cycle processes.

Figure 9.3 Program Life Cycle Process shows the typical processes of any program. These four processes often overlap one another and have an overarching process (monitoring and controlling) that moves the program forward. Monitoring and controlling tend to be the heaviest during the executing process of both programs and projects because the lack thereof would send the program out of control and possibly towards failure. Imagine that you have a program with ten individual projects that are all executing and relying on each other to complete. If the Program Manager does not watch each project closely, they could fail, which would impact the overall health of the program.

Figure 9.3 Program Life Cycle Processes

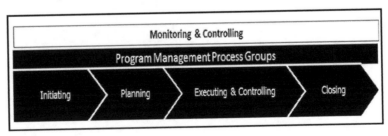

Note: This Program Management life cycle process (**Figure 9.3**) is identical to the project management life cycle process in the next chapter, "Project Management Methodology." The two life cycles are purposely the same to ensure that Program Managers and PMO Managers completely understand the two life cycle processes (program and project) and are aware that they are identical. As you go through this chapter, make sure you understand how the Program Managers focus is on a much broader and horizontal view of the larger program; whereas, the Project Managers focus is much narrower, specifically on their projects only. Therefore, even though the life cycles are the same, the different roles execute the processes depending on their roles. Consider both as you work through this chapter and the next chapter.

Knowledge Areas in the Program Management Methodology

The nine PMI knowledge areas in the program management process are identical to those in the project management methodology.

They are heavily document in Chapter 10, "Project Management Methodology." There are several tables that show the mapping between the program management life cycle and the nine knowledge areas; however, I have not included those tables for the following reasons:

- Program Managers should already have some form of project management experience in order to be successful in this role. Therefore, they should already be familiar with these knowledge areas.
- The concepts for all nine knowledge areas at the program level and at the project level are fundamentally the same, just much broader at the program level. Program Managers look wide and Project Managers look deep in each of these knowledge areas.
- The focus of this chapter is not to repeat the obvious, but to give Program Managers and PMO Managers a set of deliverables and take-away messages that they can immediately use in their programs.

Let us spend some time now and get into the program management life cycle processes, beginning with initiation. As PMO Manager, you should provide the deliverables, steps, and processes within the program management methodology to each of your Program Managers to drive their programs. You want them all to be following the processes and steps that you define within the methodology so they are all following the PMO standards and guidelines.

Bill's Thoughts:

We are just about to go down the path of initiating, planning, executing and controlling your program, and if you have any PMI background, it is going to be the same old thing you have heard in the portfolio management chapter and the same thing you will hear in the project management chapter. My thoughts are that you embrace what PMI has to offer and use the concepts and best practices and apply them to your programs and projects whenever possible. I believe so strongly that PMI has such a solid foundation and a great starting point that PMO Managers should just adopt it but then create what works for their organization and company and don't feel like you have to adopt everything. As you read through the end of this chapter, don't assume it is rubber-stamped PMI verbiage and I am suggesting you use everything you read. It is not. The processes, deliverables, and processes are all tried and tested program deliverables that I have personally created, or had folks working for me create, as part of my organizations.

Program Management Process Groups

Let's spend some time now and look at the various Program Management process groups. As you start to review the progress groups it is important to recognize that these are standard across the project industry and are the foundation for the Program Management methodology. As PMO Manager, as you review the steps and each of the areas ensure that you follow each of the major phases, but tweak the deliverables or the processes in the phase to what is suitable to your company. Also, remember, this is a guide only and it is not required to take every one of the steps, just consider them best practices and strongly recommended. You will quickly learn which processes or procedures will work in your organization.

Program Initiating Process

The process definitions and terminology at the program level are similar to the project level, but different from the perspective that there is much more of a horizontal view of the program compared to the vertical nature of projects. Therefore, the initiation process focuses on linking the vertical projects in the program and establishing the right tie-ins to ensure that there is overall coverage at the program level. Program management processes require coordination with various groups and very close ties to the projects in the program.

The program initiation process is much like initiating and kicking off a project; however, you need to have a much broader view because your program is often much more complex than a single project. Think about kicking off a new program for an airplane or an automobile and how large and complex that process would be, and then compare that to kicking off a single project. There is clearly much more to a program, but the concepts are the same and applied the same way. One of the main differences in kicking off a program compared to a project is determining which projects are part of the program and how everything in the program relates to each other.

To kick off a program, Program Managers are responsible for the tactical delivery of program deliverables. By the end of the initiation process, the Program Manager, associated Project Managers, customers, and team members will have a set of deliverables to kick off their program.

Tips & Best Practices

You get one chance to kick off your program, make sure you do it right and follow the steps that are outlined in this chapter.

One of the key questions that Program Managers often ask themselves during the initiation phase is where their program fits in the overall organization. Is their program the main over-arching program, or is it a sub program to a much larger program. Many times, even very large programs in one organization are part of an even larger over-arching program. So, understanding where your program fits is important because you will know whether you are driving all of the program requirements and processes or whether you are feeding into a larger program effort. This is an important distinction because the program initiation process deliverables, as described in **Table 9.3 Program Initiation Process** below, are a solid set of deliverables for a single program, but might not include everything that a larger program might require for its effort. When programs are part of an over-arching program, there are often other requirements or deliverables that the over-arching program requires that are specific to that program. If this is the case, and your Program Managers are part of an over-arching program, make sure the Program Managers for both programs establish a relationship and know how they will work together. As PMO Manager, both Program Managers could actually report to you, so you would have the perfect opportunity to get the two people talking and working together. Many times they won't report to you, which can be challenging and something that you may need to step in and help your program managers with. These kinds of over-arching programs and sub programs are especially common in large software initiatives. For example, there might be a large program in one organization driving a portion of the product development; however, it is only part of an even larger program. The main purpose of the larger program is to pull all the smaller programs together and ensure they are all delivering to the same timeframes, costs, goals, and so on.

The remainder of this chapter will document industry best practices and standard deliverables for creating and establishing a program management methodology that Program Managers can use in their programs. Earlier in this book, we discussed the three top types of industry standard PMOs (supportive PMOs, controlling PMOs, and directive PMOs) that could play a part in the enforcement of your Program Managers creating, or not creating, the deliverables listed in the program management methodology. Especially if your PMO models are controlling or directive, in those two cases enforcement is a common characteristic of those two models. There were also the Centers of Excellences PMO models, and if program management plays a role in your PMO, then the model you choose and the rigor you apply will have to be defined for your organization. For example, if you choose the supportive PMO, then your direction to your Program Managers would be to look at the deliverables in this methodology as best practices and recommend that they create the deliverables. You are not going to require your Program Managers to complete them in a support PMO model. However, if this is a controlling or directive PMO, the theory changes and you will require your Program Managers to complete the deliverables in this methodology. As PMO Manager, think about the importance of the model and how the model impacts the use of the program management methodology deliverables. Regardless of the PMO type, the list will not be all-inclusive, but look at it as an excellent starting point and certainly enough to get you going in the right direction.

Program Managers can use **Table 9.3 Program Initiation Process** to establish the program deliverables. This is a very busy time for Program Managers because this process only happens once and it sets the foundation as to how the program will execute from beginning to end. It is so important to get a program started correctly and to select the right projects to be part of the program to ensure that the program stays in line with the benefits it's trying to achieve. Each Program Manager, at a minimum, should complete the following deliverables for his or her program. Some companies, or industries, might have specific program deliverables that are not documented here (or they are part of a larger program) that might also need to be created during the initiation process. Be flexible and adapt any processes that your company may have into your program management methodology wherever possible.

Table 9.3 Program Initiation Process

#	Task	Notes
1.	Develop a program repository for all documentation	It is important that one of the first tasks is to establish a common repository for storing program artifacts. Establishing a repository early in the process gives all program team members a central storage place, but also an area for your affected projects to use.
2.	Develop a program charter	The program charter document should include, scope, deliverables, constraints, assumptions, risks, issues, milestones, and so on.
3.	Develop a program oversight table	This table provides a high-level view of the programs, contacts, scope items, budget, dependencies, and estimated complete dates for all projects within the program.
4.	Develop a program benefits table	This table documents all the benefits of the program. This is the BVR document. This tool is documented earlier in this chapter.
5.	Develop or utilize the Business case analysis report	This report supports the documentation and justifies why the program is being requested. This report might not be the direct responsibility of the Program Manager, such as the other deliverables in this table; however, it is definitely important to complete at this time.
6.	Develop a program organization structure	The program organization structure includes the Program Manager and the various roles that support the program. It is a best practice to include the individual project structures and the lead Project Managers for those projects.
7.	Develop a list of projects for the program	This list includes all projects that are part of the program scope. The process of authorizing projects during the initiation phase solidifies the projects to include.
8.	Develop a program stakeholder register	This register documents the major stakeholders of the program. This tool is documented earlier in the chapter.

#	Task	Notes
9.	Develop a program scope report	It is important to note that this report documents the program scope as well as the scope of the associated projects.
10.	Develop and initiate the program team	This process includes finding the team members to work on the program activities, as well as finding lead Project Managers for individual projects that are part of the program. This process is company specific, but important to ensure the team is secured during the initiation process, before starting and planning work.
11.	Develop a program status report	This report incorporates not only status at the program level, but at the project level as well.
12.	Develop the Program management kickoff material	At the end of the program management initiation process, Program Managers should officially kick off their program. The meeting materials include everything created during the initiation process.
13.	Develop applicable training plans on process or tools implemented in this phase	It is important that training plans and materials are created for any new processes or tools created during this phase.

Further Consideration Items:

Table 9.4 Program Oversight Table documents the key projects associated to the program. Having this information documented helps keep a good handle on the projects and provides Program Managers, customers, or executives a quick and easy overview.

Table 9.4 Program Oversight Table

Program Management Oversight Table					
Project Name	Key Contacts	Scope Items	Budget ($)	Project Dependencies	Est. Complete Date

Tips & Best Practices

Program Managers should always kick off their programs. Spend the time to do so, because it is worth it to put everyone on the same page.

Figure 9.4 Program Kickoff Meeting Agenda documents the key deliverables and items to cover in a program kickoff meeting. The program kickoff meeting is an important way to start out the program on the right foot and gives everyone a view into what is included in the program. There are not many tactical deliverables that need to be completed prior to kicking off the program, this is more of a way to bring together and ensure everyone is on the same page. As you would kick off a project, it is important to kick off programs as well.

Figure 9.4 Program Kickoff Meeting Agenda

Program Kickoff Meeting Agenda

➢ Welcome and Introductions
➢ Meeting Purpose
➢ Expected Benefits (Benefits Table)
➢ Program Overview/Goals
➢ Organizational Chart
➢ Stakeholder Register
➢ Program Roles and Responsibilities
➢ Program Scope Review
➢ Summary
➢ Next Steps

Program Planning Process

The planning process group creates the processes and procedures needed to execute the program. This includes planning the program itself and planning the various components that are required to run the program. The planning process describes and documents the processes as well as how the Program Manager will interface and work with the Project Managers who are driving the individual projects associated with the program. Planning the program is a very important component to driving a successful program and something that Program Managers need to be active in for their programs. As PMO Manager, one of your main responsibilities is to help your Program Managers through the planning process and ensure they are set up for success. It is your role to make sure they are completing the various deliverables for the program, but also setting up their projects (and associated Project Managers) for success.

Bill's Thoughts:

One of the biggest problems that Program Managers or PMO Managers run into is the lack of planning. Nobody spends the time they really need to plan properly. They just do not, and that is why we run into so many program and project problems. So many times, there is so much pressure to get the project started and to get people working that to spend the time and plan seems like a waste of time. We cannot continue down this path and someone must put a stop to the lack of planning. As PMO Manager, you have the perfect opportunity to sit down with your Program Manager and the program teams, or in some cases the affected project teams, and plan appropriately. Sitting down and planning all the different areas of a program will be so beneficial when you are executing the program and something happens and you have to react to one thing or another. If you have properly planned in the first place, when problems occur, they can be dealt with and the program stays on track. Lack of planning leads to Program Managers or PMO Managers spinning and reacting wildly to the events, which is not a successful way to run a program.

One of the key documents that Program Managers will create during the planning process is the program management plan. This plan is much like a project management plan: it contains the tactical processes and procedures for managing and controlling the program. It is a very comprehensive document and something that the Program Managers will use throughout the execution of the program. The contents of the program management plan will vary from company to company, based on industry, project type, and customer and stakeholder requirements. Program Managers, just by the nature of completing this very large and comprehensive document (and associated components), will have a very good handle on how they will execute their program. One of the deliverables, or outputs, of the program management plan that Program Managers will drive is a work report template. There is an example of this work report template in Figure 9.5 below. This work report template provides Program Managers a quick and easy view of the projects that are associated with the program. More details on this report later in the chapter.

Tips & Best Practices

When bringing the team together to plan your program, make sure that you include the Project Managers who are managing the projects in your program. Planning without using the full team can lead to issues down the line.

Table 9.5 Program Planning Process helps Program Managers plan and prepare execution of their program. Much like the initiation phase, the planning phase is also a very busy time and Program Managers must make sure that they give themselves enough time to plan and get their program headed in the right direction.

When entering the planning phase of a program, the Program Manager should take the time to complete the deliverables in the following table for the program. By the end of the planning process, the Program Manager, customers, and team members will have a handle on the planning components of the program.

Table 9.5 Program Planning Process

#	Task	Notes
1.	Develop program management plan	This document contains details about the overall management and integration of the program. This document includes the processes and procedures for managing all components of the program. For example, scope at the program level is handled differently than scope at the project level; this plan will document and speak to both.
2.	Develop a program resource management report	This report documents the various roles in the program. The report takes details from the projects on resource assignment and keeps this report accurate throughout the execution of the program. As staff members come and go from the program or individual projects, those updates are reflected in a timely manner in this report. A monthly resource report is sufficient for most programs. During the development of this report, the Program Manager should also start the process of obtaining staff and resources for the program and applicable project activities. Creating this report is the perfect opportunity for the Program Manager to justify the staff and resources needed. You also want to make sure that you start this process earlier than later to ensure the staff is ready to go on time.

#	Task	Notes
3.	Develop a program role and responsibilities matrix	This RACI document covers all the program roles and deliverables. The RACI focuses specifically on program deliverables and should not be confused with a project RACI.
4.	Develop scope management plan	This plan documents the processes and procedures for managing scope at the program level. Project-level scope has its own method of handling scope changes that should include reporting back to the program level.
5.	Develop program cost report	The report includes the financial details for all components of the program.
6.	Develop program communication plan	This plan includes all aspects of program-level communications, including the various communications required at the project level. This plan should include the program status report, program and project schedule updates, program cost report, program issue and risk logs, and program benefits updates (using the program benefits table). Other details are program-specific and in-line with the needs and desires of the program stakeholders.
7.	Develop program master schedule	This schedule includes all program deliverables and tasks as well as the major milestone dates for all sub projects. It is highly recommended to use an environment such as Microsoft® Project Server for creating and linking a program schedule with individual project schedules. When creating the program master schedule, it is important to create and report on the program's work breakdown structure.
8.	Develop a program interdependency mapping report	This report includes all the interdependencies among the program and the projects included in the program. Another name for this report is an interface report.
9.	Develop a program quality report	This report documents the quality metrics of the program and the projects. If the program has a large quality component, this report documents the results performed in the quality testing, summarized at the program level.

#	Task	Notes
10.	Develop a program risk management plan	This plan includes how to manage program and project risks that are raised for executive-level visibility when there is a possibility of impacting other projects in the program.
11.	Develop a program issue management plan	This plan is similar to the program risk management plan, including how to manage program and project issues that are raised for executive-level visibility when there is a possibility of impacting other projects in the program.
12.	Develop a program change-management plan	This plan includes how program changes are to occur and how individual projects interact with the program when changes occur at the project level. Documenting how to assess and report the project-level changes at the program level is often a missed component of the change-management plan. This could include creating a change-management board at the program level only—all project-level changes go through the program-level board for changes.
13.	Develop a transition plan	This plan includes how the program and project activities occur after the program and projects end. This is a very important plan and one that sets up the program for future staff movement.
14.	Calendar of programs and projects	This calendar represents the major program timelines including timelines for all applicable projects in the program.
15.	Update program benefits table	This table documents all of the program benefits. This is the BVR document and often is updated during the planning process.
16.	Update business case analysis report	This report is updated as applicable. During the planning process, quite often, the analyst on the project updates this report.
17.	Develop applicable training plans on process or tools implemented during this phase	It is important that training plans and materials are created for any new processes or tools created during this phase.

Further Consideration Items:

The **Figure 9.5 Project Work Report Template** is used to manage projects and their associated activities that are attached to the program. The work report template provides Program Managers with a mini status report from the lead Project Managers who are managing their projects as part of the overall program. It is important to note that this is not a full status report, but a communications tool from the Project Managers to the Program Manager to keep the two in sync, so as not to add a lot of overhead to the Project Manager. The Project Manager could simply say, **"Go read my status report"** to the Program Manager; however, that's going to cause communication problems and is frankly unacceptable. This simple report takes little time to complete and update, and keeps the two parties connected and communicating on a regular bases.

Figure 9.5 Project Work Report Template

Work Report Template
Program Name: _____
Project Name: _____
Percent Complete: ____%
Project Color: Red
Project Specifics

Cost:	The project is estimated to be $100,000 over budget by April. Without additional funding the project will be over budget
Schedule:	The project is already 5 weeks late on the design phase. We are meeting next week with Management team to discuss
Scope:	The scope of the project is green and approved.
Quality:	The project has a quality management plan in place and hitting the defined targets
Resources:	There is a problem with the resources. The lead design engineer has given two weeks notice and leaving the company
Risks:	There are no major risks to report
Issues:	There are no major issues to report

Figure 9.6 Program's Work Breakdown Structure documents both the work deliverables of the program as well as the associated projects. This example represents the overall program and the various program tasks, as well as the projects associated with the program and its high-level milestones. This sample Program Work Breakdown Structure is the right level for most programs to capture program tasks and associated projects. It should be at the level that Program Managers are operating at as they execute their programs.

Figure 9.6 Program's Work Breakdown Structure

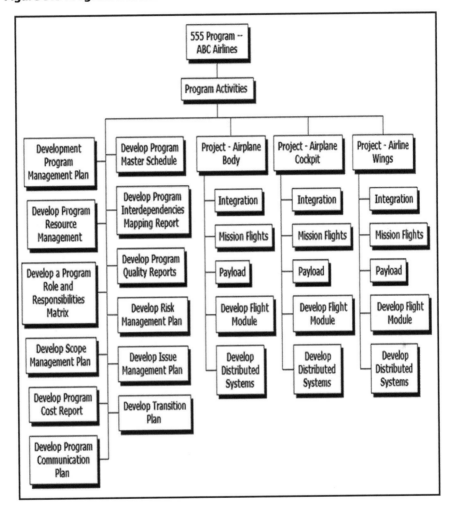

Figure 9.7 Program Calendar documents major program and project events occurring in the program. In this very simple, very basic example, you can see that there are three projects in the program that are projected to complete in April 2012. The value of the calendar tool is for the Program Manager to have the different dates readily available and to be able to communicate them whenever necessary. By using the calendar and having the major dates always in the forefront, the Program Manager will stay on top of and be alert to what is occurring in the program. The program calendar has proven to be a very valuable communication tool and is strongly suggested for every Program Manager.

Figure 9.7 Program Calendar

April 2012

SUNDAY	MONDAY	TUESDAY	WEDNESDAY	THURSDAY	FRIDAY	SATURDAY
		1	2	3	4	5
6	7	8	9	10	11	12
13	14 Design Project Complete	15	16	17	18	19
20	21	22	23	24	25 Foundation Project Complete	26
27	28	29	30	31 Architecture Project Complete		

Program Executing and Controlling Process

The executing process group contains the processes and procedures involved in driving the program work and activities related to the associated projects. The executing process from a program manager's perspective can be much more challenging than the same process at the project level due to the complexities and breadth required to keep everything proceeding in a large program. Both have challenges, but executing and controlling a program can be considerably more difficult.

The executing and controlling process involves managing the cost, quality, and schedule as an integrated plan while ensuring that benefits management, stakeholder management, and program governance are still the focus during the execution process. Oftentimes, Program Managers are tied down with the complexities of running the program, but if Program Managers pay less attention to monitoring and controlling the program's benefits, or how the stakeholders are tracking, serious program issues could arise. It is a common mistake for Program Managers to focus too much on how the program is executing and they completely forget about the benefits the program will obtain, or they don't consider the stakeholders as important. PMO Managers should make sure that their Program Managers are tracking and working closely to ensure benefits are being obtained, governance is on track, and stakeholders are satisfied and approve how the program is executing.

In **Table 9.6 Program Executing and Controlling Process**, the focus is for Program Managers to spend time driving the program through the execution process. Program Managers use this time to drive the program-specific deliverables as well as to keep track of the projects within their program. For most Program Managers, this is the busiest time after the planning phase, and this tends to be the time where most things will, and can, go wrong. Program Managers must continue to watch and report on all aspects of their programs—through the execution process—and stay in control of all aspects of their programs. I know this is easier said than done, but if Program Managers think about the key components of their role (budget, schedule management, scope, people management, and so on), they then would have the key areas where they should be focusing to manage their program. For example, think of a large program, such as the next release of a major operating system, and how many areas the lead Program Manager is responsible for to ensure that the operating system is successfully released. For a Program Manager to have all the balls in the air at one time, and have everything on track, is enormous and one of the most difficult parts of the role. You can imagine the hundreds of dependencies, interfaces, and possible things that can go wrong—the Program Manager's role is to keep it all together. The execution process is where most of these scenarios occur and where 90% of the program's life cycle occurs. The execution process occurs not only for the program itself, but also for the associated projects related to that program.

Tips & Best Practices

Remember that during the executing process, monitoring and controlling is critical to a Program Manager's success.

The controlling aspect of the Program Manager's role occurs naturally (or, should occur naturally) during the executing process. Controlling normally occurs during every process, but there is much more scrutiny that occurs during the execution process than any other. The planning process also includes a lot of controlling components as well, but the bulk of the controlling occurs in the executing process. Controlling, in this case, means much more visibility and accountability around the program and associated project schedules, budgets, risk and issue management, and benefits management just to name some of the key areas.

The following deliverables are required for Program Managers to complete during the execution process.

Table 9.6 Program Executing and Controlling Process

#	Task	Notes
1.	Deliver on program's communication plan per requirements defined in the initiation and planning process	In the initiation and planning phases of the program life cycle, the Program Manager focused on creating a program communications plan. The executing phase is the appropriate place to deliver and execute the program's communications components.
2.	Update and report program and associated project status	In the initiation phase, you created a program-level status report. Use that report during this phase, based on the requirements in the communications plan. It is important that the status report provides a realistic view of the program and associated projects. Do not sugar coat status; tell customers and management what the status is and whether it is good or bad. Exposing bad status early allows for change to occur.
3.	Update and report on the program benefits table	In the initiation phase, you created a benefits report. It is updated and reported on during this phase.
4.	Update and report project scope	In the initiation phase, you created the program's scope report. The execution phase is the perfect

#	Task	Notes
	report	time to report on how scope is progressing (or not progressing).
5.	Update and report on the program's work breakdown structure report	In the planning phase, you created the program's WBS. This is the time to update and keep it current.
6.	Update and report on the program's budget and cost report	In the planning phase, you created the program's cost report (including all budget details). This is the time to update and keep it current.
7.	Update and report on program and project resources	In the planning phase, you created the program's resource report. This is the time to update and keep it current.
8.	Update and report on program-level risks and issues	In the planning phase, you created a risk management plan and an issue management plan. This is the time to update them and keep them current.
9.	Update and report on program interdependencies	In the planning phase, you created the program's interdependencies mapping report. This is the time to update it and keep it current.
10.	Update and report on program quality components	In the planning phase, you created the program's quality report. This is the time to update and keep it current. During the execution process, quality testing and checking and auditing occurs. Therefore, it is important to update stakeholders and management on quality levels.
11.	Update and report on transition activities	This plan includes how the program and project activities occur after the program and projects end. This is a very important plan and one that is often created at the last minute by Program Managers, which is usually much too late in the program life cycle and, therefore, another area where the program gets behind and can impact the success of the program.
12.	Track and ensure project closures	At the end of project's life cycle, Program Managers should work with Project Managers to close projects in a timely manner when those projects are part of

#	Task	Notes
		the overall program.
13.	Update the program benefits table	This table documents all the benefits of the program and could certainly require updating as the program and projects are executing.

Program Closing Process

The program closing process includes the steps required to formally accept and close the deliverables of the program. It is also one of the most important processes in the overall program life cycle; however, it is also one of the processes that tends to be rushed and quickly completed with little thought or importance placed on it. As PMO Manager, it is important that you take the time and work with your Program Managers to make sure they are closing their program(s) correctly. They should ensure they have realized all possible benefits and should re-deploy all resources. Everything created during the initiation and planning phases of the program management methodology needs review and needs to be closed accordingly. Leaving loose ends or not closing programs properly often causes unnecessary overhead. For example, leaving a PO open and a vendor company billing to that same PO when everything in the program is closed is sloppy and can be easily prevented.

Consider the following key areas when closing a program:

- Did the program deliver the benefits outlined at the start of the program? Were those benefits accepted and approved by the stakeholders?
- Did the program fulfill any and all contractual obligations?
- Were the program's resources released and assigned to other areas?
- Are transition activities defined for the take-over team? (Depending on the industry, this could be the building owner, customer, operations department, and so on.)
- Were program deliverables approved and signed off by all stakeholders?
- Was it communicated to the stakeholders that the program is closing?
- Was the "lessons learned" meeting held and the information stored in a key repository for long-term reference?
- Did program and project financials get shut down (POs closed, final billing closed out)?

As you can see, there are a number of key questions and activities that need to occur to close a program. Your industry or organization might have some additional questions and you should not expect this to be a comprehensive list, but this should get you started in the right direction to closing your program. By the time the Program Manager hits this phase of the program, he or she should be able to answer these key questions and come up with many more relevant questions specific to the program. As PMO Manager, work with your Program Managers to make sure they are closing each area of their programs (cost, schedule, POs, and so on) appropriately.

Tips & Best Practices

A program might go on for many years, so hitting the closing process can be rare. If you do reach the closing process, follow these basic steps and ensure you obtain sign off before shutting everything down.

In **Table 9.7 Program Closing Process** the focus is for Program Managers to spend time and close the program deliverables correctly. Many times, program and project team members are assigned to new activities and new efforts and, therefore, closing and shutting down items is the last thing on their mind. However, that can't be the same thinking for the Program Manager. The Program Manager works with the project teams, customers, and management team to ensure that everything is closed properly.

The following deliverables are required for Program Managers to complete during the program closing process.

Table 9.7 Program Closing Process

#	Task	Notes
1.	Shut down main program repository	At the beginning of the program, you created a centralized repository for storing program and project documentation. At the end of the program, take the time to back up, and shut down the program repository.
2.	Obtain acceptance and formal approval from Program Manager	All relevant stakeholders on the project need to provide formal acceptance approvals.
3.	Conduct "lessons learned" session for program	This is an important step for Program Managers to drive for their initiatives. Program Managers should collect the lessons learned throughout the life of their program; however, having a formal meeting to wrap it up and close out is important. Program Managers should be involved in their project's respective lessons learned meetings.
4.	Seek approval and close benefits report	During the closing process, it is important for Program Manager to go over the expected program benefits with the customers or stakeholders to make sure they are happy and that the program achieved the expected benefits.
5.	Close all program documents	Program Managers should take the time to ensure that all program documents are approved, signed off, and closed.
6.	Update program benefits table	This table documents all the benefits of the program, and at the end of the program (or associated project), a final report of what

		was requested and what was delivered should be provided to the customers or stakeholders and management staff.

Summary

There are many different ways that organizations perform the program management discipline across the different industries and each has their merits and benefits. As PMO Manager, make sure that you are driving your Program Managers so that they are consistent and repeatable as to how they drive their programs. It is important to understand that there is no right or wrong way to manage programs. There is probably a much more efficient way to manage programs than how they are currently managed in your organization. You expect your Program Managers to try their best, to keep control of their programs, and report issues and risks that could prevent their programs from being successful. As PMO Manager, your role is to make sure your Program Managers are using the applicable deliverables across each of the program process areas described in this chapter to increase the chance of successfully running their programs.

PMO Build Decisions:

1. Decide based on the PMO Model you selected earlier, whether program management is part of your PMO.

2. Decide whether your PMO will have Program Managers and whether they will use a formal program management methodology.

3. Decide whether you will hire Program Managers (or will you, as PMO Manager, "share" the role)?

4. Determine if there will be a certified Six Sigma Black Belt resource available or will you have to hire them to help with the benefits realization work?

5. Decide whether Program Managers will be PgMP® certified.

6. Decide how you will audit program management processes and procedures outlined through the initiation and closing phases.

Chapter Review Answers:

1. Program Managers monitor and drive resolution on project issues, monitor and control project finances, and monitor and drive project quality across all projects in the program.

2. Monitor individual Program Managers' program management activities, drive organization planning, and drive benefits management.

3. The three steps include Value Identification, Value Analysis, and Value Planning.

4. The program kickoff meeting, which starts the program on the right foot and gives everyone a view into what is included in the program.

5. The program management oversight table is highly recommended for tracking and reporting benefits information about the program.

Chapter 10

Project Management Methodology

Figure 10.1 PMO Build Schedule - Project Management Methodology

Task Name	Resource Names
Step 5 - Design & Build or Enhance Period (Chapter 5 - 12)	**PMO Manager**
-Design PMO	**PMO Manager**
+ Design PMO Core Components	**PMO Manager**
Build PMO	**PMO Manager**
Create PMO Business Management Area on Centralized Repository Site (Sections to create are documented in Implementation Phase)	PMO Manager
+Create PMO Core Components	**PMO Manager**
+Create PMO Model (Chapter 5)	**PMO Manager**
+Create PMO Maturity Model	**PMO Manager**
+Create PMO Staffing Model (Chapter 6)	**PMO Manager**
+Create PMO Training (Chapter 7)	PMO Manager
+Create Process Methodology Areas (Chapters 8-10 - where applicable)	**PMO Manager**
+Create or Enhance Portfolio Management Methodology (Chapter 8)	**Portfolio Manager**
+Create or Enhance Program Management Methodology (Chapter 9)	**Program Manager**
+Create or Enhance Project Management Methodology (Chapter 10)	**Project Manager**
+Initiation	**Project Manager**
+Planning	**Project Manager**
+Executing & Controlling	**Project Manager**
+Closing	**Project Manager**
Document PMO Build Decisions	PMO Manager

Questions you should be able to answer after reading this chapter:

1. Why is it important to think about knowledge areas in projects?

2. What is one thing a PMO Manager should never do when rolling out a Project Management Methodology?

3. When do you collect "lessons learned" information about a project?

4. What is the difference between a life cycle area and a knowledge area?

5. What is the Circle of Communications?

One of the important components of successful PMOs is the use of a project management methodology. As PMO Manager, one of your main responsibilities is to drive and maintain the components of that methodology for your organization. There are many different project management methodologies used in the industry today, with the most popular being from PMI. PMI wrote the book, *Project Management Body of Knowledge Guide* (*PMBOK*® Guide), which outlines the components of a typical project management methodology. The nice thing about the *PMBOK* Guide is that it covers so many different industries that it is really the gold standard for project management methodologies. The downside being, however, for all the great information and comprehensiveness it provides, most organizations tend to think that it is too comprehensive and end up not using all of it. Many Project Managers assume that they need to use every aspect and component of the book, which is really far from the truth. It is actually a well-accepted practice for Project Managers to choose to use the components from the guide based on the project type, industry, and what makes sense for their projects. Think about it, it would be impossible for every component of the *PMBOK* Guide to have been used on every project. What you should consider, though, is that larger, more complex projects (building bridges or apartment buildings, for example) require much more rigor and many more components of the *PMBOK* Guide than a small software project requires.

As PMO Manager, the key to your success is to balance the flexibility and rigor that you add to your project management methodology in your organization to ensure that it makes sense for your projects. Your goal is to take the components that are fundamental to every project (schedule management, risk management, cost management, and so on) and build a methodology that will work for your projects, your organization's dynamics, and the amount of rigor you feel is necessary. Too much flexibility might cause Project Managers to ignore the methodology, while too much rigor around the methodology might cause them to feel like they do not have enough flexibility. You will hear that you are inflexible or that there are too many processes getting in their way. The key message to understand here is that there is a balance to what makes sense while still applying some level of rigor and process. As PMO Manager, in most companies you control that balance.

Throughout the book, we continue to talk about the importance of resources, procedures, and infrastructure and how those three areas are focus points for the PMO

Manager to adhere to and continually check on and validate as he or she builds and then executes the PMO. In the project management methodology, all three of those areas are applicable in this process. This is just another reminder to consider those factors as you look at the project management methodology and validate the three areas as you look at skill sets, new processes and deliverables, and the different project management tools we will cover in the details of the methodology.

Implementing a project management methodology in your PMO is just one component for a successful PMO. As PMO Manager, you also need to consider the PMO model you selected and how that model works with project management (as we discussed in earlier chapters, with portfolio and program management). PMO Managers need to watch what PMO Model they choose closely and the impact that project management methodology has on that model. As PMO Manager, the decisions on how Project Managers will execute on their projects is your responsibility and therefore the model and the processes and procedures that are in the project management methodology need to be aligned.

Other considerations PMO Managers need to think about when implementing a project management methodology are staffing, training, and possible mentoring opportunities. One thing a PMO Manager should never do is administer a project management methodology to Project Managers without support, training and ongoing guidance. Otherwise, the methodology could become a huge disaster and do more harm than good for the organization.

Finally, as with the portfolio and program management methodologies, you need to design and determine the right components for the project management methodology as well. No single project management methodology will work exactly for your company, so work with your Project Managers to design the right methodology for your organization, and then create and implement that methodology.

Let us move now into a project management methodology that will give you, the PMO Manager, the hands-on, tactical processes and steps to implement within your organization.

Project Management

In Chapter 8, "Portfolio Management Methodology," we established a portfolio management process. In Chapter 9, "Program Management Methodology," we created and outlined the program management methodology. Our next step is to create a project management methodology. Project management will most likely be the bread and butter and the basis of your PMO, as it is for most other PMOs, but it may not be the only component. Remember the four P's of PMOs? Well, you might recall that project management is just one of those P's and there are three other P's that can also be part of your PMO (one being the PMO itself). The other two are critical components: the portfolio management methodology and the program management methodology, but they are not required components of your PMO, while the project management methodology is not required, but will most likely be the dominant methodology in your organization. If you look across most PMOs, project management tends to be included in most of them, doesn't have to be, but usually is for most companies. That's also why having a solid project management methodology is so important to the success of your PMO. Also, the project management methodology will likely be special to you and something that, as PMO Manager, you can really own and drive for your organization because, in most cases, you come from a project management background and, therefore, it is probably near and dear to you. So, embrace this step of building your PMO because it is the one area in most companies that falls to you, the PMO Manager, to own and drive for your organization, where portfolio and program management can sometimes fall outside of the PMO purview in some companies.

What Is Project Management?

Project management is the discipline of planning, organizing, and managing resources to achieve specific goals. A project is a temporary endeavor with a defined start and end and, in most cases, a defined objective in mind. PMI developed a structured process for project management professionals that is industry leading and the crème de la crème of the project management industry. There are very few individuals in the project management industry who don't at least acknowledge the PMI framework and the impact it has had on the industry. The *PMBOK®* Guide is considered the bible for most Project Managers. As PMO Manager, you own and drive this methodology for your organization. As PMO Manager, it is a best practice for you to be the one who creates the project management methodology as well, so that you understand it, and can help drive your employees and provide them what you want done in each area. It is so important for you to drive your project management methodology for your organization and most successful PMO Managers find that out very quickly in their careers.

If you do not drive the project management methodology and set expectations for your Project Managers, you could definitely run into trouble managing and leading your PMO. However, when the PMO Manager spends the time to develop the processes/procedures, templates and the mechanisms for the project management methodology, and then works with his or her Project Managers to drive the projects using the methodology, he or she is much more successful. It is also a good way to test that the methodology is working, by working alongside of your employees and making updates and enhancements to the methodology where applicable. Now compare how successful this PMO Manager would be compared to another PMO Manager who finds a generic project management methodology on the web, and then tries to force fit it into the PMO, which typically doesn't work so well.

Tips & Best Practices

Executives in the software industry are often confused by the differences between a project management methodology and a software development methodology. Help drive clarity around the two and clear up the confusion whenever possible.

Throughout this chapter, the *PMBOK* Guide is the main source of the project management methodology that we will cover; however, it is impossible to implement the *PMBOK* Guide by itself. There are many more deliverables, tools, and best practices noted for your Project Managers to follow. If you have not developed a project management methodology before, that is okay, the process is simple. We will use the high-level components of the *PMBOK* Guide through this chapter, and your main job will be to take what we have here and enhance it based on your organization and project management requirements. By following industry standards for project management, across the five life cycle processes, and the nine knowledge areas, you will have an incredible advantage and will be able to put your Project Managers on the best path to success.

Who Are Project Managers?

Project Managers are unique individuals who require many different skills to be successful. There is great debate on what makes a good Project Manager. It depends on a number of factors, but the following are some qualifications to consider when selecting Project Managers for your PMO.

These qualifications include, but are not limited to the following:

- Leadership skills—a Project Manager is a leader; therefore, strong leadership skills are essential.
- People management skills—Project Managers must motivate, sustain, and keep the team working toward a common goal.
- Technical or business-related skills—Project Managers should have some skills or knowledge about the project type that they are managing. A software Project Manager will likely struggle to manage a construction project.
- Great communication skills—there is no question that 90% of a Project Manager's job is communicating; this is an essential skill.
- Problem-solving skills—Project Managers must be able to get in and lead, not necessarily solve every technical project problems, that can easily be done by the project team members.

This is just a sample list of some of the key skills required by Project Managers and a good starting point for PMO Managers who are hiring Project Managers for their PMOs. As PMO Manager, hire the people who are best suited in the Project Manager role—those who have the qualifications and skill sets to drive successful projects. Hiring people in order to grow them or force them to have these skill sets is frustrating for you and the individual. It is highly recommended to match the qualifications of the individual with the skills needed for the Project Manager role.

As PMO Manager, follow this chapter closely and use the *PMBOK* Guide as your reference point. By the end of this chapter, you will have what you need to create your own project management methodology, following the same concepts that we did for both the Portfolio Management and Program Management chapters.

As noted above, the *PMBOK* Guide is comprised of two major themes or topics that, as PMO Manager, you will need to create your PMO's project management methodology. They are: life cycle processes and knowledge areas. If you have spent any time in the industry, you would agree that every project includes each one of these components. Therefore, your project management methodology must have these same components as well. You will determine which components will work and are required for your organization, but it is important to make sure that you have at least something for each area. Not all projects are going to require all components of the life cycle process, or even all of the knowledge areas, but most will require at least some. Planning for everything and allowing Project Managers to decide what is right for their projects makes the most sense.

Before we get too far, let us review the life cycle process and document the knowledge areas as well.

The life cycle process group includes the following:

- Initiation/Initiating
- Planning
- Executing
- Monitoring and Controlling
- Closing

The knowledge areas include the following:

- Project Integration Management
- Project Scope Management
- Project Time Management
- Project Cost Management
- Project Quality Management
- Project Human Resource Management
- Project Communications Management
- Project Risk Management
- Project Procurement Management

Within each process or area, there will be activities that the Project Managers in your organization are responsible for performing during project execution. Exceptions to this process only occur when you, as PMO Manager, discuss and agree to them with your Project Manager. In some cases, that's the reality of project management: not all projects are going to require the same level of project management deliverables and the same level of rigor. What a PMO Manager needs to worry about the most is when your Project Manager doesn't use any rigor or any type of project management methodology on their projects.

Tips & Best Practices

Every project will incorporate the life cycle process. As PMO Manager, make sure you are driving the right standards and practices in those areas.

Project Management Life Cycle Process

As we start the process of creating your project management methodology, it does not matter whether you start by creating the tasks within life cycle process or by breaking down and creating the specifics of the knowledge areas. Both areas are just as important as the other, and both are needed to round out your completed project management methodology. You cannot really have one without the other, and it is best practice to follow the order in this chapter to create your own.

Before we start, though, let us make sure we understand the different life cycles of every project, regardless of size, industry, type, and so on. No matter what you think, and how hard you might fight it, every project will go through this life cycle process. It is an interesting dynamic really, because sometimes people do not realize that they are in a particular process or do not specifically call out that they are in one process or another. If you break down the life cycle process, you can't miss any of the following processes and still be doing a project.

- **Initiation/Initiating**—You have to start a project. Formal or informal, there is someone who says, "get this effort or thing started," and you start the activities to kick things off.
- **Planning**—This process is debatable because many Project Managers will say that they do not plan or have time to plan and, therefore, they do not really complete this process. I would debate that and say that planning is the most important process for kicking off a project and driving it forward. Even if a Project Manager isn't considering the time (limited, as it may be) in this process, he or she is indeed planning. Preparing the scope of the project, hiring resources, and generally getting prepared to drive the project all falls into the planning process.
- **Executing**—Executing is not something Project Managers call out as being a process; however, it is not really debatable whether every project includes this process because Project Managers acknowledge this as the phase where all the work gets done. In software, this tends to be when the coders are programming, or the testers are testing; and in construction projects, this tends to be when the plumbers are plumbing, the electricians are running wires, and the concrete folks are laying concrete. The "work" happens during this process.
- **Closing**—This process also does not get much attention from Project Managers, which again is a little short sighted of them because every project eventually ends. It can end successfully or end very badly, but it does end.
- **Controlling and Monitoring**—Project Managers rarely acknowledge this process as officially part of the project. They will all acknowledge, however, that without it, it is more difficult to keep projects on track, but there is no set timeframe associated to controlling or monitoring a project, it just happens throughout the project. When looking at **Figure 10.2 Project Life Cycle Process Group**, below, you will see how this process becomes over-arching and is completed throughout the life of the project. Most Project Managers do

not formally acknowledge this process. But remember, implementing change control or a sign-off process is a controlling function.

So, the life cycle processes will occur, but it is up to the Project Manager to decide what to do in each phase and whether to call out which process the project is in at any given time. As PMO Manager, though, it is definitely your responsibility to ensure that your Project Managers understand what to do during each process, know when they are in a process, and in the end successfully drive each process of the project. Therefore, it is also your responsibility to make sure that each process has specific activities outlined in your project management methodology and that you keep a watchful eye on your Project Managers to ensure they are completing the necessary steps in each process.

Figure 10.2 Project Life Cycle Process Group depicts the typical processes for any project. The processes will often overlap with one another and they have an over-arching process (Monitoring and Controlling) that helps move the project forward. Monitoring and Controlling tends to be the heaviest during the Executing & Controlling process because the lack thereof would send the project out of control and possibly toward failure. For example, imagine you are going to build a house. Would you give a team of people all the money they need to build that house and say, "See you in six months when you are done"? No, you would want to manage and watch the construction throughout the process and if anything were to come up, (for example, more budget needs), there would be processes in place to handle them. That is: Monitoring and Controlling, which is definitely a crucial process for any successful project life cycle.

Figure 10.2 Project Life Cycle Process Groups

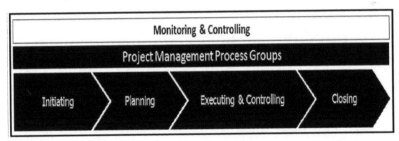

Does this figure look familiar? Many PMO Managers have seen it, or something like it, many times in different shapes and forms. However, even if you have seen it in different variations, one of the most important takeaways is that the Executing and Controlling processes are lumped together into one process and not separate processes. This is important because Executing and Controlling happens mainly during the execution of the project and rarely, if ever, do Project Managers execute projects with no control. As you can see in the figure, Monitoring and Controlling occurs during the entire life cycle process. Some might argue differently, and that is up to you and what you have experienced, but it is a best practice for PMO Managers to think about these processes as depicted in the figure.

Tips & Best Practices

Consider the overlap between the different life cycle processes. It is important to keep the overlap in mind while executing on your projects.

To conclude the life cycle process, it is important that as PMO Manager, you understand the process well and are able to guide your Project Managers through them on their projects. The ultimate reference for this material is in the *PMBOK* Guide; however, what you will find in this chapter that because it is tactical you should have what you need to implement in your PMO today.

Let us start with the Initiation/Initiating process.

Project Initiation Life Cycle Process

The Initiation/Initiating process is one of the most important processes for Project Managers, and those who do it right tend to be more successful. As PMO Manager, it is very important that you stay in touch with your Project Managers as they kick off their projects. Project Managers should execute the following set of tasks and deliverables for every project in your organization. The caveat being that projects and organizations will be very different and there is not one big comprehensive list that covers every possibility for every type of project. That is impossible. There are nine knowledge areas in every project, and the Initiation/Initiating process is the one place in the project where the Project Manager can think about those nine areas. **Table 10.1 Project Initiation Process** is just a starting point and a guide for the Initiation/Initiating process, but the key components are certainly there and applicable to most, if not all, projects. As PMO Manager, you should enhance this list for your organization.

It is also important to note that the order in which the Project Manager develops the project management deliverables is not important as long as the deliverables are created and ready for the planning phase of the project. The important thing is that you have them and you use them to drive your project.

As we move through the remainder of this chapter (also discussed in Chapters 8 and 9), we will document industry best practices and standard deliverables for Project Managers to follow as they execute their projects. Also, as noted above, the enforcement that you, as PMO Manager, follow for your Program Managers is the same for your Project Managers. It is important that you treat the Portfolio, Program, and Project Managers the same when it comes to enforcing standards and best practices. Refer to the Chapters 8 for Portfolio Management Methodology and in Chapter 9 for the Program Management methodology for more information on those methodologies.

Remember, projects are different across the various industries and because of that, there is a no single comprehensive list of all activities in the project life cycle process. The lists are comprehensive, but not complete. As noted previously, it would be impossible to create such a list for anyone. The deliverables in the following table will definitely give your Project Managers a great starting point and will give you, the PMO Manager, a starting point for auditing your Project Managers' work as they execute their project.

Tips & Best Practices

An important note about the following table is that the tasks and deliverables are specific to the Project Manager on the project. Other roles on the project will likely have other deliverables to create, but this table purely reflects the items for the Project Manager.

Table 10.1 Project Initiation Process outlines the tasks and deliverables for the Initiation phase of the project. This is a very busy time for most Project Managers because not only is there pressure to get the project up and running, but there are a number of deliverables needed to start the project.

Table 10.1 Project Initiation Process

#	Task/Deliverables	Notes
1.	Develop a project charter document	This important document formally authorizes and kicks off the project. Most projects, with few exceptions, require a project charter document. This document provides the scope, objective, and participants in a project. Some companies have existing project charter templates (or you can find hundreds of templates on the web).
2.	Develop a project management plan	This plan includes all the major steps to drive the project. Common items include: resource management, communication management, and scope management plans...etc. Some companies have existing project management plan templates (or you can find hundreds of templates on the web).
3.	Develop project kickoff materials	Most companies have predefined tasks for kicking off a project. Complete those tasks at this time and make sure that you understand your company's processes/procedures to initiate a project. These kickoff tasks will also vary from industry to industry, so look for company specific requirements to kicking off your projects.
4.	Obtain project budget information and create a budget spreadsheet	It is imperative to understand the budget from the beginning of the project and to establish a reporting process. Project Managers must report financial status weekly, throughout the life of the project. Again, the timing (weekly) need to match what is applicable to your project. A multiple year project for example, it is not likely that a weekly financial report would be that valuable, in that case a monthly report would be more appropriate.

#	Task/Deliverables	Notes
5.	Develop an initial project schedule with initial dates and high-level deliverables	It is important to have at least a high-level schedule at the beginning of the project.
6.	Develop a "lessons learned" process and repository for storing ongoing lessons learned information	Collecting and storing Lessons Learned information allows Project Managers to have this information to make course corrections on their projects. Tracking this data from the beginning of the project prevents trying to scramble and collect it at the end when team members have moved onto other efforts. Having the information at the start and throughout also allows course corrections along the way. This process is very important to stress to your Project Managers.
7.	Create a centralized project repository for storing all project information	This centralized location is for sharing project information. It is critical to make sure that everyone on the project has access to the information they need. This can be an internal website, a shared directory, drive, and so on.
8.	Develop a project communications plan	This plan includes all aspects of how Project Managers communicate project information.
9.	Develop a project roles and responsibilities document	This very important document should be created during the Initiation/Initiating process to ensure that everyone is on the same page regarding roles and responsibilities throughout the life of the project. Creating this document late in the project can lead to project team members not being responsible or accountable for tasks and items being missed.
10.	Prepare purchase orders or any acquisition-type documents to ensure you have the right staff identified for the project	The Initiation/Initiating process is the time to define which resources (staff or other resource types) and to start the process for hiring them onto the project.

#	Task/Deliverables	Notes
11.	Develop the project's change control process	This process will be used and tested through the life of the project. Therefore, it is important to create the change control process before the project gets too far. This includes all templates, forms, processes, and the project team locking this process on obtaining approvals for changes, long before there is ever a single change request. Some companies have existing project change requests processes already (or you can find hundreds of Change control processes on the web). If you don't already have a change request process in your organization, see Chapter 12, "PMO Tools and Processes."
12.	Develop a project governance	This process acts as governance for controlling the direction and path of the project. All projects require a governance process to ensure stakeholders, management are aligned and tracking with the direction of the project. **Note:** In the Program Management methodology (Chapter 9), we also talk about creating a Governance structure. Work with your Program Manager and determine if you want both a Program and Project Governance structure.
13.	Develop a project escalation process	This process acts as an escalation path and provides project teams with the path to management and stakeholders to make decisions, provide status, and guide the direction of the project.
14.	Develop the project organization chart	This organization chart is so important, simple to create, but powerful in that team members and management can see who is on the team. It is highly recommended to use the project organization chart where possible on your projects.

#	Task/Deliverables	Notes
15.	Develop a project status reporting process	This includes the initial project status report, defining the template, timeframes for report delivery, working with the customer on what they want to see in the report, and so on. It is important that your different project leads (software would include Dev. Lead, Test Lead...etc.) also define and work through their status reporting process. Project Managers work with their leads and define this process.
16.	Develop a human resources plan that includes any and all resources required for the project	This is the perfect time to review staffing and resource needs and to document those needs in this plan. Complete this prior to the Planning process because of the time it generally takes to obtain resources and how short most planning cycles are for projects, you don't want to have resources missing at critical times in the project.
17.	Develop a quality management plan	During this early phase, the quality of the product, service, or end result is the last thing on anyone's mind. It is the Project Manager's responsibility to start this plan now and to get people thinking about it early in the process. This plan is often left for the end or is never produced. Starting it now gets people thinking about quality very early in the process.
18.	Develop the scope management plan	Scope management is often one of the most difficult components of a project to manage and is often tough to manage without some sort of plan in place as to how you will manage changes through the life of the project.
19.	Develop an action item log	Action items are very important for project delivery and having a formal log to assign and track action items is important to keep projects organized and on track.
20.	Create a project transition plan template	The Project Manager creates the project transition template for their project. The purpose of the document is that it acts as a

#	Task/Deliverables	Notes
		transition plan when one project manager leaves and another one has to take over. The document is to be kept up to date at all times and stores the critical information about the project allowing transition between the two project managers to go smoothly.
21.	Develop project milestone presentation templates	Project Milestone presentations are used on all major milestones for the project. Project Managers should take an active role in driving the creation and use of these presentations for their projects.
22.	Develop applicable training plans for process or tools implemented during this phase	It is important that training plans and materials are created for any new processes or tools created during this phase.

To conclude the Initiation/Initiating process, there are a tremendous number of processes and procedures to set up your Project Managers for success. Many Project Managers are faced with a lot of pressure to get the project started and to get team members working, which tends to rush Project Managers through this process. Taking the time to perform the activities and create the deliverables listed in **Table 10.1 Project Initiation Process** will help your Project Managers be successful. As PMO Manager, you can use the items in the table as a checklist for your Project Managers to follow as they work and execute their projects.

Project Planning Life Cycle Process

The Planning process is one of the shortest but most difficult components of the life cycle process group. You will be surprised to know that many Project Managers often blow right past this phase. They do; it is one of the most important areas of project management, yet it gets the least amount of time and attention. As PMO Manager, instill in your Project Managers the importance of taking the time to plan projects appropriately. The Planning process is the time to set up and establish what your project is going to be all about. From a Project Manager's perspective, this is the time to establish how to run the project. Allow your Project Managers to spend the time to develop the core documents for driving and running their projects.

In the project management methodology, especially in this planning section, you will notice that many of the plans are created during the Planning process (if you are following PMI's *PMBOK* Guide). It is highly recommend, however, that Project Managers start this process during the Initiation process, as noted in the table above. As PMO Manager, you should also support this decision and understand that starting (not finishing) these documents sooner rather than later is preferred. Project Managers spend much more time in the Initiation process of the project than they do in the Planning process, even though planning is really the most important component of the various project life cycles. If you don't plan the project properly, think about the problems you will have executing and controlling the project.

Table 10.2 Project Planning Process puts the focus for Project Managers on time and energy for planning the execution of the project. Some of the items not necessarily important during the Initiation process are important here. Risk and issue management, for example, can be completed during the Planning process and not necessarily during the Initiation/Initiating process. The tasks in the following table are specific to project planning.

Table 10.2 Project Planning Process

#	Task/Deliverables	Notes
1.	Update and enhance the master project schedule	The initial plan has already been started, the project's methodology has been created with the schedule, and a separate project management arm has been created. During the Planning process, the plan continues to be refined and major deliverables are added to the plan. Resources and assignments are also refined. It is also important that Project Managers are starting to develop a work breakdown structure (WBS) from the project schedule. Make sure the WBS is broken down to the lowest possible level and that level aligns to your reporting period.

#	Task/Deliverables	Notes
2.	Develop the risk management plan	Document and define the processes for capturing and tracking risks on the project.
3.	Develop the issue management plan	Document and define the processes for capturing and tracking issues on the project.
4.	Update and enhance the budget spreadsheet with information obtained during the Planning process	Budget tracking and budget requirements often vary from company to company. Project Managers must ensure that they follow the financial processes of the company.
5.	Update the governance model for the project	Governance models are required for good project control and for leadership visibility. All projects require some form of governance. Ensure that during this phase the model is agreed upon and signed off.
6.	Update the escalation model for the project	In some cases, escalation is part of the governance model, but often it is not. Either way, make sure it is documented and approved during the Planning process. For more information, see Chapter 12, "PMO Tools and Processes" for an escalation process that you can follow if you don't already have one in your PMO.
7.	Update a quality management plan for the project	During the Planning process, it is a perfect time to determine what level of quality will be accepted on the project. Updating this plan during Planning process will get everyone thinking early in the project about how to tackle this very important component.
8.	Update procurement documents, purchase orders, or any other purchasing related documentation	It is crucial that the procurement process is locked and executed before the project officially starts. It is also important that all resources are hired and in place during the Planning process, long before the official work on the project begins. Hiring resources early, before the scheduled work starts, will help to ensure that your project has the resources available when needed.

#	Task/Deliverables	Notes
9.	Develop applicable training plans for process or tools implemented during this phase	It is important that training plans and materials are created for any new processes or tools created during this phase.

To conclude the Planning process, there are many items to complete in a very short period. As in many organizations, the Initiation/Initiating and Planning processes are often short changed from a time perspective and management and leadership are usually pushing Project Managers to get going on the project and deem planning as unnecessary or not that important. When that occurs, Project Managers need to push back and enforce the creation of the planning deliverables listed in **Table 10.2 Project Planning Process**. Without these deliverables, Project Managers struggle with their projects. Several projects have failed due to lack of up-front project planning. As PMO Manager, help your Project Managers be successful and fight for them to get the time they need to plan their projects accordingly.

Project Executing and Controlling Life Cycle Processes

The Executing process is one of the most important processes in managing a project. As PMO Manager, your Project Managers will look to you for support throughout this process. You might be asked to review a presentation before a big meeting or confirm the contents of a communication plan—Project Managers will constantly be looking for support and guidance. It is important to combine the two processes (Executing and Controlling) into one process. PMI keeps the two processes separate in their documentation, and that makes sense, but for a project management methodology, it is a best practice to keep them together. Hence, it was decided to combine them for our purposes in this book.

This is also where, as you create a project management methodology, you need to have as many processes and procedures in place as possible, so that if your Project Managers run into issues on their projects, they have a process and procedure to follow. This is usually the busiest time of the project for the Project Managers because, like people often say, "This is when the real work gets done" and Project Managers are most active in driving and providing status on the progress of the project. As PMO Manager, support your Project Managers during this process and dive into the details of the projects and help out where you can.

Project management deliverables for the Executing and Controlling processes, in most cases, are the deliverables that were created during the Planning and Initiation/Initiating processes. The focus for the deliverables is to communicate project information to customers, leadership, and to anyone who is interested in project status. The various status reporting tools in the Executing and Controlling processes ensure that you are providing project information to the right people, at the right time, to make the right business decisions.

Table 10.3 Project Executing and Controlling Processes focuses on updating or enhancing most of the existing tools already developed prior to moving to this process in the project. Again, the order in which you create these project management deliverables is not relevant, just having and driving the project management deliverables for your project is an important part of setting up your project for success. Because this process is about executing, not necessarily planning or kicking things off, you will notice that this table is much shorter than the Initiation/Initiating process or Planning process tables.

Table 10.3 Project Executing and Controlling Processes

#	Task/Deliverables	Notes
1.	Update the project management plan	This is an important time to review the project management plan to determine whether you are managing the project the way you expected. What you decided during the Initiation/Initiating process might not be how you are actually managing it. Change directions where applicable, but take the time and update this plan during this process.
2.	Update the project schedule and report progress throughout this process	As the project progresses, it is important to make sure that management, customers, and others are watching and tracking the project schedule. Make sure that you are reporting the project schedule as defined by the customers in the communication plan.
3.	Update and track finances, weekly	Using the financial spreadsheets set up during the Initiation/Initiating process, watch project finances on a weekly basis (see note earlier about appropriate timing). Project Managers track the financial costs of their projects weekly and should have a snapshot-in-time each week of their project's financial data.
4.	Update "lessons learned" information	Make sure that you are tracking lessons learned information throughout the life of the project, especially during this process when most of the work is occurring. It is very important not to wait until this phase to start tracking lessons learned because you might have missed issues that happened during the Initiation/Initiating and Planning processes.
5.	Perform a communications check with customers, leaders, and appropriate stakeholders	Making sure that the right people are getting the right information is a critical component to being successful during this process. Sit down with stakeholders and make sure they are getting the information they need.

#	Task/Deliverables	Notes
6.	Review how the team is performing against the RACI	With the team in the Executing process, this is a perfect time to check in and determine if everyone is closely following the RACI. Project Managers must ensure that team members are following the RACI throughout the project.
7.	Status reporting and leadership presentations	Project Managers should make sure they are sending project status information based on the timing requirements of the customers, leaders, or other stakeholders. Most software projects, for example, send out weekly status reports; however, a weekly status might not be applicable for large construction projects that might find using a monthly status report more appropriate to the timing of those larger types of projects.
8.	Update the change control process, where applicable	The change control process will likely be used the most during this process, so make appropriate updates to the process.
9.	Update the scope management process, where applicable	As the project is executing, one of the trade-off decisions that often becomes part of project execution is the project's scope. A scope management process is often tested and used during this phase. There might be areas where this process needs updating.
10.	Update the quality management plan, where applicable	As the project is executing, make sure you are tracking the quality of deliverables. The defined quality parameters made during the Planning process are put to the test during this process. Update the quality plans, tests, and parameters during this process.

To conclude the Executing and Controlling processes, the tasks and processes are about controlling every area of the project, not necessarily about creating new deliverables. The majority of project deliverables are created by Project Managers during the Initiation/Initiating and Planning processes. This phase is much more concentrated on status and keeping the project moving forward towards a successful end. There are definitely deliverables in this process, but they are not the focus. The focus is on how the team is executing towards the end result, product or service. As PMO Manager, you have a clear set of deliverables and areas where you can focus your

Project Managers to help them drive their projects. You can look for consistency from your Project Managers as they execute their projects if they follow the components in these tables. Make sure that you are helping your Project Managers keep constant control and oversight on their projects and be active in reviewing their project deliverables and status reports and help out where you can on their projects. Oftentimes, Project Managers need someone to listen to them, someone to bounce questions off of, and someone to run scenarios by of what is occurring on their projects or where they are having trouble. This is an extremely busy time for your Project Managers, so be there to support them where you can.

Project Closing Life Cycle Process

The Closing process is one of the quickest, but one of the least addressed, processes of all of them. However, it is actually very important and something that should not be taken lightly by any Project Manager. Project Managers work on projects from the Initiation/Initiating process through the Closing process, so they need to take this process as seriously as all the other processes and not rush through it. As PMO Manager, it is important to define the Closing process and procedures for your Project Managers to follow and ensure that they keep their eye on the ball and shut down the project appropriately, completing all the processes defined in this section. Of course there will be differences among the various industries, but the core Closing process to close a project generally remains the same.

Table 10.4 Project Closing Process focuses on closing down a project's activities. The processes defined here wrap up the project as a whole, release the resources, close all financials, and shut down the project. By the end of this process, the Project Manager should be able to walk away from the project with no outstanding activities.

Table 10.4 Project Closing Process

#	Task/Deliverables	Notes
1.	Project documentation cleanup	Has the project documentation (Business Requirements Document, Functional Specifications document, or Technical specifications documents been updated and close off with all applicable approvals.
2.	Project team roll-off plan	Have the project resources moved onto new roles? Do you know their new roles or have you worked to secure them new roles?
3.	Support team handoff	Regardless of the industry, typically when a project completes, a new team takes over. This could be an operations team, a building maintenance company, and so on. Someone or some team will generally take over. As Project Manager, ensure you have identified this team and understand who you "turn the keys over to" when the project is complete.

#	Task/Deliverables	Notes
4.	"Lessons learned" review	Perform the lessons learned process established by the company. If Project Managers have tracked the Lessons Learned information from the beginning of the project, they would have been recording their lessons learned throughout the project. Therefore, by the time they are at the Closing process, they should have a great deal of lessons learned information to share with the team, customers and the leadership team.
5.	Obtain official signoff and approvals from customers, managers, and stakeholders	Typically, it is critical to obtain official signoff from the customers, and managers on acceptance and transferring of the project from the current project team to an ongoing team. Every industry will be different on how they handle it, but every project must a formal acceptance process.
6.	PO and financial closeout	Close all open POs, SOWs, or anything related to the financials of the project. Work with your financial team to close requisitions or any open spending for the project. This is something that Project Managers often forget and therefore important to call out.
7.	Close all documentation	This is a good opportunity to close all project documentation. The documentation needs to be finalized, and then shared in the document control system for future reference. Review the various documents for the project and finalize them.
8.	Send final project status information, thanking everyone involved in the project	It is important for the Project Manager to send the final email with the project wrap-up information and thank you(s) to the project team. It

#	Task/Deliverables	Notes
		is a very professional way to close the project as well as end the project on a high note. As PMO Manager, strongly encourage your Project Managers to send the final email to the customers, team, management, and any relevant stakeholders.

To conclude the Closing process, it is important for Project Managers to focus on closing the project in an organized manner. Very often, Project Managers will complete the project as quickly as possible to move onto a new project. When this occurs, they tend to forget items that are important to properly closing the project. Forgetting to get approval signatures, recording lessons learned, shutting down POs or any procurement activities because they are rushed to start their next project is a major issue and happens all the time. As PMO Manager, work closely with your Project Managers during this time to ensure they close their projects in a timely manner. It is the proper thing to do for everyone.

As we summarize this section, PMO Managers, it is important that you stay on top of the different activities and processes/procedures outlined across the five life cycle processes. Organizations are very dynamic and things change all the time; therefore, you must remember not to stall or stagnate processes within your methodology or your Project Managers will feel like these items are overhead and will not complete them. Keep these processes fluid and keep things flexible and make sure, at the minimum, you do a yearly review of the materials and make changes only if necessary.

Project Management Knowledge Areas

It is important to understand the five life cycle processes and ensure that all Project Managers follow the processes in their projects. Project Managers also need to understand the nine knowledge areas. Again, these are defined by PMI and are industry standards for all projects, regardless of the industry, size, or type. If you have a project, you will hit most of these knowledge areas somewhere during the life of managing your project. The only exception might be Project Procurement Management; you might not necessarily have a project with procurement activities. All others areas, though, tend to be in most projects.

One of the important tasks that PMO Managers need to consider when working with the different knowledge areas is to ensure that they have defined the right processes and procedures for each knowledge area. This allows your Project Managers to have something to follow during project execution. There is nothing worse than a Project Manager who is only loosely executing the different knowledge areas and only working the areas they deem necessary. For example, one Project Manager follows Project Scope Management, using best practices and techniques, and another Project Manager lets scope go haywire. You want to control how Project Managers are executing the processes so you can step-in and provide guide whenever necessary. If your project managers are making new processes or not following the standard processes/procedures, if you need to step in and help, you will be stuck learning something new. This could be time consuming and have a negative impact on the project. By having a standard set of processes, it lends nicely to having a standard approach to how your Project Managers work with each knowledge area on their projects. Establishing rigor and a standard set of processes for Project Scope Management, for example, gives the PMO Manager the ability to not only understand how the Project Managers are executing scope management, but also gives the customers a consistent experience from the different Project Managers they are working with across all of their projects. It is a best practice to give customers a consistent experience across multiple projects and not vary processes from project manager to project manager.

So, let us move now into each knowledge area. As PMO Manager, ensure that your project management methodology has each knowledge area documented and that you have defined the processes and procedures for your Project Managers to follow on their projects. There is definitely some flexibility based on project type, size, and other complexities, but generally, the details outlined in each knowledge area are a minimum and should be followed across all projects.

Tips & Best Practices

Knowledge areas and life cycle processes are very different. Both are needed on every project.

Figure 10.3 Knowledge Area Circle specifies the various knowledge areas applicable to most projects. An interesting component of the knowledge area circle is that there is no order to how Project Managers work the knowledge areas, with one exception. That exception is the Project Integration Management knowledge area, which is always the first area to start with on projects. The eight other areas do not need to follow a particular order. There are more details below about integration, but this is the one area that Project Managers must process first for their projects. The interesting thing about looking at the knowledge areas in a circle is that there is a perception of no order to how they are worked. There appears to be no start or end to the process, and finally, no dependencies, which is a bit of a misnomer because the knowledge areas are definitely connected. We will go into the connection of the knowledge areas later in this chapter.

Figure 10.3 Knowledge Areas Circle

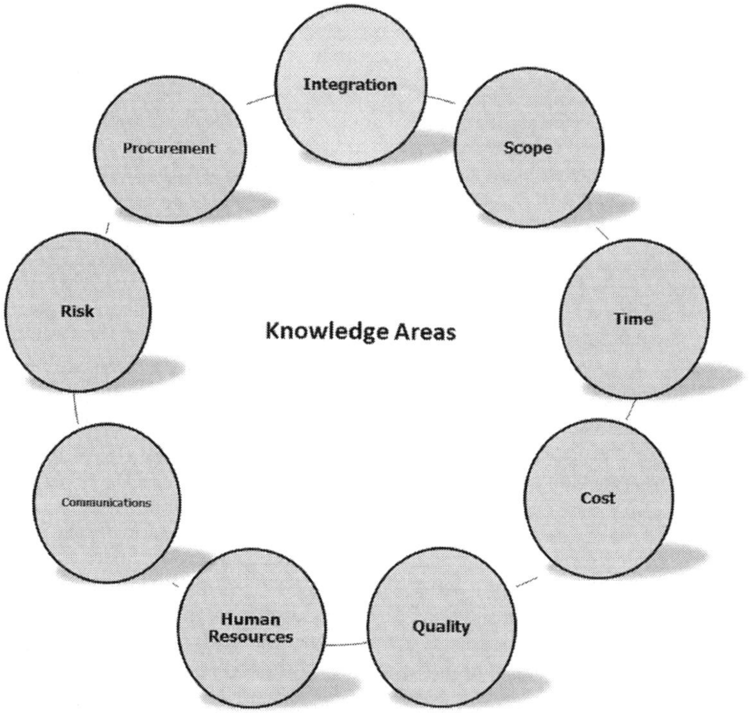

There is such a great significance of this circle from a project execution perspective. It is expected that PMO Managers will quickly grasp the relevance of this circle and how different knowledge areas work together. As PMO Manager, you should work with your Project Managers to ensure they grasp this concept as well, and that they are driving their projects thinking about how the different knowledge areas all work together. Let us look at one example now on the Project Communications Management knowledge area and how it connects to the other knowledge areas.

Figure 10.4 Project Communications Management Knowledge Area Circle
shows the most prevalent knowledge areas applicable to the Project Communications
Management knowledge area. That's complex right? Well, actually it's simple because if
you think about the main knowledge area (communications), and then think about all
the different things that need to be communicated during the project and which
knowledge areas they fall into. Clearly, a few come to mind: scope, cost and time are
the three that most people care about on projects. All three are knowledge areas and,
therefore, they are most relevant to the Project Communications Management
knowledge area. There is no right or wrong answer to which areas are the most
relevant and which are not; however these circles provides a guideline for project
managers to follow and consider on their projects. Project Managers will make their
own choices as to which areas they feel they need to connect or not and the knowledge
area circles just give them a starting place.

Figure 10.4 Communication Knowledge Area Circle

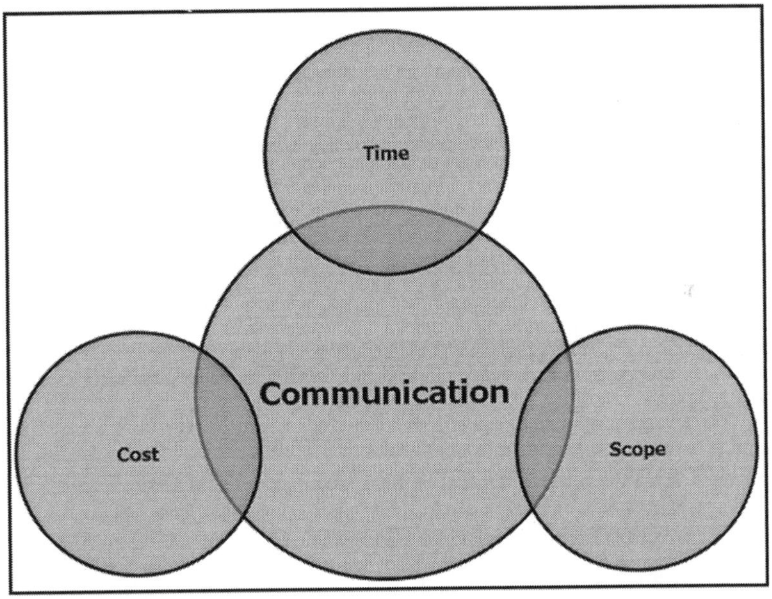

In the sample Project Communications Management knowledge area circle, I associated
the following three knowledge areas are closely associated with communications:
Project Scope Management, Project Time Management, and Project Cost Management.
Because communication is crucial in project management, this circle could include many
more associated knowledge areas and we will see the full example later in the chapter.
Again, this is just a small example to get you to understand the concepts of the various
knowledge areas working and associating with one another.

When Project Managers think about the circle concept (which knowledge areas work
together), as PMO Manager, you can feel comfortable that your Project Managers are at

least considering the key components of each knowledge area. Because they are likely watching them closely, they are set up for a better chance of success on their projects. As PMO Manager, it is important that you continue to give them the guidance and direction around these knowledge areas and show them how they tie together with other knowledge areas so that they continue to think about them as they execute their projects. Just thinking about the different knowledge areas and how they work together is a huge start for many project managers.

Let us move now into the first knowledge area: Project Integration Management, as this is the first knowledge area that Project Managers face when establishing and kicking off a project. Look for the Project Integration Management knowledge area circle as the starting point for all projects.

Project Integration Management Knowledge Area

The Project Integration Management knowledge area includes the various processes and procedures to ensure that the elements of driving a project are coordinated, such as the project plan development and execution, and project control (for example, the change control process). This knowledge area is such an important process and often considered low priority to Project Managers who tend to be in such a hurry to start a project. The Project Integration Management knowledge area is closely associated to the project Initiation process documented earlier in this chapter. There is also a tie between the Project Integration Management knowledge area and the Closing process but, in reality, the two are rarely associated with each other. During the Project Integration Management phase, one of the components includes the project Closing process and closing documentation, which occurs at the end of the project, not at the beginning, where the other components of Project Integration Management are associated. This is a disconnect that is in the *PMBOK* Guide, and at this point, has not been corrected. It is something worth noting and, as PMO Manager, something to make sure that your Project Managers are aware of while managing their projects.

Tips & Best Practices

The Project Integration Management knowledge area ties in very nicely with the Initiation/Initiating life cycle process. Make sure to understand them both and how they are aligned.

The **Figure 10.5 Project Integration Management Knowledge Area Circle** shows the various knowledge areas applicable to integration. The following knowledge area components are directly related to Project Integration Management: Project Communications Management, Project Cost Management, Project Scope Management, and Project Human Resource Management. These areas are the most relevant because this is the first time in the life cycle of a project where processes are being kicked off so Project Managers are focusing their time and efforts mainly in these four areas. As noted above, Project Integration Management is about pulling the key components and processes together to ensure that the project is driven in a coordinated manner; these four areas are crucial to making that happen. Project Communications Management is important across the board and specifically communicating how the Project Manager is kicking off the project is an important step in this process. By communicating "how" he or she is going to manage the project is important so that everyone understands what is happening through the Project Integration Management process. Communicating the cost, scope, and resources of the project early and often is critical in driving a successful project. The communication techniques that the Project Manager establishes during the Project Integration Management phase of the project sets the foundation for how they will communicate throughout the project. If those practices are also documented in a communications plan, the project communications will be formalized and everyone will be on the same page as to what and how communications occur during the project.

Figure 10.5 Project Integration Management Knowledge Area Circle

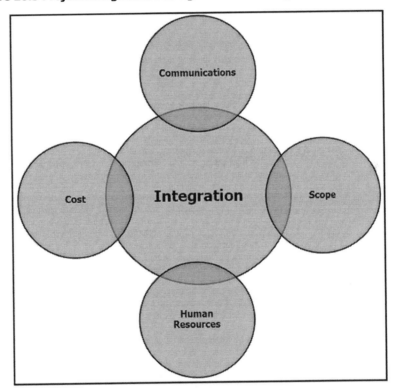

Table 10.5 Project Integration Management Knowledge Area focuses on many components of managing a project ranging from project plan development to project execution and control. The processes outlined in this table below all focus on setting up and kicking off a project. It is important to look at this tasks or activities as a minimum

set during the initial stages of a project and can certainly be added too based on industry or company standards.

Table 10.5 Project Integration Management Knowledge Area

#	Task	Notes
1.	Develop the project's document control system	Create a central repository where all project documents are stored. This can be an intranet site, a drive on a local area network (LAN), and so on.
2.	Implement the project charter	**Note:** The project charter document was created during the project Initiation process, which was discussed earlier in this chapter.
3.	Implement the project management plan	**Note:** The project management plan document was created during the project Initiation/Initiating process, which was discussed earlier in this chapter. Project management plans are underutilized project documents; however, they are critical for establishing how Project Managers will drive their projects.
4.	Implement the change control process	**Note:** The change control process was established during the project Initiation/Initiating process, which was discussed earlier in this chapter.
5.	Develop a help wanted log	A help wanted log in a document control system is a great way to understand the various asks on your project.
6.	Develop a configuration management plan	This document manages how you make changes to the deliverables and the resulting documentation.
7.	Develop a project escalation process	This process should be included in your project governance process, however some projects do keep these separate sometimes. This documents how the escalation process should occur on the project. Escalations occur all the time and not having an escalation process can quickly derail the project.

#	Task	Notes
8.	Develop a decision tracker log	Tracking decisions is a very mature project management technique and something that Project Managers sometimes neglect to set up on their projects.
9.	Develop the project's status meeting and report cadence	This is such an important process and one that requires getting on top of early in the project. It is important to align the meeting agenda and the expected items to report on in the status report. Often, Project Managers have one opportunity a week to pull together the project team and therefore have to make best possible use of the time.
10.	Develop the project's organization chart	This communication tool is so important to have available for the project team, customers, and management. Knowing who's who on a project can be valuable in bringing the team together, driving morale, and helping the team connect as unit.

To conclude the Project Integration Management Knowledge area, it is one of the more important areas in understanding how to start, control, and close your project activities. This knowledge area is about pulling everything together and kicking off your project successfully. As PMO Manager, make sure your Project Managers use **Tables 10.1 Project Initiation Process Table and Table 10.5 Project Integration Management Knowledge Area table** documented above, to set up a successful project. Because the project Initiation/Initiating process and the Project Integration Management knowledge area are so closely tied together, connecting the activities outlined in the two tables is important.

Project Scope Management Knowledge Area

The Project Scope Management knowledge area includes the processes to ensure that all of the work that is required for the project. This area also includes documenting work that is not required as part of the project (out of scope)—and it can't be stressed enough how important it is to document out-of-scope work as well. By doing so, questions, and missed expectations of what is in and out of scope for the project are limited.

Project Scope Management includes the processes and procedures the team follows to ensure that the project includes all the work, and only the work required for the project. Anything that is not part of the project's scope is deemed "out of scope" and is not included in the activities for the project. How Project Managers manage project scope is an important part of their role. This is something that Project Managers can share with other members of the team so that everyone is aware of the Project Scope Management process. For example, PMO Managers have seen Project Managers share the scope setting responsibilities with Business Analysts and Functional Analysts on some projects.

Figure 10.6 Project Scope Management Knowledge Area Circle shows the various knowledge areas that are applicable to the management of the project's scope. As shown in this knowledge area circle, Project Communications Management, Project Risk Management and Project Integration Management are the most relevant knowledge areas that closely align with Project Scope Management. Project Communications Management is closely aligned because it is important to ensure that everyone is aware of and agrees to the project scope. Project risks are always an important component of Project Scope Management process as well because they document potential problems with the scope and can play a major role in whether some scope can be included in the project. For example, the risk involved by not receiving the appropriate budget for the project can dramatically reduce the project scope. Project Integration is an important of the Scope Management process as it is the process that drives the setup, planning, execution and control of a project and therefore would important and critical to the scope management process. The other knowledge areas are important to scope management, just not as important as these three areas.

Figure 10.6 Project Scope Management Knowledge Area Circle

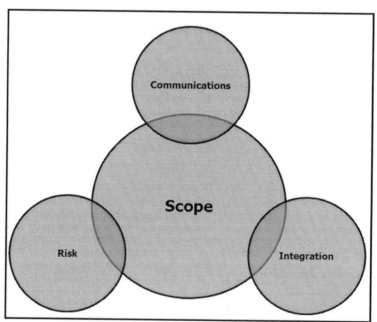

Table 10.6 Project Scope Management Knowledge Area focuses on documenting what is in and out of scope for the project. Not only does the Project Manager lock the project's scope, but he or she also documents the scope and obtains formal signoff and approval by all parties. The Project Manager also drives the use of the project's established change control process to control scope throughout the life of the project.

Table 10.6 Project Scope Management Knowledge Area

#	Task	Notes
1.	Develop the project's requirements document	This document includes what is in and out of scope for the project. The definition of the project scope is articulated within this document. In some cases, depending on team structure, the Project Manager might not be responsible for creating this document; however, it is his or her responsibility to ensure the activity is completed.
2.	Create the scope definition document	This document defines and documents the project's scope. Sometimes, scope definition is solely done in a project requirements document, other times it is documented in a scope definition document.
3.	Create project's WBS document	This document includes all project scope, as well as any additional activities by specific roles working on the project.
4.	Incorporate the use of the change control process	This knowledge area often causes the most use of the change control process. As projects enter the Executing process, the project's scope continually comes under question and, therefore, a change control process is often utilized. This process is documented in **Table 10.1 Initiation Process**.
5.	Create a scope management document	This document outlines the process and procedures to change the project's scope. This process includes a change request process, but it might have other organization or company requirements documented as well.

Project teams manage five main areas when dealing with project scope. Out of the five areas, two of those areas work nicely as one area. It is easy to perform WBS creation and scope verification together. Let us look at those areas now.

The Project Scope Management knowledge area includes:

Collecting project requirements—Regardless of what ultimately lands in and out of scope, this is the first and most important process of Project Scope Management.

Defining scope—Scope definition specifies what is in scope and out of scope for the project. The scope planning process is a negotiation process where one or two project team members meet with the customer and determine the minimum "must have's" and what is possible to do on the project to come to an agreement on the project scope. During this same conversation, it is important to document the areas not covered, or deemed out of scope.

WBS creation and scope verification—One of the key processes of Project Scope Management is the creation of a WBS. The WBS is an incredible tool to document what is in and out of the project's scope. This process helps you document the project deliverables and break down those deliverables (when applicable) into smaller and more manageable components. It is important to remember when creating a WBS to make sure that you also create a section for project management. Project Managers have many project activities to complete, but some are not part of the project's scope or the project's main deliverables, so it is important to include a project management section in the WBS for all projects and add the non-scope deliverables to that section.

Scope verification has been added to this area as well because when you create your WBS and communicate the WBS as the work of the project, it is natural to also verify that the scope you documented is correct. This is not a separate process because part of scope verification is obtaining signoff, and part of creating and documenting a WBS is also obtaining signoff. There was not enough reasons to keep these two separate, so it is best to combine them.

Scope control—Scope control is one of the hardest and most challenging components of a Project Manager's job and something that he or she will face throughout the life of the project. Project scope can constantly change due to a number of factors that can occur on the project, such as change in budget, requirements change, and timeline pressures. Project Managers must continue to keep a handle on project scope using a formal change control process.

Each Project Scope Management process is handled differently by different Project Managers. As PMO Manager, you role is to ensure they are handled correctly and consistently by your Project Managers. It is important to understand that you cannot micro-manage Project Managers in "how" they do it, just whether they do it. It is not best practice to micro-manage anyone, but keeping an eye on your project managers and guiding them through the execution of their project is a main part of your role.

Your success is helping your Project Managers execute each of the components of their projects.

To conclude the Project Scope Management knowledge area, it is a very important area and tends to be very close to the customer because it culminates in the project's end result. Customers often want more scope than what is possible due to time, money or other considerations on a given project, so Project Managers must watch this area closely. As PMO Manager, keep your Project Managers on top of project scope and ensure that they have a formal change control process for their projects. Following the tasks outlined in **Table 10.6 Project Scope Management Knowledge Area** will definitely help Project Managers maintain project scope and if they need to make trade-off decisions, they can do so with the right information and provide their customers with the right choices and outcomes for those decisions.

Project Time Management Knowledge Area

The Project Time Management knowledge area is one of the more important components of managing projects and something Project Managers should watch very closely throughout the life of the project. In Project Time Management, the Project Manager needs to understand what the project's resources are working on, in what order they need to work on tasks, and how long they will be working on them. Having that information for each of the project's tasks is essential for Project Managers. If they do not have that information, they will have to rely on a number of resources for it and they might not necessarily be providing you all the information you need.

Project Managers need to keep a close eye on project timelines throughout the project to ensure that they are making the dates promised by the team members and expected by the customers. One of the techniques that Project Managers can use during Project Time Management is performance reporting. Performance reporting is a great technique that Project Manager can take advantage of to show how well the team is executing the project. The Project Manager completes the performance reporting technique throughout the project and constantly reports and adjusts project assignments depending on the results of the performance report and, of course, how well the team is performing on the project. Performance reporting aligns perfectly with the Project Time Management process. In Chapter 14, "PMO Measurements and Performance Tracking" of this book, we go over performance reporting in detail, so for further information, you can always go review that chapter. Project Time Management is often a very tricky and a difficult aspect of the project to manage. Project Managers really only get better at it when they do it repeatedly and they learn trick and techniques (i.e. performance reporting) along the way.

Figure 10.7 Project Time Management Knowledge Area Circle shows the various knowledge areas that are applicable to the project's time management. In the Project Time Management knowledge area, there are four other knowledge areas that are closely associated to Project Time Management: Project Communications Management, Project Cost Management, Project Human Resource Management, and Project Procurement Management. These four areas were selected due to the important component that time plays in managing and controlling those specific knowledge areas.

Think about how important that Time plays in cost and human resource management on a project. Take costs for example, when a project goes longer than planned it generally makes the project cost more. In looking at resources, as you bring one or more of them either human or equipment, the timing of those resources also plays an important role in the success of the project. If resources start too late on a project, they might not be able to catch up and help complete the project on time. Bringing resources on too early, however, tends to cost more and it might not be beneficial to have them on the project that soon and potentially not assigned to any tasks. When you think about the important of communications when it comes to time, it is literally a no-brainer. Project Managers are communicating the time components of their projects on a continual bases, and there this is a very tight connection between communications knowledge area and the time knowledge area. Finally, and we spoke about it earlier the procurement process (bring on outside resources) onto a project and the timing of those activities are critical in the time management knowledge area. Those two knowledge areas are critical for the project manager to think about and ensure they are managing them closely together.

Figure 10.7 Project Time Management Knowledge Area Circle

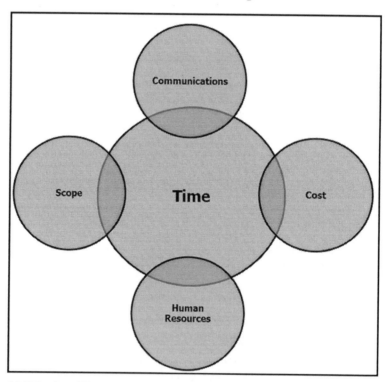

Table 10.7 Project Time Management Knowledge Area focuses around managing the time components of the project. Time is associated with everything you

do. Therefore, the Project Time Management area is watched very closely throughout the project by Project Managers, customers, and management. The Time component is part of the famous project triple-constraint triangle that occurs on most projects as the mechanism for project trade-off decisions. The triple constraint, as you might recall, focuses on time (schedule), cost, and scope, therefore it is an area that project managers must watch closely and be active in managing. Although there are several versions of the triangle, this combination (schedule, cost, and scope) tends to be the most popular used in the industry today, and therefore will be the one that most project managers are familiar with. Better yet, it is one that most customers are familiar with and therefore an important component for project managers to drive on their projects.

Table 10.7 Project Time Management Knowledge Area

#	Task	Notes
1.	Develop a project schedule management plan	This plan is vital to use on large projects especially when there is a separate role of project schedulers who are responsible for managing the project schedule.
2.	Create a high-level project calendar	Project Managers should use one of the various tools to create a high-level project calendar for their projects. The schedule can be at a high level at this point and it does not need to be detailed or even in a software tool at this time. A high-level project schedule gives customers, management, and the project team an idea of overall timing and is an amazing communication tool and just as powerful on paper or in a software tool.
3.	Document and define the project activities in the project schedule	Project Managers should follow best practices around creating a project schedule for this process.
4.	Create a WBS for the project	The WBS is an important component to help Project Managers keep their project teams on track and on schedule. Ensure the timeframes for each task are visible when communicating this schedule.

The Project Time Management knowledge area consists of the following six main components:

Defining project activities—Define the activities required for executing the project. This is not necessarily just the project deliverables, but the tasks to create or obtain those deliverables as well.

Activity sequencing and ordering—Define the sequence and the order of the project activities. Oftentimes, you must complete one activity before starting another. Occasionally, some activities can occur at the same time, so this whole process entails spending the time and understanding the exact order in which tasks need to be completed. If you don't do this correctly, it can cost a large amount of money to correct, and in other cases, it can be life threatening. This is often an underestimated exercise because it often comes natural to project teams when following a predefined methodology or set of processes/procedures. Other times, ordering the activities can be time consuming and takes full project team participation.

Activity resource estimation—This process defines and documents the resources, both human or equipment, needed for the project. This process also documents the types of resources, the number, into a complete project schedule for the Project Manager and team to use.

Activity duration estimating—This process determines the expected time allocation for each activity. The times are estimates, not actual times, where actuals get captured during project execution. There are many methods and techniques Project Managers can use to capture estimates and there are a number of factors to consider. The most common technique being the PERT technique and, as PMO Manager, it is your responsibility to define which estimating technique your project teams will use to capture project estimates across your PMO. Ensure your Project Managers are consistent in how they collect the estimates.

Schedule development—The project schedule development is the process of understanding the different activity sequences, time estimates and durations, resources required (people/equipment) and any constraints tied to those various activities in developing an actual schedule for the project. Project schedule development, in the end, is about creating a schedule that is ultimately going to take you through the life of the project, so this is a very important process for any Project Manager. PMO Managers should ensure that Project Managers are consistent in the way they create their project schedules and should recommend some minimum standards that Project Managers should apply to their schedules.

Schedule control—Control all aspects of how updates, corrections, or changes are made to the project schedule. Project Managers establish, at this point, very strict control over schedule changes and should limit the number of people who have the ability to make changes during this process. A Project Manager who loses control of the schedule loses control of the project. In some projects, Project Managers hire schedulers to make all project schedule changes under the direction of the Project Manager. In these larger efforts, this is where many project managers will create and ensure there is a project schedule management plan in place and utilized. In smaller projects, the Project Manager (or a Project Coordinator) is responsible for making project schedule changes.

As PMO Manager, it is important for your Project Managers to understand this very important knowledge area and how it influences the success of your project. When looking at activity sequencing, it is going to be critical that you understand which order the different activities have to occur and what constraints are on each activity that will prevent them from occurring in that order. Without that knowledge, you could have huge project execution issues.

Another important component of this process is duration estimating and the process to do so. There are many different estimating processes and many Project Managers will have their favorites, or the company might be driving a particular method based on the types of projects or industry. There is no right or wrong estimating model; there are just different models and Project Managers need to evaluate which one works for the project they are managing. It would be impossible for anyone to offer one model over another model as being better for your organization due to the hundreds of industries and the thousands of types of projects there are today. However, as PMO Manager, you do need to define this for your organization. The estimation model choice you make needs to be tested and determined if it will work for your organization. After you've made the decision, your role is to support your Project Managers and project teams through the learning process on the estimating model as they apply it to their projects. As PMO Manager, complete an assessment of your organization, industry, project type(s) and determine which is the right estimating model for your organization. There are many different websites and lots of information that you can find to help you choose the right model based on what you need at your company. Again, there is no right or wrong model per say, but you definitely should create an estimating model to help your Project Managers be successful.

To conclude the Project Time Management knowledge area, one of the key things for Project Managers to consider is how time plays such an important role in the successful execution of a project and how each of the six components of this process are critical to managing time and keeping your project on track. Successfully driving this phase of the project starts during the Initiation/Initiating process and Project Managers must be diligent in getting on top of their project activities and understanding how well the team is meeting the scheduled date for each activity.

Project Cost Management Knowledge Area

The Project Cost Management knowledge area is another area in project management that falls into the triple constraint triangle, like the Project Time Management process, however cost is a bit different. Most of the customers, managers, and project team members usually watch the project's costs very closely and generally question and raise issues and concerns around project spending, more than any other area of the project. Budget is always a top concern for management and the customer. To drive a successful project, Project Managers must stay on top of their project budgets.

Figure 10.8 Project Cost Management Knowledge Area Circle specifies the various knowledge areas applicable to the management of the project's costs. In the Project Cost Management knowledge area, the following six knowledge areas are closely associated to Project Cost Management: Project Communications Management,

293

Project Time Management, Project Human Resource Management, Project Procurement Management, Project Quality Management, and Project Integration Management. Each plays an important role in influencing, either positively or negatively, the project's costs. As you can imagine, there are actually a number of items on a project that influence the cost or the budget of a project. These include time (how long the project is scheduled—longer projects tend to be more expensive), resources (human and other) greater or fewer resources can dramatically impact project costs, quality (how much or how little rigor on quality management is required), and the procurement process. The procurement process works hand-in-hand in executing the project costs and thus plays a role in the process. Each knowledge area plays an integrated role in how the Project Manager allocates costs on the project and each needs careful managing throughout the project. If any of the areas goes off the mark, the project costs can rise dramatically.

Figure 10.8 Project Cost Management Knowledge Area Circle

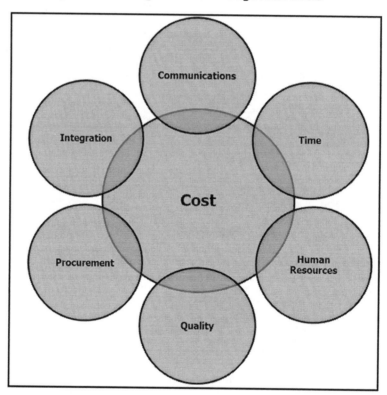

Table 10.8 Project Cost Management Knowledge Area focuses on managing the project costs. There is a cost component to almost every part of a project, and the tools and deliverables within this table will help Project Managers control the cost components of their projects.

Table 10.8 Project Cost Management Knowledge Area

#	Task	Notes
1.	Develop a project estimating tool	The estimating tool is for high-quality and accurate project estimates. This tool provides an accurate estimate based on hours, rates and other associated costs. Develop this tool as one of the first deliverables of project cost management.
2.	Develop a project cost estimation for each project activity	There are a number of tools to perform the cost estimating process; however, one of the best tools to use for this process is a scheduling tool, such as Microsoft Project. Any automated scheduling tool will do and will allow you to track more effectively throughout the project. Using a tool such as Microsoft Excel, although handy and much faster, is yet another tool that needs to be managed.
3.	Develop a project budget estimate using a budget spreadsheet	In most cases, budgets are handed to the project team. However, by going through the process of developing a project budget request lets you present your estimate and compare it to what was actually allocated. Project trade-off decisions (such as triple constraint) are made if there are differences between the two figures.
4	Develop a cost control process	It is important for Project Managers to have a project cost control process in place for their projects. What happens when projects go over budget, what happens if they are too far under budget...etc. A cost control process helps with that.

Best Practice: Weekly cost management

After creating a project budget spreadsheet, one best practice recommended for all Project Managers is to track project accounting on a weekly basis. Most financial systems process actuals on a monthly basis however do track forecasts real time. Real-time entry and ever-changing of project forecasts require Project Managers to track weekly as the only method to keep coordinated with what is occurring on the project from a financial perspective. This real-time changing of project cost data is quite challenging to manage and can be a Project Manager's nightmare if he or she is not constantly on top of it. Without this visibility, it's very difficult for Project Managers to keep control of project estimates when they continue to change randomly. Although actuals hit on a monthly basis, the random approach we see when project team members enter their project forecast estimates is frustrating and therefore can be controlled if project managers are capturing it weekly and then following up on forecasts that don't appear accurate or valid.

This weekly cost management process is very simple, take a week-to-week snapshot of the project's cost data and compare the previous week's data to the current week's data. If there are any differences, resolve or document those differences. Regardless of how the project's cost data spreadsheet is set up, the goal is to run the same comparison report week after week and catch anything that has changed. If there are any differences (and you find changes), work with the resources who changed the estimates and find out why they made the changes. When Project Managers stay on top of project costs, they can make project trade-off decisions and are in the best position to keep a great handle on their finances.

To conclude the Project Cost Management knowledge area, it is important to understand how critical cost management is to your project. Without it, you could have some major project problems and no ability to solve those problems because you don't know your budget. Without cost management processes or control, projects can quickly go over budget, which can cause cancellation, or are forced to reduce workforce. Project Managers need to keep a weekly handle on their projects from a finance perspective and provide a constant stream of communications about how a project is progressing, cost wise. As PMO Manager, it is highly encouraged to stress to your Project Managers to refer to **Table 10.8 Project Cost Management Knowledge Area** and the different deliverables in that table to give them a great set of tools to help them manage their costs and increase their project's chance of success.

Project Quality Management Knowledge Area

The Project Quality Management knowledge area includes the activities that determine how to manage project quality. Project quality includes policies, any specific quality-related objectives, and how team members drive quality for their own roles and responsibilities. Every project should include quality management of one form or another, and Project Managers should ensure they are driving quality to the highest level whenever possible.

Figure 10.9 Project Quality Management Knowledge Area Circle shows the various knowledge areas applicable to the management of the project's quality. In the Project Quality Management knowledge area, the following four knowledge areas are closely associated with quality management: Project Communications Management, Project Cost Management, Project Risk Management, and Project Time Management. These knowledge areas drive or influence the project's quality. For example, Project Communications Management plays an important role in Project Quality Management as it does in any other knowledge area, but around quality, the Project Manager must ensure he or she is communicating and driving quality metrics and measurements for the entire project. If the Project Manager fails to communicate constantly about project quality, the project quality will not be an important part of the project, which could cause quality problems at the end of the project.

Project Cost Management plays a big role in quality because to increase quality, you usually increase cost. For example, running additional test cases, hiring more testers, spending additional time (driving the project longer), or improving one component, all drive the project cost up. Project Managers who drive quality will also understand the cost component and will keep both in mind when making project-level decisions.

Project Risk Management also plays a role in Project Quality Management. The risks of the project and the quality of the project go hand in hand. The lower quality, the more risk the Project Manager introduces to the project. These two knowledge areas help force project quality decisions throughout the project. Increase quality, lessen the risk, but in most cases, increase the costs. Depending on the project, these might be very hard or easy decisions to make for Project Managers and, as PMO Manager, you need to be there to support your Project Managers during this process because many times Project Managers have little to no experience in Project Quality Management.

Finally, Project Time Management also plays a big role in the quality of project deliverables. Often, adding and improving quality adds more time to the project, especially if quality was not discussed or planned for in the planning phase of the project, thus influencing the project schedule. Project Managers will have another trade-off decision to make about adding time, increasing quality, or leaving the allotted time to what is in the schedule and accepting the level of quality that fits into the time-period. For example, if the project allocates two weeks for testing, and the two weeks of testing only gives the project the bare minimum level of quality that is acceptable to the customer, then both the Project Manager and the Customer must decide if that level of quality is enough. If not, the Project Manager and Customer can choose to add more time to the schedule. If the Project Manager thinks the level of quality is enough, but the customer does not, the Project Manager is faced with having the team start over and add more time and increased quality on the project. This is never a good thing for a project; it only adds unexpected time and cost to the project. This situation is avoidable if the Project Manager keeps an eye on project quality from start to finish and especially ensure that it is a major component discussed and planned for in the planning phase of the project.

Figure 10.9 Project Quality Management Knowledge Area Circle

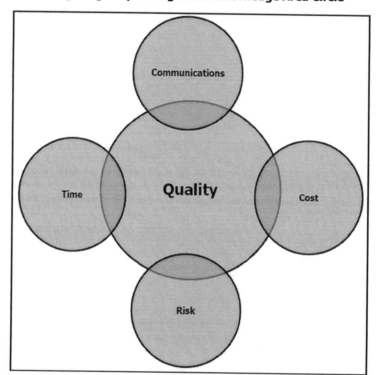

Table 10.9 Project Quality Management Knowledge Area focuses activities around managing the quality components of the project. There is a quality aspect to every component of your project; however, the quality management process tends to focus on improving the quality of the final project deliverable (the house, the software, the bridge, and so on) not necessarily on the deliverables or the processes along the life of the project. However, it would be a huge miss if Project Managers did not look at both aspects and ensure that they are driving quality in both areas because they are so tightly integrated. As PMO Manager, ensure that your Project Managers are driving project quality for both the final product and the project deliverables along the way.

Table 10.9 Project Quality Management Knowledge Area

#	Task	Notes
1.	Develop the quality management plan	This plan ensures that the activities completed during the project strive for the highest level of quality. The plan documents the customer's acceptable level of quality for the final deliverable. Other areas include defining quality requirements, standards, and how quality can be measured and displayed.
2.	Develop quality management tools	During the quality management process, one of the tasks Project Managers should consider is lining up and securing the quality management tools they need for the project. Tools include, test plans, control charts, and scatter charts.
3.	Perform quality assurance audits	At this point during the project, the Project Manager ensures that the quality of the processes and deliverables to build the final product are being audited and that standards are being adhered to for the project.
4.	Direct the performance of quality audits, including ongoing communications	Project Managers ensure that quality management processes and procedures are performed and that the standards established in the quality management plan are being met.

Project Managers should not underestimate how important Project Quality Management is on their projects. As PMO Manager, you must drive the importance of this concept into them and guide them into making the right quality decisions for their projects while balancing time, scope, and budget. It seems that Project Quality Management is one thing that is often overlooked by the whole project team, not just the Project Manager. Nevertheless, it is the Project Manager's job to drive the conversations around quality. The Project Manager owns the responsibility of attaining the highest level of quality on the project.

You can imagine how much more successful a project would be if the Project Manager focuses and communicates quality throughout the life of the project instead of at the end when product testing occurs. Imagine how different the project team would behave if the quality of the project was tied to bonuses, or end-of-project payouts. It would be extremely different and something that some teams would react to very positively. As PMO Manager, this may be something that you test on some pilot projects and reward your team when they deliver a high quality product (regardless of what it is) to their customers.

To conclude the Project Quality Management knowledge area, you can see that there are many areas that Project Managers and team members can follow to improve a project's quality—not just the quality of the end-result, but the quality of the deliverables created to run the project. As PMO Manager, you need to stress to your Project Managers the importance of using the documents, tools, and procedures in **Table 10.9 Project Quality Management Knowledge Area** and you should continue to drive the quality conversation with your Project Managers as they execute their projects.

Project Human Resource Management Knowledge Area

The Project Human Resource Management knowledge area includes the activities and processes that organize, manage, and drive the project team to a successful execution of the project. Project Human Resource Management is one of the hardest processes to manage on a project. Project Human Resource Management differs from company to company and industry to industry. As PMO Manager, work with your Project Managers to make sure they are aware of the processes. If you think about the different companies and organization structures, you can only imagine how many different team configurations there are, so managing human resources will be different from project to project. One of the tasks that project managers have to consider about this knowledge area is that it is not only about the management of humans (project team members), but the management of other resources as well. Examples of other resources include cranes, computers, and tractors.

Project Managers need to keep both human and equipment organized and managed; therefore, are responsible for performing all resource management during the life of a project.

Figure 10.10 Project Human Resource Management Knowledge Area Circle shows the various knowledge areas that are applicable to the management of the project team members and specific equipment during the life of the project. The following four knowledge areas are closely associated with managing the resources on the project: Project Communications Management, Project Cost Management, Project Procurement Management, and Project Integration Management. These knowledge areas were selected due to their important role that they each play in managing resources on projects. Project Communications Management is one of the key areas that Project Managers need to be on top of to execute a successful project and therefore will be spending a great deal of time and effort on communicating the various resources reports or equipment usage reports throughout the life of the project. These two knowledge areas are very applicable to each other. Project Cost Management is important when considering the human resource knowledge area because the majority of project budgets are based on the costs of the humans working on the project. As project team resources come on and off the project, that movement of resources will positively or negatively impact the project's budget. Project Procurement Management and Project Integration Management knowledge areas both play a big role in the Project Human Resource Management knowledge area. Project Integration Management closely impacts the Project Human Resource Management knowledge area because it deals with how to drive the project in a coordinated manner and ensures the resources are tightly aligned. The Project Procurement Management knowledge area plays a big role in human resources because you must follow the procurement process to obtain resources for the project. Project Managers must be aware of the procurement process for their organization especially if the project requires the use of vendors or contractors to offset employees on the project team.

All four knowledge areas play such an important role in the execution of a project and, as PMO Manager, your role is to ensure that your Project Managers are seeing the connections and managing these areas as efficiently as possible.

Figure 10.10 Project Human Resource Management Knowledge Area Circle

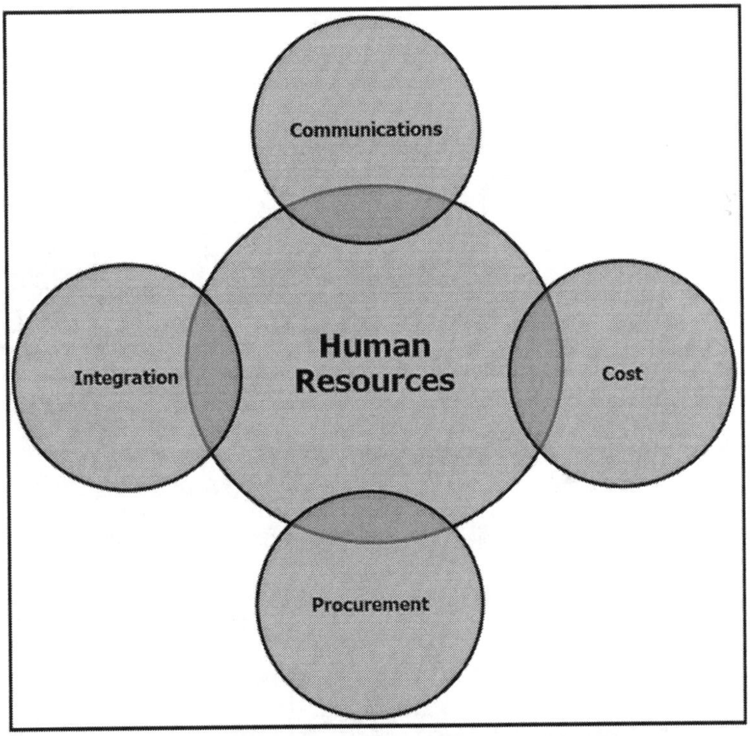

Table 10.10 Project Human Resource Management Knowledge Area focuses on managing the resources on the project. It is a best practice to manage both human

and equipment resources during this process. This table shows the tasks and activities to manage both. Otherwise, managing resources falls into the Project Procurement Management knowledge area only and would not be part of this process which could have a negative impact on the project.

Table 10.10 Project Human Resource Management Knowledge Area

#	Task	Notes
1.	Develop a human resource plan, including how other resources, such as equipment, will be managed as well	This plan documents various project roles, responsibilities, skills required, and organization relationships. This plan is needed to create a staffing management plan.
2.	Create a staffing management plan	This plan ultimately documents and explains the staff and other resources needed for the project. The plan is essentially a portion of the human resource plan and the contents are determined by project type, organization parameters, size of the project, and is tailored to the project.
3.	Acquire project resources, including staff and equipment/hardware or non-human resources	Obtain the project team. It is that simple. Gather the team members who are required for the project. Team members consist of employees, vendors or contract resources. The process of obtaining the resources is different from company to company. At this point, it is also important to obtain other types of resources required for the project. Depending on the project type, there could be many different processes for obtaining non-human resources.
4.	Develop a project roles and responsibility matrix (RACI)	The RACI matrix is such an important tool for any Project Manager and project team. It can be used in any industry. This document drives accountability and responsibility ownership, per task, to team members at the beginning of the project and before any work begins.
5.	Perform resource leveling throughout the life of	Resource leveling is a concept or technique that reviews and examines the unbalanced use of the project's resources

#	Task	Notes
	project	(usually people or equipment) over time, and resolves any over-allocations or under-allocations. Oftentimes, Project Managers look for who is over-allocated and miss the under-allocated resources who also need correcting.

To conclude the Project Human Resource Management knowledge area, it is important to understand that projects are only successful when the project team works well together and when they are committed to each other's success. When the team is not committed to one another, or there is a lot of fighting among resources, the project will struggle to deliver its intended goals. Regardless of industry, when team members are not focused on the goals of the project, there tend to be project problems. Project Managers have a huge task to build and drive teams that are committed and want to succeed together. It is not an easy task, but this is one of the knowledge areas were Project Managers do not give a lot of attention and tend to let team dynamics work themselves out. To increase the chance of success on projects, Project Managers must be diligent in team management and, as PMO Manager, your role is to encourage your Project Managers in this work. You can look for training and offer your own guidance, but make sure Project Managers get the skills they need to lead high performing teams. Also, as PMO Manager, ensure your Project Managers are following and performing the processes outlined in **Table 10.10 Project Human Resource Management Knowledge Area** to increase their chance of driving a successful project team.

Project Communications Management Knowledge Area

The Project Communications Management knowledge area is the most important component of project management. Time and time again, projects fail due to lack of proper communications from the Project Manager—regardless of any other specific reason called out, it always comes down to project communications. Project Communications Management includes ensuring that the right information is getting into the hands of people who can make the right decisions; a Project Manager owns that responsibility throughout the life of the project. No other person on the team holds that same level of accountability on a project. As PMO Manager, help your Project Managers communicate as effectively as possible. It is your role to ensure their customers, management, and project team members are getting the project information they need to drive the project to a successful completion. It is important that Project Managers consider themselves as the "Circle of Communications" and control all project communication aspects of their projects.

Figure 10.11 Circle of Communications represents a Project Manager who is fully connected and in control of project communications. In this example of a software project, the Project Manager is the center of all communications and is linked to the various functional leads on the project. The functional leads control communication among their functional areas and are responsible for controlling communication to and from the Project Manager. It is also important to note that the leads for the different functional areas will have workers or teams within their respective areas who will communicate through their functional leads for all project updates. Also, it is important to note that, in this example (software project), the Dev. Lead and the Test Lead can communicate without the Project Manager through the life of the project, but if either party has official status or project communications about the project, that information must be vetted and approved by the Project Manager before communicating to other parties. This protocol ensures that the Project Manager is always aware and involved in official project communications. This is definitely a concept that you, the PMO Manager, should stress to your Project Managers and have your project teams set up for their projects. It will drive accountability and clarify who is ultimately in control of project communication.

Figure 10.11 Circle of Communications Chart

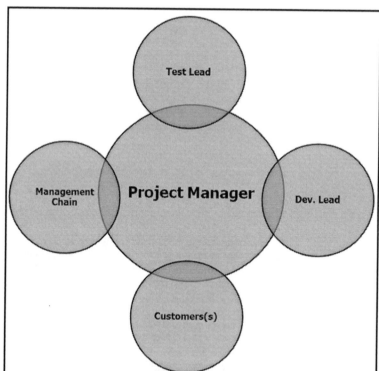

Figure 10.12 Project Communications Management Knowledge Area Circle shows the various knowledge areas that are applicable to the management of project communications. The remaining eight knowledge areas are all closely related to the

project communication knowledge area. As you can imagine, there is a component of project communication to every area on a project, so it makes sense to link all of the knowledge areas to project communications. Project Communications Management is the only knowledge area that is applicable to every other knowledge area and is a critical component for the successful execution of the project.

Figure 10.12 Project Communications Management Knowledge Area Circle

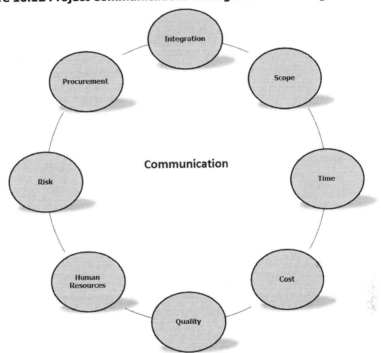

Table 10.11 Project Communications Management Knowledge Area focuses the activities around managing project communications. There are many tools available to Project Managers for communicating various project components and selecting the right tool for the right level of communication is very important. Project Managers must ensure they know their audience members and that they are sending the right level of information to the right level of audience. It is common to hear that an executive will want a high-level summary of the project and a tactical manager will want much more details. However, that is not always the case, and a project manager must sit down, work with each stakeholder, customer, and executive, and determine exactly what level of information he or she needs. You may be surprised, some executives want a lot of detail, and if you present them with a high-level status, you may be hearing from them that they are not getting the information they need. A Project Manager's credibility is hurt if he or she doesn't communicate effectively.

Table 10.11 Project Communications Management Knowledge Area

#	Task	Notes
1.	Create the project's stakeholder register	This is a very important and valuable communication tool for understanding the "who's who" of your customers.
2.	Create the project communications plan	This plan is one of the most important documents in the execution of your project because it drives the success of your project. Some important tools to include in this document: • Circle of communications chart • Communication requirements matrix • Role report matrix • Project calendar **Note: More information on some these tools can be found in my first book "Project Management Communications Bible"**
3.	Develop a plan to distribute project information and associated communication rhythm	This information can be included in the project communications plan or in a separate document, but documenting how to distribute project information is critical to a project's success. Establishing a communication rhythm is important when defining the project's communication requirements. If, for example, you want to send monthly status reports, but your customer wants weekly status reports, knowing that information early allows you to work through the disconnect and come to an agreement.
4.	Develop a stakeholder reporting cadence	This is an opportunity to sit down with the customer or stakeholders and manage expectations, communicate status, and develop relationships and partnerships through the execution of the project. It is important when you are sitting down talking to your customers ask them about the level

#	Task	Notes
		of information they need. I.e. Summary type information or detailed information.
5.	Develop a performance reporting matrix and tracking process	Determine how you will track various performance measurements on the project. For example, you might include schedule or cost performance measurements, but you as project manager will need to determine what is right for your type of project.
6.	Develop all other communications tools	This is a great opportunity to develop specific communication tools needed for your project. Spend the time while planning the project's communications to develop tools, such as the following: • Project document control systems (centralized repository for storing project information) • Project newsletters • Project status reports • Others??

To conclude the Project Communications Management knowledge area, this is the one area that will determine a project's success or failure depending on how much or little the Project Manager controls communications. Project Managers who focus less on project communications tend to have more problems in execution of their projects, than ones who apply the right balance and tend to care more about communications. As PMO Manager, you must play an active role in how your Project Managers communicate about their projects. Spend the time to ensure Project Managers are communicating effectively by checking presentations, looking at internal websites or document control systems, or reading status reports. If you stay on top of their communications, you will be there to offer guidance and support where needed.

Project Risk Management Knowledge Area

The Project Risk Management knowledge area includes the process of planning, identifying, responding, and controlling a project's risks. Many Project Managers recognize that risk management is one of the most difficult components of managing a project due to the unknown and uncertainty around them. It is the uncertainty of whether a risk event occurs and the impact to the project that makes it so difficult. As PMO Manager, you definitely should spend time with your Project Managers to ensure that they have a handle on project risks. You want to make sure they are aware of any major events that could occur on their projects. It is also important that your Project Managers have contingency plans in place that cover issues, such as budget or additional days, in case a risk event occurs. Contingency planning can make or break the success of a project. Therefore, work with your Project Managers to ensure they are ready for possible risk events.

One of the components of Project Risk Management that is not formally recognized by the *PMBOK* Guide as a standalone knowledge area is Project Issue Management. The *PMBOK* Guide refers to issues as problems that can keep a team from reaching its goals and identifies safety issues, performance issues, and compliance issues, but does not formally call out Project Issue Management as a project management area of responsibility or as a specific knowledge area. As PMO Manager, ensure your Project Managers have formal processes and procedures in place to manage project issues. Project issues, such as lost resources, lost budget, or losing customer sponsorship, can kill projects. It is important for Project Managers to remember to close their project issues when they are resolved, because leaving them open leads to confusion on the project and team members or the customers not knowing the latest status of the issue.

Proper management and closure is so important because of the alignment between risks and issues. Project Managers must work the two areas closely and stay on top of them both as they execute on their projects. As risk events occur, they become project issues and need resolution to prevent long-term negative impact to the project. Issues can occur and temporarily negatively impact the project, but solid Project Issue Management will prevent long-term negative impact.

Figure 10.13 Project Risk Management Knowledge Area Circle specifies the various knowledge areas that are applicable to the management of a project's possible risk events. In the Project Risk Management knowledge area, the following five additional knowledge areas are closely associated with managing a project's risk events: Project Communications Management, Project Scope Management, Project Time Management, Project Cost Management, and Project Quality Management. In each of these areas, Project Risk Management plays a large role and can drive the success or failure of that area. In Project Scope Management, for example, Project Risk Management plays a big part of the project's scope when determining which scope items to include in the project. It might be too risky to bring in one item over another item, so the Project Manager is constantly balancing the risks and the scope of the project. Project Time Management is another area that plays a role in the Project Risk Management process. When risk events occur, they often push out the project schedule, so by keeping the two areas tightly aligned is a best practice of most Project

Managers. Project Cost Management and Project Risk Management are also tightly aligned because of the impact that the project's risks can have on the project budget. If risk events occur, projects can run out of budget or go over budget. Finally, Project Quality Management and Project Risk Management need to be tightly aligned through the execution of a project. These two knowledge areas are aligned by the possibility of risk events occurring and the impact they would have on a project's quality. For example, if there is a risk event where a construction firm has to pull out of a project due to a higher priority, the construction project might have to bring in a lesser qualified organization to complete the work on their behalf, thus impacting the quality of the end result. The new construction company might be known to have had quality issues and delivery problems, but might be the only one available. This is just one of the many examples of how risk events and quality problems are tightly aligned.

It is important to note that Project Issue Management is not included with this knowledge area purposely because it is not a recognized knowledge area in the project management industry. However, when thinking about which knowledge areas work together, Project Issue Management definitely applies to the Project Risk Management knowledge area and should be considered here. **Table 10.12 Project Risk Management Knowledge Area** includes the Project Issue Management processes, and other work items because of the close alignment to Project Risk Management.

Figure 10.13 Project Risk Management Knowledge Area Circle

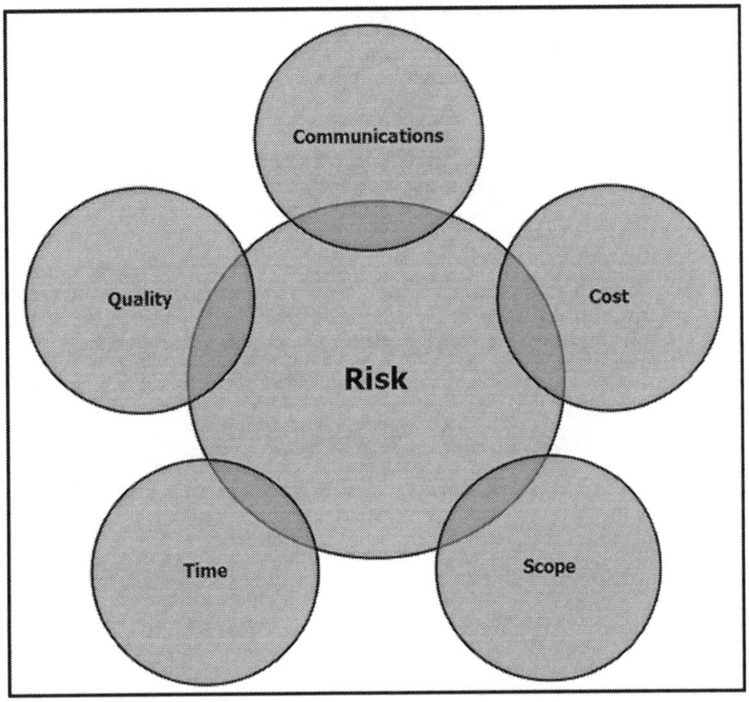

Table 10.12 Project Risk Management Knowledge Area focuses the activities around managing the project's possible risk events. There is so much uncertainty around what could happen to a project; therefore, Project Risk Management is about managing that uncertainty. Project Risk Management is about planning, preparing for what might happen, and having processes, procedures, and budget in place to prepare for risks (if that is the right decision) without influencing the execution of the project. There is a lot of great information about risk management, great training, and some unbelievable experts in the art of managing project risks. There are also some easy processes to follow for any Project Manager. As PMO Manager, keep your Project Managers driving these processes consistently on their projects. These basic steps and processes will assist any project manager in driving a successful project.

The following table also includes the documents, deliverables, and processes for Project Issue Management. Like Project Risk Management, Project Issue Management is an important component for driving a successful project.

Table 10.12 Project Risk Management Knowledge Area (including Project Issue Management items)

#	Task	Notes
1.	Develop a risk management plan	This plan documents how to manage and control risks throughout the project.
2.	Develop an issue management plan	This plan documents how to manage and control issues throughout the project.
3.	Develop risk and issue management storage locations	Ensure that risks and issues are tracked separately in two separate tracking tools whenever possible. The characteristics of a risk event are different from issues, so they be tracked in two locations, however in some cases, they are able to be tracked together. Many Project Managers combine these, which is not a best practice, but can be done. Make sure to calculate the expected monetary value for each risk event and develop and capture risks on the project. This is important to remember when creating the repository to hold risk events.
4.	Develop qualitative and quantitative risk analysis processes	These two processes are important to develop early during the risk management process because they are the same processes used throughout the life of the project. Developing these

#	Task	Notes
		processes early is going to better prepare you when risk events do arise.
5.	Develop a monitoring and controlling process for both risks and issues	It is important to create this process early during the project for monitoring, and controlling project risks.

To conclude the Project Risk Management knowledge area, this risk management process is certainly an area that if managed incorrectly or without structure can make or break the success of a project. Project Managers must be very diligent when managing risks on their project. The processes and documents outlined in **Table 10.12 Project Risk Management Knowledge Area**, if completed by the Project Manager early in the life of the project, will set them up with a good set of tools to manage both risks and issues throughout the project. Project Managers who very diligently manage both risks and issues typically have more success and keep customers and team members engaged and working together in order to prevent risk or to reduce issues on projects. Some Project Managers spend many hours managing risks and issues, which can be time consuming, but is definitely important for driving a successful project.

Project Procurement Management Knowledge Area

The Project Procurement Management knowledge area is one of the least known and least utilized knowledge areas in a project's life cycle. Most Project Managers never think about how they will manage the project procurement area. If Project Managers, for example, do not have to purchase any resources, products, or if the project uses internal resources only, they feel that the procurement area is less important and, therefore, should receive less attention. This is true to a point; however, what happens is that most Project Managers think this knowledge area is only about procuring resources (human or equipment) for their project. This is not the case, and there is much more to this knowledge area than simply obtaining resources or adding material or parts for a project. That is a big component for sure, but not the only component. For example, other processes in the Project Procurement Management area include establishing a central repository for project deliverables, documenting lessons learned, and obtaining all official project sign-offs. Each of these areas is not typically viewed as a procurement activity, but due to the nature of the activities and timing, they make sense to be included in this knowledge area.

Figure 10.14 Project Procurement Management Knowledge Area Circle shows the various knowledge areas that apply to procurement management activities. The four knowledge areas that are closely associated with Project Procurement Management are: Project Communications Management, Project Scope Management, Project Time Management, and Project Human Resource Management. Project Scope Management plays a major role within the procurement activities because scope can play a role in whether the Project Manager needs to bring resources onto the project

311

that are not already available. For example, if the project is to build a large swimming pool and there are no available backhoes to dig the hole, the Project Manager needs to procure a backhoe and a person to run it. Depending on the scope and the different items needed that are unavailable, the only means to obtain those items is to use the procurement process. Time Management plays a big part in the procurement process because of how long it can take to obtain resources for the project if having to procure them from inside or outside the organization. Therefore, the procurement process plays a big role in the project's schedule and Project Managers need to manage this timeframe accordingly. Finally, human resources (or other resource types) is one of the most utilized areas of the procurement process. In many cases, projects supplement their project teams with outside vendors or contractors and use the procurement process to obtain those resources. It is very common for Project Managers to hire individual resources or hire complete teams to perform project activities. This process is the same for non-human resources (for example, the backhoe). Generally, the only way to obtain these resources is to go through a procurement process. In all four cases, each knowledge area plays such an important part of the project life cycle and, therefore, plays an important part in the procurement process.

Figure 10.14 Project Procurement Management Knowledge Area Circle

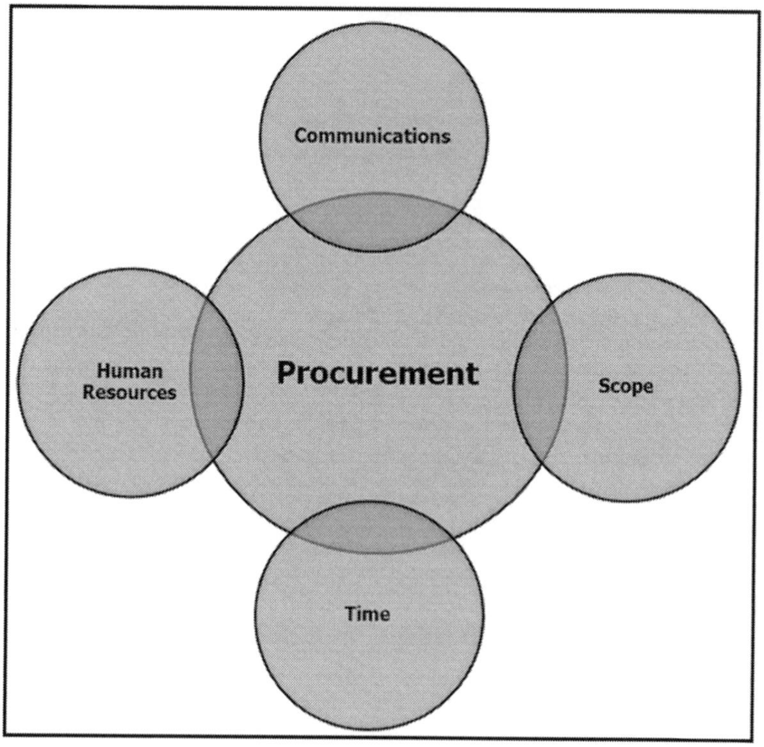

Table 10.13 Project Procurement Management Knowledge Area focuses the activities around managing the project's procurement activities. Included in this table is the minimum set of requirements that Project Managers should complete while performing their procurement activities for their projects. As PMO Manager, help your Project Managers through this process as most of them will have little experience with these processes and will need your guidance. If the project, however, does require a large procurement component (for example, hiring teams of vendors), than prior to getting into this phase it would be good to understand how the internal procurement activities work within your company. Understanding your company's procurement process early and knowing how to work the process, if there is ever a time where you do need to hire a vendor or outside help, this will allow you to properly plan for this activity and not let it impact the flow of the project.

Table 10.13 Project Procurement Management Knowledge Area

#	Task	Notes
1.	Close and approve all procurement documents	These documents include any SOW documents, purchase orders, contracts—any document needed to purchase resources in the company. This will vary greatly from company to company.
2.	Document administration	After obtaining resources, there is a process of administration and paying for those resources throughout the life of the contract.
3.	Develop acceptance documents and associated acceptance approval process	Create the formal acceptance documents and determine the process to obtain approvals before actually requiring them. This seems like a simple process, but this can often be very time consuming that takes longer than expected.
4.	Hold "lessons learned"/post-mortem meeting	It is highly recommended to collect lessons learned during the life of the project; however, at the end of the project there needs to be a final session where the project team and stakeholders talk about the project and capture the areas that they did well so they can use again on future projects.
5.	Close out all project documents	This process closes everything. There should be no resources left and the documents should be closed and backed

#	Task	Notes
		up.

Further Consideration items:

Lessons learned information—It is important that throughout the life of a project, Project Managers collect "lessons learned" information. The best opportunity to collect lessons learned information is during the project team's weekly status meetings and during 1:1 sessions with project team members. In both meetings, team members are engaged and can track this type of information.

By Project Managers tracking lessons learned information during the course of the project instead of waiting until the end it eliminates the problem of people leaving the project or having to remember the events that took place on the project which could have occurred months ago. Many times, people move on and simply forget what happened over such a long period.

Capturing this information can be fun and does not always have to be a negative process. Capturing what people are doing well and celebrating the success of individuals along the way is a great thing and something that helps improve team morale. There is also the need to capture some of the mistakes and some areas to grow as well, which should prevent those same things from happening again.

One of the best practices when collecting this information (especially if it is not very positive) is to keep it in a separate file and with limited visibility. Information from someone venting does not always belong in a lessons learned file and does not need sharing.

To conclude the Project Procurement Management knowledge area, it is an interesting knowledge area from the perspective that so many Project Managers have the feeling that it is just one unique area of the project life cycle (obtaining resources), yet it is actually so much more than that. If you think about all the different areas covered in this chapter, procurement actually spans the life of the project. These processes are heavily used at the beginning of the project (obtaining resources), during the life of the project (collecting lessons learned, paying for resources), and at the end of the project by closing the project, obtaining signoff, and shutting down project activities. As PMO Manager, it is important to ensure you focus your Project Managers on this very important process and keep them thinking about and managing this process throughout the life of the project.

The Tactical Guide for Building a PMO

Knowledge Area Mapping Chart

One of the key aspects of what we covered in this chapter is linking the various nine knowledge areas together while executing the project deliverables. **Table 10.14 Knowledge Area Mapping Chart** shows the mapping for easy review and use on your projects. It is important to note that there is no right or wrong linking among the knowledge areas in this chart, and there certainly can be great debate on the links chosen. As PMO Manager, this is a great chart to stress to your project team members about how important it is for them to be thinking about which knowledge areas work together so that they don't miss the opportunity to connect the different process areas when managing their projects.

Table 10.14 Knowledge Area Mapping Chart

	Integration	Scope	Time	Cost	Quality	Human Resources	Communications	Risk Management	Procurement
Integration		X		X		X	X		
Scope	X						X	X	
Time				X		X	X		X
Cost	X		X		X	X	X		X
Quality			X	X			X	X	
Human Resources	X			X			X		X
Communications	X	X	X	X	X	X		X	X
Risk Management		X	X	X	X		X		
Procurement		X	X			X	X		

Tools, Templates, Processes and Procedures

As you look through this chapter, there is a lot of mention of tools, templates, processes/procedures. In most cases, you will find that they are not included any of these in this chapter. That was done so on purpose, because the main goal of this chapter is not to provide you the exact templates or examples, but to provide you, the PMO Manager, a project management framework. The activities that your Project Managers follow when managing their projects are broken down by the different knowledge areas. Most Project Managers do not think of managing projects by thinking about these different knowledge areas, but think about how much better of a job they would do if they did and they were specifically focusing on those different areas throughout the life of the project. As PMO Manager, it is 100% your responsibility to go out and establish these items for your PMO and to select the right template and processes/procedures for your Project Managers, but that can't be done in one, two or three books. It requires some experience, searching the Internet, and determining what makes sense for your organization. With the different types of industries, projects, companies and all the variations, there is no way to have a single template that works for everyone across every project.

Many of the tools discussed in this chapter and throughout the book are located in my first book, *Project Management Communications Bible*, which is highly recommend as a companion guide to this PMO book. If you need to find some templates, well they are in that book and on the companion CD. The CD includes working templates, tool examples, and book has the full explanations of how to plan, create, and use each tool.

Summary

There are hundreds of different methodologies in the project management industry about how to execute a project across the many industries and project types. There is no methodology that is going to work for every project, so it is important that we all come back to the industry standard established by PMI, which is documented in the *PMBOK* Guide. It is also important to note that this particular book, unlike the *PMBOK* Guide is specific enough that anyone could pick it up and use it on his or her projects today. This chapter documented a methodology that you can pick up and use with real-world examples. It also explains to any project manager what to do at a minimum in each knowledge area on their projects. As PMO Manager, the project management methodology will most likely be the foundation or your PMO and therefore it is important that you are active in its creation and understand all aspects of it. Have your Project Managers follow it as closely as possible as they execute their projects and be there for them to support them along the way.

PMO Build Decisions:

1. Decide, based on the PMO model you selected how project management is completed in the PMO. If it is a controlling PMO or a supportive PMO, decide how project management will be done based on that model.

2. Decide whether the PMO will have Project Managers and, if so, will they each follow a formal project management methodology?

3. Decide whether the Project Managers will be Project management Professional (PMP®)-certified.

4. Decide how you will audit project management processes/procedures outlined from the Initiation/Initiating through the Closing processes.

5. Decide whether the PMO Manager will also manage projects.

Chapter Review Answers:

1. Most of the knowledge areas are used and addressed in every project. Therefore, it is important to think about them and ensure you have a solid understanding.

2. A PMO Manager should never administer a project management methodology to Project Managers without support, training and ongoing guidance.

3. You should collect "lessons-learned" information throughout the project. Start collecting it during the kickoff meeting and don't finish until you close the project.

4. A "life cycle" is a phase that the project is in at a given time, and a "knowledge area" is a particular area of the project. For example, the Initiation/Initiating phase is part of the life cycle; Project Communications Management is a knowledge area.

5. The Circle of Communications chart shows the Project Manager fully connected and in control of project communications.

Chapter 11

PMO Reporting

Figure 11.1 PMO Build Schedule - PMO Reporting

Task Name	Resource Names
Step 5 - Design & Build or Enhance Period (Chapter 5 - 12)	**PMO Manager**
-Design PMO	**PMO Manager**
+Design PMO Core Components	**PMO Manager**
-Build PMO	**PMO Manager**
Create PMO Business Management Area on Centralized Repository Site (Sections to create are documented in Implementation Phase)	PMO Manager
+Create PMO Core Components	**PMO Manager**
+Create PMO Model (Chapter 5)	**PMO Manager**
+Create PMO Maturity Model	**PMO Manager**
+Create PMO Staffing Model (Chapter 6)	**PMO Manager**
+Create PMO Training (Chapter 7)	PMO Manager
+Create Process Methodology Areas (Chapters 8-10 - where applicable)	**PMO Manager**
+Create PMO Reporting (Chapter 11)	PMO Manager
Review Past, Current, and Future Reporting Requirements	PMO Manager
Assess and Enhance any existing PMO Reports	PMO Manager
+Create Process Methodologies Specific Reports (Portfolio/Program/Project)	**PMO Manager**
Review and Capture Management/Customer Reporting requirements	PMO Manager
Determine processes for report creation Automation vs. Manual Reporting	PMO Manager
Review and determine various Report Data Sources	PMO Manager
Create PMO Dashboards if applicable and funding available	PMO Manager
+Company Reporting Timing Requirements	**PMO Manager**
Document PMO Build Decisions	PMO Manager
PMO Reporting Complete	PMO Manager

Questions you should be able to answer after reading this chapter:

1. When setting up the PMO reporting components, what are the three time perspectives to consider and why?

2. Name four considerations of building the reporting component of your PMO.

3. How does the PMO model play into PMO reporting? How are they tied?

4. Which tool can you use to help your organization report on company events?

5. Which PMO role is highly recommended to handle all reporting requirements and produce all reports?

As we continue to build your PMO, one of the areas that you, the PMO Manager, needs to keep top of mind is PMO reporting. PMO reporting provides a great way to show the value of the PMO to your management team and customers. It is important for PMO Managers to understand exactly what data is *available* in the PMO and what data the management team and customers *want*, and then compare the two to understand any differences. Sometimes there are mix-matches between what is being asked for and what is actually available, and those disconnects can be troublesome for any PMO Manager. Those disconnects can be very difficult to resolve for a variety of reasons and, as PMO Manager, somehow you will need to resolve them. Actually, PMO Managers deal with a number of factors and considerations when thinking about PMO reporting, such as tools, management and customer requirements, automation and manual processes, timeframes and staffing, and so on. In addition, PMO Managers need to think about the concepts of past, current, and future reporting on their PMO and drive their PMO report development based on those three factors. More details will follow on these concepts, but for now, think about the three time concepts as the foundation for how you will drive your PMO reporting in your organization.

PMO reporting is actually a complicated process and keeping everything on-track and balanced can be time consuming for anyone. Typically this responsibility falls onto the PMO Manager. Some PMO Managers hire a PMO Reporting Analyst to produce various reports and dashboards of PMO data. In those PMOs, the PMO Reporting Analyst's role is very valuable and something you too should consider when you are thinking about service offerings and staffing needs of the PMO and what a full time reporting analyst could offer to your customers or management by having them on staff producing reports for your organization. Many PMO's use PMO reporting analysts in their organizations.

PMO Managers only have one way to approach PMO reporting with any chance of being successful. PMO Managers, as a best practice, should approach PMO reporting as they did with the other components they built when creating the PMO—start slowly, and as the PMO matures, let the PMO reporting mature as well. Starting this process off too quickly or offering too many reports and exposing what is going on in the PMO before it is mature enough to handle any kind of exposure can spell major trouble. If PMO Managers decide to control how fast they roll out reporting and the release of PMO information in the manner to which is beneficial to the organization—not too quickly and not too slowly—then the reporting component and the organization, as a whole, has a much better chance of success.

It is very easy as a PMO Manager to create dashboards and generate a ton of useless reports that nobody is ever going to use and still not focus on what you, your management team, or your customers actually require to make business decisions. Making accurate and timely PMO information available is a key component to PMO reporting. Understand that the data that you provide people use it to make decisions and course corrections. As PMO Manager, your job is to make sure that the data is accurate, timely, and provides value to your recipients. Using these three key factors when thinking about your PMO data is critical, and if you continually use these as guiding principles, you will be forced to make the right decisions around your data. Think about the negative impact on the PMO and the company if you create reports or dashboards that show bad or late data and force people into making decisions without the right information. It **will** hurt your credibility, which could reflect negatively on you in the eyes of management and your customers. You, as PMO Manager, may never recover.

As it came up in previous chapters, it comes up in PMO reporting too: the PMO model that you select for your organization also plays a role in establishing and setting up PMO reporting. The PMO model plays a big role in the type of reporting you do for your PMO. We will get into more detail later in the chapter, but think about the different reports you would produce if you were a supportive PMO, compared to a directive PMO, compared to a coaching PMO, and so on. This is just another area that PMO Managers need to factor in when building the reporting components of the PMO.

Other common areas that are just as important to consider as the PMO model choice are the resources, procedures, and infrastructure we have talked about throughout the book. Even in PMO reporting, the same three areas are very relevant and something the PMO Manager needs to consider when establishing a reporting plan for the organization. Keep those areas in mind as we continue through this chapter.

Lastly, when PMO Managers think about reporting, there must be some thinking around dashboards and metrics. Metrics are going to be a PMO Manager's greatest friend and worst nightmare—all at once. With metrics, PMO Managers can expose the great work their Program Managers and Project Managers are doing, on one hand, and on the other, those same metrics will expose problems and trouble areas. Metrics play a big role in PMO reporting and are something that PMO Managers need to figure out quickly how they will incorporate into their organization.

Let's move now into PMO reporting and look at which areas you need to consider when building your PMO and determine the types of reporting you will do for your organization.

Setting up PMO Reporting

Before you get too deep into setting up and creating a series of reports for your PMO, it is important to understand the concept of past, current, and future reporting in more depth because that concept and thought process will be the foundation of how to create reports for your PMO. PMO Managers who approach their thinking in that way are preparing themselves nicely for any possible reporting questions they will be asked by management, customers, and team members. When thinking about the three categories, you cover all options and set yourself up nicely for years to come. Let us look at these three areas now from a PMO reporting perspective.

Past reports—When thinking about creating or setting up reports that have historical data (data from the past), you do so mainly to understand performance-related data based on how well the team performed from a time, cost, scope, quality, and so on, perspective. These types of reports are very valuable when it comes to establishing budgets, timeframes, scope items, and more, for future portfolios, programs, or projects. These types of reports, when there is data over a several year period, are important because they give a longer performance history of how the programs and projects have performed, and are not even possible to produce with current or limited data. These reports are in the past—the results cannot be modified or changed. What is done is done!

Current reports—The primary purpose when thinking about creating and setting up reports based on current data is to understand both performance and the current state of the activities. Regardless of whether the reports are portfolio, program, or project reports, they all need current information to allow management and customers to make business decisions about the information. Programs might be tracking over-budget, projects might be missing key dates are just some of the examples of the types of reports and information that is important to provide to management and customers to course-correct and get the various efforts back on track.

Future reports—When thinking about setting up and establishing future-type reports, you do so for predictive modeling, where you build reports to predict future outcomes. Earned-value reporting is a perfect example of creating schedule and cost performance reports that help understand and predict how the team is doing from schedule and cost perspective. It is best said that future reports are based on trends, and performance data (schedule/cost) is one type of data that you can trend very easily and therefore make available for reporting by any PMO Manager.

Tips & Best Practices

Think hard about the three different types of reporting (past, current, and future) and as a best practice try to bucket your reporting requests into them.

When starting to think about some of the various PMO reporting areas, it is important to consider the right level of reporting (high-level vs. detailed reporting) for your

322

management team and customers, and the different factors and considerations you will face building out the PMO reporting component of your PMO.

Some of these considerations include:

- PMO model
- Process methodologies (portfolio, program, and project)
- Management and customer requirements
- Automated vs. manual reporting
- Data sources for generating reports
- PMO dashboards
- Reporting timing requirements
- Reporting staff workload consideration
- Reporting tools

These are just some of the considerations that PMO Managers must factor in before rolling out formal PMO reports. Your organization will vary, and of course, some of these considerations will apply and others will not apply, but this list provides a good starting point for you. As PMO Manager, you need to understand each of these areas, in detail, in order to determine how to set up reporting in your organization.

Let us spend some time now and break each consideration down, in detail. Once we complete that process, you will have a great foundation to establish reporting in your PMO.

PMO Model

There is a significant relationship between the PMO model you have in your organization and your various PMO reports. Depending on the PMO model you are using, reporting can play a big part of a PMO Manager's role. Let us look at how the PMO model and PMO reporting will work together allowing you to see how you would drive reporting based on the PMO model.

Supportive PMO model—In a supportive PMO, your PMO reports "support" the Program Managers and Project Managers in the PMO. The reports include:

- Program and project status reports
- Financial and budget reports
- Risk reports
- Issue reports
- Schedule reports

Most of the reports in a supportive PMO model focus on getting the Program Managers and Project Managers the information so they can be successful. These same reports also go to your management team and customers, so it is important to understand the same reports that are used to help Program Managers and Project Managers are also used to potentially expose problems, issues, and performance issues to your management team and customers. PMO reports generally, though, are very beneficial to both roles to highlight information that is occurring in the programs and projects and then allow everyone to work together and focus on improving and course correcting.

Coaching PMO model—Most of the same reports used in the supportive model are also used in the coaching model. However, when in the coaching model, the reports are then used to help coach the Program and Project Managers into correcting any areas where they are having problems and getting their efforts back on track.

Directive PMO model—In a directive PMO, the PMO reports focus on program and project "compliance" and/or "auditing" and are used by management and the Program Managers and Project Managers to determine how well their efforts are in some cases complying to the standards setup by the PMO Manager. In other cases, the PMO reports are used by everyone to understand and report the current status of the programs and projects. The reports can include:

- Financial and budget reports—is the budget on track?
- Methodology audit report—have the programs and projects completed all deliverables?
- Schedule reports—is the project on time and achieving its planned milestones?

These are just some of the PMO models that highlight the ties between the PMO models and the PMO reporting. As you can see, even in these few examples, the reports tend to be for different purposes. By understanding the PMO model, you have to start thinking about the various PMO reports important to that model. It is important to also understand that the choice of PMO model will drive the majority of the type of reports required and asked for by your management team or your customers, but it won't be the only thing. Other factors, such as management and customer-specific reporting needs also drive a lot of the reporting requirements.

Bill's Thoughts:

The PMO model plays such a big role in determining which PMO reports you generate for your organization. My last two PMOs were directive PMOs and, therefore, many of my reports were around understanding the current status of programs and projects and trying to help my Program and Project managers to keep everything on track. Do not underestimate how these two PMO components work so closely together.

Process Methodologies (Portfolio, Program, and Project)

As you can imagine, when thinking about the various process methodologies that make up your PMO, it is important to consider the types of reports that each generate as they execute through their respective processes. If you think about the concepts of past, current, and future reports as well, it is easy to think about the types of reports needed in each of those process methodologies. Let us look at just a small sample of the many reports available in each area (refer to the specific chapters (Portfolio, Program, and Project) for more information).

Portfolio Management Reports

Typical portfolio management reports include:

- **Past Reports (historical versions of current reports)**
    - Historical Portfolio Roadmaps
    - Historical Planning Report
    - Historical Budget Report
    - Historical Business Value/ROI Report
    - Historical Performance Report
- **Current Reports**
    - Yearly Planning Report
    - Program and Project List Report
    - Product Revenue Report
    - Portfolio Status Report
    - Financial Planning Report
    - Strategic Plans
    - Portfolio Schedules
    - Resource and Capacity Report
    - Portfolio Optimizing Report
- **Future Reports**
    - Future Year Planning Roadmap
    - Portfolio Earned-Value Report
    - Portfolio Continuous Improvement Report
    - Portfolio Performance Report

There are a number of portfolio management systems, such as Microsoft Dynamics® CRM, that companies use to manage their portfolios. A portfolio management system is a key tool for your Portfolio Manager or PMO Manager roles to use for portfolio-level reporting. Portfolio management systems include many features and functionality that provide some great portfolio-level reports and span the requirements for past, current, and future reporting.

Program Management Reports

Typical program management reports include:

- **Past Reports (historical versions of current reports)**

- Historical Program Performance Report
- Historical Program Customer Satisfaction Report
- Historical Program Financial Report
- **Current Reports**
  - Business Value Report
  - Customer Satisfaction Report
  - Program Status Report
  - Program and Project Matrix Report
  - Program Budget Report
  - Program Interdependencies Report
  - Program Risk Report
  - Program Schedule
  - Program Quality Report
- **Future Reports**
  - Program Trending Report
  - Program Earned-Value Report
  - Program Performance Report

Project Management Reports

Typical project management reports include:

- **Past Reports (historical versions of current reports)**
  - Historical Performance Report
  - Historical Budget Report
  - Historical Scope and Requirements Report
- **Current Reports**
  - Project Status Report
  - Project Budget Report
  - Project Schedule Report
  - Project Risk & Issue Report
  - Project Performance Report

- Project Resources Report (including both human and electronic utilization)
- Project Earned-Value Reports
- **Future Reports**
    - Earned-Value Reports
    - Project Execution Trend Report
    - Project Resource Utilization Report
    - Project Performance Reports

A number of portfolio, program, and project management reports that were covered earlier in the book, as part of their specific chapters, were purposely excluded from these lists, but **should definitely be included** when determining all the reports required for your PMO reporting. It would be a mistake to leave those reports out of your reporting scope and more applicable to detail those in their respective methodology chapters compared to re-listing them here in this chapter as well.

In addition, these report examples are just a small sampling of the thousands of reports available today. Many of these reports are tool-agnostic, which is a consideration for you, as PMO Manager, to consider when selecting your PMO tools. However, some of these reports will be included with your tools, so taking the time to research the tools and their reporting features is definitely time well spent. More details and information about PMO tools are later in the book, but they are important to consider now when you are building the various PMO report offerings—and you need some tools to make this happen.

Management and Customer Reporting Requirements

Your management team and customers are the main requestors of PMO data that you will encounter. Your program and project teams will also request specific type of reports, but their requests will pale in comparison to what your management team will ask for on a regular basis. It happens all the time, your management team will ask for a variety of reports ranging from program and project status, to financial reports, to information they need for an important meeting...in the next hour. Management reporting can be very demanding and can include countless unexpected hours of pulling data that may or may not be readily available or even possible to locate. This is a big part of a PMO Manager's role and many get caught in unexpected situations because they have not prepared or worked with their management team enough to inform them of what kind of data is available and what is just not possible to obtain for one reason or another. Another thing for PMO Managers to consider when they are working with their management team, and depending on the expected volume, is hiring a PMO Reporting Analyst. A PMO Reporting Analyst is available for generating reports as well as supporting other groups and customers who ask for reporting data. More details and a job description for a PMO Reporting Analyst are provided later in this chapter, including a sampling of the type of skills needed for this type of analyst role.

Tips for working with your management team when establishing PMO reporting:

- Communicate, communicate, communicate. Ensure you are spending time with your management team regularly and sharing the data you have (and do not have) in your PMO for reporting.
- Seek feedback about existing reports and any communications with the management team. It is not a good idea for PMO Managers to throw reports over the wall to the management team without seeking valuable input about what is working and not working for them.
- Ask your management team if they want to see charts and graphs in their reports or do they prefer raw data. This is an important way to connect and understand if your management team is "pictures and graphics" people or "raw data" people who get distracted by charts and graphics.

Tips & Best Practices

Spend the time and capture your management and customers reporting requirements. This is time well spent to ensure they have the reports they need to make business decisions.

Bill's Thoughts:

This last point about your management team being "graphic and chart" people compared to people who connect with just raw numbers and text is so important, and something not just for PMO Managers, but for everyone to understand. There have been a couple of times in my career where I have been in situations where I never had the chance to ask my management team what format they preferred before sending reports to them. As you can imagine, when I sent the reports without first asking which format they preferred, the reports came right back with complaints and issues from my management team. The minute I talked to them and asked them what they preferred, and then updated the reports, my reports were accepted. Simply adding a chart to a Microsoft Excel spreadsheet can make a huge difference to some people.

Automated vs. Manual Reporting

When thinking about the various types of reports for your PMO, one thing to consider is how to create the reports. You will also need to know what data is readily available in the system you are using and what data will need to be generated manually. This is important for PMO Managers to understand because it could mean adding a couple hours or more to your employees' existing workload, or adding mere minutes by having the data pulled and the reports automatically generated by the software. The PMO Manager should be responsible for determining which reports are available with the PMO software they are already using. There could easily be a lot of reports and data available for reporting with limited effort. Often, large project portfolio systems have powerful reports included with the software, but the PMO Manager needs to ensure someone is entering the appropriate data so the reports don't become useless. PMO Managers need to understand which reports are available in the various PMO tools, and then determine if there is data to support reporting.

Think about the time commitment and the extra workload that manual reporting adds to PMO employees' existing workload, and then balance that with the asks of your management team and customers. Not every requested report is possible or worth the manual effort to create. As PMO Manager, one of your roles is to understand the requested reports and ensure they are feasible and worth creating. Sometimes, standing up for your employees and saying no to creating reports that are not feasible or that will take an exorbitant amount of time is necessary.

Data Sources for Generating Reports

Understanding the various reporting data sources is often a very difficult problem for PMO Managers to resolve. This is because it is often difficult to understand what sources are available to pull PMO data from to provide meaningful reports to your management or your customers. There is certainly no lack of available data, but getting access to it or knowing how up to date it is often provides a challenge. The following are some possible data sources that PMO Managers can draw from for generating PMO reports.

- Project portfolio systems
- Company-wide status systems
- Company-wide financial systems
- Company-wide project repositories
- Company-wide time tracking systems
- Program and project quality tracking systems
- Company-wide program and project risk and issue repositories
- Company-wide project schedule repositories, such as Microsoft® Project Server

These are just some of the many examples of the different types of company applications that have data available for PMO reporting. As noted above, even though there is a number of systems that companies have to track program and project data, it is not known whether the data in those systems hold valuable PMO data and if it is readily available for reporting purposes. That is up to you, as PMO Manager, to work through and understand and determine exactly what systems hold the data you need for reporting. As PMO Manager, it is important for you to spend some time and learn about these systems and the data they include, and then figure out what types of PMO reports you could offer based on that analysis. Nothing is better than having systems full of data and automated reports all ready to go when your customers or management team asks.

PMO Dashboards

One of the greatest tools PMO Managers can offer to their management team, customers, and program and project teams is the PMO dashboard. PMO dashboards have been around for many years, come in every shape and size, and are always customized for the organization. Rarely do PMO dashboards come out of the box and ready for organizations to use without some customizing. **Figure 11.2 PMO Dashboard Examples** shows some samples of PMO dashboards that are available and created via software products on the market today. It is important to understand what the PMO dashboards look like because the software products can produce such a wide variety, and if you choose one piece of software over the other without understanding what the dashboard looks like or how to customize it, you might end up regretting your choice of software. (Matteucci 2012)

Figure 11.2 PMO Dashboard Examples

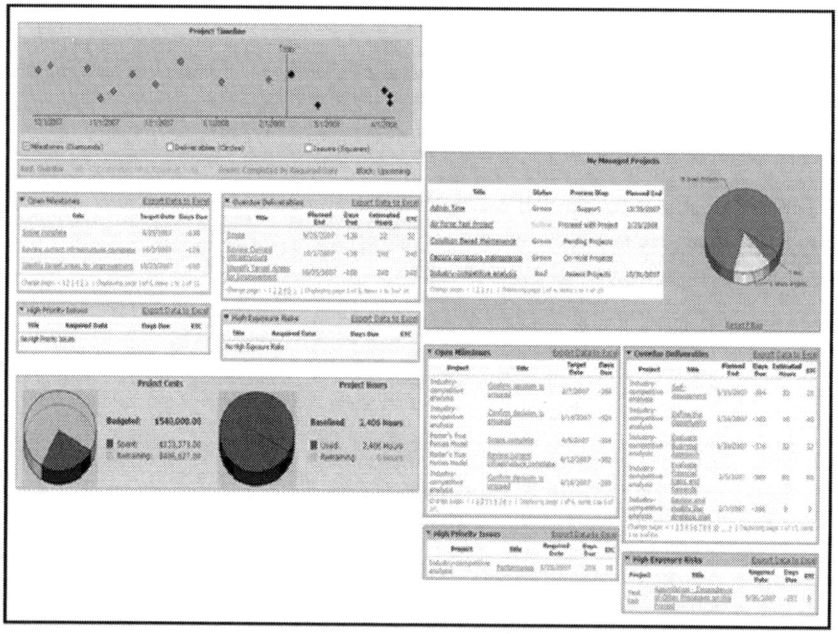

Dashboard example provided by VCSonline.com and called "VPMi dashboard for project management. More information can be found at: **http://www.vcsonline.com**

As PMO Manager, sit down with your management team and customers and understand their PMO dashboard requirements. Document those requirements and compare what they are asking for and what is available in the various PMO type software (Portfolio Management, Program Management...etc.) on the market today. Discuss the differences and whether management and customers can live with those differences. Spend the time and review different packages and try to match the requirements as closely as possible.

Hidden Cost of PMO Dashboards

One of the traps that PMO Managers fall into and are not aware of when they commit to setting up and running a PMO dashboard is the cost of running the dashboards— either by existing staff or by hiring new staff. When creating PMO dashboards, there is a cost associated to running and maintaining those dashboards that needs to be considered with the PMO staffing model, as well as the cost of running a PMO. The PMO dashboard team is mentioned in Chapter 6, "PMO Staffing Models." When companies get serious about creating PMOs— maybe not during the first year—but if they prove to be successful, a PMO dashboard is a common tool that is requested and supported by management. When that occurs, remember to factor in the PMO dashboard team costs and the overhead of running it within your organization.

Bill's Thoughts:

I worked in a number of companies that have PMO dashboards and they have been incredible. I can't stress enough how important they are and how valuable they can be toward running a large PMO. If possible, spend the time and money setting up a PMO dashboard, I don't think you will regret it; I know I never did. It provided the real-time updates that my management team and customers always wanted with my PMO data.

Reporting: Timing Requirements

One of the factors that PMO Managers face when determining their PMO reporting requirements is their company's internal reporting deadlines. For example, most companies have a deadline of end-of-day Friday for program and project status reports. As PMO Manager, you may be in the position to establish or change those deadlines, but you will be subject to follow or adhere to them as well especially if they are company deadlines, not necessary PMO created deadlines. This is a good process that companies have established because it sets the foundation for status reporting; program and project teams must get in line to ensure their data is up to date and accurate at least once a week. As PMO Manager, these deadlines make your life easier because you have a deadline for everyone to hit, and you see who hits and who doesn't hit that deadline. You can do your summary-level reporting based on the updated program and project data.

One of the easiest and most effective ways for PMO Managers to keep the reporting timeframes top of mind and easily remembered is by creating a PMO reporting calendar. **Figure 11.3 PMO Reporting Calendar** shows key dates on the calendar. These items include status reporting dates, financial reporting dates, and PMO newsletters, for example. As PMO Manager, you can add any event you feel is relevant and important to the organization to this calendar.

Figure 11.3 PMO Reporting Calendar

May 2012

SUNDAY	MONDAY	TUESDAY	WEDNESDAY	THURSDAY	FRIDAY	SATURDAY
	1 — Monthly Financial Report due by EOD	2	3	4 — Program/Project Status Due by EOD	5	
6	7	8	9	10	11 — Program/Project Status Due by EOD	12
13	14	15	16	17	18 — Program/Project Status Due by EOD	19
20	21	22	23	24	25 — Program/Project Status Due by EOD	26
27	28	29	30 — PMO Newsletter Due by EOD	31 — PMO Newsletter Sent by EOD		

You can add a PMO reporting calendar directly to an intranet site—anywhere users access PMO data regularly and can see upcoming events such as program and project deadlines. As PMO Manager, ensure you create a PMO reporting calendar for your organization. It is a critical PMO reporting tool that you are responsible for maintaining and it helps set the rhythm of reporting for you and your PMO team members to follow.

Tips & Best Practices

Another PMO calendar to use in the organization is a PMO employee out-of-office calendar. This allows you as PMO Manager to understand and see when your PMO team members are away from the office.

Reporting: Staff Workload Considerations

Earlier in this chapter, I mentioned the time it takes to create reports for the PMO, which is worth considering again because the time employees or contractors spend creating PMO reports is time spent away from working on programs and projects—unless reporting is built into the project life cycle. Typically, reporting is not built into the schedule, which is something the industry needs to improve upon, in general. As PMO Manager, work with your project teams to ensure they allocate time for cycles to spend toward report requests so that when they do come in, they are not as much of a burden to complete. In addition, make sure you consider the number of requests you are making of your team members without taking into account their current workload. You might be adding to the problem and not realizing it. If it becomes administrative overhead (team members having to produce PMO reports in addition to their current duties), one of the options you have is to hire a PMO Reporting Analyst (as noted earlier). The analyst can take a huge amount of workload off team members, Program Managers, or Project Managers and can be a tremendous amount of help to you by running administrative reports. Later in the chapter we talk in more specifics about the PMO Reporting Analyst role.

Reporting Tools

The various reporting tools that are available for your PMO will vary greatly from company to company. Factors will depend on the state of your PMO (new vs. existing PMO), management support, budget availability, company standards, and so on. It is safe to say that most PMOs have some tools already available to them. As you build your new PMO, however, picking additional tools is not a trivial task. Think about spending thousands of dollars on a reporting tool, and then not having the processes and procedures in place to enter the required data so the tool becomes useless to you and your organization and a waste of money.

PMO Reporting Tool Considerations

When selecting PMO reporting tools, consider the following:

- Budget availability
- Process methodology maturity
- Management support
- Timeframe of PMO—if the PMO is just starting, adding a large, formal reporting tool may not be the right time
- Manager, customer, program, and project team feature requirements
- Organizational policies
- Licensing fees and yearly payment commitments

Taking these factors into consideration will help drive which types of PMO reporting you put into your new or existing PMO. There is much more information about PMO tools later in the book.

Assessment of Existing PMO Reports

Earlier, it was mentioned that there are a number of factors and considerations for creating PMO reporting when you, as PMO Manager, are starting from scratch and building a new PMO. However, reality says that not all PMO Managers have the ability to create their PMOs from scratch and more often walk into an existing PMO where they must assess the existing PMO's reporting. This is actually very common for PMO Managers, so you need to be aware of how to assess an existing PMO and its current set of reporting. Here are the items to look for when assessing existing PMO reporting—your recommendations and adjustments will be based off your existing findings and not on preconceived notions of what you feel will work. It would be an unprofessional move to come in and suggest a process, tool, or a procedure without first doing a proper assessment of the existing state of reporting. You must remember, someone suggested the current set of reports, so there must have been a valid reason at one time, and it would be naïve to ignore those initial thoughts and reasons why those initial reports were there in the first place.

Some of the assessment considerations include, but are not limited to, the following:

- Current management and customer reports
- PMO reporting budget availability
- Current reporting tools and status of tools (updated regularly vs. never used)
- Current reporting timeframe requirements (weekly vs. monthly, for example)
- Existing reporting requirements documentation, if it exists
- Current list of issues or concerns from management, customers, program, and project teams
- Current reporting staff—or is reporting done on top of employees' current workload
- Assessment of automated or manual reporting process

After arming yourself with these considerations, you should have a good starting point to assess the current state of reporting in the existing PMO. You must approach these assessment activities with a rigor and structure and with an end goal of creating a PMO Reporting Recommendations document. The documented results will help you with conversations and making decisions with your management team and customers about how to move forward with any PMO reporting changes.

Problems with PMO Reporting

While assessing the existing PMO, you will quickly run into some of the problems that management and customers are having with the current PMO reporting. There could be a variety of reasons as to why the existing reporting is not working, and your role is to assess those reasons quickly and make improvements where possible. These improvements could include training staff, shutting down reports that are no longer valuable, changing or updating processes, and so on.

The following list includes some of the common problems you will run into as you assess existing PMOs:

- Reports are not presented in a professional or standard format (a lack of consistency in reporting formats is a big problem).
- Reports take too much time to produce—the manual process takes too much time to create.
- Reports are not timely or do not come out consistently each week or month, for example.
- No dynamic or automated reports are available.
- Reporting tools are difficult to work with or there is a lack of data to produce consistent reports.
- Inconsistent data due to multiple data sources.
- Management and customers are not getting the reports they need to make business decisions.
- Program and project teams are unwilling to spend the time to create meaningful reports.

This list is just a small sampling of all the problems and issues you can find when evaluating existing PMO reporting. Your role, as PMO Manager, is to review each problem and determine if there are quick and simple solutions to turn around some of the problem areas. Not every problem can be resolved overnight, but start with some of the high-priority items that make the most sense and provide the biggest impact.

PMO Reporting Analyst

One of the common themes that you might have noticed pop up repeatedly during the course of this chapter is the suggestion to hire a PMO Reporting Analyst for your PMO. The reason it is continued to be mentioned is because of the incredible value this role can bring to the PMO at a relatively low cost. The PMO Reporting Analyst works with the PMO Manager, directly supporting the management team, customers, and the Portfolio, Program, and Project Managers with reporting. The PMO Reporting Analyst collects project status, analyzes information, creates reports (including dashboards), to then be presented to senior management. This is generally a full-time role, but this person could also perform the Project Coordinator duties as well, directly supporting individual project teams.

Some of the various responsibilities of the PMO Reporting Analyst include:

- Collecting, analyzing, updating, and publishing weekly and monthly project status reports.
- Regular and ad-hoc resource forecasting and utilization report generation, including identification of gaps or risks to resourcing.
- Communicating and following up with Project Managers and the management team to ensure high-quality reporting of status.
- Preparing senior management presentations with the ability to translate and professionally communicate data-driven results.

It is understandable that not all PMOs have the available budget to hire a full-time PMO Reporting Analyst, however, if your hire a low-cost or newly graduated university student who is looking for a break into the business world, you will quickly see that the cost for an analyst becomes less of a factor.

It is also recommended that you hire a PMO Reporting Analyst later in the PMO report creation process. It is far more important when first creating your PMO reporting processes and sets of reports that you focus on getting the right reports to satisfy the needs of your management team and customers first, and then as your PMO matures, you can hire a PMO Reporting Analyst. **It will be worth every penny you spend!**

Summary

To summarize the PMO reporting chapter, we have covered a wide range of areas for PMO Managers to consider when establishing the reporting for their organization. As we review the processes and procedures outline in this chapter, one of the main takeaway's for PMO Managers is to focus on the PMO reporting requirement(s) from their management team and customers because those requirements will actually drive many of the initial reports for the organization. Then, as the PMO grows, the reporting requirements will grow as well and there will be a need for more and more reporting. In addition, it is important to consider the role that the PMO model (supportive, controlling, and so on) and the various process methodologies (portfolio, program, and project) each play in the reports needed in the organization. Each play a role because they will define the type of reports needed. A supportive PMO might have different reports than a controlling PMO, and so on. Finally, as you think about reporting, consider the workload added to your PMO employees and how hiring a PMO Reporting Analyst might be cost effective and a great way to take the reporting deliverables off those employees and onto someone who can do it full time.

PMO Build Decisions:

1. Decide on your management teams' and customers' key reporting elements for the PMO.

2. Decide on the whether any of the reporting considerations covered will be a factor or not in your PMO.

3. Decide what will be the initial set of reports to create.

4. Decide whether you will create a PMO dashboard.

5. Decide whether you will hire a PMO Reporting Analyst.

Chapter Review Answers:

1. Time perspectives to consider are: past reports, current reports, and future reports. They give you three possible time frames to think about when reporting data and give you a foundation on which to create all of your reporting.

2. Four considerations for building your PMO's reporting component include: management and customer requirements, automated vs. manual reporting, report data sources, and PMO dashboards.

3. The PMO model drives the types of reports you use. A supportive PMO model is quite different in its reporting requirements than a directive PMO model.

4. Use a PMO reporting calendar to help you report on company events.

5. The PMO Reporting Analyst role can handle all reporting needs.

Chapter 12

PMO Tools and Processes

Figure 12.1 PMO Build Schedule - PMO Tools and Processes

Task Name	Resource Names
Step 5 - Design & Build or Enhance Period (Chapter 5 - 12)	**PMO Manager**
-Design PMO	**PMO Manager**
+Design PMO Core Components	**PMO Manager**
-Build PMO	**PMO Manager**
Create PMO Business Management Area on Centralized Repository Site (Section)	PMO Manager
+Create PMO Core Components	**PMO Manager**
+Create PMO Model (Chapter 5)	**PMO Manager**
+Create PMO Maturity Model	**PMO Manager**
+Create PMO Staffing Model (Chapter 6)	**PMO Manager**
+Create PMO Training (Chapter 7)	PMO Manager
+Create Process Methodology Areas (Chapters 8-10 - where applicable)	**PMO Manager**
+Create PMO Reporting (Chapter 11)	PMO Manager
+Create PMO Tools & Processes (Chapter 12)	**PMO Manager**
Review the Communication Tools Process by analyzing 5 W's	PMO Manager
Review PMO Standard Tools & Process for Organization	PMO Manager
Review and Select Portfolio Management Tools	PMO Manager
Review and Select Program/Project Management Tools	PMO Manager
Perform PMO Tools Evaluation (where applicable)	PMO Manager
+Create PMO Processes	**PMO Manager**
+Create PMO Generic Process (used across Portfolio/Program/Project Management Processes)	**PMO Manager**
+Create Portfolio Management Processes	**PMO Manager**
+Create Program/Project Management Processes	**PMO Manager**

Questions you should be able to answer after reading this chapter:

1. What are the five critical questions of communication tools?

2. Name three standard PMO tools.

3. What are the pitfalls of the "magic pill"?

4. Name three PMO generic processes.

5. Name three PMO processes tips and best practices.

One of the most critical parts of building a PMO is selecting the tools (for example, software) for the organization. PMOs generate so much information that having a good set of PMO tools makes finding and reporting the data much easier. For you, the PMO Manager, the tool selection process is critical because, in most cases, you not only are in the position of making the recommendation, but also in the position of implementing it for your organization. Another thing to be aware of during the tool selection process is that, as PMO Manager, you will find software companies approaching you and suggesting that their tool will save the day—you will continually be bombarded with their hard sales tactics. These tactics rarely work out in your favor and can end up costing you a lot of time and money. This is not a good position to be in with your PMO employees or management team if you fall for a one-size-fits-all solution and your employees are then stuck using a tool they do not believe adds value.

One of the best practices for PMO Managers to follow when implementing tools within their organization is to approach the process very slowly and carefully—don't be tempted to jump at the first "all-in-one-box" solution that comes through the door. Taking a slow but structured approach allows you to understand the needs of your management team and employees to find a solution that will work for everyone.

Another component of PMO tools that often gets lost when building a PMO is the cost and expenses associated with purchasing or building the tools and the ongoing costs to maintain, train employees, and support the tools as you run your PMO. As PMO Manager, remember the cost ramifications of these tools and work with your management team to ensure you have the budget now (and ongoing) to support the PMO tools. In some cases, you will not have any budget issues and not a problem; whereas, in other cases, especially if you are just building and proving the value of the PMO, budget might be limited and, therefore, your options are limited. Consider budget a key component in the PMO tools process.

Aside from tools, one of the other components to understand around building a PMO is to ensure you're building the foundation on PMO processes. PMO processes, such as governance, change control, and escalation processes, are critical to define and drive in the PMO so that you, as PMO Manager, can control, change, and make adjustments as necessary. Defining these standards in one process methodology, such as program management, makes it very simple to adopt the same principals and process across portfolio and project management as well, which helps drive repeatability and consistency across your PMO.

Communication Tools

When selecting PMO tools, it is important to approach the decision from a communication perspective. That is right, look at the various procedures/processes, resources, and information needed in your PMO and test those against the various communication tools available in the project management industry. It is actually an easy process to view your PMO from a communications perspective, and it is the same process used by newspaper reporters when they approach writing a story. Before reporters write a story, they ask the following questions: **who, what, where, when, and how**. In this case, the "how" will actually get you thinking about the tools that you might use to report this data. Asking these five questions gives you a huge advantage in understanding the PMO tools you might need and gives you the structure to start this process. Let us look at these questions now:

Who—"Who" from management, leadership, and team members needs PMO data? This is generally a very large list, consider including more people than fewer and you should be fine. Focus on having your PMO data available to everyone, and then determine the process for limiting the data if and when the situation arises.

What—"What" type of information should your PMO produce? This answer will vary depending on who is asking and what level the person is in the organization. Think about the types of high-level information an executive, such as Vice President, would want from your PMO data compared to an individual team member on a single project looking for a risk register item. Clearly, these are very different needs and very different levels of individuals asking for PMO data. As PMO Manager, make this data available by selecting the right tools that can satisfy all types of requests. Other considerations of "what" PMO tools you need depend on the roles in the PMO as well. If you have Portfolio Managers, Program Managers, and Project Managers, the data you need to satisfy them will be different than if your PMO just has Project Managers. Think about the organizational structure and how it plays a role in the data and, therefore, the data your organization needs.

Where—"Where" will the PMO data be available for reporting purposes? When thinking and focusing on the "where," think about the location where the PMO data is stored and how to access the information for reporting.

When—"When" will the data be available and current for reporting purposes? As PMO Manager, your focus on the "when" will have you thinking about any internal administration timeframes or company-specific deadlines to know when your PMO employees must enter their data to satisfy those "when" requirements. For example, many companies have end-of-week status report deadlines, so company employees, including your PMO employees, enter their data by end-of-day on Fridays, so focusing on the "when," you won't have data to report each week until Saturday and forward. It is important to look across all the various types of information that might be needed and understand the various timeframes as to when the data is needed and when it will be available for reporting. Another example is monthly finances, another popular process at most companies that only occurs once a month.

How—"How" is one of the most important questions to answer when thinking about the PMO data needed for your audience. How the data is extracted, how the data is reported—your role is to focus on whether there is data available automatically, or you have to pull it manually and the timing around data availability. These are just some of many decisions to factor in when evaluating various communication tools.

These are definitely important questions to consider when determining which tools to use in your PMO. It is also important to realize that by going through these questions, you will learn how to look at the different tool requests and how to generally approach this process.

As PMO Manager, you should understand how to evaluate PMO tools so you can hold off those pushy sales people and make sure you are asking the right questions when reviewing and testing specific PMO tools for your organization. Later in this chapter, we cover a tool evaluation process, which gives you an approach to follow when evaluating your PMO tools for your organization.

Finally, from a communication tool perspective, there is no better book on the market that goes into more detail and provides a huge selection of tools than the book, *Project Management Communications Bible* (Dow and Taylor 2008). Every PMO Manager should have a copy because it provides over 70 tools to help Program Managers and Project Managers communicate effectively.

Standard PMO Tools

Two of the most exciting areas when building your PMO is determining the tools and processes/procedures to use for your organization. When you have the authority to buy tools and create processes, you are literally setting the foundation for how your organization will run and you influence the execution across all programs and projects in the PMO. This is definitely something that should excite you, as PMO Manager, and is one of the best parts of the job. It is definitely a best practice for every PMO Manager to use a hands-on approach to both the tool evaluation process and the process for generating PMO processes/procedures. When using a hands-off approach, you can end up with PMO tools that might not be what you need and the processes might not align with what you are expecting for your PMO. There is a balance between how much you, as PMO Manager, take on and create, and how much you enlist your PMO employees to do. You can expect your PMO employees to help evaluate the PMO tools and help create the PMO standard processes. These should be part of their job responsibilities. Their input in this process is valuable because they are the ones who use both the tools and the processes as they execute their programs and projects. Remember, you cannot do this alone and you need their help; it would be bad politically not to involve them. This balance is something every PMO Manager faces. Be careful and do not take too much on yourself—share the load, but do not dump the work on your team members as well. With both of these areas being so important in how your PMO operates, it is a best practice to be heavily involved throughout selecting and evaluating the tools and the creation of the various processes and procedures in your organization.

Tools for the PMO Organization

When deciding which tools your PMO needs, one of the first places to look is at your company's standard tools. The standard tools will be incorporated into your PMO from a company requirement perspective, not necessarily from a PMO perspective. Here is a list of some standard company tools:

- Microsoft® SharePoint®, or other centralized repository for information
- Centralized status system
- Centralized financial system
- Centralized human resources performance system
- Centralized timesheet system
- Centralized purchasing processes and systems for processing POs and work orders
- Centralized employee training system

Each of these tools are not PMO-specific; however, they are usually important for PMO employees to use regularly as company employees. As PMO Manager, do not recreate or purchase these kinds of tools without checking with your management team first to determine if there is already a tool in place to use.

Tools & Best Practices

Ensure you also document the PMO Manager's requirements for PMO tools when capturing your management and team member's needs. Because you are running the PMO, you might also need specific tools to run your organization, that your management or team members never consider themselves.

However, that is not to say that the PMO will not need specific tools, so remember to focus on those five critical questions (who, what, where, when, and how) so you can apply that logic across the list of tools to review. You also need to think about the different tools you will use to drive and run the PMO. In most cases, the tools you use are the same tools your Portfolio Managers, Program Managers, and Project Managers need as well, but think about the types of reports you need to stay on top of your organization. Consider these eight major components of a project: communications, scope, cost, quality, schedule, risk, procurement, and resources—these knowledge areas will drive many of your own PMO reporting requirements and force you to look at different tools with those areas in mind. For example, financial tools give you cost information, and scheduling tools provide time and resource information, and so on. Combining the five critical questions with these eight major project knowledge areas provides a very structured approach for determining which tools are right for your PMO. Here are some tools specific to the PMO:

- **Centralized project repository, LAN directory, or website**—It is important for project teams to have access to and store project deliverables in a central location that the IT department both backs up and secures. The PMO Manager can review project deliverables such as project milestone decks, program and project risks and issues, communication plans, and so on without having to trouble the team or interfere with the Program Manager or Project Manager directly.
- **Centralized scheduling system**—The organization can require the use of a centralized scheduling tool, such as Microsoft® Project Server, for all programs and projects regardless of whether they all roll into your PMO. If there are projects that do not roll into the PMO, then a best practice is that they still follow the same processes as the ones that do and store their project schedules in a central location for easy retrieval and reporting.
- **Centralized status reporting system**—It is so important for PMO Managers to be able to pull reports and data on the how the programs and projects are executing toward their plans. This system **must come** with some sort of reporting abilities that pull the data into summarized or management type reports such as dashboards and weekly program and project status reports.

Bill's Thoughts:

The centralized reporting system is critical to every PMO Manager because it is the one repository to store and hold program and project status. In my PMOs, I ensured that these systems were in place and that I could control the data entry to those systems by the Project Managers on my team. It is so important to know what information is stored about the programs and projects because you are going to be the one in most cases that is reporting this data to your management team and customers.

- **Centralized financial reporting system**—This systems is critical for the PMO Manager to understand how programs and projects are executing against their budget.
- **Centralized auditing system**—This auditing system tracks how well the Program Managers and Project Managers are tracking and creating their specific work deliverables. The PMO Manager is able to review specific deliverables and audit items.
- **PMO engagement list**—This is a centralized list to which PMO employees and vendors add their work efforts and percentages worked on each effort. For example: "Bill Dow, Door Repair project, 60%." Having this list for everyone in the PMO gives the PMO Manager an ongoing understanding of PMO resource allocation and the project names they are working on. When new efforts come into the PMO, the PMO Manager can check this list first for availability.
- **Program and project transition plans**—These plans document all the information about the program and project that is utilized when resources (usually, Program Managers and Project Managers) roll off the effort and you need to ramp up the next person who is taking over. Typical transition plans include the following sections for both programs and projects:
  - Schedules
  - Centralized repository
  - Nine PMI knowledge areas
  - Governance process
  - Change control process
  - Resource list
  - Critical links
  - Other Information

PMO Managers should ensure from the start that their program and project teams have these plans in place. If there is a change in leadership (for example, a Program Manager or Project Manager), the transition document saves hours of resource time ramping up on the project.

Each tool should provide the PMO Manager with the information needed to run the organization from a pure PMO perspective—not necessarily from a portfolio, program, or project perspective. Let's look at the industry leading brands for these software products.

Where do you start with PMO tools?

As PMO Manager, one of the more difficult and costly decisions you make is choosing the software for your PMO. This is not an easy decision and mistakes made from a bad decision can be costly. Mistakes not only cost money, but also hurt from a credibility and process perspective. Each of the factors in the following list can go a long way in helping your overall success as PMO Manager, or they can have a lasting negative impact. Therefore, to give you the best chance in choosing the right software, you should understand the different factors you face. These factors include, but are not limited to, the following:

- **PMO model (controlling, directive, supportive, and so on)**—The PMO model you choose will be one of the main deciding factors for the software tools you need for your PMO.
- **Available budget**—There needs to be available budget to purchase the software and to provide training. Some of the budget considerations include the costs for ongoing maintenance, licensing costs, or third-party support. The less mature the company is from a process perspective, the less likely it is that you will get funding and the ability to purchase PMO software. When the PMO starts providing value, then it is often much easier to obtain budget for purchasing PMO software.
- **Buy or build decision**—Some PMO software products can be built in-house rather than purchased.
- **Results of pilot programs**—It is important to conduct a pilot program for any software that you bring into the PMO. The results of the pilot program will direct you in your decision.
- **Methodology process groups**—Portfolio, program, and project methodologies all play a role in deciding the type of software to purchase for the PMO. If your PMO is a program and project only PMO, for example, you do not need portfolio-level software.
- **Management team expectations**—The types of reports and expectations your management team has for your PMO will drive many of the factors in deciding which software you require.
- **Software features and various options**—Here are some of the common options available in PMO software:
    - Cost
    - Professional support and yearly maintenance fees
    - Email notifications to task owners
    - Dashboards
    - Web-based interface
    - Time tracking
    - Task lists
    - Access control
    - Budget tracking and reporting
    - Calendars and schedules
    - Third-party calendar integration
    - Task assignments

- Resource allocation
- Advanced reporting, including charting and graphs
- Multilingual support
- Mobile device support

When is the right time to bring in tools?

As PMO Manager, the decision as to when to invest in software for your PMO is another variable you need to consider in this process. Some of the factors to help you decide when to invest in software include, but are not limited to, the following conditions:

- Available budget
- If your projects are continually running late and missing internal deadlines
- If your projects are of poor quality
- If your projects are continually running over budget
- If your management team and customers require hand-holding and constant reports on program and project progress.

It is a best practice for PMO Managers to follow the same process for purchasing software that we have been following throughout the book: crawl, walk, run. Do not bring in software if the PMO team is not ready for it, but do not delay bringing in software until teams are struggling to execute their programs and projects. As PMO Manager, your focus is to help and support your teams to be successful. Software products, such as a project scheduling tool (for example, Microsoft® Project), are critical tools for all teams and should be brought in at the right time. Let us review the tool evaluation process now so you can start purchasing tools for your PMO through a formal and structured process.

Tool Evaluation Process

One of the main processes when building a new PMO is the evaluation of PMO tools. If there are not any PMO tools available, or there are key products that are simply missing, then your role is to evaluate the different PMO tools on the market. You goal will be to run a tool evaluation process and select the tools that are most suitable for your organization. As PMO Manager, you should own and drive this process. Your team members can assist you in the process, but you need to own and drive it. If you do not drive this process, you will end up suffering the most because you could end up being stuck with these tools for years— PMO team members will come and go faster than you do, so it is important that you take ownership of the process and you know what software tools you are purchasing and why.

There is a fairly simple process to follow when evaluating PMO tools. Make sure to look into any company-specific rules and procedures before you get too far into the process because if you are unfamiliar with your company's rules, and you bring in software, you could end up getting into some trouble. You do not want to break any company polices during the evaluation process, so meet with your company's IT department or support desk to ensure you are on the right track. Here is a simple process to evaluate PMO tools:

Tips & Best Practices

Ensure you get a broad audience for running your pilot programs—do not limit this PMO tool evaluation process to just PMO employees.

Select Evaluators

It is important to have a good cross group of individuals who will test and try the PMO tool. It is also important that all levels of the organization are involved in the process and that you have at least one program and project team that will try it out. It is best practice to include, at a minimum, these people:

- Executive or leadership team
- PMO team members
- Program and project team members—include at least two teams
- Customers or external staff outside of the PMO

Create Evaluation Criteria

The first step in this process is to create the evaluation criteria. Make sure you spend the time, and gather the PMO software requirements using the following factors:

- Executive or leadership team requirements
- Customer requirements
- PMO team member requirements
- Costs—up-front and ongoing, support, and maintenance
- Tool functionality
- Tool reporting capabilities
- Tool processes and any associated processes that come with using the tool
- Other company- or industry-specific criteria

Perform Evaluation (including testing and pilot programs)

The next step is to perform the evaluation. Look to answer at least these minimum questions:

- Is the tool easy to use across a wide range of employees?
- Does the management team find value in using the tool?
- Did the pilot program teams use the tool? Did they find it valuable?
- Did the tool provide required reporting capabilities across various evaluators?
- Does the tool fit within available budget?

Create Recommendation Document

Finally, create the Recommendation document and present to management and customers. Follow at minimum these steps:

- Create the Recommendations document
- Review and approve the recommendations documented by PMO employees before presenting to management.
- Deliver and present the Recommendation document to management and customers.
- Develop a training plan for the process or tool. Make sure you have a training plan laid out and part of the recommendation process because management needs to be aware of training activities.

Bill's Thoughts:

It is very easy to make mistakes in evaluating and purchasing PMO tools. I know, I made them myself. My mistake was that I brought in a risk management tool too early and my PMO employees were not ready to use it on their projects. Luckily, it was not too expensive, and it didn't break the bank, but it was still a perceived waste of money in the long run because it was clear the PMO employees where not at the level of maturity that they could use the tool. I need to take blame as well, but I never thoroughly did my homework and understand completely the maturity level of the organization. Make sure your organization is mature enough to use the tools you bring in and that you start slowly by only purchasing a few copies of the software to begin with, and then expand and buy more copies if the tool proves to be useful for your organization.

Let us now look at the list of portfolio management tools, and then we will spend time looking at the list of program and project management tools. As PMO Manager, embrace these lists, but do not be overwhelmed by the number of products because there is no way you are ever going to use them all in your PMO. However, by having the list—especially while you are building or enhancing an existing PMO—you can search and see if there is a tool listed that may be close to what you are looking for and that matches your needs.

Portfolio Management Tools

As we look across the project management industry, specifically at portfolio management tools, the market is much more mature in the software products available than companies are at executing portfolio management. This is a positive because, in many cases, immature companies can use tools to raise their maturity. However, be forewarned, just because a tool says it can do this or that and is sold as the "magic pill," you need to balance the adoption and implementation of the tool across the company, which could easily fall flat if not executed correctly. In addition, if a company's processes (portfolio, program, and project) are immature, forcing the use of a tool may not be the answer. As PMO Manager, this is another area where you need to balance how much of the tool you implement with the organization being ready to adopt (or not) what is needed to move it forward. It is a tricky combination to balance and it is highly recommend that you work with your management team to get their full support.

Tips & Best Practices

Do not bring in a tool without your management team's support. Tools often require process change, and without management support, process change in organizations are next to impossible.

In Chapter 8, "Portfolio Management Methodology," there is a list of some of the top portfolio management tools widely used throughout the industry. What you see below in **Table 12.1 Software for Project Portfolio Management** is a much larger list of the same type of tools, but even this list is incomplete. There is no way to include a complete list of something so dynamic and that is constantly changing. This is a great starting point, though, for you to see some of the tools available and determine those that might be useful for your organization. Use this list as a guide to help you understand the tools available and as a reference. It is important that you determine the right tools for your organization. Some software sales people can be quite convincing, so ensure you have a structured methodology for evaluating and piloting software products before you even think about bring them into the organization. Many companies will let you pilot their software before purchasing; therefore, you should work with each company directly to understand their evaluation processes.

Bill's Thoughts:

Most companies will use one (or two at the most) portfolio management tools and will focus on getting those tools working before expanding any broader. Portfolio management is so different from company to company and yours will be different too. I do not recommend that you spend a lot of time evaluating and bringing in tons of tools for portfolio management. Definitely, though, look at everything available and talk to other PMO Managers or IT Managers about what they are using to understand what is working for them. I have a number of different PMO Managers and industry experts I use to bounce ideas off and share ideas. It is highly recommend you get a group of individuals yourself to bounce ideas off of as well.

Let us look at the list of software for project portfolio management.

Table 12.1 Software for Project Portfolio Management

This list includes, but is not limited to, the following products:

Software for Project Portfolio Management		
(Please check suppliers' websites to ensure accurate information)		
Provider	Product	Focus
1000Minds	1000Minds	General / collaborative ranking, conjoint analysis / New Zealand / on site, SaaS
3 Olive Solutions	Portfolio Intelligence™	General, mid-sized firms / project planning, tracking, scoring / USA / SaaS
4c Systems	4c Portfolio Manager	General / project scoring / suite / UK / on site
Algorithmics	Algo Risk	Financial institutions / cap. allocation, risk, real-time market data / Canada / on site
Artemis	Artemis 7	IT, new prods., gov / proj. & resource management, scoring / Int'l / on site, web
Asta	Teamplan	IT, professional services / project & resource management / UK / on site
Atlantic Global	PPM	IT, gen., mid-sized firms / demand, resource & financial management / UK / SaaS
AtTask	@Task	General, IT / proj. & resource management, workflow, suite / Int'l / SaaS
BMC Software	PPM	IT / financial, governance, compliance, vendor management, suite / Int'l / on site
Borland	Tempo™	IT / project & demand management, scheduling, alignment / USA / on site, web
BOT International	Processes on Demand PMO	General, gov / project management, templates, scoring / Int'l / SaaS
CA	Clarity™	IT, new products / project & resource management, suite / Int'l / on site, SaaS
Canea	Canea Framework	Gen. / proj. & resource planning, prioritization, suite / Sweden / on-site, web
Cambridge	Prioritascs™	Transportation / prioritization, custom models / USA, Netherlands / on site, web
Clarizen	Clarizen	General / project & resource management, status reporting / Int'l / SaaS
Compuware	Changepoint	IT, prof. services / proj. & resource management, suite / Int'l / on site, SaaS

Software for Project Portfolio Management		
CorasWorks	PPM Version 1.3	Gen., gov / project tracking & reporting / Microsoft Sharepoint app / USA
Cranes Software	InventX™ ePM	New prods. / statistical analytics, customizable, suite / India / on site, web
Daptiv	PPM	IT, HR / proj. & resource management, collaboration / Int'l / SaaS
Deltek	Deltek Enterprise	General, gov / proj. & resource management, compliance, suite / USA, UK / web
EDC Technology	Portfolio Intelligence	Mid-sized firms, schools / scheduling, tracking, ben scoring, modular / USA / SaaS
Folio Technologies	Folio Priority System	Various / portfolio optimization, internal modeling platform / USA / on site, SaaS
Fujitsu	sDIS+	Banking, finance / price & liquidity risk / Int'l / on site, web
Genius Inside	Genius Project	IT, new prods., prof. services / planning & execution, suite / Int'l / on site, SaaS
GenSight	Gensight® PPM	Various / stage-gate, scalable, alignment / genetic algorithms / UK, USA / web
Glomark-Governan	GeniusCompare/Optimizer™	Tech buyers / bus. case preparation, prioritization / USA, Mexico / standalone
Guidon	GuidonVue	Prof services / Six-Sigma, multi-project management / USA / SaaS
HP Software	PPM Center	IT / project & resource management, alignment, suite / Int'l / on site, SaaS
IBM	Rational Focal Point	IT / proj. & resource management, ALM, benefit scoring, suite / Int'l / on site, SaaS
i-lign	i-lign	Gen. / proj. & resource management, alignment / New Zealand / Java, web, SaaS
InfoHarvest	Criterium DecisionPlus®	General / multi-criteria decision software, custom models / USA / desktop
Innotas	PPM Solution	IT / governance; resource, financial & time management, alignment / USA /SaaS
Instantis	EnterpriseTrack™	IT, new prods. industry modules / project tracking, six sigma / USA, UK / SaaS
Inventx®	SP2M™	Industry templates / project & resource management, suite / India / web
iPlanWare	TeamWorks	IT, prof. services, R&D / project, time & resource management / UK / SaaS
i.s.edge	Project Network	General / Dashboard, project management, resource planning / USA / web

Software for Project Portfolio Management		
Logical Decisions®	LDW Portfolio	General / budgeting, prioritization, custom MCDA models / USA / desktop
Lumina	Analytica	General / custom models, analysis, optimization / USA / desktop, on site
MaestroTec	Maestro-PPM	Prof services, IT / proj. & engagement management, suite / USA / on site, SaaS
Microsoft	EPM	Gen., IT / proj. & resource management, alignment, AHP, suite / Int'l / on site, web
Mindmap	MindManager	IT / project planning, collaboration, strategic alignment / USA / Mac, web
Onepoint Software	Project Enterprise	Manufacturing / project, resource & collaboration / Europe, USA / on site, SaaS
OpenAir	Enterprise	Prof. services / project management, tracking & billing, EVM / USA / SaaS
Oracle	Crystal Ball®	General / risk analysis, simulation & optimization, custom tools / Int'l / spreadsheet
Oracle PeopleSoft	PeopleSoft PPM	Prof. services, general / templates, project versions / Int'l / on site, web
Oracle Primavera	Primavera Enterprise PPM	Gen, construction / accounting, planning, resource mgmt. / Int'l / on site, web
Palisade	Decision Tools Suite	R&D, gen. / decision & risk modeling, customizable optimization tools / Int'l / Excel
Planisware	Planisware 5	New prods, IT, pharma, aero & defense / balance, alignment / Int'l / on site, SaaS
PlanningForce	Portfolio Planner	Gen. / proj. plan. & res. schdlg, direct priority assgnmt. / Belgium / desktop, onsite
PlanView	Enterprise™	IT, new prods. / proj. & resource management, collaboration, suite / Int'l / web
Portfolio Decisions	Customized software	General / consulting, process improvement, custom tools / USA / on site
Portfolio Decisionware	PDWare™	Gen., small firms / demand & capacity management, time tracking / USA / on site
ProjectObjects	ProjectFolio	IT, new prods. / strategic alignment, targets, suite / Ireland, Italy, India / web
Projectplace	Projectplace	Gen. / collaboration, proj. planning, doc. mgmt. / Europe, India / SaaS, plug-in
ProModel	Portfolio Simulator	General / project management, collaboration, alignment / USA / desktop
QuickArrow	PSA Solution	Prof. services / proj. & resource management, billing / USA / SaaS

Software for Project Portfolio Management		
SAP®	Port. & Proj. Management	Gen., IT, new products / lifecycle management, alignment, suite / Int'l / on site
Saviom Software	Saviom Project Management	Gen. / program, resource, proj. & time management / Australia, India / on site
Sciforma	Sciforma 4	Gen. / proj. management, scheduling, collaboration / USA / SaaS, on site
Smart Org	Portfolio Navigator™	R&D, new prods. / simulation, custom value models, risk analysis / USA, UK / web
SOA Software	Eclipse PPM	IT / governance automation, alignment, suite / USA / mainframe, on site, web
Solution Q	Eclipse	General / risk balancing & reporting / USA / web
Sopheon	Accolade™	New prods. / roadmapping, simulation, strategic alignment / Int'l / web
Stand by Soft	RationalPlan Multi Project	General, small firms / multi-project & resource management / Romania / SaaS
Syncopation Software	DPL Portfolio	Gen. / decision trees, influence diagrams, portfolio optimization / USA / desktop
TeamDynamix	TDPortfolio Planning	Gov., colleges, construction / proj. management / USA / on site, web
Tenrox	PPM	Gen. / time & cost management, proj. execution, suite / Int'l / SaaS
UMS Group	POP©	Utilities / asset mgmt., optimization, custom models / Int'l / spreadsheet apps
UMT	Enterprise Portfolio Management	General / project & resource management, scoring / USA
VCSonline	VPMi	General / project & resource management, scoring / USA / SaaS
XenLogic	TOBi	Prof. services / business intelligence, reporting, suite / USA / on site

Reprinted with permission from Lee Merkhofer, of Lee Merkhofer Consulting. Lee continually updates this list. For the full list, visit his website at: **http://www.prioritysystem.com/**

This is only a sampling of the master list from Lee Merkhofer's website. There are well over a hundred portfolio management products available to any company.

This is certainly a long list of portfolio management software, and there is no way you will use all of them in your PMO. Depending on your budget, your industry, and some factors we will explore in the sections that follow, having this list available to you is valuable for any PMO Manager. As different conditions come up in your portfolio, it is highly recommended that you refer back to this list. It will keep you in touch with the latest software—and if you want to expand on the current products in your PMO, it gives you some options.

Program and Project Management Software Tools

As we begin to look at the software available to PMO Managers to offer their Program Managers and Project Managers, it becomes much more difficult to find software that is specific for program management and not also relevant to project management. Essentially, the software products will work with both Program Management and Project Management very nicely. That is the nice thing about how closely aligned these two different methodologies are. In most cases, you can use the same software across both methodologies. For example, you can just as easily use Microsoft® Project Server for reviewing a program schedule as you can to review an individual project schedule.

As you review the program and project management software tools list, below, you will also notice that there are many software products available—each with their own features and functionality that might align nicely to what you need in your organization. As noted in the previous list, this list can also be over whelming and, as PMO Manager, you should take the time to filter through the list and determine what is right for your organization. You certainly do not need to buy or use all the software listed, but you should study the list and choose wisely the applications that you will end up piloting in your PMO.

Table 12.2 Software for Program and Project Portfolio Management provides a list of program and project management software packages available on the market today. PMO Managers should review this list and determine what is feasible for their organizations.

Table 12.2 Software for Program and Project Portfolio Management

Product Name	Product Details
@Risk ®	@RISK performs risk analysis using Monte Carlo simulation to show you many possible outcomes in your Microsoft Excel spreadsheet—and tells you how likely they are to occur. This means you can judge which risks to take and which ones to avoid, allowing for the best decision making under uncertainty
AceProject ®	AceProject is a project management tool that helps organizations get organized using a collaborative approach.
AtTask ®	AtTask has Project Scheduling, Reports & Dashboards, Resource Management, Team Collaboration, Issue Tracking, Time Management...etc.

Basecamp ®	Basecamp has Project Dashboards, To-Do Lists, Calendars, Messaging and full of wonderful features.
Brightwork ® pmPoint	Brightwork pmPoint is a SharePoint add-on for managing work and projects of different sizes and types. There are countless templates and SharePoint reporting available.
Celoxis ®	Celoxis is an online Project Management tools that offers comprehensive web based project management software
Clarizen ®	Clarizen is a cloud based project management software tool, that is robust, integrates with Google Docs, Accounting apps, Outlook...etc.
ConceptDraw Project 6 ®	A full-featured project management solution with all the necessary functions including, extensive reports on project and task statuses, embedded documents and hyperlinks, and multi-project dashboards.
Copper Project ®	Copper is a project management software tool that helps teams manage projects, tasks, clients, contacts, and documents online.
CS Project ®	Project scheduling and management software for Manufacturing and Mining
Deltek's Risk + ®	Deltek's Risk+ seamlessly integrates with Microsoft Project to provide Monte Carlo simulation capability. This tool allows you to quantify cost and scheduling uncertainties, making risks easier to identify and assess.
DeskAway ®	DeskAway is a web-based project collaboration software that provides teams a central location to easily organize, manage and track their projects & work.
Easy Projects ®	Easy Projects is a scheduling tool that includes a view of multiple projects, batch operations, custom fields, Gantt charts and many other features.

Endeavour Software Project Management ®	Endeavour software many features including Use Cases, Project Plan, Change Requests, Tasks, Dependencies, Defect, Tracking, Test Cases, Document Management.
HP Project & Portfolio Software ®	This software features Top-down project portfolio management and planning that interfaces with bottom-up project plans. There are many controls in the software to increase visibility to maintain compliance, and reduce costs.
MacProject ®	The SharedPlan family of project management software for Mac OS X. It has a ton of services, and because it is the Mac, definitely work checking out.
Mavenlink ®	An online software package that has a tremendous number of features. They have project workspaces where you manage communications, documents, schedules, budgets and payments.
MicroPlanner X-Pert ®	Micro Planner X-Pert is a powerful project management program developed to enable you to take full advantage of the power of the very latest computer technology. A prime objective in the design of the software is to provide a simple and efficient man-machine interface. We believe that you will find it the most responsive project management tool that you have ever used.
Microsoft Office Project Server 2010 & 2012 & Microsoft Project ®	MS Project ® is the market leader in project management software. It enables project planning, resource scheduling, multiple types of diagrams and reports, project costing, project control and project status update.
Microsoft SharePoint Server ®	Microsoft SharePoint 2010 makes it easier for people to work together. Using SharePoint 2010, your people can set up Web sites to share information with others, manage documents from start to finish, and publish reports to help everyone make better decisions.

Microsoft Team Foundation Server ®	Visual Studio Team Foundation Server 2010 (TFS) is the collaboration platform at the core of Microsoft's application lifecycle management solution. TFS automates the software delivery process and gives you the tools you need to effectively manage software development projects throughout the IT lifecycle.
Milestones Professional ®	Milestones Professional is the fast, easy way to create schedules and reports for projects. When you manage and schedule projects you need software that is powerful, fast and easy to use.
Onepoint Project ®	Onepoint Project software has a number of features including Project Pipelines, WBS, Trend Analysis, Resource Utilization, Gantt charts and project templates
Critical Tools - Pert Chart Expert ®	PERT Chart EXPERT is a Windows-based project management software application that is used to create PERT charts (also known as Network Charts, Precedence Diagrams and Logic Diagrams).
Planbox ®	Planbox is a full-featured - yet easy to use - Agile Project Management Software that lets you plan, collaborate and deliver.
Planisware 5 ®	Meticulous project management is imperative to ultimate product success – and Planisware 5's proven system provides users with a toolbox of the most advanced applications to support project management processes.
Primavera ®	Oracle's Primavera P6 Professional Project Management gives today's project managers and schedulers the one thing they value most: control. Primavera P6 Professional Project Management, the recognized standard for high-performance project management software, is designed to handle large-scale, highly sophisticated and multifaceted projects.
Principal Toolbox	The Principal Toolbox software makes professional PRINCE2 project management easier than ever. This Toolbox includes Web-based interface, document management, central database, reporting, project dashboards and many more features.

Project KickStart	Project Kickstart has a six-step wizard to help you with project creation, professional Gantt charts, budget and resource tracking and many other features.
ProjectManager.com	This is online project management software that includes, dashboards, project planners, reporting, team management, and collaboration online.
Projectplace	Projectplace offers many features such as project management, project planning, document management, issues management.
ProjectSpaces	ProjectSpaces is a simple, secure, and powerful online workspace and extranet tool to help your project teams, workgroups, committees, partners, and others easily connect, share and collaborate.
Task Enterprise Project Management ®	@Task is a comprehensive enterprise project management system that includes: project planning, task management, resource management, project costing, and document management.
TeamworkPM ®	TeamworkPM is online project management software with many features including, Task Management, Milestone Tracking, Messaging, File Management, Time Tracking, People & Contacts
UMT Project Essentials ®	This product has many features and very robust. It includes, Governance Workflows, Financial Structures and controls, Financial Estimates, Top Down & Bottom Up Project Tracking, Performance Measurement, and extensive Reporting.
VPMi ®	VPMi Professional includes features across Project Management, Program Management, Portfolio Management, Resource Management, Governance , Personal Management

Critical Tools - WBS ChartPro ®	WBS Chart Pro is a Windows-based project management software application that is used to create and display projects using a Work Breakdown Structure (WBS) Chart. A WBS chart displays the structure of a project showing how a project is organized into summary (phase) and detail levels. Using a WBS chart is a more intuitive approach to planning and displaying a project.

As you can see, there is more software on the market than companies can handle. This is good because it gives PMO Managers an incredible choice of products for use in their PMOs. However, that many products to choose from also makes things more complicated for PMO Managers because it gives them too many choices. Careful consideration is required before selecting and buying any tool for your PMO.

It was mentioned when reviewing the list of portfolio management software earlier in the chapter, PMO Managers cannot use this much software in their PMOs, and it is important that the focus is not on the number of tools that you buy and make available, but that you choose the right tools for the organization. Overburdening your PMO employees with too many tools can make them less efficient and can affect the execution of their portfolios, programs, and projects. However, not providing enough tools can be an issue as well. Think about the balance of bringing in the right number of tools into your PMO to help your PMO employees.

PMO Processes

As PMO Manager, one of the many tasks in building a PMO is to create PMO processes. These processes should be generic when working across the PMO, but must be specific when working across portfolio, program, and project management. Generic processes will not necessarily work on the portfolio or across a program, that's where you need more specific processes that are applicable to those types of work efforts. Also, make sure you don't create too many processes too quickly and drown your PMO team. Too many processes can cause issues and concerns around program and project execution and is something to be avoided. However, having too few processes is not good because too little rigor causes different kinds of problems in program and project execution.

The following are some of the processes that are common to most PMOs. This list does not cover all processes, but it specifies the main ones that each PMO Manager should create for their PMOs:

Create Generic PMO Processes (used across portfolio, program, and project management)

- Governance process
- Escalation process
- Change control process
- Financial process
- Lessons-learned process
- Procurement process
- Resource management process
- Portfolio review board process

Portfolio Management Processes

- Create portfolio, program, and project initiation processes
- Create portfolio planning process
- Create portfolio status reporting process

Program and Project Management Processes

- Create program and project status reporting process
- Create issue management process
- Create risk management process
- Create schedule update process
- Create program and project quality processes
- Create performance reporting process

As PMO Manager, these should be the minimum processes you create for your PMO. It is common to create processes that are industry or company specific processes, but those become known when in the midst of creating the PMO processes—as you start implementing the processes, missing processes quickly appear. A key process for programs and projects is the performance reporting process. PMO Managers tend not to think about establishing and setting up this process until much later in the PMO life cycle; however, one of the best processes is to establish performance reporting immediately. By doing so, your program and project teams will focus on performance reporting from the very beginning and, therefore, will act and behave very differently (for the better) while executing their efforts.

This book does not go into the details behind any one of the 17 processes, not even performance reporting, because of various nuances that would make it almost impossible to explain a single process and have that process work exactly the same in every company. However, details for processes are all over the Internet, from your peers, or at a number of online sources starting with some of the specific program and project online communities. Most companies practice many of these processes already, so your role is to look at the processes that the company already has from a PMO perspective and update them accordingly, and then add any processes that the company is missing.

Process, Process, Process

It is very important when creating and introducing process that you do not just implement it, and then leave it for the organization to figure out. That could be one of the worst things you do for your credibility and you might end up driving people away from using your process altogether. The best practice for any process is like the tool process—pilot and evaluate the process first, and then introduce a wider rollout after the process has been tested and proven effective. As PMO Manager, you are in charge of driving process change, including creating process, training, and mentoring and coaching where applicable.

When rolling out a new process, focus first on your high-performing teams. Let your high-performing teams vet each process first and figure out any kinks or issues, and then have that team adopt and use the process regularly on their programs and projects before rolling the new process out to the general population. This will go a long way in overall acceptance across the organization. You will find very quickly that some teams will not necessarily be ready or accepting of any new process for a number of factors and your role sometimes is to encourage them to take on the process. Some projects will be in a specific stage (initiating, planning, and so on), so balancing the right time to implement a process while not affecting the team's execution is something that the PMO Manager, the Program Manager, and the Project Manager will have to negotiate. The end-result being that the organization as a whole adopts all new processes implemented by the PMO.

PMO Processes: Tips and Best Practices

As PMO Manager, there are things that you can do to guide your team through process adoption. The following are some simple things to think about when rolling out processes in your organization.

- **Pilot the process**—You have no idea if your proposed process will be effective until some groups actually try it on their programs or projects.
- **Program and project stage**—Determine which stage the program or project is in, and then determine whether adding a new process at that stage of the project is appropriate. For example, introducing a new process during the closing phase would not make sense.
- **Time impact**—How much time does the new process add to team members' schedules?
- **Tools to support the process**—Are there software tools available to support the new process or will it be a manual process for team members?
- **Training**—Has the team member's been trained and do they understand the process?

As we conclude discussing processes, you, the PMO Manager, play a key role in rolling out processes across your PMO. If you implement too many processes, PMO employees and various team members will feel hampered and overburdened; too few processes, and the rigor and structure of portfolio, program, and project management goes out the window. As PMO Manager, you need to control and balance rolling out new processes to your organization. Increase the maturity level of all PMO employees by adding processes that add value, increase efficiency, and move your PMO forward.

Follow these processes and steps when you roll out any new processes or procedures within your PMO for a better chance of acceptance and adoption across the organization.

PMO Round Table and Best Practices Sharing Sessions

If you think about the various PMO tools and processes we just covered, the next challenge you face is how to roll them out to the organization in both a formal and informal manner.

In an earlier chapter, there was a lot of discussion about training and education and the process of educating PMO employees, but what was not discussed in detail were any informal processes. After viewing the long list of software tools and the various PMO processes, this is an appropriate time to discuss the various informal procedures for rolling out tools and process training. One of the best practices PMO Managers can follow when rolling out these items is the use of PMO round table meetings and best practice sharing sessions. The meetings are exactly like they sound; they are simply open-forum meetings that the PMO Manager drives where there is informal training of the latest PMO tools and processes driven by the PMO. All PMO employees are encouraged to come, but anyone working with the PMO is also welcome. The goal is to bring awareness to what the PMO is rolling out and pick up some tips and tricks about a tool or process that you might not be aware of already. A sample meeting agenda includes the following:

Meeting duration: 1 hour

Time: Lunch hour (local time)

Attendees: All company employees and contractors

Topics include: Microsoft® Project Server 2010, change management, project planning, WBS training, and risk & issue management

These meetings are a best practice and highly recommended for a PMO Manager to implement in the PMO. Do not miss the chance to continually update the organization about the tools and processes within your organization.

Summary

We covered a wide range of topics in this chapter, from listing the various tools available, to evaluation process, to bringing in tools for your organization. As PMO Manager, driving the adoption of the various software tools and PMO processes is so important for how your organization operates and delivers their efforts that this is something you need to take seriously and spend time on continually.

It is important to remember that you do not need to purchase all of the various software products mentioned. Just because the software is available does not mean it is right for your organization. Also remember that there is no "magic pill" in software packages and just because a sales person says that a product can do this or that, it probably will not be the case. It is a best practice to pilot any software product you are thinking about purchasing for your PMO. The evaluation process does not have to be long or take a lot of effort from team members, but the time spent will be valuable and could prevent long-term adoption of a product that won't work for the organization.

Embrace the tools and process work efforts during the building of your PMO because it can be exciting to bring in new tools and introduce new processes (adding rigor and structure).

PMO Build Decisions:

1. Decide on the standard PMO tools and processes to initially create for the PMO.

2. Decide on the various portfolio, program, and project management software packages that you will purchase for your PMO.

3. Decide on your tool evaluation criteria and how you will run this process in your PMO. Will it just be for tools or all processes? How long will it last?

4. Decide which of the generic PMO processes, such as governance, change control, issue and risk management you will create initially for your PMO.

5. Decide how you will use your PMO employees in creating and rolling out PMO process training.

Chapter Review Answers:

1. Critical questions for communication tools are: who, what, where, when, and how?

2. PMO tools include: a centralized status system, a centralized financial system, and a centralized timesheet system.

3. Not all tools accomplish what they promise. You could buy a product that says it can do this or that, and then end up stuck with a tool that is worthless to your organization.

4. Some generic processes to create include: a PMO governance process, a PMO escalation process, and a PMO change-control process.

5. Conduct a pilot program for the process, understand the time impact for using the new process, and understand any training needs for the new process.

Part Three

Chapter 13

Implementing the PMO

Figure 13.1 PMO Build Schedule - PMO Implementation Process

Task Name	Resource Names
-Step 6 – Implementation PMO Deliverables/Processes Period (Chapter 13)	**PMO Manager**
Review the PMO Recommendations Document from Recommendation period.	PMO Manager
Review all PMO Decisions in the PMO Build Decision Table.	PMO Manager
Continue to work with Executive team and re-confirm support for Implementing PMO	PMO Manager
Obtain PMO Budget, or at least get an understanding on what your role is in the budget process	PMO Manager
+Implement PMO Business Management Area on Centralized Repository Site	PMO Manager
+Implement Core PMO Items	**PMO Manager**
+Hire PMO Team members – This will include employees, vendors & contractors across all roles.	**PMO Manager**
+Implement PMO Training Including all Training Materials	**PMO Manager**
+Implement PMO Reporting	**PMO Manager**
+Implement PMO Processes	**PMO Manager**
+Implement Process Methodologies where applicable (Portfolio, Program, Project)	**PMO Manager**
+Select and Purchase PMO Tools (Portfolio, Program, Project)	**PMO Manager**
PMO Implemented & Ready for Ongoing Enhancements	PMO Manager

Questions you should be able to answer after reading this chapter:

1. What are the three input items for implementing a PMO?

2. Why aren't all the steps required?

3. What is the most important step in implementing a PMO?

4. What role does budget play in the implementation process?

5. Defined in the table "PMO Implementation Steps" there were key steps noted, can you name the first four steps?

The implementation phase of building a PMO is one of the most difficult components of the whole process. You are probably wondering where to start. It is understandable and very common to have doubts and questions at this point. So far, we covered all the components of building the PMO, or what to look for when enhancing a PMO, but we haven't learned how to implement anything. That was by design; when you build a PMO, you need to get into the mindset of that particular component and there is a lot of research and things to accomplish when you are creating new ideas. Remember the concept: crawl, walk, run and how that concept is applicable to the build process? Well, it is applicable during the implementation phase as well. From a build process perspective, "crawl" to build the initial components of your PMO, and then "walk" to enhance the PMO components that you built, and finally "run" to apply best practices and procedures throughout your PMO. The "running"
phase takes years to get to, but if you use PMO maturity model (covered in Chapter 5 of this book) correctly, it will guide you in determining when and how fast you mature different components of your PMO.

Make sense? Great. Are you ready to move into the implementation phase now? You should be; you did a ton of work to get to this point, and your management team and your customers want you to start building this PMO.

Bill's Thoughts:

*There are a couple of different ways that PMOs get started from an implementation phase perspective, and your management team will likely drive you hard to do this or do that. You need to be organized in how you approach this task; **do not** force the PMO. This is your chance to do things right, do not mess it up because you are under pressure to get things done quickly because your management team has pressure on you. Even if you are in the situation where you are enhancing an existing PMO, do not be tempted to force new processes or components because management is forcing you to do so. Go slow, be thoughtful, and think about what you are doing.*

Okay, let's get started. This is exciting, this is your chance to create a PMO from scratch using industry best practices and processes that have been tested and proven to work. It's also your chance to prove to management that you are the right person for the job. Embrace the implementation phase—things are going to move quickly—you are going to try things that don't work, things that do work; the whole experience will be a learning process for you. Have fun, it will be a wild ride!

PMO Implementation Steps

Implementing a PMO will be one of the most rewarding experiences of your professional career. You have spent hours reviewing and deciding on this or that component, and now you have the opportunity to build it in a real environment. As you move into the implementation phase, you start to implement all the decisions you made. This is also the time when you test various processes and procedures that might end up being used for years to come. That's exciting, but also scary because you need to get them right. So, approach this work carefully and slowly and make sure you bring the right people with you through the process. Bring in the people slowly and they will support you along the way.

The key to running any successful organization, but especially one as political as a PMO, is the people. The same people you interact with every day can make or break your PMO. You will deal with all kinds of personalities—people who are naysayers and others who support everything you do. These people will range from top-level management to individual team members. Regardless of whom you are dealing with, or what level they are at the company, you must build relationships with them—especially if they are working in your PMO. It is your role to ensure people at all levels see value and support the PMO work at all times. It is not an easy task, and not everyone is successful, but it's one of the reasons you were hired. Part of your role as PMO Manager is to be part salesperson and part marketer, tooting your PMO's horn at all times. You need to continually show value of your PMO and work with people to gain their support. Ideally, you want everyone who is working in and with your PMO to be a **"true believer."** You will know you have accomplished that when you hear that they are supporting and speaking highly about your PMO to others and when they continue to want to work with your PMO. There is no better feeling at that point because you know you are providing value, making a difference, and in the end, helping your organization. If you are aware of how important people are in your PMO and how those people can help your PMO be successful, you should be fine. You have to focus on it, though, and make an effort to build relationships.

Tips & Best Practices

Start Implementing your PMO by building a Microsoft® SharePoint® intranet site or other common repository site because it gives you a central location from which to drive everything.

It is time to move into the implementation phase of the book and, ultimately, into the steps to build the PMO. This is the fun part, so let's get started and focus on building a world class PMO. One of the best places to start in a complex process like this is to reference the **PMO Build Decision Chart** that you have been using while reading chapters 4 through 12 and documenting the various PMO build decisions. Do you remember that chart and the questions at the end of each chapter? Did you document your decisions? You need them documented for this part of the process. Let's look at

Table 13.1 PMO Build Decision Chart again and review the information (or the template) that you completed.

Table 13.1 PMO Build Decision Chart

Chapter	PMO Build Decision Questions	Decisions Made
Example Row Chapter 4	1, 5	My PMO mission statement is, "To drive excellence in the management and delivery of projects." MY PMO will focus on program & project management
5	2,3,4,5	The P's of the PMO will represent program and project management. My PMO model is supportive, but will include parts of the directive model in terms of methodology processes. The categories of my maturity model include…, and so on.
6	1,3,5	……
7	1,2,3	…….

Is your PMO Build Decision Chart handy and complete? Did you document your decisions for every chapter? If not, go back and do it now, because you need this information to move forward. If you did answer each question, you actually answered a huge list of different questions through the build process. That's right, you made a number of important decisions while going through the different build chapters and you took my recommendation and documented them along the way using the PMO Build Decision Chart. Great work, that's was half the battle. You should be ready to start implementing on all those decisions. Now, these are important decisions, but they are not all critical. Remember that during this process, just because you made a decision about what you were going to do, not every decision has to be implemented right away. Remember, we talked about it earlier: crawl, walk, run—when you think about implementing your PMO build decisions, you are in the "crawling" phase. When you look at the decisions outlined in your completed PMO Build Decision Chart, look at them through that lens because some decisions are critical and some are necessary, but they are not all critical to implement when getting your PMO off the ground. The best example of this is the PMO mentoring program, although, a best practice and highly recommended, it is not critical—you can wait some time before implementing a mentoring program in your PMO, it does not have to be done immediately.

Okay, let's look at your PMO Build Decision Chart. Also, remember the PMO Recommendation Report you created in Chapter 4, "How to Build a PMO"? Have it handy too because that work and analysis plays a role in implementing the various components of your PMO.

PMO Implementation Process

The PMO Build Decision Chart will be the key tool to help you move through the implementation process. Another process that you will follow during the implementation phase is focusing on the required components versus the nice-to-have components. Remember, not everything you documented in the PMO Build Decision Chart and the PMO Recommendation Report is required when you start implementing your PMO; some of it can wait until the PMO grows and matures. Do not try to implement everything at once, lay down the basic foundation and the key components first, and then grow and mature the PMO, add more processes, best practices, tools, templates, and so on. PMOs have their own peaks and valleys when they are being built. At the very beginning of the build and implementation process, everyone is very busy and there are lots of things occurring, this is known as the peak times. But, as everything settles down and matures (and it will), this is known as the valley times (slower times), your role will be to continually look for ways to improve and make processes and life easier and more efficient for everyone. For example, imagine how much easier it is for your management team to pull overall status of all the programs and projects in your PMO from an automated dashboard. PMO Managers usually don't implement PMO dashboards right away, but rather mature into them as they grow their organization. They also would not take on the effort of implementing a dashboard during the peak or very busy times, they would be smart to wait until things slow down and the organization and management are ready for an automated tool like a dashboard.

Critical Decisions for Successful PMO Implementation

As noted, there are some decisions that you need to make when implementing your PMO. Let us spend some time and review those items now:

- **Management support**—How well received, politically, is the PMO?

- **PMO budget**—How much money or budget does the PMO have and do you have the authority to spend that budget?

- **P's of your PMO**—Which of the P's (portfolio, program and project management) will you implement in your PMO?

- **PMO model**—Which PMO model did you choose (directive, supportive, and coaching, and so on)?

- **PMO roles**—What kind of staff (for example, permanent, vendors, contractors) do you need?

PMO Implementation Steps

It is time now to start the implementation process, but before we do, let's make sure you have the right things in place before you begin. **Figure 13.2 PMO Implementation Input Deliverables** outlines the top three input deliverables needed to start the PMO implementation process. Take a look and gather the materials now before moving onto the tactical implementation steps.

Figure 13.2 PMO Implementation Input Deliverables

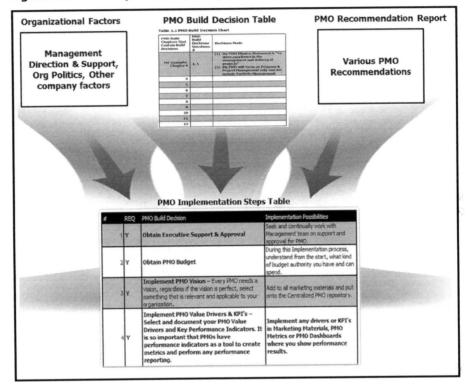

As illustrated, the following three key input items will drive the implementation of your PMO:

- **Organizational factors**—What does the company and management team think about the PMO, and what are the political factors involved in making the PMO work at your company? Who supports it, who is against it, how bad is program and project execution today? These factors will impact what you initially will be able to implement for your PMO.

- **PMO Build Decision Chart**—This chart includes the documented decisions you made while mentally going through the build process. These decisions made sense before you were actually building anything, but now at the time of implementation, you need to consider these decisions again and make sure your management teams supports your decisions.

- **PMO Recommendation Report**—This is the report for areas of improvements and proposed changes you created early on during the assessment process when you were looking at the organization and determining or recommending changes to management. This report plays a role in the implementation process. There could be other various PMO recommendations as well that also factor into this input that maybe outside of what is documented in the PMO Recommendation Report.

These three items are important and key inputs for the next process: the actual PMO implementation steps.

Let us now look at the steps in **Table 13.2 PMO Implementation Steps** to help you create the PMO for your company. In this table, you will see a REQ (required) column, which represents the need to implement that particular task at the time of implementing your PMO. Not all tasks are required, but review and check that column for each task. A Y/N indicator in the table signifies something you decided during the build process. Let us look now at the table and the steps to implement your PMO.

Table 13.2 PMO Implementation Steps

#	REQ	PMO Build Decision	Implementation Possibilities
1.	Y	**Obtain management support and approval** *** This is a key implementation step ***	Continually seek and work with your management team for PMO support and approval. There is no implementation without support. How you handle obtaining that support will be company specific, but ensure you collect and obtain that support before moving forward.
2.	Y	**Obtain PMO budget**	The budget process will be re-examined and addressed during the implementation process just as it was during the build process. You may have a second ask for budget during implementation.
3.	Y	**Implement the PMO centralized repository site**	Implement this intranet or repository in a central location for your company. Make sure everyone can access the information and pull data from it.
4.	Y	**Implement a PMO mission statement**—Every PMO needs a mission statement that sets the guiding principles of the PMO.	It is important to add the mission statement to all marketing decks, presentation materials, and your centralized repository for visibility.
5.	Y	**Implement a PMO vision statement**—Every PMO needs a vision statement; select	Add the vision statement to all marketing materials and the

#	REQ	PMO Build Decision	Implementation Possibilities
		something that is relevant and applicable to your organization.	centralized repository.
6.	Y	**Implement PMO value drivers and KPIs**—Select and document your PMO value drivers and KPIs. It is important for PMOs to have performance indicators as a tool to create metrics and performance reporting.	Implement drivers or KPIs in marketing materials, PMO metrics, or PMO dashboards where you show performance results.
7.	Y	**Implement the P's in your PMO**—Selecting and determining which methodologies will be in your PMO is critical. Select whether your PMO will have components of portfolio management, program management, or project management. This is the defining factor for your PMO and will drive many components of what you do in your PMO on an ongoing bases.	After selecting the different methodologies, there are many implementation considerations. Depending on your selection, you will set up organization groups, repositories, and complete operations around the methodology selected.
8.	Y	**Implement the PMO model**—The PMO model includes supportive, directive, controlling, and so on. Every PMO has a combination of different models, but you should have a major theme or preference. *** This is a key implementation step ***	The implementation choices of the PMO model are critical. You will make multiple decisions based on the model(s) you choose for your PMO.
9.	Y	**Implement the PMO maturity model**—You must understand the different categories and rating system to use in your PMO. *** This is a key implementation step ***	Add the maturity model to your centralized repository, marketing decks, and PMO presentations. Make sure you can speak to this model with everyone. Your measurement of our PMO is critical and done mainly through the use of a PMO Maturity Model.

#	REQ	PMO Build Decision	Implementation Possibilities
10.	Y	**Implement your PMO service offerings**—The offerings, such as a centralized repository, best practices, auditing, and so on, define your PMO. *** This is a key implementation step ***	The PMO model plays a big role in the service offerings you decide to implement. Implementing service offerings also includes creating the processes around those offerings, creating training materials, and creating pilot programs to ensure each of the offerings are successful.
11.	Y	**Create the PMO roles to service- offerings matrix** *** This is a key implementation step ***	This is an important step in the implementation process for understanding the staff you need to hire. Use this matrix on marketing materials, PMO presentations, and in staffing conversations to justify staffing requests and costs.
12.	Y	**Hire PMO team members**—This includes employees, vendors and contractors across all roles. *** This is a key implementation step ***	The implementation process for hiring PMO team members entails hiring them and getting them ramped up in their respective roles.
13.	Y	**Create and implement training plans** *** This is a key implementation step ***	Create a PMO training plan and the budget request to support the execution of that plan. This includes creating an initial training plan, and then determining the training details. (e.g. Project Communications training)
14.	N	**Create a PMO Mentor Program or PMO Buddy System**	Implement this program slowly, following the steps documented earlier in Chapter 7 of this book. This is not a critical step or something that needs to occur immediately, but certainly a best practice and highly recommended when the organization is ready.

#	REQ	PMO Build Decision	Implementation Possibilities
15.	Y/N	**Implement the portfolio management methodology** *** This is a key implementation step *** In this case you see both a Y and a N. This is where you will decide Yes or No whether you will use Portfolio Management or not in your PMO.	Depending on the type of PMO, which P's are in the PMO, and if portfolio management is part of the implementation process, follow the details in Chapter 8, "Portfolio Management Methodology" to implement portfolio management. ** It is highly recommended that you take the components of portfolio management and make pocket-sized copies of the methodology for your Portfolio Managers. The miniature version provides help to the Portfolio Manager going through the portfolio process and gives them a handy pocket guide that they can use on a daily bases. **
16.	Y/N	**Implement the program management methodology** *** This is a key implementation step *** In this case you see both a Y and a N. This is where you will decide Yes or No whether you will use Program Management or not in your PMO.	Same as the portfolio description, it depends on whether program management is part of the PMO. ** Create handy pocket guides that they can use on a daily bases. **
17.	Y/N	**Implement the project management methodology** *** This is a key implementation step *** In this case you see both a Y and a N. This is where you will decide Yes or No whether you will use Project Management or not in your PMO.	Same as the portfolio & program management descriptions, it depends on whether project management is part of the PMO. There is a good chance it will be as most PMOs do include it. ** Create handy pocket guides that they can use on a daily bases. **

#	REQ	PMO Build Decision	Implementation Possibilities
18.	Y	**Implement PMO reporting—** It is important to think about the minimum set of reports to use when starting to implement your PMO.	From an implementation perspective, PMO reports during the initial implementation phase should include basic program and project data only. These reports can focus initially on on-time and on-budget tracking. Enhance reporting only as the PMO matures and do not add too many reports initially.
19.	Y	**Implement PMO tools—**The tools will be specific to the different P's selected for the PMO (portfolio, program, and project) and any software products required to run the PMO. **Examples include:** • Centralized status system • Centralized financial systems • Centralized HR performance system • Centralized timesheet system • Centralized purchasing system for processing POs and work orders • Centralized employee training systems *** This is a key implementation step ***	The implementation possibilities around PMO software are endless. Think about implementing only limited PMO software packages to start, and then add additional packages as the PMO matures. Think about software training and the processes needed to use the tools anytime you add them.
20.	Y	**Implement PMO processes—** These are the key PMO processes that are specific to running and driving the PMO.	The implementation possibilities around PMO processes include timeframes for submitting status reports, running financial

#	REQ	PMO Build Decision	Implementation Possibilities
		Examples include: • PMO governance process • PMO escalation process • PMO change control process • PMO financial process • PMO lessons-learned process • PMO procurement process • PMO resource management process • Portfolio review board process *** This is a key implementation step ***	processes, running change control, and so on.

Tips & Best Practices

Focus on the "key implementation steps" outlined in the table. They can make or break the implementation process if you do not get them right.

Bill's Thoughts:

In a couple of my PMOs, I created pocket-sized guide books for my Program Managers and Project Managers, and people loved them. They were great marketing collateral to show day-to-day responsibilities, but they were also incredible job aids. I highly recommend creating these guide books for your organization. Regardless of the subject or material, they will go over well with management, customers, and your PMO team members.

Follow these 20 steps for an excellent foundation for a world class PMO. As PMO Manager, your role is to actively drive each phase and continue to refine and grow each PMO process where applicable, while maintaining a speed that the company can handle. Do not expect that your company can adopt the processes as quickly as you can think of them; go slowly and be methodical in your approach. Be careful during this process and do not underestimate the importance of communicating changes to your organization (e.g. known as Organizational Change Management) and slowly moving your people through the different processes or tools that you are implementing in your

PMO. People often struggle to embrace new ideas or processes quickly, so make sure to consider how your new PMO idea might impact the execution and flow of existing programs and projects. Aggressive PMO Managers often implement too many processes and procedures too quickly and end up not lasting long in their roles. But, PMO Managers who can grow into the role and understand and balance the needs of the PMO with the needs of the company, while continuing to show and prove value of the PMO, tend to be the ones who last the longest and have the ongoing support of their management team. Understand this balance and consider how important it is during the implementation process.

Implement and Sustain

Now that you have implemented your PMO and built the foundation, you can move into an ongoing process of improving and refining your PMO. One of your main responsibilities as PMO Manager is to constantly look for areas to grow and improve while being aware of areas that are not working well and removing them, when necessary. You must have a constant understanding of what is working and what is not working.

Having this knowledge of what is working and not working is such an important point because, as you may recall, earlier in the book it was mentioned the shelf-life of a typical PMO Manager and the various reasons why they do not last long (typically, three-four years) at any one company. You do not want to be in that position; you want to ensure that your PMO is providing value and that your program and project teams are executing and meeting customer expectations.

Celebrate Success

As PMO Manager, remember to celebrate your PMO employees' successes throughout the year. In **Figure 13.3 PMO Build Schedule**, you will remember we talked about a **Celebrate Period** where the PMO Manager takes the team to an offsite event, usually once a year, to celebrate everyone's great work. This event is very important and highly recommended, but it may not be enough for some employees, so what else can you do during the year to celebrate success?

Figure 13.3 PMO Build Schedule

Task Name	Resource Names
-PMO Build Schedule	PMO Manager
+Step 1 - Grow PMO Manager Skills - Ongoing Activity	PMO Manager
+Step 2 - Obtain Executive Support (Chapter 3)	PMO Manager
+Step 3 - Assessment Period (Chapter 4)	PMO Manager
+Step 4 - Recommendation Period	PMO Manager
+Step 5 - Design & Build or Enhance Period (Chapter 5 - 12)	PMO Manager
+Step 6 – Implementation PMO Deliverables/Processes Period (Chapter 13)	PMO Manager
+Step 7 - Refine, Enhance and Grow Period (Chapter 14 - Chapter 16)	PMO Manager
+Step 8 - Celebrate Period	PMO Manager
+PMO Built & Implemented - Time to Mature and Grow - PMO Project Complete	PMO Manager

Well, that is easy, and something that any PMO Manager can do while keeping the costs low and morale high. One of the best practices for celebrating success during the year is creating a "PMO Professional of the Month" award. This award process includes the recipient receiving a trophy and PMO certificate that celebrates their great work for the month. The PMO Manager can take a picture of the individual with the trophy and certificate and post the picture on a centralized repository for everyone to see and acknowledge the great work of the individual.

Bill's Thoughts:

I have created a "Project Manager of the Month" award in my last couple of PMOs and they have been incredibly successful. The employees loved it, it was low-cost, it boosted morale, and it was basically a great way to keep highlighting the great work the PMO employees were doing throughout the year. This is a highly recommended best practice.

Summary

As we conclude the implementation process, you should have a solid foundation for your new or enhanced PMO. How exciting is that—and was it not a fun process to go through? Most people say it is very fulfilling to do. Now you have the organization and you have the foundation to make it even better. It is in your hands to grow and mature the organization and to make changes and enhance it as the company matures.

Depending on the choices and the "crawl, walk, run" process you followed throughout the implementation phase, you should have a good handle on areas you need to work on to grow your PMO.

Remember the people in this process and how implementing a new PMO impacts them. Think about the impact on them from a tactical perspective and how you just added a new level of rigor and structure to their projects that they may not be comfortable with. They also might not be in the best position to snap to a new set of structure and you might need to work with them to understand how they can adopt some of the new PMO processes you just implemented.

Also, it is important to not forget about the concept of "resources, procedures, and infrastructure" we have talked about all along during the PMO build process. Think about how each area is critical for everything you implement in your new PMO. We talk about people, procedures/processes, and infrastructure throughout building our PMO and focus you on thinking about each continually during the build and implementation processes.

Finally, remember that new procedures or processes can be a struggle for project teams to adopt and so do not force it during this implementation process. It can take several years for every program and project to use a common set of processes. Keep working on them, though. Your role as PMO Manager is to ensure that as many program and project teams are using the processes and procedures and are following the best practices you outlined in your PMO.

The PMO implementation process is a slow but rewarding journey. Eventually, the teams get there and, if you do it right, your PMO has a great chance of being successful.

Chapter Review Answers

1. Items for implementing a PMO include: management support, PMO budget, and the P's of your PMO.

2. Not all steps are required due to a variety of factors. For example, if you are creating a PMO that is only a program management PMO, you would not implement the portfolio or project management methodologies.

3. Trick question—there is not one single most important step when implementing a PMO; every company and situation is different, but if you have to pick one thing, Management Support tops the list.

4. Budget plays a significant role during the implementation phase because the available budget impacts how much money you have to hire people, offer different service offerings, purchase tools, and so on. The more budget you have, the more flexibility you have growing your PMO.

5. Obtain management support and approval, implement the PMO model, implement the PMO maturity model, and implement the PMO service offerings.

Chapter 14

PMO Measurements and Performance Tracking

Figure 14.1 PMO Build Schedule – Performance Tracking

Task Name	Resource Names
-PMO Build Schedule	**PMO Manager**
+Step 1 - Grow PMO Manager Skills - Ongoing Activity	**PMO Manager**
+Step 2 - Obtain Executive Support (Chapter 3)	**PMO Manager**
+Step 3 - Assessment Period (Chapter 4)	**PMO Manager**
+Step 4 - Recommendation Period	**PMO Manager**
+Step 5 - Design & Build or Enhance Period (Chapter 5 - 12)	**PMO Manager**
+Step 6 – Implementation PMO Deliverables/Processes Period (Chapter 13)	**PMO Manager**
+Step 7 - Refine, Enhance and Grow Period (Chapter 14 - Chapter 16)	**PMO Manager**
+PMO Measurements & Performance Tracking (Chapter 14)	**PMO Manager**
Review the PMO KPI's established during the build phase	PMO Manager
Define PMO Level Metrics. Ensure the PMO Metrics are aligned to the company's	PMO Manager
Work with management, customers and PMO team members to understand metrics	PMO Manager
-PMO Measurement Process	**PMO Manager**
+Create KPI Metric Data	**PMO Manager**
+PMO Performance Tracking	**PMO Manager**
Review different areas of PMO where Performance reporting was possible	PMO Manager
+Create Performance Reporting	**PMO Manager**

Questions you should be able to answer after reading this chapter:

1. Why should PMO metrics align with company metrics?

2. What is the difference between qualitative and quantitative metrics? Why does that difference matter?

3. How does the PMO maturity model help with creating metrics and measurements?

4. What are the three most popular PMO metrics?

5. Why is auditing important? Why do it?

Your PMO is now up and running and things seem to be working nicely. Your Portfolio Manager has the portfolio in shape, the planning process is complete, and programs and projects are executing well—some problems occasionally crop up, but generally things are going well. Now, it is time to turn your attention to establishing measurements and metrics for your PMO. You and your management team feel that it is time to start measuring progress to see if the PMO is providing value for the organization. You had some initial KPIs already in your PMO—you created them earlier when you were first building your PMO. It is time to buckle down and get serious about recreating or readdressing those KPIs with much more rigor and process to start proving that your PMO is valuable and worthwhile to the company.

However, before you go too much further, reconfirm with your management team your PMO model (Controlling, Supportive...etc.), and whether you are in the position to create and measure programs and projects. You just may not be using the right type of PMO model that is conducive to collecting and reporting PMO metrics. For example, if you have a directive PMO, you are definitely set up and ready to run metrics against how the program and project teams are executing, but if you are a supportive or coaching PMO, you may not yet be ready to create and drive metrics. Work closely with your management team and make sure they fully understand your PMO model. If they do, you might not need to create metrics and measurements. For this chapter, though, we are going to assume you are in a PMO that is set up to create and drive metrics for the organization.

Any time your management team or customers ask you to look at metrics and measurements, take a step back first, and look at how you are currently measuring the success of your PMO. You might have the right processes and procedures in place already to track and record performance, but you might not be reporting it in a manner that is resonating with your management team. If that is the case, you just need to change how you are reporting. On the other hand, you might realize that you are not generating any performance measurements, in which case, you need to get serious about this ask from your management team and make it happen.

Tracking and reporting measurement data is critical to the success of a PMO because it validates and exposes how well the PMO is executing and performing. On the other hand, tracking this data also exposes issues that are occurring within the programs and projects. Having this measurement data will help you, as PMO Manager confirm whether the processes and procedures that you created and implemented while building your PMO are working or whether they need updating. Alternatively, if you inherited an existing PMO, and your task was to evaluate the PMO and find out what is working and what isn't, you could look at the existing KPIs to determine whether they need updating. Reviewing the measurement data, or KPIs, of an existing PMO helps determine how well the PMO is executing, which helps you understand where changes are necessary. If there are problems around program and project delivery, review the KPIs the PMO was using to find immediate areas on which to focus. In most cases, the KPIs will need refreshing within the PMO, and now that you are the PMO Manager, you'll probably want to change them anyway.

We considered throughout the PMO assessment process, and into the PMO build and implementation processes, how resources, procedures, and infrastructure might be affected. Resources, procedures, and infrastructure are critical to building and implementing PMOs, which continues to be true and as we look into metrics and measurements. As PMO Manager, remember to always keep these three areas at the forefront and consider the impact to those areas for anything new you propose during this process.

Let's look at these three areas and the important roles they play in this process:

- **Resources** play an important role in the metric and measurement process because they collect the measurement data and it is their work that the Project Manager rates. Think about that for a minute, someone might tell you that they can do a task in five days, but instead they take ten days (scheduling performance). Who does the Project Manager blame for that slip? The person who initially made the estimate—we expect people to hold to their estimates and do the task in the time they said they could do the work. Therefore, if you think about this process across all the various performance reports possible, you quickly see that all resources play a huge role in collecting this metric and measurement data.

- **Procedures** plays a critical role in the metric and measurement process as well because procedures/processes are used to create and capture metric data. Without these steps, there would be no way to create the data and no meaningful way to capture the data. As PMO Manager, think about new processes or procedures that are needed and how PMO employees will use them as you create different metrics and measurements. Some teams will easily accept new procedures and processes while other groups will struggle and take much longer to adopt it.

- **Infrastructure** also play a role in the metric and measurement process because you use a variety of tools to capture and generate performance reports. Tools include project scheduling tools, financial tools, and quality tools.

These are just some of the considerations that PMO Managers encounter for the three areas (resources, procedures, and infrastructure) during the metrics and measurement process. As noted earlier, keep them at the forefront of your mind during this process and consider each one carefully as you create metrics and measurements for your PMO.

A best practice is to focus on establishing metrics around business value because it is the driver behind the project. We went into detail about business value in in Chapter 9, "Program Management Methodology," and this is the point in the process where you actually start creating them for your PMO. Review the section about business value in the "Program Management Methodology" chapter and think about it as you create your new metrics and measurements for your PMO. Remember, do not rush into creating business value KPIs; use those already in use by the organization. If you have to suggest, name, or create new value KPIs, ensure that they align with the top goals of the organization (for example, revenue, market share, cost reduction (balance sheet KPIs), and so on). Creating metrics and measurements around business value is valuable for any organization because it keeps your PMO connected with your customer requirements (around business value) and your programs and projects will be set up to deliver that value. PMO metrics do not solely need to be based on on-time or on-budget performance. More mature PMOs include business value metrics because they realize that sometimes the customers would rather track to how well the program or project is tracking towards business value compared to the standard performance measurements (on-time or on-budget).

A best practice when creating measurements and metrics is to ensure that you are setting them up only where you have control and responsibility over that part of the organization. Naming KPIs that are outside your span of control, or outside the direct impact of your project or effort, jeopardizes your credibility and shakes the image of the PMO—whether those KPIs are headed in the right direction or they unexpectedly falter. There are two sets of metrics that PMOs usually track: PMO performance metrics or KPIs, and organizational metrics and KPIs. PMO metrics are based on project and program cost, delivery, and quality. Organizational KPIs are the secondary measures that are impacted by the effort—short or long term. Your metrics and measurements will be program and project execution related, which is expected, but depending on the PMO model, the metrics and measurements might be very specific for that model. For example, if you are driving a coaching PMO, you might have a metric for the number of Project Managers involved in PMP training for the year. You would not, in that case, have a metric around on-time performance; it would be an irrelevant PMO metric for that PMO model. Therefore, PMO models play a role in the types of measurements and metrics possible and applicable in your organization.

Let's move into creating PMO metrics and measurements for your PMO.

Establishing PMO Metrics and Measurements

Establishing PMO metrics and measurements is a very rewarding process because the end result is a set of goals and measurements that everyone in the PMO can measure their programs and projects against and know whether they are tracking to management's expectations. PMO measurements give program and project teams goals to strive for and increases the efficiency of the organization, overall. Metrics and measurements are a key management and customer tool for measuring how program and project teams are executing. As PMO Manager, if you do not have metrics in place, it is important that you establish some sooner rather than later. To drive an efficient and effective PMO, you need metrics in place so that all programs and projects can align to them.

PMOs must have organizational level (top-level) metrics. These metrics measure how well the organization is performing. PMO Managers will be critical in establishing these metrics.

Here are three examples of PMO-level metrics that you can use in your PMO to get you started in this process:

- Successful implementation of programs and projects

- Ensuring the adherence of programs and projects to standard methodologies

- Successful completion and sustainment of programs and projects

These examples set the foundation for all other metrics in the PMO. As new KPIs are created, they should be tested against these to ensure alignment; otherwise, the metrics become useless and non-meaningful.

Tips & Best Practices

Work with a certified Six Sigma Black Belt or Six Sigma Master Black Belt Process Engineer to create PMO measurements and metrics. These individuals are key for creating good measurable metrics and instrumental to you being successful in this process.

You will hear the terms: metrics, performance metrics, and KPIs, and you might get confused about the different meanings. Sometimes, you might ask yourself, what are they anyway? Well, these terms, or metrics, (regardless of what you call them) are *measurements of an organization's activities and performance*. Your management team and customers will drive metrics requirements and you, as PMO Manager, drive the processes and procedures that program and projects teams perform to make these metrics happen. In PMOs, performance-based metrics assess the health of programs and projects. One of the key responsibilities for PMO Managers is to use metrics to measure a project's health, depending again on the type of PMO they are leading. If you are running a supportive PMO, you might not be as worried about program and project health data as you would be if you were running a directive PMO. However, without metrics, there is no true way of understanding how well programs and projects are executing or performing. Your management team and customers won't have that information either, which could cause some real problems. Metrics are necessary in the world of PMOs. When you add metrics to your PMO, you give everyone the ability to measure the progress of your project data and make transparent the true state(s) of programs and projects within your organization.

Here are a few of the many reasons as to why you should use PMO metrics:

- Help control programs and projects
- Helps with risk mitigation
- Help drive and manage team performance
- Help drive management and customer satisfaction
- Help evaluate program and project progress and overall health

Metrics and KPIs need to be relevant. How you use metrics in your PMO depends on what you are trying to accomplish across the PMO. For example, if you create a performance metric to improve on-time delivery, the purpose of the metric is not to track at a single program or project level, but to track at an organizational level. So, all on-time metrics for programs and projects are tracked and the results of each are calculated for a *total* score at the organizational level.

The other term you hear often in metrics and measurements is the Key Performance Indicator (KPI). It is interesting to know that a KPI is a metric, but not all metrics equate to a KPI. Think about that when you create metrics and measurements for your organization. In simple terms, it means that when you establish key criteria for a KPI, not every metric will match all of the criteria.

Let's look at some of the criteria for creating KPIs. Use these conditions when creating KPIs for your PMO. The conditions include, but are not limited to, the following:

- They are defined by your management team and customers
- They cascade throughout an organization
- They are based on corporate standards
- They are easy to comprehend
- They empower users
- They lead to positive action

Another important part of creating and establishing metrics is to ensure that there is a mixture of both qualitative (observed, but not measured) and quantitative (measurable data) in place. Having both allows PMO Managers, management, and your customers to have two sets of measurement data they can use in this process. Let us look at some of the different examples when working with PMO data.

Qualitative

- Applied risk management processes result in less critical impact to project execution
- Structured issue management processes result in quicker turnaround on project impacting issues
- Continued delivery of on-time programs and projects improve PMO reputation

Quantitative

- The number of Programs and Projects completed on time
- The number of Programs and Projects completed on budget
- The number of customer requirements exceeded
- The length of time it took to escalate project items

PMO Managers need to show a balanced view for tangible and intangible KPIs. PMO Managers, management teams, and customers often ignore intangible KPIs in favor of classic KPIs, such as revenue, cost savings, and efficiency goals. Successful organizations often prioritize intangible values over conventional short-term revenue and market-share goals. Intangible KPIs tend to improve the future of the business more than immediate financial gain.

PMOs and project stakeholders often ignore intangible KPIs because intangible KPIs are often difficult to deconstruct or establish an equivalent dollar value. For example, what is the impact of customer satisfaction on future revenue? There are many techniques to establish the approximate value for each customer or product-facing activity, but it is equally good for the PMO to obtain consensus on the project percentage contribution to the actual all-up intangible value. Many organizations hire professional quality consultants to help establish these criteria.

It is much more difficult to find examples of qualitative PMO measurements and metrics because PMOs tend to focus more on measureable data and hard facts around program and project execution than they do around non-measurable data. However, it is common for PMO Managers to forget to measure the "how" or the "qualitative" value, which is an important part of the overall measurement. This typically happens because Project Managers each manage their projects very differently—even when they are following the same processes and templates, which is acceptable but it is also important to understand their management styles. Management teams and customers focus on "how" Project Managers accomplish tasks; therefore, this is a fair and acceptable measurement for them as well. As PMO Manager, look at how your PMO team members are performing and don't ignore this qualitative measurement.

Qualitative measurements should focus on measuring and understanding emotional behavioral data, such as how the Project Manager works with team members and interacts with customers, or how he or she reports to and works with the management team. This is not critical data, but it is important data and something to include in the measurement process.

The reverse is also true: if the Project Manager only focuses on the "how," and although the team and customers enjoy working with that Project Manager, the project(s) are always late and over budget, that is also an issue. In this case, the "how" is measured partially as a positive measurement, but around the execution, the Project Manager would have a negative rating. When the Project Manager focuses solely on doing the right thing for the customer, he or she could find other issues that delay the project from completing. However, this could be a good thing because the product might not be ready yet, so the Project Manager knows that the customer would be unhappy with the product if they were to get it at this time. Therefore, the Project Manager who spends more time on the "how" and less time driving the tactical areas could actually be right in this scenario. This is just an example that you, as PMO Manager, might run into where you can see how qualitative data is something you might use in the measurement process. This is another balancing act that the PMO Manager needs to contend with, but is very important.

Your role in the PMO measurement process is to ensure that your management team and customers are active in this process. They will often be very active in defining measurements and metrics for the organization, specifically, PMOs. Make sure you keep both groups engaged and involved during the measurement and metric process. There is no sense in creating a measurement process in a vacuum without already having approval or buy-in. Keep them involved throughout the process and check in yearly for metric updates or changes to the measurements.

Remember, as PMO Manager, you are the value protector. If a project has no envisioned value, then it's best not to start work on it in the first place.

Before we go too deep into establishing and creating measurements and metrics, let's look at where some organizations struggle so you don't run into those same problems in your PMO. Some organizations struggle with how to process metric data. Here are some of the issues they might find in the metric data from the respective programs and projects:

- Measurements are not useful

- Data quality is poor

- No baseline performance data, so there is no starting point from which to start comparing the program and project efforts

- Too busy to analyze the data

- Management team is unfamiliar with metrics or they don't give them time or attention

- Too much data collected—no idea where to start to analyze.

These are just some of the many different problems that organizations run into around metric and measurement data. These problems are common for most organizations where the focus is to perform as many programs and projects as quickly as possible without spending the time to figure out how to measure themselves on an ongoing basis. These problems are centered around having too much data and not enough time to analyze it. Your role as PMO Manager is to work through the various problems and create a formal process to complete as many programs and projects as possible. You need to balance the information coming in and use it to help the organization become more effective so that you can exceed the expectations of your management team and customers.

Creating PMO Metrics and Measurements

Creating PMO metrics, as noted above, comes from management and customers and is something you should take very seriously. When starting this process, meet with your management team and customers to gather their requirements and continue to work with them as you implement their requirements in your PMO. Having their support and approval is critical, so work closely with them throughout this process.

It is time to start walking through the process to create PMO metrics for your organization. Luckily, you already have a great starting point for this process by having created your PMO maturity model when you were first building your PMO. Go back to Chapter 5, and review the PMO maturity model you created because it is the basis for how you will create these PMO metrics. As shown in **Figure 14.2 PMO Maturity Model KPI Process**, start with the PMO maturity model you built, and then create the KPIs (at least one for each row of your maturity model) that define the key data elements of each KPI. In this figure, there are three steps which are the same procedures you followed when creating your KPIs for your PMO. The existing PMO maturity model is a great starting point for you in this process.

Let's look at the process and go into more detail after we review the model.

Figure 14.2 PMO Maturity Model KPI Process

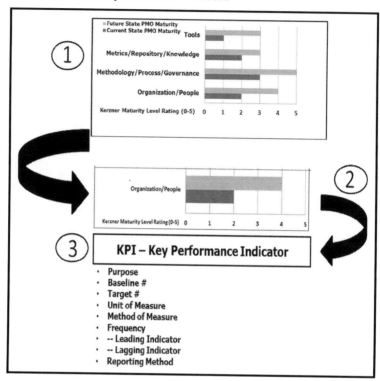

In reviewing the process, you can see that it is straightforward and relatively easy to do. Remember, though, keep your management team and customers involved throughout this process to ensure the greatest chance of them accepting the KPIs you create for your PMO.

Process for following the maturity model:

Step 1: Use your existing PMO model as a starting point for KPI metric creation. Remember the PMO organizational level metrics.

Step 2: Pull one of the PMO maturity categories from the model and develop specific KPIs for that category.

Step 3: Create a KPI for each category by completing and filling in the KPI data for each row. There can be more than one KPI for each row.

Metrics require very basic data, and at the core, include:

- Purpose
- Baseline number—what is the starting point for this metric?
- Target number—what target do you want to reach with this metric?
- Unit of measure—how will you measure the metric?
- Frequency
    - Leading indicator (e.g. customer complaints)
    - Lagging indicator (e.g. days lost due to injuries)
- Reporting method—when and how will the data be reported?

Note: See examples below for more information about each data point.

When completing the details for each metric, you can add additional data for every metric, but it is important to start with the minimum fields first, and then add more if needed.

Repeat Step 3: Create additional KPIs for each category, where applicable.

Step 4: Process complete!

After completing the process, you will have, at a minimum, four KPIs—one row for each row of your maturity model—if you selected only four categories for your initial PMO maturity model. If you have more than four rows, you will still have one row for each category. It is a best practice to keep the KPIs to a limited number (four is fine) to start with, especially because the PMO is new and still maturing; it is much easier to manage a fewer number of KPIs. Managing a large number of KPIs is difficult and, therefore, decreases your chance of success.

Tips & Best Practices

Remember to tie these KPIs back to the PMO organizational (or top-level) KPIs because they are interrelated and should be connected.

Use the following examples as starting points for creating your own metrics in order to help you understand which KPIs to use for each maturity model category.

KPI and Metrics for the PMO Maturity Model Process

As noted earlier in the chapter, the PMO maturity model that you created during the PMO build process is an important first step when creating PMO metrics. The PMO maturity model provides you the key areas for your PMO and establishes the different categories where you can measure and track the performance of your programs and projects. Let's look at the different PMO maturity model categories from the initial maturity model noted earlier in the book and review some possible KPIs for each category.

PMO Maturity Category: Organization/People

KPI and Metric: Percent of Project Managers to be PMP certified

- **Purpose**: PMP certification enhances Project Managers' skill sets to deliver projects with improved consistency and repeatability.
- **Baseline number**: 60%
- **Target number**: 90%
- **Unit of measure**: PMP certifications
- **Frequency**
    - Leading indicator: Number of Project Managers scheduled for PMP exam.
    - Lagging indicator: Number of Project Managers not interested in taking the PMP exam.
- **Reporting method**: This metric is reported monthly to the PMO management team, including functional managers, where applicable.

PMO Maturity Category: Methodology/Process/Governance

KPI and Metric: Percent of programs and projects that use a standard program or project methodology

- **Purpose**: Standard methodologies use the same set of deliverables to maintain consistency in project delivery. Using consistent project delivery methods help correct and steer projects in the right direction if they get off track. Projects that do not use a methodology are much more difficult to correct because part of your time is spent understanding how they operate before you can even begin to start to help them.
- **Baseline number**: 40%
- **Target number**: 90%
- **Unit of measure**: Projects following methodology
- **Frequency**
    - **Leading indicator**: Number of projects that are following a standard methodology.
    - **Lagging indicator**: Number of projects that are not following a standard methodology.
- **Reporting method**: This metric is counted and reported when projects hit major milestones and associated sign-off meetings.

PMO Maturity Category: Metrics/Repository/Knowledge

KPI and Metric: Number of project teams that use a centralized project repository

- **Purpose**: Centralized repositories increase communication to management, customers, and team members about project health data. By using a centralized repository, PMO Managers can review and apply audits to programs and projects.
- **Baseline number**: 75%
- **Target number**: 95%
- **Unit of measure**: Program and project websites
- **Frequency**
    - **Leading indicator**: Number of projects that use a central repository, such as an intranet site.
    - **Lagging indicator**: Number of projects without a central repository that continue to use multiple areas to store program and project deliverables.
- **Reporting method**: Project Managers are accountable for counting and reporting this metric when their project hits a major milestone and its associated sign-off meeting.

PMO Maturity Category: Tools

KPI and Metric: Percent of projects using Microsoft® Project

- **Purpose**: Scheduling tools automate project management processes, drive project dependencies, and produce automated performance reports.
- **Baseline number**: 70%
- **Target number**: 100%
- **Unit of measure**: Project teams using Microsoft® Project
- **Frequency**
    - **Leading indicator**: Number of Project Managers using Microsoft® Project
    - **Lagging indicator**: Number of Project Managers who are not using Microsoft® Project
- **Reporting method**: Project Managers are accountable for counting and reporting on this metric when a project hits a major milestone and associated sign-off meeting.

These four metrics provide basic examples that you could use in your PMO. These metrics will help you get started in the process so your management team and customers are aligned and your program and project teams can focus on the metric process.

In summarizing metrics and measurements, you should now have a good feel for creating some initial metrics and KPIs for your PMO. When your PMO is just starting, these metrics should be very basic so that everyone can understand how to use them and why they are beneficial to the PMO. As your PMO matures your metrics mature, and as you start to collect and gather real metric data, make changes to the metrics to continue to enhance them.

PMO Performance Tracking

One of the reasons for capturing metrics and measurements is performance reporting. The metrics can become meaningless very quickly if you do not track how well you are doing against them. As PMO Manager, you will continually generate various performance reports, so you need to understand the processes for creating the reports and understand the data available for reporting. The advantage of knowing performance data is being able to identify where programs and projects are going off the path and need course correction. Without these types of performance reports, there is no way of really knowing how well programs and projects are doing or whether the project health data is an accurate representation of what is really happening.

There are many different performance reports available from a PMO perspective. Some reports include: schedule performance, financial performance, quality performance, and so on. One of the most basic performance reports is a schedule performance report. As long as the projects are using a scheduling tool, generating this report is simple. Schedule performance gives Project Managers an accurate view of how well the team is performing and whether they are tracking to the dates they committed to at the beginning of the project. As PMO Manager, you will see a lot of benefit from this kind of report because you can look across your PMO and get a feel for how all programs and projects are executing.

Reporting around project scheduling is an important performance-related tool and provides clues into how the team will deliver the project. When, for example, project team members say they can complete a task in five days and they end up taking ten days, you get a view into the accuracy of the schedule across the board—especially if multiple team members repeatedly miss their scheduled dates or, at the minimum, hit very few of them. On the other hand, when team members provide estimates for tasks and they take less time than originally planned, this is also performance data. In this case, the performance data is positive and allows you, as PMO Manager, to make larger cross-PMO decisions when you see your project teams are coming in on their efforts ahead of schedule. If you have a project team that consistently hits their scheduled dates, you could definitely be in a position where you are saving on budget, and having to find new projects for your PMO resources to work on. These types of scenarios are excellent for PMO Managers because you are seeing the performance levels of the program and project teams regardless if they are good or bad, and you are then in a position to make course corrections or leave things alone.

Many PMO Managers only look for negative data in performance reporting when there is both negative and positive data. There should be a balance of changes to make on both sides of the data. If a project team is struggling, missing dates, or over budget, there are changes to make that are completely different from changes you might make to a team that is performing at, or surpassing, expectations. For these teams, PMO Managers might not want to make changes to the team, but might look for ways for a high-performing team to mentor or coach struggling teams to share some best practices and processes to help make them successful. As PMO Manager, look for both positive and negative data in performance reports and react accordingly.

Project scheduling performance reports are one of the quickest and easiest ways to develop performance reporting. If project teams are using a scheduling tool such as Microsoft® Project, this process becomes that much simpler. Let's look at creating project scheduling performance reports using Microsoft® Project at the highest level.

Project scheduling performance reporting using Microsoft® Project is a very simple process. **Figure 14.3 Microsoft® Project Performance Process** shows the five steps for creating schedule performance-related reporting using Microsoft® Project. This type of data reporting is priceless to PMO Managers who are looking for data and trying to determine how well projects across the whole PMO are executing. It is also a mandatory performance report for all program and project managers.

Figure 14.3 Microsoft® Project Performance Process

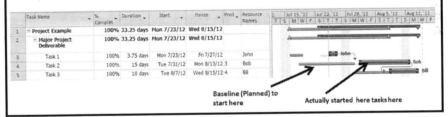

Review the five steps in the figure, and then look closely at the results in Microsoft® Project, shown after the steps, for a powerful performance data report. You can see that the three project tasks were scheduled to start on one date, but ended up starting several days later. When Project Managers link all their tasks using Microsoft® Project (or any scheduling tool) and use proper task dependencies and best practices so that when tasks slip, all tasks that are dependent on that task slip. When the first task slips, all tasks slip. It becomes a chain reaction of project schedule slips, which is only visible by creating a performance report on project schedules.

It is important to note that there must be a formal scheduling management process associated with obtaining scheduling data within each project. This example shows the results after establishing a formal set of processes that both the Project Manager and team members follow to collect and capture the data. This process is critical as well to producing another type of performance report, the cost performance report. You will see that it is also important to have a formal process for establishing and gathering all cost related data in order to create cost performance reports as well.

As noted, another popular performance report that PMO Managers use is the financial (or cost performance) report. This is another type of performance report that gives PMO Managers, Program, and Project Managers a view of how well the programs and projects are executing from a financial perspective. You can easily create financial reports using Microsoft® Project or any of the other scheduling tools. Cost reporting is just as important in some companies as schedule performance reporting is and another area that Program and Project Managers need to watch closely. When determining the costs for each project task, the end result of this process is the budget request for the project. When you start executing the project and if the team constantly goes over budget at the task level, the whole project could quickly go over budget as well. This is why it is so important to track costs at the project task level and why it is important to have cost performance reports. In doing so, you will know exactly how well the team is tracking towards going over budget on staying on track.

When looking at the various tools to create cost performance reports, it is recommended to go back and look first at the scheduling tool to see if there are cost reports available before looking at other tools. If there is, use that tool because it includes your scheduling data. You should capture and report cost and schedule data from the same place, if possible. Some companies use separate tools to track cost data, so you might need to use that tool for cost performance reporting, otherwise if possible use your scheduling tool.

If you are tracking cost-related data within your scheduling tool, such as Microsoft® Project, the process to pull cost performance reports is simple. There is data that you need to enter to be able to pull these reports, but the process is straightforward.

Let's look at that process for Microsoft® Project. Using Microsoft® Project to perform project cost performance reporting is a very easy process. **Figure 14.4 Microsoft® Project Cost Performance Process** shows the basic steps for creating cost performance-related reporting using Microsoft® Project. As you know, there are many different methods for tracking and reporting costs—this is just one example. As with scheduling reporting, this type of reporting is priceless because it allows Project Managers and PMO Managers to keep tight control on financial costs.

Figure 14.4 Microsoft® Project Cost Performance Process

Cost Performance Reporting

Create Baseline with Costs

1) Create a project baseline in Microsoft® Project
2) Add resources to tasks. Ensure there is a rate associated with each resource.

Report Project Progress

1) Set Status Date for reporting period.
2) Using the current schedule, update the tasks with actual Start, Finish dates and actual costs.
3) Change Table in MS Project from the Entry table to Cost table to obtain the example below for your project.

Task Name	Fixed Cost	Fixed Cost Accrual	Total Cost	Baseline	Variance	Actual	Remaining	Jul 15	Jul 22
Project Example	$0	Prorated	$685	$600	$85	$685	$0		
Major Project Deliverable	$0	Prorated	$685	$600	$85	$685	$0		
Task 1	$125	Prorated	$125	$100	$25	$125	$0		John
Task 2	$250	Prorated	$250	$200	$50	$250	$0		
Task 3	$310	Prorated	$310	$300	$10	$310	$0		

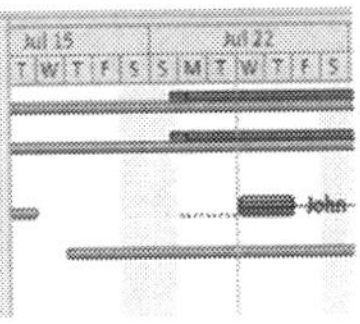

Your variance per task is noted here

It is interesting to note that the processes (schedule and cost performance reporting) are generally the same, but include a different set of fields that need data for tracking. For example, to track cost performance, you need to enter data into the cost fields.

In this view, the **Variance** column shows the difference between your baseline costs and your actual costs. As PMO Manager, or the Project Manager, you can see how well the team is tracking costs at the task level. In the example, you can see that the project is going over budget on every task versus what was planned when the project baseline schedule was created. If this trend keeps up, the project will quickly go over budget.

It is important to note that there must be a formal cost management process associated with obtaining cost data within each project. This example shows the results after establishing a formal set of processes that both the Project Manager and team members must follow to collect and capture the data. This process is critical for producing cost performance reports.

Finally, another very popular performance report for PMO Managers is quality performance reporting because it shows the quality levels of the individual projects or efforts. There are many examples of quality reports available— work with your Project Managers to create the right quality of performance reports for their projects.

Let's look at one example of a Quality Performance Report, **Figure 14.5 Quality Performance Report** shows a quality job that spanned ten days and the results for each day. You can see the trend line for this data trending positive. This, as PMO Manager, is something to investigate, especially as you can see spikes in the number of hours from day to day. E.g., Day 4 takes six hours to run a job, and just one day later the same job takes three hours. This report provides an excellent way to understand how well the project is performing from a quality perspective.

Figure 14.5 Quality Performance Report

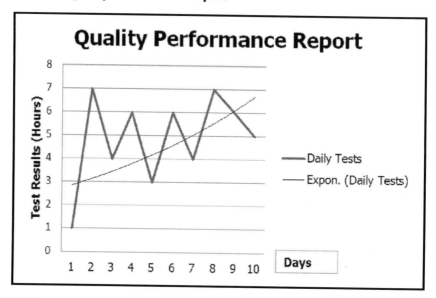

Bill's Thoughts:

In a couple of my PMOs, I immediately created at least two of these three metrics. I created processes for the Project Managers to track scheduling and cost performance reports, and then during my 1:1 meetings with them we would review the reports to understand how their projects were proceeding. Think about these three performance reports as the bread and butter of your PMO and use them as indicators to show how your teams are delivering to what they said they would deliver at the beginning of their efforts.

In summarizing the different quality reports, you can quickly see the power of this data and the decisions that you can make as PMO Manager if you had this data for all the programs and projects in your organization. Think about how valuable these reports (even the examples) are to your management team and customers and what they can do with the data. They too can make business decisions based on what they are seeing and they can get involved at the program and project level to course correct and move things forward. Performance reports are critical in maturing and growing a PMO, so get started with them immediately; however, you must also make sure that your organization is prepared for them. Don't attempt to roll out processes when the organization is not ready or cannot adapt easily to them.

PMO Audits and Auditing

Another way to measure performance is to understand how programs and projects are executing internally and if they are using standard and repeatable processes. Many projects make scheduled dates, stay on budget, or even lower their quality scores in order to move the project into a production environment, although, internally, the project is a disaster. This ranges from not following project management best practices to ignoring key deliverables and outputs of a development life cycle. The range of bad to worse is all over the place in some projects and, as PMO Manager, this is an important component for you to understand and get a handle on in your organization. There are Project Managers who can go for years barely getting by using some project management process and be relatively successful. However, the issue to consider is long-term stability and support when projects like this are put into a production state and there are further enhancements down the line. The next Project Manager, or PMO Manager, who tries to find an issues list or a risk register will struggle if the project was not managed using some of the best practices established by the various portfolio, program, or project methodologies used across the industry and referenced throughout this book. As we discussed earlier, each of these methodologies (Portfolio, Program, and Project) have many processes and procedures for Program and Project Managers to follow and there should be no excuses as to why they are not on their efforts. Across the board, you should work with your PMO employees to ensure they are following a formal methodology whenever possible.

How do you do that? Well, one process is to work with your employees every week and review their project deliverables to ensure that they are creating the required deliverables for each phase of the project while balancing the required list with what is needed for the particular project type, size, and so on. There are definitely factors that impact how closely a Program Manager or Project Manager follows a methodology, which is fine because no methodology will work for every project. However, the conversation about what is required and what is optional must occur between the PMO Manager and the employee at the beginning of the project. That way, everyone is on the same page and has the same expectations.

The other process is to set up a formal auditing system where Program Managers and Project Managers self-manage auditing their deliverables against different methodologies. The auditing process is straightforward and usually consists of a list of all the deliverables outlined by the different methodologies (portfolio, program, and project).

Table 14.1 Project Management Audit Process is just one of the multiple audit tables that PMO Managers use to audit their Project Managers' deliverables. You can create a similar table for your Portfolio Managers and Program Managers. Only you can decide how much rigor is needed in your PMO.

Table 14.1 Project Management Audit Process

Project Management Process	Tasks & Deliverables	Exists for Program /Project (Y/N)	Comment	Score (1 if Delivery Exists)
Initiating				
	Project Charter document			
	Project management plan			
	Project kickoff materials			
	Budget spreadsheet			
	Initial project schedule, including initial dates and high-level deliverables			
	Lessons-learned process and repository for storing ongoing lessons-learned information			
	Centralized project repository			
	Project communications plan			
	Project Roles and Responsibilities document			
	Purchase order or acquisition documents			
	Project change control process			
	Project governance process			
	Project organization chart			
	Project status reporting process			
	Human resources plan			
	Quality management plan			
	Scope management plan			

Project Management Process	Tasks & Deliverables	Exists for Program /Project (Y/N)	Comment	Score (1 if Delivery Exists)
	Action-item log			
	Project transition plan template			
	Project milestone presentations templates			
	Training plans for process or tools			
Planning				
	Master project schedule			
	Risk management plan			
	Issue management plan			
	Budget spreadsheet			
	Governance model for the project			
	Escalation model for the project			
	Quality management for the project			
	Procurement documents, purchase orders or any other documentation related to purchasing			
	Training plans for process or tools			
Executing & Controlling				
	Project management plan			
	Project schedule and report progress throughout this process			
	Weekly finances			
	Lessons-learned information			
	Communication check with customers, management team, and appropriate stakeholders			
	RACI			

Project Management Process	Tasks & Deliverables	Exists for Program /Project (Y/N)	Comment	Score (1 if Delivery Exists)
	Status reporting and leadership presentations			
	Change control process			
	Scope management process			
	Quality management plan			
Closing				
	Project documentation cleanup			
	Project team roll-off plan			
	Support team handoff			
	Lessons-learned review			
	Obtain official signoff and approval from management team and customers			
	P.O. and closeout of financials			
	Send final project status and thank everyone involved in the project			

The purpose of this table is to specifically audit and track project management deliverables; however, you must also consider the deliverables for the engineering process you are using. Think about how software uses a software development process, manufacturing uses its own processes, and so on. There is great value in also tracking the many different engineering practices that may not exactly align with program and project deliverables.

Table 14.2 Software Development Audit Process shows a small sampling of a software engineering process that you can use. These deliverables are very different from those shown earlier in **Table 14.1 Project Management Audit Process**, which included project management deliverables only. Because this is just a sampling, as PMO Manager, you will need to update it for your specific engineering methodology.

Table 14.2 Software Development Audit Process

Software Development Process	Tasks & Deliverables	Exists for Program/ Project (Y/N)	Comment	Score (1 if it Exists)
Project Initiation/Kickoff				
	Project schedule			
	Project Budget			
Business Requirements				
	Business Requirements document			
System Requirements				
	System requirements			
	System Requirements document			
Design				
	Product design			
	Usability or customer feedback			
Build				
	Product build			
	Bug database			
	Final software build			
Test				
	Test plan			
	Final software test plan			
User Acceptance Approval Phase				
	Usability test			
	Usability feedback and implementation plan			
Production Phase				

	Product release			
	User approval			
Post Production Support and Warranty Period (if applicable)				
	Support training and product rollout			
	Warranty period (one year)			

Again, unlike the project management table, the engineering process table includes just a sampling of deliverables and provides an engineering audit template to get you thinking about how to capture and track the engineering deliverables for your organization.

You might be wondering whether you can combine the project management audit table with the engineering table to make one big table. These tables **should remain separate**. It would not be a best practice to combine them and would be confusing because the tables serve two purposes: one is for project management compliance and the second is for software compliance.

Initially, you might find it best to create these tables in a spreadsheet, such as Microsoft® Excel, and then as the PMO matures, and the processes around collecting and reporting the data matures, you can automate the process by incorporating a database system or using an intranet site. This would be a very valuable system for any PMO manager who is looking across all their programs and projects to understand how they are adhering to the auditing process.

Lastly, it is important to note that the auditing process is not applicable to every PMO model. A directive PMO should definitely have an auditing process in place, but a coaching or supportive PMO is highly unlikely to use one. Because no single PMO model works for every PMO, work with your management team to ensure that your particular PMO requires auditing. If you are driving a PMO that is set up for auditing, it is best practice to start an auditing process and work with your PMO employees to ensure that they are following the methodologies on their programs and projects.

In summarizing auditing, PMO Managers should work to develop an auditing process for their PMO. You might not need a formal process initially, but as the PMO matures the rigor and processes around auditing should mature as well. Support your PMO employees and work with them on their programs and projects to ensure that they are following the different methodologies closely. They don't always need to follow the methodology to the letter, but it is unacceptable to not follow it at all. Program Managers and Project Managers should find the required level of rigor needed for their efforts as they are in the best position and, at least initially, in the right position to make the call. When they do, they should then work with you, the PMO Manager, to jointly figure out the final level of rigor to apply to their efforts. You might not necessarily agree with the level of rigor they propose, but you should at least hear them out and make sure you let them tell you why they feel the level of rigor is appropriate for the program or project. This is not a decision they should make alone, or without telling you, and you should not force your expected level of rigor on them without listening to them first.

Summary

As we conclude the metrics and measurement chapter, we covered a number of important areas in which you, as a PMO Manager, need to drive for your organization. The many different processes and topics covered should give you the foundation to start measuring and tracking your organization's performance. These processes will move your PMO forward and start maturing areas of the PMO that need maturing. Remember though, you do not have to rush into creating metrics and measurements if your PMO or the organization is not ready. You will have to start sometime, just understand when the right time is for the PMO and don't rush into it or it can many negative effects.

We also covered the importance of creating PMO metrics and measurements and discussed the fact that they need to align with the company's metrics to ensure that there is consistency between the company and the PMO. As PMO Manager, you need to know how your PMO will support the company as a whole, so aligning your metrics to the company is very important.

Through the chapter, we also discussed how to create metrics and to use the PMO maturity model as a starting place to create metrics and to build on what you are already doing to drive your PMO; take advantage of the PMO maturity model you are already using and do not attempt to start this from scratch. Using the PMO maturity model as the basis for creating PMO metrics gives PMO employees a method to let them see how their work affects and influences the organization's performance.

We also covered the importance of performance reporting in PMOs. In that discussion, we covered how PMO Managers can work with their management team and customers to use performance results (good or bad) to drive business decisions and course corrections on programs and projects where necessary. We covered, in detail, the top three types of performance reports: on-time, on-budget, and quality for PMOs, and then outlined in tactical steps how to create cost and schedule performance reports using your own scheduling tool.

Finally, we covered auditing and the process for setting up and driving auditing within PMOs. A Project Management Audit Process table that follows the project management methodology (discussed in Chapter 10, "Project Management Methodology") and the Software Development Audit Process table shows a small sample of an audit table for a software project, which would need to be adjusted to include tasks for the full methodology. Both examples provide an excellent starting point for PMO Managers to use in their own PMOs. We also talked about the importance of determining the level of rigor needed for each project. Not all projects are created equal, so the level of rigor needs to be determined between the PMO Manager and the Program Manager or Project Manager based on project size, type, and so on.

In the end, the take-away for all PMO Managers is that metrics and measurements are required in your PMO. Embrace the chance to start measuring your performance and grow and learn from what you discover during the process. Learning will only help the PMO mature and provide even more value to the organization.

Chapter Review Answers:

1. PMO metrics should align with the company's metrics to ensure the PMO is aligned to support and help achieve company goals.

2. Qualitative metrics are observed, but not measured, and quantitative metrics enable you to measure the data. You need a mixture of qualitative and quantitative metrics to ensure you have tangible data from which to measure performance.

3. The PMO maturity model determines which KPIs you create for your PMO.

4. Popular PMO metrics include: schedule, cost, and quality performance.

5. Auditing helps achieve a level of consistency in the organization. Auditing helps you assess your PMO employees' work and helps you ensure they are following PMO standards and guidelines.

Chapter 15

PMO Capabilities Assessment

Figure 15.1 PMO Build Schedule—Capabilities Assessment

Task Name	Resource Names
-PMO Build Schedule	**PMO Manager**
+Step 1 - Grow PMO Manager Skills - Ongoing Activity	**PMO Manager**
+Step 2 - Obtain Executive Support (Chapter 3)	**PMO Manager**
+Step 3 - Assessment Period (Chapter 4)	**PMO Manager**
+Step 4 - Recommendation Period	**PMO Manager**
+Step 5 - Design & Build or Enhance Period (Chapter 5 - 12)	**PMO Manager**
+Step 6 – Implementation PMO Deliverables/Processes Period (Chapter 13)	**PMO Manager**
+Step 7 - Refine, Enhance and Grow Period (Chapter 14 - Chapter 16)	**PMO Manager**
+ PMO Measurements & Performance Tracking (Chapter 14)	**PMO Manager**
+Project Management Office - Capabilities Assessment (Chapter 15)	**PMO Manager**
+Create a PMO Capabilities Assessment Process	**PMO Manager**
-Assess needs & identify gaps of PMO employees	**PMO Manager**
Create a PMO Capabilities Checklist	PMO Manager
-PMO Employees to learn & update their skills based on gaps	**PMO Manager**
Create PMO Capabilities Opportunities	PMO Manager
PMO employees skills updated (where applicable)	PMO Manager
PMO Capabilities Assessment process complete	PMO Manager

Questions you should be able to answer after reading this chapter:

1. Describe the importance of the capabilities assessment process.

2. Define the three steps for the capabilities assessment process.

3. Name three skills in the PMO capabilities checklist.

4. Name two PMO capabilities improvement opportunities.

5. Name three PMO capability results.

One ongoing challenge for PMO Managers is evaluating employees to ensure that they are competent, professional, and capable of doing their jobs. You will be surprised as you spend more time in the role of PMO Manager how often you are required to assess your team's capabilities in order to determine whether they have the right skills and capabilities to manage their assigned programs or projects. As PMO Manager, you must be committed to performing these assessments for your employees; it is an important responsibility as their manager and you want to staff your programs and projects with competent staff to ensure the greatest chance of success. An interesting fact about the PMO Manager role is that you never know the kinds of programs and projects that will come into your PMO, so it is in your best interest to retain the most capable and competent staff as possible. Capability assessment is an ongoing evaluation of your PMO employees to determine whether they are capable of doing the work assigned to them.

This is not an easy task and it requires PMO Managers to constantly analyze and work with their employees by reviewing deliverables, spending time on the projects, and assessing how well they are performing. If your PMO includes more than a handful of Program Managers and Project Managers, you can see how quickly your time can be filled assessing and reassessing the capabilities of your staff. No one wants to be evaluated all the time, but you want to make sure your employees are capable of handling their programs and projects. PMO Managers must balance what is right for the employee and what is right for the program or project. Sometimes, a Project Manager's skills don't match the job requirements and you find yourself in the position of reassigning the Project Manager or letting him or her go. It happens, and when it does, it is the best solution for both the employee and the program or project. Sometimes, these decisions work out best for everyone.

One of the common themes throughout the book has been to always consider resources, procedures, and infrastructure. The capabilities assessment process falls into the "resources" area. As discussed, everything around building and implementing a PMO touches these three areas. Understanding the skills a person needs to do their job, and then outlining their gaps in those skills gives them information they can use to improve. Generally, everyone likes to improve so the capabilities assessment process simply highlights the areas that need improving for them. Consider the impact to the

PMO employees during this process and recognize the sensitive nature of identifying skill gaps.

Let's look into the capabilities assessment process to ensure that you, as PMO Manager, know how to evaluate your PMO employees and vendors.

Capabilities Assessment Process

How often have you worked with Project Managers who, despite trying their hardest, will never meet the required skills? Project management is a learned skill, yet inherent to those who are the most successful at it. As a PMO Manager, you will quickly learn who on your team has it and who is struggling and might not be in the right role.

So, what do you do when you have an employee who you know will never be successful at project management? How do you rate your employees and where do you start this process?

First, know that when you talk about capabilities assessment there are two indicators you use to assess your PMO employees: quantitative and qualitative ratings—one without the other would not give you a full assessment of your employee. We just covered both concepts in Chapter 14, "PMO Measurements" so it is not important to readdress the definitions now, but they are both very relevant to this discussion. Think about both indicators as you read this chapter.

Figure 15.2 Capabilities Assessment Process outlines the three steps that PMO Managers follow during the assessment process. Follow this process for each employee regardless of their role in the PMO. Because this is an employee assessment, all roles in the PMO fall into the assessment process. Let's look at the process now, and then delve into the details of each step.

Figure 15.2 Capabilities Assessment Process

PMO Capabilities Assessment Process

1
Assess needs & identify gaps of PMO employees

2
PMO employees to learn & update their skills based on gaps

3
PMO employees skills updated (where applicable)

- Understand the position needs for each role in organization.
- Determine PMO employees needs regardless of their current position.
- Perform capabilities assessment for each PMO employee.
- Determine and document the gaps between PMO employee skills and position needs.

- Provide PMO Processes to employees to utilize in their jobs.
- Provide on-the-job training & experience.
- Work with PMO employees and have them develop their own career plans.
- Provide specific PMO tools training.

- Newly acquired skills reflected with on-the-job assessment of work performed.
- Programs and projects delivering with additional rigor and consistency.
- Management & customer's improved relationships & confidence in PMO employees.
- PMO employees are capable of larger and more complex efforts.

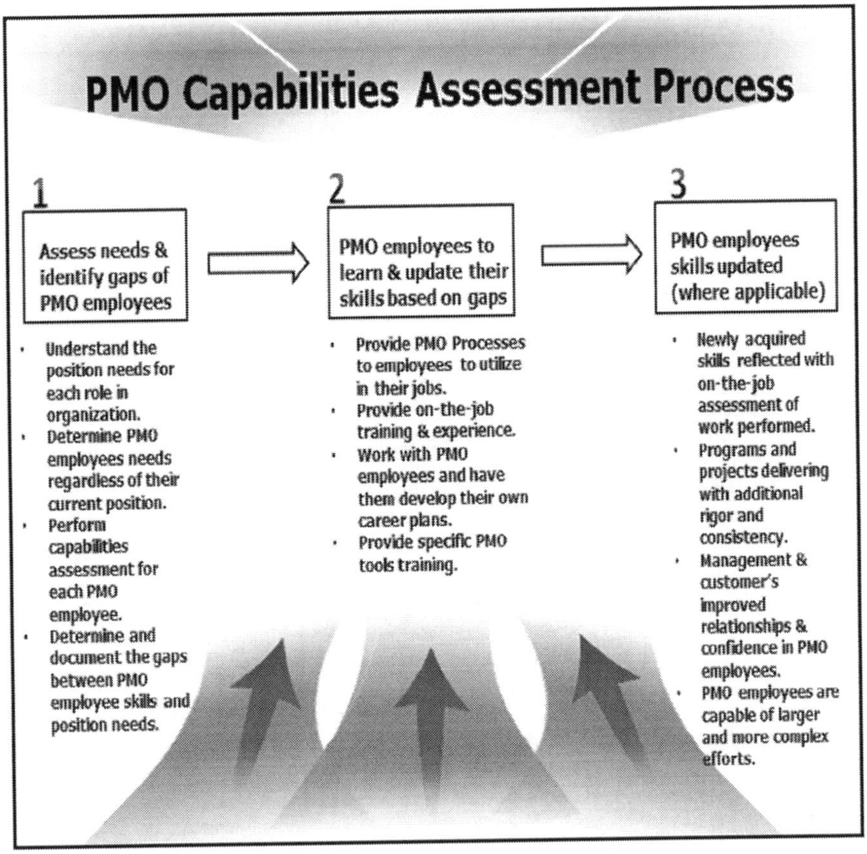

In reviewing **Figure 15.2 Capabilities Assessment Process,** it is important to provide some additional context for each area so that you, as PMO Manager, can adopt this process directly in your organization.

Bill's Thoughts:

I have used this type of process before and it works. Make sure that you understand what each role in your PMO is expected to perform and that you hire the right people with the right skill set to perform that role. Not everybody is a good fit for every role, so be mindful of that as you assess your employees.

Capabilities Assessment Process Breakdown

Step 1: Assess needs and identify skill gaps of PMO employees—At this stage, you assess and evaluate your PMO employees' individual skills and capabilities to determine the right role for them in your organization. Some employees are not a good fit for the Program Manager or Project Manager role, so you will need to determine the right role for them in the organization. During this time, you will also document the gaps and areas for improvement for each employee. Make sure the skill gaps are role-specific and clear so that employees understand how improving in these areas will help them progress in their careers.

Step 2: PMO employees learn and update their skills based on gaps—At this stage, PMO employees recognize their skill gaps and start to improve upon them. They do this by working and learning on the job, taking formal and informal training, and finally, making a personal commitment to improve in those skill gap areas. You will never see an employee improve if he or she does not want to improve in that area. You, as PMO Manager, have the responsibility to provide employees with the right opportunities for improving their skills by offering the right training (on the job, or funding for formal training) and working with them to perform their current duties. PMO work must continue through this process, so employees need to balance their skill improvement areas with their current duties. This is just a reality of the current business environment that everyone should be aware of and work with.

Step 3: PMO employees' skills updated (where applicable)—In this final stage of the capabilities assessment process, employees use their improved skills and training on their assignments. The results of these newfound skills are often relevant to program and project execution by allowing more rigor and structure that helps increase the overall satisfaction of your management team and customers. As PMO Manager, celebrate and recognize the good work your employees are doing with their newfound skills. This might mean assigning employees to much larger and more complex efforts or even financially rewarding them with promotions or bonuses. The results of this process must be beneficial to the employees as well as the PMO, and you, as PMO Manager, own this recognition process. If your employees gain new skills and do not see any rewards from that effort, you might lose those employees.

This three-step process is simple and easily adaptable for any PMO. There are certainly other capabilities assessment models, but this is an excellent foundation for any PMO Manager to get started. Start this process sooner rather than later so that you can evaluate your PMO employees on an ongoing basis.

Tips & Best Practices

Make sure you continually perform this assessment process. As PMO Manager, make this one of your main responsibilities and something you continually do as a regular part of your job.

One common question that is often asked about capabilities assessments is the participation of vendors or contractors in this process. Well, it is a simple and important answer and outside of the capabilities assessment process. The capabilities assessment process, in most scenarios, is not applicable to vendors or contractors within your PMO. Actually, most companies have rules that don't allow vendors or contractors to participate in formal training events—and don't treat them like permanent employees in any way. As PMO Manager, watch this very closely and make sure you draw a clear line between vendors and permanent employees; otherwise, you could end up in trouble with management or the human resources department. You should also not allow vendors or contractors to participate in formal on-the-job training—in which case, a better question might be to ask whether that person is a good fit for that role. Assigning them to a different program or project, or hiring a different vendor or contractor, might be the appropriate course of action.

The closest area where you might consider using a vendor or contractor is in **Step 1: Assess needs and identify skill gaps of PMO employees** of the capabilities assessment process. In this step, there is a sub step where the PMO Manager needs to understand the position qualifications for every role in the PMO. When that assessment and understanding is complete, the PMO Manager can choose to hire a vendor or contractor for those positions. However, that is the only connection and not really a component of the capabilities assessment, which focuses on permanent employees' skills and gaps.

To understand PMO roles and specific qualifications for each PMO employee, let's review a checklist that PMO Managers can use to ensure that they are hiring the best employees for the organization.

PMO Capabilities Checklist and Evaluation Criteria

One of the challenges that PMO Managers face when assessing and identifying the skill gaps of their PMO employees is determining what capabilities they should expect from each employee. Different job roles factor into this checklist; however, there are PMO qualifications that are common to every role. Review the "Portfolio Management Methodology," "Program Management Methodology," and "Project Management Methodology" chapters and the different qualifications for each role and the foundation for filling those roles.

Tips & Best Practices

This checklist is not comprehensive, but is something you can use as a starting point, and then add to or enhance as you see fit. You need something to start with, so use this and supplement as necessary.

PMO capabilities checklist:

1. **Communication skills**—There are many data points that say 90% of a Program Manager's or Project Manager's role is communication; therefore, this is a "must have" capability for each PMO employee.

PMO Manager evaluation criteria for communication skills:

- Have you read your employees' current program and project status reports? Do they make sense?

- What communication tools do they use?

- How happy is management with your employees' communication?

- Have you talked to customers about your employees' communication skills?

- Have you reviewed the content in their centralized repository?

2. **Portfolio, program, and project management methodologies**—PMO employees must have some experience or background using a structured methodology.

PMO Manager evaluation criteria for portfolio, program, and project management methodologies:

- Do employees understand the difference between an engineering methodology and the portfolio, program, and project management methodologies?

- Do you receive from your employees suggestions about how to improve existing portfolio, program, and project management methodologies?

- Can you see evidence of a methodology used on their programs or projects?

3. **Self-starters and go-getters**—PMO employees must be self-starters and go-getters. Because they will drive large, complex programs and projects, you want employees who are self-sufficient and can get the job done.

PMO Manager evaluation criteria for self-starters and go-getters:

- Do employees sit and wait for assignments?

- Do they market and expose their work to peers, customers, and management regularly?

- Do they teach, present, or offer to share their experiences and best practices?

- Do they tackle their projects head on, or are they shy and cautious about their approach?

4. **Portfolio, program, project management skills and background**—Hire PMO employees who have the background and experience that works well on any type of project, in any situation. If a project is going well, you want the Project Manager to work and deliver that project, but if a project is in trouble, you want that same Project Manager to control the project and turn it around. Therefore, all PMO employees need some skills in the areas of portfolio, program, and project management, depending on their role.

PMO Manager evaluation criteria for portfolio, program, and project management skills and background:

- What previous work experience do employees have in portfolio, program, or project management?
- How well are their current projects progressing?
- In what state are the current deliverables?
- Have they completed a PMO audit? What were the scores from those audits?

5. **Confidence**—It is important for PMO employees to have confidence in how they approach their work activities and do their jobs. Regardless of role—from Portfolio Manager to Project Manager—each employee must be confident. If employees have a chance to work closely with your management team, you want to know that they are comfortable presenting and providing management with the information they need.

PMO Manager evaluation criteria for confidence:

- Do employees have role clarity, leadership, and a sense of confidence to get the job done?
- Have you seen them make presentations to management and show a level of confidence in how they present and communicate to management or their customers?
- Do they have confidence when working with peers and do they help them be more confident in their work activities?
- Do you see them motivate and instill confidence in everyone they work with?

6. **Customer-focused**—It is important for PMO employees' to focus on and care about their customers.

PMO Manager evaluation criteria for customer focus:

- Do employees have their customers best interest in mind when executing on their programs and projects?
- What interactions have you seen your employees have with their customers? Is it been a positive or negative experience for the customers?
- Have they built a trusted partnership with their customers?

7. **Technical skills**—We work in a highly technical environment these days, regardless of the company you work for, your PMO employees need some level of technical aptitude. The different roles in the PMO will dictate the specifics for

technical aptitude (for example, Project Managers need scheduling tool knowledge); however, everyone needs some basic abilities to work in a technical environment.

PMO Manager evaluation criteria for technical skills:

- Do employees have technical skills or are they completely lost in a technical environment? Can they demonstrate those skills to you?

- What kind of background or experience do they have working in a technical environment? How does that experience align with the roles in the PMO?

- Do they have any engineering-specific technical skills (for example, development or test background for a software company)?

8. **Risk taker**—PMO employees, especially Program Managers and Project Managers, need some skills and capabilities in risk assessment and tracking. There will be times when they need to take risks. PMO Managers should be careful not to punish employees who take occasional risks.

PMO Manager evaluation criteria for risk takers:

- What were the risks that the employees took on their Programs or Projects? Did they work with you before they made those risk decisions?

- Were the risks calculated or were they safe risks?

- Did a risk fail and how did the employee handle the failure? Alternatively, did the risk work and how did the employee handle success?

- Does the employee seem risk adverse or a risk seeker during your conversations? You can typically get a good feel for this in general conversations with employees.

9. **Does the employee love his or her job**—When hiring and working with your PMO employees, one thing to be aware of is whether they love their jobs. As PMO Manager, you want to surround yourself with people who love their jobs and are eager to learn and do the best for themselves and for the company. When you have employees who hate their jobs or who are constantly looking for a different role, it affects their overall performance and their chances of being successful in the PMO.

PMO Manager evaluation criteria for employees who love their jobs:

- How is the relationship between you and your employee? Does he or she show excitement and willingness to do the job?

- Has the employee openly expressed interest in moving on to another role outside of your PMO?

- Is the employee an active member of the team? Does he or she participate in team events and support team functions?

- What are the employee's long-term goals?

Bill's Thoughts:

I have worked with employees who hated working in the PMO and hated working for me directly. You will likely experience that too; it's something every PMO Manager faces. Help the employee get a different role outside of your group. He or she might be the best company employee ever and might be frustrated and dissatisfied in the current role. It is in both of your best interests for him or her to move on as soon as possible.

10. **Political savvy**—One of the key skills employees need is political sense. When times get difficult, especially with customers, they need to know what levers to pull and what levers to leave alone.

PMO Manager evaluation criteria for political savvy:

- How have employees handled political situations within their programs and projects?

- How political do the individuals act in general? Are they all about themselves or do they have a team mentality?

- When working with you directly, do they understand the political dynamics of the environment or are they clueless as to what is going on around them from a political perspective?

As you implement the capabilities assessment process within your PMO, think about using these ten points as the foundation to assess the current skill sets of your employees.

Now that the assessment process is complete, your next step is to allow employees the opportunity to gain new skills.

PMO Capabilities Opportunities

The capabilities assessment process is important because it lets each employee know the areas they need to work on to improve their skills. As PMO Manager, you will likely be their functional manager as well and you are responsible for providing your employees the opportunity to work on areas where they needed improvement.

This process will only work if employees are interested in improving their skills. If they are not, you can point out the areas for improvement and highlight the gaps, but it likely will not matter to them. They might pacify you to make you think they are interested in improving, and they might take formal feedback or criticism during performance reviews, but if they are not interested in improving, they will not improve. There is nothing you can do about it. The only change you can make is to remove or reassign the employee outside of the PMO or completely out of the company. Both of these options should be a last resort, so only use them when appropriate.

Before you reach the last resort options, you owe it to your PMO employees to provide different ways where they can improve their skills and improve within your PMO. Most employees look for ways to improve and most want to continue to improve. Remember, this was a criteria for hiring them.

So, what are some areas within the PMO where employees can improve their skills? Before going too far, it is an opportune time to review Chapter 7, "PMO Training" about formal and informal training, as well as information about the PMO mentoring program and the informal PMO Buddy System. Remember those points as we examine other areas for improving PMO employees' skills.

Let's look at some of those areas now:

- **On-the-job training**—Nothing beats learning on the job and gaining firsthand experience. Make it a safe environment and allow employees to make mistakes without threat of punishment.
- **Formal training**—Occasionally, employees need to take formal training that is specific to their jobs. This training should be PMO-specific.
- **PMO-focused conferences**—PMO employees should attend industry-specific conferences to learn the latest and greatest best practices and to learn what is happening in the industry.
- **Mentoring and coaching**—Mentoring programs and one-on-one coaching are extremely valuable for PMO employees, especially if the coaches and mentors are experts or very experienced in the program or project field. Having a senior employee who is willing to coach PMO employees can be extremely valuable and a way to improve the skills of employees faster than on-the-job training or taking a class.

This is certainly not a comprehensive list, but it is a good starting point to offer your employees once you get the three or four areas set up in your PMO—later, you can add additional areas. Anything you do along the same lines will only enhance and improve your employees' skills, which is exactly what you are trying to accomplish during the capabilities assessment process.

After assessing your PMO employees for skill gaps and giving them specific skills to improve, make sure to track the results. The capabilities assessment process is costly in both budget and time. This process will impact programs and projects, so there must be a long-term benefit to the process.

Let's examine the benefits of this process.

Results of the PMO Capabilities Assessment

There is nothing like a high-performing PMO full of employees and vendors who are passionate and driven about the portfolio, program, and project management disciplines. The end-result of the capabilities assessment process gives you a high-performing PMO team that lives and breathes the world of portfolio, program, and project management. This is every PMO Manager's goal and end vision that often takes many years and sometimes a lot of turn over to reach. It's realistic to expect staff turnover in the PMO for those who lack the right skill set or don't want to contribute toward building a world-class PMO.

So, what are the results PMO Managers should look for in their PMO and across programs and projects at the end of the capabilities assessment process? Here are some of the process outcomes:

- High morale and increased employee satisfaction
- PMO is the "number one" organization to work for in the company
- Great results across programs and projects
  - Increased on-time delivery percentage
  - Increased on-budget delivery percentage
- Business value realized and tracked
- Improved customer satisfaction scores
- Fewer projects managed outside the PMO
- Improved management acceptance
- Decreased employee turnover rate
- Increased ROI

This list can go on and on, but most PMO Managers quickly realize what a successful organization looks like when they are running it. Most PMO Managers recognize when things are not going well, but they also know when things are running smoothly and they have support and acknowledgement from their management team. It's a satisfying feeling for PMO Managers to identify the PMO employees' skill level and to give them the opportunity to improve areas they need to, and then take advantage of those new skills in the PMO.

Summary

In summarizing the capabilities assessment process, it is important to recognize for any PMO Manager how important this process is for running and maintaining a PMO. You cannot be successful in your role as PMO Manager if you do not understand your staff's strengths and weaknesses. You need to know this information so that you can make the right program and project assignments and help them improve their skills where they need it.

As PMO Manager, your success depends on the success of your employees; therefore, it is in your best interest to ensure that you are providing opportunities for them to gain the skills for the best chance of being successful.

The most difficult phase during this process is performing the capabilities assessment and working with each employee to identify areas for improvement. This is often difficult because most employees do not want to hear from their manager that they have areas to improve and work on. A best practice for this difficult and uncomfortable process is for you, the PMO Manager, to hire a vendor or a contractor to drive the assessment process and provide you the results of the analysis.

Regardless of the challenges you run into during this process, it is a "must do" for every PMO Manager who wants to mature the skill sets of his or her employees. The results from and benefits of performing the capabilities assessment process far outweigh the difficulties of obtaining the information for each employee and developing specific training catered to each employee. It is important to improve the various skills of your employees to help you drive your PMO into the future.

Chapter Review Answers

1. The capabilities assessment process helps you determine how strong your PMO employees are and their areas for improvement.

2. The three steps for the capabilities assessment include: assess needs and identify skill gaps for each PMO employee, PMO employees continue to learn and update their skills based on previously identified gaps, and PMO skills updated where applicable.

3. Three skills in the checklist include: communication skills; portfolio, program, and project management methodology skills; and being a self-starter and go-getter.

4. Improvement opportunities include: on-the-job training and formal training (for example, instructor-led classes).

5. Results of improving PMO employees' capabilities include: increased morale and improved employee satisfaction, improved results across programs and projects, improved customer satisfaction scores.

Chapter 16

PMO Change Agents

Figure 16.1 PMO Build Schedule – Change Agents

Task Name	Resource Names
-PMO Build Schedule	PMO Manager
+Step 1 - Grow PMO Manager Skills - Ongoing Activity	PMO Manager
+Step 2 - Obtain Executive Support (Chapter 3)	PMO Manager
+Step 3 - Assessment Period (Chapter 4)	PMO Manager
+Step 4 - Recommendation Period	PMO Manager
+Step 5 - Design & Build or Enhance Period (Chapter 5 - 12)	PMO Manager
+Step 6 – Implementation PMO Deliverables/Processes Period (Chapter 13)	PMO Manager
+Step 7 - Refine, Enhance and Grow Period (Chapter 14 - Chapter 16)	PMO Manager
+PMO Measurements & Performance Tracking (Chapter 14)	PMO Manager
+Project Management Office - Capabilities Assessment (Chapter 15)	PMO Manager
-Project Management Office - Changes Agents (Chapter 16)	PMO Manager
Understand Change and Change Agents	PMO Manager
Understand Industry Change Models	PMO Manager
Understand the Organization Change Management	PMO Manager
Understand the role of the PMO Manager in the Change Process	PMO Manager

Questions you should be able to answer after reading this chapter:

1. What role does a PMO Manager have in the change process?

2. Name two similarities between PMO Managers and change agents.

3. What does "OCM" stand for and what does it do?

4. What is the J-Curve effect?

5. What are the three things a PMO Manager can do immediately as a change agent?

When deciding to change an ocean freighter's direction in the middle of the sea, the decision can be easy, but the execution of that decision is the difficult part. Turning a ship in the middle of the ocean is not easy and takes time. On the other hand, a rower in a rowboat can change direction fairly easily. Organizations are like ocean freighters when it comes to change—it takes a lot of effort and time to make it happen. Projects produce deliverables that involve change in order to accomplish organizational goals. Projects involve change and the PMO Manager who is at the helm naturally plays a change agent in the organization.

It is human nature to want to feel good about yourself. PMO Managers are not immune to that feeling and want to succeed in the organization. Yet, not many PMO Managers feel good if they are maintaining status quo results. After all, across many sectors—for-profit organizations or non-profit organizations—there are portfolio, program, and project management offices that are responsible for the work of the organization; therefore, those offices control and manage change. You, as PMO Manager, need to feel empowered and in charge of managing change within the organization. You need to feel confident that you are helping the organization through the change process.

Within the organizational structure, a PMO is established to effectively manage the work in the organization. PMOs help increase customer satisfaction (both internal and external), increase revenue, improve profit margin, use resources efficiently, create and launch products, and capture more market share. PMOs achieve these results not by maintaining the status quo, but rather through program and project execution. This typically means that "something is changing somewhere, for someone." To be a successful PMO Manager, you must reach beyond the status quo, which means being an effective change agent.

Throughout the book, the three areas that are critical to building and implementing a PMO have been discussed: resources, procedures, and infrastructure. Well, change management is largely focused on your resources and the impact the change has on those resources. As PMO Manager, you will likely play a significant role in the process of helping your employees understand and work through change. Think about the impact and effect on your resources (in this case your people) during this process, and think about how you can guide them through change. Again, PMO Managers need to be change agents.

In this chapter, we will cover change agents, methodologies, and best practices so that you, as PMO Manager, can embrace this part of your role in order to help your organization understand and manage change. Let's get started by examining change and change agents.

Change and Change Agents

Change is merely what happens between the current situation and the future desired result. Sounds simple, and yet it is not. If it were, more PMO programs and projects would reach their goals with fewer struggles, and employees would not complain about change fatigue. Organizational change typically revolves around process, technology, and other things at that tactical level. Change is achieved through programs and projects and by getting people involved. Getting people involved, however, tends to be where things get messy and change agents are needed. Enter the PMO Manager wearing the "change agent" hat.

A change agent understands change and how people emotionally deal with change. A change agent does not force compliance, but knows how to positively help make change happen. Even if your job description, as PMO Manager, does not include the responsibility of being a change agent, it is implied and it is a required skill. This skill includes influencing, implementing, and supporting positive change in order to deliver the organization's programs and projects.

Bill's Thoughts:

I have been a change agent in my last couple of PMOs and have worn the role very proudly. PMOs are in a constant state of change, and as the leader, I felt that I needed to constantly wave the change-agent flag in order to sell and market the PMO. Not only did I have to sell the existence of the PMO, but also the value it brought to the organization, while helping my employees process change. I was constantly trying to change people's opinions about the PMO and the value it brings to the company. You too will be the change agent—many factors will determine what you need to change, but expect it to be an ongoing part of your role.

Similarities Between PMO Managers and Change Agents

A change agent need not be a PMO Manager. There are people in your organization who are not PMO Managers, yet they influence others with new ideas about how to solve problems. Being talented and skillful at persuading people with ideas or resolutions to a problem is not limited to a job description or a level in the company. While a change agent does not need to be a PMO Manager, a PMO Manager needs to be a change agent to deliver results.

PMO Managers and change agents have the following similarities:

- Focus on the vision, future state, and outcome
- Approach work holistically, as a system
- Develop consensus and participant alignment
- Proactively achieve desired outcomes

Change agents naturally focus on people and how they affect the desired outcome. PMO Managers who do not recognize the need to also act as change agents are not as successful reaching stated and implied goals. As PMO Manager, make sure you are aware of your role as a change agent and do not fall into the trap of letting change just happen.

Let's spend some time looking at change models and how they relate to programs and projects.

Industry Change Models

There are several leading industry change models that organizations have been using for many years. These models include the Burke-Litwin (12 dimensions) change model, Kurt Lewin's change model (Unfreeze, Change, Refreeze), and Daryl Conner's change model Each model has its own unique characteristics and, as PMO Manager, it is important to have a general understanding (or some awareness) of change models to help you be successful in your role. Also, it is important to help your organization through the change process. You certainly do not have to be an expert, but you do need to have some knowledge about the process.

Let's look at one of the industry-leading change models and see how that model works in a PMO environment. If you want more information, you can search the Internet, buy books, and become very well versed in the subject of change management.

Tips & Best Practices

As PMO Manager, it is certainly in your best interest to understand different change models. Your company might use one model, but if you move to a different company, they might use a different model; therefore, you need to have a general understanding of the different models.

Sponsor, Agent, and Target Model

Daryl Conner's sponsor, agent, and target change model can be nicely overlaid onto projects. In **Figure 16.2 Daryl Conner's Sponsor Agent Target Change Model**, the sponsor is the authorizer and owner of the change, and the agent in the model represents the change agent who is responsible for carrying out the change. The target in the model defines who is involved in the change, typically customers.

The world of PMOs includes Programs and Projects and each have an associated sponsor. Those sponsors are the same as the sponsors represented in Conner's model. The Project Manager is the agent (in Conner's model), and the targets are the customers, or anyone else who is impacted by the change. Does that make sense? Therefore, Conner's model works perfectly when looking at program and project structures. It's often said, "A picture is worth a thousand words," so let's look at Conner's model now.

Figure 16.2 Daryl Conner's Sponsor Agent Target Change Model

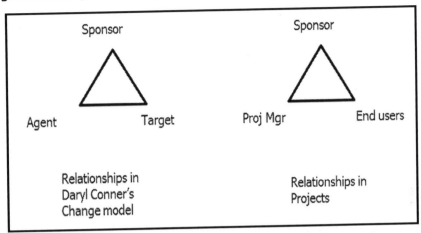

Conner's model is just one of the different models in use. If you have an interest to become an expert in these models, spend the time and research the internet, buy books, and become familiar with the subject. It is an important part of your job, and so anytime learning and understanding the models better would be beneficial. Let's move onto organizational change management and look at how change affects people.

Organizational Change Management

Organizational change management (OCM) focuses on how people are affected by change. This is not the same as the change management process in a project management methodology or a formal change control process, no, this is very different. OCM centers around how people manage and deal with change.

Some of the original models for change involved three phases that are part of most OCM models today. **Table 16.1 Organizational Change Management Models** shows the three OCM models commonly used in the industry today.

Table 16.1 Organizational Change Management Models

Phases of change:	Stage 1	Stage 2	Stage 3
Kurt Lewin, father of organizational development and the action research model (1940's).	Unfreeze current state	Change	Refreeze the new state
William Bridges' phases of transition. Author of, *Managing Transitions: Making the Most of Change.*	Ending, letting go of the old	Neutral zone, the transition activity	Beginning, the new is in place
Prosci's change management methodology	Planning for change	Managing the change	Reinforcing the change

A PMO Manager cannot go wrong as a change agent and thinking about change in the three phases and spending time to learn about the different models. There are a number of resources on the web that you can use to learn about OCM models to help your organization and your employees handle change.

Organizations and Individuals During Change

Senior management in organizations set strategy and goals. Goals are achieved through ongoing work on projects, and it is commonly understood that changes happen during project execution. Some examples of change include policy changes, process changes, software changes, and so on. The commonality in these examples is that a person is experiencing the change. Employees are working on changing how things happen in the current state to how things are going to happen in a desired future state. While organizations handle change at a tactical level (projects execution), people handle change at an emotional level. It is just the way it is, and as an effective change agent, you need to respect their emotions during the life of a project. **Figure 16.3**

Organizations and Individual Change Model outlines how organizations and individuals handle change and the different paths that each go through in the process.

Figure 16.3 Organizations and Individual Change Model

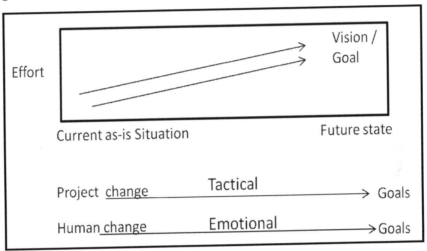

Generally, people do not change because someone tells them they have to change. Advancement in neuroscience tells us that humans are hardwired to resist change. The human brain is programmed to detect anything in an environment that is different. Fear rises when a change represents loss and uncertainty. Give a construction worker a new state-of-the-art hammer to build a widget and the brain detects something in the environment has changed and resists the change until it recognizes things are okay.

If someone must adopt something that will be different in the future state than its current state, multiple kinds of communication must happen before the person is expected to perform differently. The person must deal with the emotional change to be receptive toward new behavioral training and to perform differently.

J-Curve And Change

The J-curve effect is popular for thinking about improved productivity through change, and it's highly applicable to PMO Managers. This notion originated with Edward J. Murphy, a United States Air Force Engineer who was testing some new technologies and noticed that a system's performance generally gets worse before the targeted benefits are reached. Murphy's theory led to the J-curve effect and what is commonly known as, "Murphy's Law." **Figure 16.4 J-Curve Change Model** shows that things usually get worse before they get better (the J-curve effect).

Figure 16.4 J-Curve Change Model

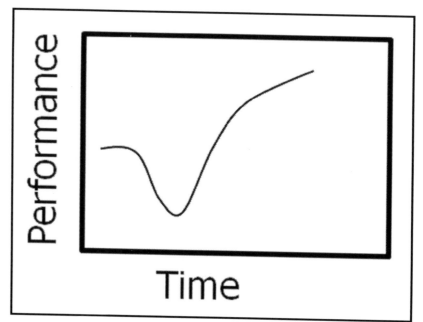

Dr. Jerald Jellison, author of, *Managing the Dynamics of Change*, applied his five stages of change to the J-curve, from left to right. Jellison's five stages are: plateau, cliff, valley, ascent, and mountaintop. During the current state (the plateau), news is communicated that there will be a change. After falling off the cliff and into the valley, a person starts the ascent and ends up at the mountaintop, which is the desired future state of the change. **Figure 16.4 J-Curve Change Model** shows what it looks like to use Jellison's model. The last stage (the mountaintop) is where you want people to be when change is implemented.

Change Strategy and the Human Element

If you want individuals to adopt change when implementing something new (for example, adopting a time-sheet system), it is a best practice to develop a change strategy to help people move from the current state (for example, no time tracking), through the emotional stages ("I hate this tool; I'm not using it"), to the future state ("I love this tool"). Only when you reach this last stage ("I love this tool") does the individual emotionally accept the change.

As a good change agent, develop an effective change strategy by identifying who is impacted by the change and analyzing the pros and cons for implementing the change with the change impact.

It is important for PMO Managers to recognize what the stages of change look like and how to help people proceed through the stages to successfully reach the future state. As PMO Manager, work with your Program Managers and Project Managers to ensure they have change management plans, updated communication plans, and training plans in place to help people through the change process. Program and project success depends on it. In some companies, you might have dedicated OCM groups that you can work with to help you develop the strategy, change management, communication, and training plans.

Role of PMO Manager During the Change Process

Why is change information important to PMO Managers? It is simple, you are a leader in the organization and often part of the company's management chain; therefore, you should understand the change process. Your role is to work with programs and projects to help drive change into the organization; you will play part change agent, part OCM, and so on. In some companies, working around change is a major part of one's daily responsibilities—especially in newer, less mature companies that do not have processes or OCM procedures in place. In these companies, employees tend to struggle with handling change; thus, making your role that much more important during the change process.

Advantages of Managing Change

If PMO Managers do not see themselves as change agents and do not give change any thought, then the probability of achieving their program and project goals decreases. Otherwise, if they impact the role and are change agents and focus on helping their employees through managing change, there is an increased chance of success and achieving the goals set by the programs and projects. Managing the people side of change is part of the cost of doing business. A PMO Manager cannot afford the cost of *not* being a change agent!

Change has a bad reputation because people often fear uncertainty and know from experience that things often do not go well when change is introduced. When a change occurs and the people side of the change is not addressed, achieving project goals often falls short. Overcoming negative history about implementing change is critical for PMO Managers to face and to help their organizations face.

PMO Manager as Change Agent

As PMO Manager, you should have enough information now to know that you will play a role in the change process. You might be a change agent, or you might support a change agent, so it is definitely in your best interest to understand the change process. You should now be thinking like a change agent; here are some solid takeaways that you can start implementing in your organization now:

- Identify the current situation of a particular effort and the change that needs to happen in order to reach the desired future state.
- Understand what is driving the change and the level of urgency for the change.
- Find a champion to approve the change—someone who can approve the change and be a champion for it.
- Build a case for the change.
- Identify the stakeholders who will be impacted by the change.
- Build a coalition, including stakeholders, to support the change.

- Create ownership by involving the impacted stakeholders in creating the change from the current state to the desired future state.
- Develop a change strategy with a change management plan that includes communication plans and training plans.
- Deliberately plan for individuals to experience the "stages of change" and include resistance management in your change management plan.

Everyone can learn from each other's failures, and change process is no different. You should never adopt a Pollyanna attitude when implementing change; it is a surefire way to lose trust with your stakeholders.

It is so important to be respectful and champion the people dealing with the change. When people are forced to be compliant with change, results fall short. Put yourself in their shoes and walk the talk of a change agent for a greater chance of success.

Summary

To summarize this chapter, it has been often said that PMO Managers play a huge part of the change management process—not only by acting as a change agent, but by supporting change agents as they move through the change process. There is certainly no expectation that PMO Managers be industry experts in managing and handling change, but they need to have some knowledge, background, and curiosity about the subject. It is highly recommended that PMO Managers spend some time understanding the change process to determine where and how they can be a champion during this process.

It is also important for PMO Managers to understand the OCM process—understand the different models and focus on people and how they handle and process change. This is important. In this chapter, we only covered a very small amount of the different industry OCM models, but enough to give PMO Managers a taste to what OCM means and how it plays an important part of running and maintaining your PMO. There is much more information on the Internet, in books, and from resident experts on the OCM process.

Change happens, we all have to deal with it, and we all have to process it, but it is the savvy PMO Manager who embraces change, starts waving the change-agent flag, and is critical in helping the organization through the process. These PMO Managers are successful and they help their programs and projects be successful too.

Chapter Review Answers:

1. As PMO Manager, you will likely play a significant role in the change process by helping your employees understand and work through change. Think about the impact and effect on your resources (in this case your people) during this process, and think about how you can guide them through change. Again, PMO Managers need to be change agents.

2. PMO Managers and change agents approach work holistically (as a system) and develop participant consensus and alignment.

3. Organizational change management (OCM) is about handling the "people" side of change.

4. The J-curve effect is popular for thinking about improved productivity through change.

5. PMO Managers acting as Change agents should identify the stakeholders who are impacted by the change, build a coalition for the change that includes the stakeholders, and create ownership by involving stakeholders when making the change from the current state to a future state, including reaching goals.

Chapter 17

PMO Summary

Figure 17.1 PMO Build Schedule—PMO Complete

Task Name	Resource Names
PMO Build Schedule	**PMO Manager**
+Step 1 - Grow PMO Manager Skills - Ongoing Activity	**PMO Manager**
+Step 2 - Obtain Executive Support (Chapter 3)	**PMO Manager**
+Step 3 - Assessment Period (Chapter 4)	**PMO Manager**
+Step 4 - Recommendation Period	**PMO Manager**
+Step 5 - Design & Build or Enhance Period (Chapter 5 - 12)	**PMO Manager**
+Step 6 – Implementation PMO Deliverables/Processes Period (Chapter 13)	**PMO Manager**
+Step 7 - Refine, Enhance and Grow Period (Chapter 14 - Chapter 16)	**PMO Manager**
+Step 8 - Celebrate Period	**PMO Manager**
PMO Built & Implemented - Time to Mature and Grow - PMO Project Complete	**PMO Manager**

Well, you did it; you successfully built and implemented a new PMO! Or, perhaps you inherited an existing PMO and used the best practices and key concepts out of this book to update and enhance it. Either way, it's finished and you should be proud of the work you did because it took hours to reach this point. This has not been an easy process; you certainly completed an enormous amount of work and you deserve a tremendous amount of credit. Don't forget that you didn't accomplish this alone. Your team, including management, deserves a lot of credit as well; you could not have done it without them.

Through this process, you considered the importance of resources, procedures, and infrastructure and how each area was a key contributor to successfully running and driving your PMO forward. As you completed each PMO stage (including building, implementing, and maturing), you kept each area at the forefront of your mind. This is a best practice that you must remember. Although you are the leader, these three areas remain critical to your success. Do not forget that!

Let's recap the process that you followed to build, implement, and mature your new PMO. This is a good reminder because during the hustle and bustle of setting up your PMO, there might be areas that you want to revisit to make sure you didn't miss anything.

In Part 1, we looked at a couple of different PMO-specific surveys and talked about why PMOs across the industry fail. Recall, that it's important to watch these areas closely to help prevent yours from failing in the future. Because your PMO is new, there is no fear of it failing right now, but be mindful of the signs that point to possible failure.

Then, we looked at the history of PMOs. Understanding the history of project management and PMOs, in general, will help set context for the importance of building and driving your PMO. The history chapter covers why PMOs are important, what value they bring, and so on, which will arm you for specific and detailed conversations with anyone during the PMO build process. These questions are common and you can expect to answer them over and over again during the process. It also provides a nice history lesson to give you a perspective about what others, like you, have done in the past so that you can potentially learn from their successes and mistakes.

We then moved to the important subject of obtaining executive support. You need executive (management-level) support or you should stop and not move forward. We covered the political nature of PMOs; the only way to initially be successful is by getting management to acknowledge that they support the PMO's creation—you need their full confidence and support to move forward.

In Part 2, we got our hands dirty and started to build the foundation of the PMO. At this point in the book, we went tactical and rolled up our sleeves to start creating the PMO Build Schedule. Using a Microsoft® Project schedule to help build a PMO is the foundation that PMO Managers should use to move forward. We also started to define the PMO and looked at different mission and vision statements to use in the PMO. The concept of KPIs was lightly introduced because they're covered in much more detail later in the book. KPIs were mentioned early so that you could start thinking about them and create some initial KPIs. The concept called, "the four P's of PMOs" was introduced and definitions were provided for portfolio, program, and project management so that you were grounded with the concepts to understand them well. Eventually, you would have to decide which one you were going to use in your PMO, so this provided a good initial view into those three areas. There were a couple different industry methodologies covered and we looked at how engineering methodologies differ from project management methodologies. Examples were provided and hopefully now you are much clearer on the concepts after having created a PMO. This methodology discussion was important to cover in this book and important for every

PMO Manager to know well. It is often confused by so many people and you must be very clear on this concept yourself so the confusion doesn't perpetuate. The **PMO Build Decision Chart** was also introduced. At the end of every chapter in this section, there are a series of PMO build decision questions and you were asked to keep running documentation about your decisions by using the chart. This chart is relied on heavily during the implementation process.

After covering the basics for creating a PMO, we looked at PMO models including the various models used across the industry today. Remember, not one model will fit every company, so mix and match the best parts and pieces of the various models to make a model that works for your organization. Then, PMO maturity models and PMO measurement systems were defined. The maturity model becomes the foundation of your PMO—what you will use to grow and mature your PMO going forward. Dr. Harold Kerzner developed the industry standard project management measurement system, which also works well with PMOs. Finally, PMO service offerings were explained—you create and develop service offerings for your PMO. The offerings can be simple and limited at the beginning of the PMO, but as the PMO matures, the service offerings should also mature.

From there, staffing models were considered; if you build a PMO, you will need staff. Next, created a staffing model matrix to match service offerings with the people required to provide the service you created for your PMO. This provided a model to determine your staffing needs as well as an excellent tool for you, as PMO Manager, to justify your staffing requirements with management. PMO qualifications for staff, career paths, and the various industry-standard certifications available were explored. It's important as PMO Manager (and, often as functional manager) that you have conversations about career progression with your staff to set expectations on how they advance their careers. Vendor management and the nuances of working with vendors who often become a major part of your PMO staffing were also discussed.

We then moved onto training and education and the various types of training that PMO Managers should provide for their PMOs. After going over the different types of skills and training required for PMO employees, PMO mentoring programs, and the more informal PMO Buddy System, were explored. These programs allow ongoing training for PMO employees. Mentors and coaches give an employee someone to turn to if he or she needs help on a program or project. These programs are highly recommended as a best practice and something you should be offering within your PMO.

Then, at this point in the PMO build process, we shifted our focus onto the different industry-standard methodologies (portfolio, program, and project) and went into detail about each methodology across three chapters. The methodologies were explained, in detail, as were the qualifications for the roles, so that you could then create step-by-step deliverables to implement immediately across your PMO. The three methodologies are the core work products of your PMO; therefore, there is a tremendous amount of detail and information that is important for PMO Managers, Portfolio Managers, Program Managers, and finally Project Managers to know and understand. Each PMO employee should understand the three methodology chapters inside and out for their particular role—and as a stretch for all the roles. This allows career growth as well as an overall better understanding of how PMOs work.

PMO reporting became the next hot topic in the build process and how to create PMO reporting calendars and PMO dashboards. In the reporting chapter, we covered the concepts of past reports, current reports, and future reports—using the concepts as ideas for how the PMO Manager can focus on creating PMO reports for their organization. We also covered the importance of the PMO model and how it dictates the different types of required reports. For example, a supportive PMO model requires different reports than a controlling model requires.

Being in the building process, it then made sense to cover the various PMO tools and processes. Communication tools and the four W's (who, what, where, when, and how) were explored. The tool evaluation process was discussed and we established guidelines and processes to evaluate tools within your PMO. Don't forget to reference the large list of portfolio management, program management, and project management software tools. These lists are starting points to help you, the PMO Manager, determine which tools you need for your organization. These lists are starting points only; do not use them as buying guides. PMO Managers must be smart about which tools they purchase and how quickly they bring them in, so this process requires careful consideration. Finally, PMO processes and the best practices around those processes were defined. These are the minimum processes that PMO Managers should adopt in their organizations. Different companies require different processes for various industry nuances, such as Sarbanes-Oxley, or regulatory rules, and as PMO Manager, you should look for those areas to incorporate, but the standard processes in the chapter are consistent and important to add to your PMO.

Part 3 moves into the implementation process. Hours and hours were spent building some amazing PMO deliverables and Part 3 explains how to implement them into the organization. The implementation process is ongoing; there is no single point in time when you can say you're implementing the PMO. One of the largest tactical areas in the book covers the results of the PMO Build Decision Chart where you implement the answers to the questions that you provided during the PMO build phases. Examples include creating the official PMO mission statement, deciding which of the 4 P's of PMOs to use, hiring staff, selecting tools and processes, and so on. Remember, this is also where you implemented the different PMO build decisions during this phase.

Then, once the PMO is built, the focus turns to measurements and metrics. Measurements and metrics drive a high-performing PMO to become even better. We covered the concepts of performance reporting and provided the steps to immediately create three main performance reports in your PMO. These are great starting points for any PMO Manager and will be the launching pad for future additional reports. Review that chapter, there are some great maturity items there, and know for a fact that the metrics and measurements are the right areas to help you move your PMO forward. At the end of the same chapter, PMO audits and auditing were covered as another method to drive maturity into the PMO. The procedure for setting up audits across both program and project management methodologies, and across engineering development methodologies, was provided. These processes have been practiced across many PMOs in the industry and are best practices to establish in yours as well.

After covering metrics and measurements, creating a capabilities assessment process was explained. During this process, you assess the capabilities of the PMO employees and provide them with various learning opportunities to improve their skills. Not only did we cover the simple three-step process, but employee evaluations, based on the key skills needed to be a PMO employee was discussed. This gives every PMO Manager areas to work with each employee and drive career advancement conversations forward.

Finally, we covered the change process and the importance of the PMO role in handling and processing change. Different models were covered, such as the OCM model, and the role of PMO Managers as change agents was also explored. The focus and goal of the chapter was to bring some much needed exposure to PMO Managers about how to handle change and how to drive the change process throughout the organization. There is no expectation that you, the PMO Manager, would become a change expert after reading this chapter, but there was definitely enough exposure to get you thinking about how you will handle change.

Summary

To summarize, it has been a long haul, but you made it and the work is done.... Actually, the work is never done. PMOs continue to grow and expand. You, as PMO Manager, should be active in the industry, attend conferences and continue to grow your own skills. Strong PMO Managers share best practices and work to grow the industry inside and outside their own company. Allow others to take advantage of and learn from what you are doing. It is in everyone's best interest to share the good work we are all doing because there are always opportunities to learn and grow from each other.

This is it, you are done with the book, and you now can officially be called a PMO Manager. If you followed every process, every step, every tool in this book, and then implemented each of them in your PMO, then darn right, you are a PMO Manager. You deserve that title because that was one hell of a lot of work to complete.

Good luck and have fun because you are in one of the greatest jobs in the industry!

Chapter 18

Appendix

Table 17.1 Table of Tables

Table Number	Table Name
1.1	PMO Build Decision Chart
4.1	Portfolio, Program, and Project Manager Roles
5.1	PMO Model and Process Methodologies
7.1	PMO Mentoring Program Initiation Tasks
7.2	PMO Mentoring Program Startup Steps
7.3	PMO Buddy System Startup Steps
8.1	Evaluation Criteria
8.2	Portfolio Initiation Process
8.3	Portfolio Planning Process
8.4	Portfolio Executing Process and Portfolio Controlling Process: Planning Process
8.5	Portfolio Executing Process and Portfolio Controlling Process: Execution Process
8.6	Portfolio Closing Process
9.1	Program Benefits Register Table
9.2	Stakeholder Register
9.3	Program Initiation Process
9.4	Program Oversight Table
9.5	Program Planning Process
9.6	Program Executing and Controlling Process

Table Number	Table Name
9.7	Program Closing Process
10.1	Project Initiation Process
10.2	Project Planning Process
10.3	Project Executing and Controlling Processes
10.4	Project Closing Process
10.5	Project Integration Management Knowledge Area
10.6	Project Scope Management Knowledge Area
10.7	Project Time Management Knowledge Area
10.8	Project Cost Management Knowledge Area
10.9	Project Quality Management Knowledge Area
10.10	Project Human Resource Management Knowledge Area
10.11	Project Communications Management Knowledge Area
10.12	Project Risk Management Knowledge Area
10.13	Project Procurement Management Knowledge Area
10.14	Knowledge Area Mapping Chart
12.1	Software for Project Portfolio Management
12.2	Software for Program and Project Portfolio Management
13.1	PMO Build Decision Chart
13.2	PMO Implementation Steps
14.1	Project Management Audit Process
14.2	Software Development Audit Process
16.1	Organizational Change Management Models
17.1	Table of Tables
17.2	Table of Figures

Table 17.2 Table of Figures

Figure Number	Figure Name
2.1	History of Project Management
3.1	PMO Cycle
4.1	PMO Build Schedule

Figure Number	Figure Name
4.2	The Four P's of the PMO Lifecycle
4.3	Portfolio Management
4.4	Program Management
4.5	Project Management
5.1	PMO Build Schedule – PMO Models
5.2	PMO Maturity Model Using Four Categories
5.3	Dr. Kerzner's PM Measurement Model
6.1	PMO Build Schedule—PMO Staffing Models
6.2	PMO Roles and Responsibilities Staffing Model RACI
6.3	PMO/PMI Certification Career Path
6.4	PMO Organization Model
7.1	PMO Build Schedule—PMO Training
8.1	PMO Build Schedule—Portfolio Management Methodology
8.2	Six Strategic Steps in the Creation of Portfolio Management
8.3	Doing the Right Things Right Chart
8.4	Project Approval Process Example
8.5	Portfolio Selection Under Multiple Criteria
8.6	Resource Supply vs. Demand Summary—Shortages (highlighted) and Surpluses (un-highlighted)
8.7	Example of a Portfolio Schedule
8.8	Precedence Diagram
8.9	Portfolio Network Diagram
8.10	Resource Pool Description
9.1	PMO Build Schedule—Program Management
9.2	Program Governance Body—How It Works
9.3	Program Life Cycle Processes
9.4	Program Kickoff Meeting Agenda
9.5	Work Report Template
9.6	Program's Work Breakdown Structure
9.7	Program Calendar

Figure Number	Figure Name
10.1	PMO Build Schedule—Project Management Methodology
10.2	Project Life Cycle Process Group
10.3	Knowledge Area Circle
10.4	Project Communication Management Knowledge Area Circle
10.5	Project Integration Management Knowledge Area Circle
10.6	Project Scope Management Knowledge Area Circle
10.7	Project Time Management Knowledge Area Circle
10.8	Project Cost Management Knowledge Area Circle
10.9	Project Quality Management Knowledge Area Circle
10.10	Project Human Resource Management Knowledge Area Circle
10.11	Circle of Communications
10.12	Project Communications Management Knowledge Area Circle
10.13	Project Risk Management Knowledge Area Circle
10.14	Project Procurement Management Knowledge Area Circle
10.15	Knowledge Area Mapping Chart
11.1	PMO Build Schedule—PMO Reporting
11.2	PMO Dashboard Examples
11.3	PMO Reporting Calendar
12.1	PMO Build Schedule—PMO Tools and Processes
13.1	PMO Build Schedule—PMO Implementation Process
13.2	PMO Implementation Input Deliverables
13.3	PMO Build Schedule
14.1	PMO Build Schedule – Performance Tracking
14.2	PMO Maturity Model KPI Process
14.3	Microsoft® Project 2010 Performance Process
14.4	Microsoft® Project 2010 Cost Performance Process
14.5	Quality Performance Report
15.1	PMO Build Schedule—Capabilities Assessment

Chapter 19

Bibliography

Resources

Books

Bridges, William with Susan Bridges. <u>Managing Transitions: Making the Most of Change, Third Edition</u>. Philadelphia, PA: Perseus Books Group, 1991, 2003, 2009.

Dow, William and Bruce Taylor. <u>Project Management Communications Bible</u>. Indianapolis, IN: Wiley Publishing, Inc., 2008.

Jellison, Jerald. <u>Managing the Dynamics of Change: The Fastes Path to Creating an Engaged and Productive Workplace</u>. New York, NY: McGraw-Hill, 2006.

Perry, Mark Price. <u>Business Driven PMO Setup: Practical Insights, Techniques and Case Examples for Ensuring Success</u>. Fort Lauderdale, FL: J. Ross Publishing, Inc., 2009.

Project Management Institute, Inc. <u>The Standard for Program Management, Second Edition</u>. Newton Square, PA: PMI Publications, 2008.

Project Management Institute, Inc. <u>A Guide to the Project Management Body of Knowledge (PMBOK® Guide), Fourth Edition</u>. Newton Square, PA: PMI Publications, 2008.

Online

Kerzner, Harold. "Project Management Maturity Model Online Assessment." 2002-2012. <http://www.iil.com/kpm3/default.asp>.

Matteucci, Nick. "VPMi dashboard for project management." January 2012. <http://www.vcsonline.com>.

Merkhofer, Lee. "Software for Project Portfolio Management." 2002-2010. <http://www.prioritysystem.com/>.

Conference Material

Linenberg, Y. and Stadler, Z. and Arbuthnot, S. (2003). Optimising organisational performance by managing project benefits. PMI EMEA conference.

Linenberg, Y. and Rynn, D. (2005). Improving project success through effective project selection: the efficient frontier technique. PMI EMEA conference.

Trademarks

Microsoft is a trademark of the Microsoft group of companies.

"PMI" and "PMP" are registered marks of Project Management Institute, Inc.

Chapter 20

Index

A

B

C

H

I

J

Q

R

S

T

V

W

51935291R00257

Made in the USA
Charleston, SC
07 February 2016